CUBA

in your hands

TOURIST
GUIDE

escandón
EDICIONES

infotur

Through our offices across the country, Infotur offers updated tourist information on the Cuban Destination.

Free printed or digital supports will help you choose the best deals for your enjoyment.

www.
cubatravel.cu
infotur.cu
cubainfotur.cu
cubageotur.cu

INFORMATION CENTERS ACROSS CUBA

» PINAR DEL RÍO
Hotel Vueltabajo.
Tel. (53 48) 72 86 16
Viñales
Tel. (53 48) 79 62 63

» LA HABANA
Habana Vieja
- Obispo # 524
Tel. (53 7) 866 33 33
- Obispo esq. San Ignacio.
Tel. (53 7) 863 68 84
Plaza
Hotel Habana Libre.
Tel. (53 7) 832 92 88
Playa
Ave. 5ta y 112.
Tel. (53 7) 204 70 36
Aeropuerto Int. "José Martí"
Tel. (53 7) 642 61 01
Playas del Este
- Guanabo.
Tel. (53 7) 796 68 68
- Sta María.
Tel. (53 7) 796 11 11

» VARADERO
Calle 13
Tel. (53 45) 66 29 61
Centro Comercial Hicacos
Tel. (53 45) 66 70 44
Aeropuerto Int. "Juan G. Gómez"
Tel. (53 45) 24 70 15 ext.2564

» CIENFUEGOS
Tel. (53 43) 51 46 53

» TRINIDAD
Tel. (53 41) 99 82 58

» VILLA CLARA
Santa Clara
Tel. (53 42) 20 13 52
Aeropuerto Int. "Abel Santamaría"
Tel. (53 42) 21 03 86

» CIEGO DE ÁVILA
Edificio 12 Plantas (Bajos)
Tel. (53 33) 20 91 09
Aeropuerto Int."Jardines del Rey"
Tel. (53 33) 30 91 09

» CAMAGÜEY
Tel. (53 32) 25 67 94
Aeropuerto Int. "Ignacio Agramonte"
Tel. (53 32) 26 58 05 / 26 58 07

» LAS TUNAS
Parque Vicente García
Tel. (53 31) 37 27 17, 37 15 12

» HOLGUÍN
Edificio Pico Cristal.
Tel. (53 24) 42 50 13
Aeropuerto Int. "Frank País"
Tel. (53 24) 47 20 26

» GRANMA
Bayamo
Tel. (53 23) 42 34 68
Aeropuerto Int."Sierra Maestra"
Tel. (53 23) 57 44 34
Hotel Guacanayabo.
Manzanillo
Tel. (53 23) 57 4412

» SANTIAGO DE CUBA
Lacret, # 701
Tel. (53 22) 68 60 68
Aeropuerto Int. "Antonio Maceo"
Tel. (53 22) 69 20 99 / 69 88 64

» GUANTÁNAMO
Tel. (53 21) 35 19 93
Baracoa
Tel. (53 21) 64 1781 / 64 1782

CUBA
in your hands

One of the main purposes of the *Cuba in Your Hands* tourist guide is to offer the greatest possible information on the island. Thus, the publication will be your constant companion in all your journeys throughout the largest island in the Caribbean. In texts and images lies the essence of a country that is discovered as a territory wealthy in history, art, culture and traditions.

The most general information, as well as curios and legends that identify each region, appear in the present pages divided in several parts to make it more user-friendly. *Cuba in Your Hands* opens with a general index and a map that sets guidelines for easy consultation. The guide is divided in five chapters: "An Overview of the Island;" "History, Art, and Tradition;" Regions of Cuba;" "Useful Information;" and "Tourism Directory".

The first chapter depicts in a very general manner geographic, economic, political, social and cultural data, as well as the nation's symbols. The guide's second chapter covers history, art, and the island's traditions through figures and representative images that will make readers understand the evolution of the country. *Cuba in Your Hands* offers a third chapter dedicated to the Western, Central and Eastern regions in an itinerary that runs from one end of the island to the other. Regions are divided by provinces and tourist destinations, described in a general manner and with references to historical and tourist sites, as well as the area's curiosities and characters. Every region is preceded by an introductory text and an index, complemented with maps, references and photographs.

After the East to West overviews, the guide includes a chapter with useful information for visitors, and lastly a tourism directory with the most up-to-date data. The present guide, published by Escandón Editions, also has the added value of including the two newest Cuban provinces, a product of the most recent modification of the country's political and administrative division that came into effect on January, 2011. *Cuba in Your Hands* will be your perfect traveling companion to this Caribbean island, which discoverer Christopher Columbus called "the most beautiful land human eyes have ever seen."

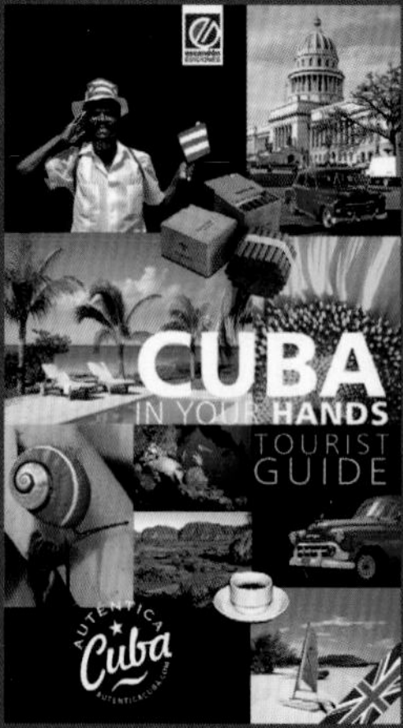

A tourist guide published by
ESCANDÓN EDICIONES
Seville, Spain

Publisher:
Germán Escandón Martín

Editor:
Lilibeth Bermúdez

Design:
Masvidal

Photography:
Julio Larramendi

Translation:
Germán Piniella

Printing and binding:
Escandón Impresores
www.escandon.com

Legal Dept: SE-845-2013

ISBN: 978-84-939380-2-4

2013 Edition

Published in three languages: Spanish, English and French.

contents

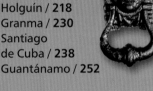

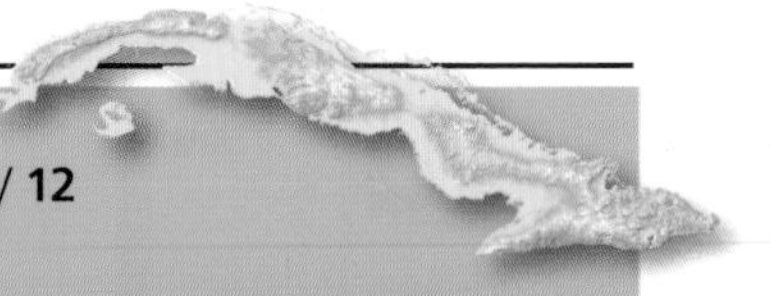

HOW to Use this guide

Structure of **CUBA IN YOUR HANDS GUIDE:**

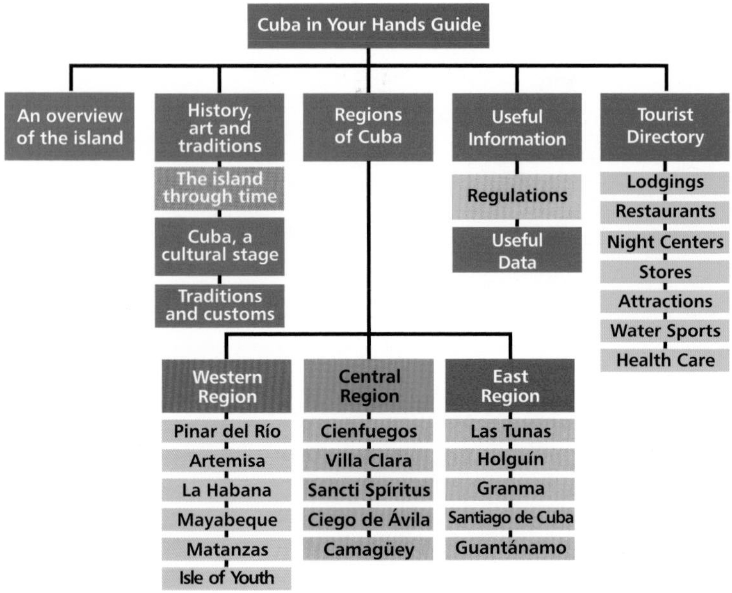

The *Cuba In Your Hands* guide is structured so that readers may find with ease and promptness on any page the context of the country. Readers will also find in the guide maps of the main provincial capital cities, as well as those of Cuba's different regions. The following examples illustrate the option on every page:

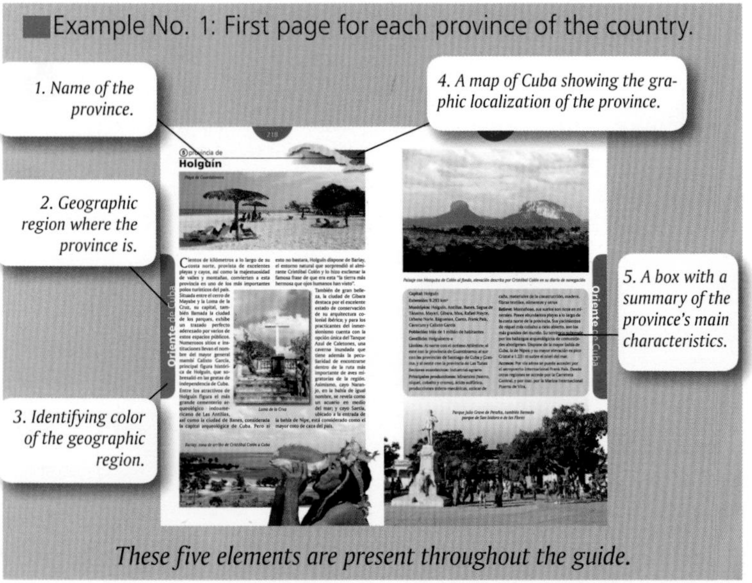

Example No. 2:

Cities, sites or significant geographic elements in a province are emphasized with a background color and all identifying elements of Example No 1 are maintained:

In this example you can see the town of San Juan de los Remedios, in the province of Villa Clara and pertaining to the Central Cuba region.

Villa Clara
lugares de interés
Villa de San Juan de los Remedios
Centro de Cuba

Example No. 3:

In the guide you will find the following symbols:

6

White circle: Signals locations you will find in the maps of the Western, Central and Eastern regions.

6

Black circle: Locations that you will find in the maps of provincial capitals and cities such as Varadero, Trinidad and Baracoa.

Example No. 4:

In the Tourist Directory at the end of the guide, you will find all the services offered at each region, divided in categories, with the same identifying codes as in the rest of the guide:

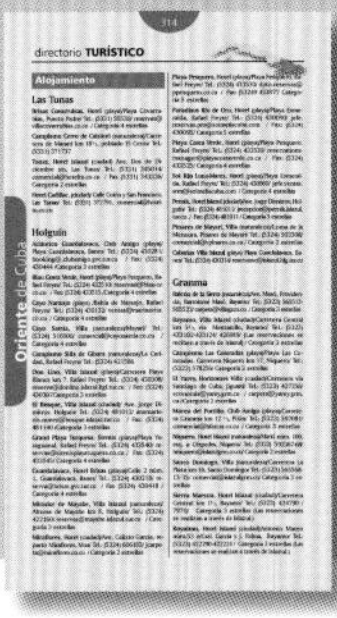
directorio TURÍSTICO
Alojamiento
Las Tunas
Holguín
Granma
Oriente de Cuba

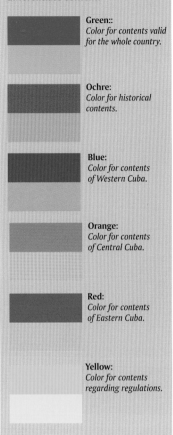

In this example you will find lodgings in the provinces of Las Tunas, Holguín and Granma, in Eastern Cuba, identified in red.

Chromatic code

Throughout the book you may guide yourself by the colors used to differentiate content:

Green::
Color for contents valid for the whole country.

Ochre:
Color for historical contents.

Blue:
Color for contents of Western Cuba.

Orange:
Color for contents of Central Cuba.

Red:
Color for contents of Eastern Cuba.

Yellow:
Color for contents regarding regulations.

Map Legend

- Site of interest
- Monument
- Museum
- Hotel
- Church
- Hospital
- Theater
- Cave
- Sports center
- Train station
- Bus station
- Marina
- Diving site
- Beach
- Lighthouse

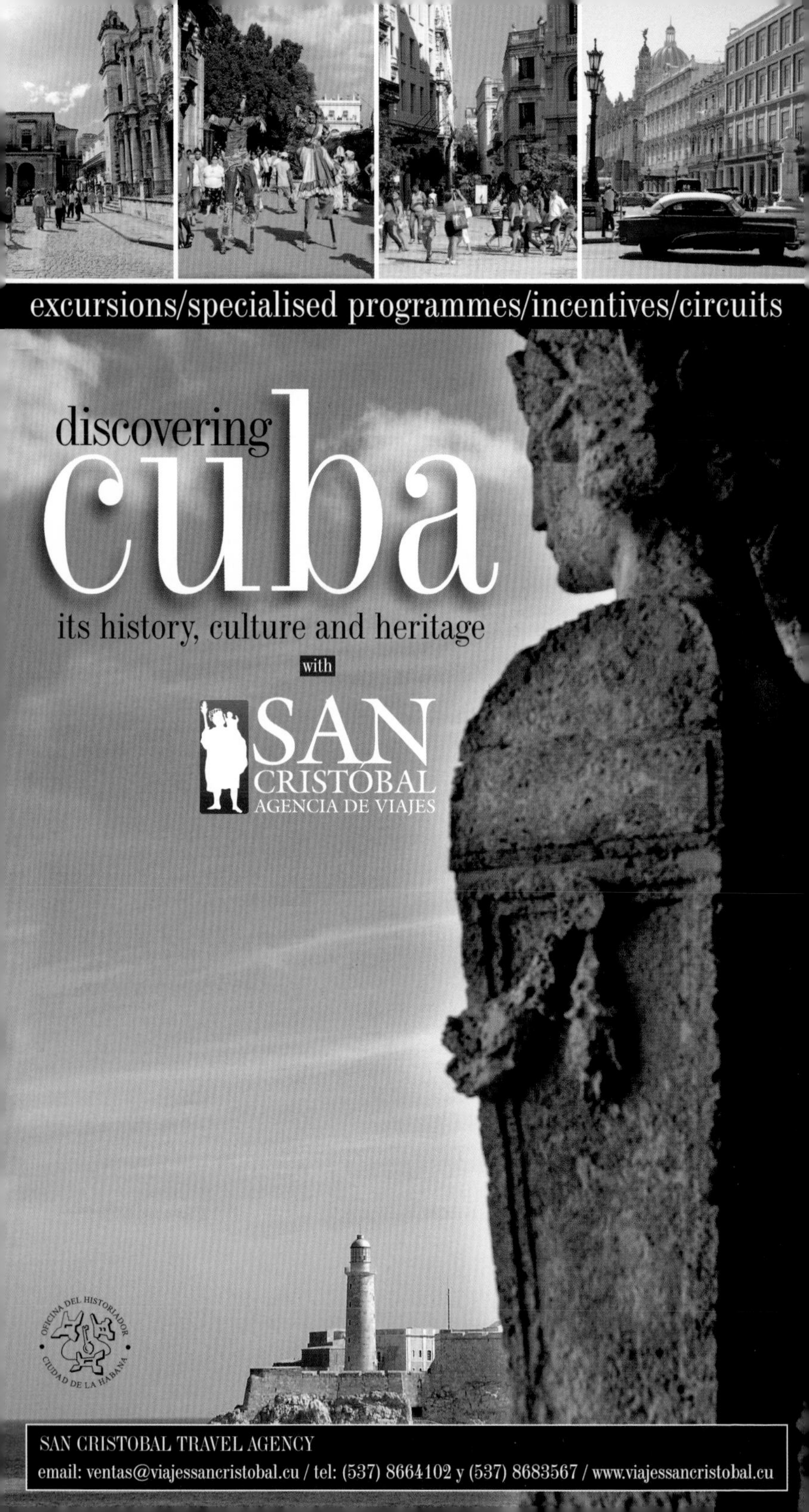
excursions/specialised programmes/incentives/circuits
discovering
cuba
its history, culture and heritage
with
SAN
CRISTÓBAL
AGENCIA DE VIAJES
OFICINA DEL HISTORIADOR
CIUDAD DE LA HABANA
SAN CRISTOBAL TRAVEL AGENCY
email: ventas@viajessancristobal.cu / tel: (537) 8664102 y (537) 8683567 / www.viajessancristobal.cu

An overview of **the island**

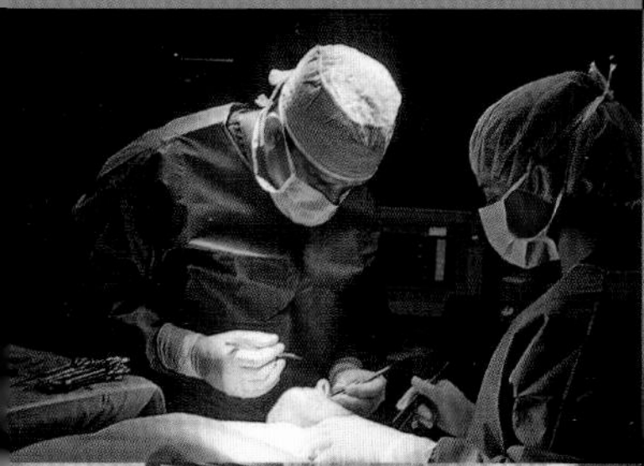

An overview of **THE ISLAND**

Location

Cuba is an archipelago bordering to the North with the Florida straits and with the Nicholas and Old Bahamas Channels; to the East with the Windward Passage; to the South with the Caribbean Sea; and to the West with the Yucatán Peninsula. The nearest lands are: to the North, Florida, USA (180 km) and the Bahamas (21 km); to the East, Haiti (77 km); to the South, Jamaica (140 km); and to the West, the Yucatan Peninsula (210 km).

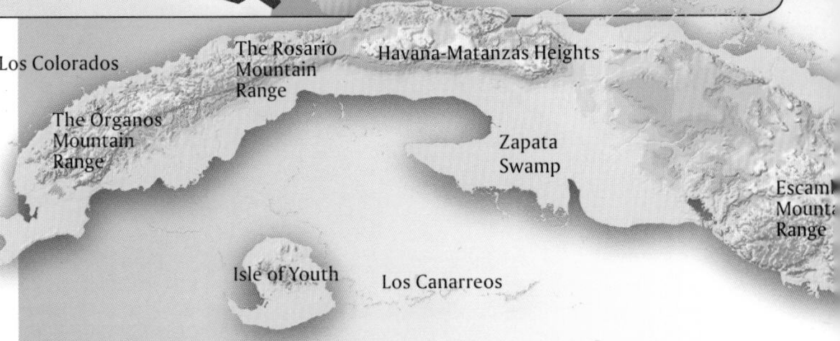

Area

The island of Cuba, the largest and westernmost of the Greater Antilles with 104,556 Km², has a length (East-West) of 1,250 Km, and a width (North-South) between 32 and 210 km. The length of its coasts is 3,209 Km on the north, and 2,537 Km. on the south. Usually compared to a caiman because of its elongated and narrow shape, Cuba is the 15th largest island on the planet.

Island groups

Cuba is an archipelago formed by two larger islands –Cuba and the Isle of Youth– and 4,195 smaller islands, keys and islets. The Cuban archipelago has a total area of 110,922 Km², and has four additional island groups: Los Colorados, Sabana-Camagüey (also known as Jardines del Rey), Jardines de la Reina, and Los Canarreos. The latter is the most important, since it includes the Isle of Youth, the second largest in the archipelago, with 2,204 Km².

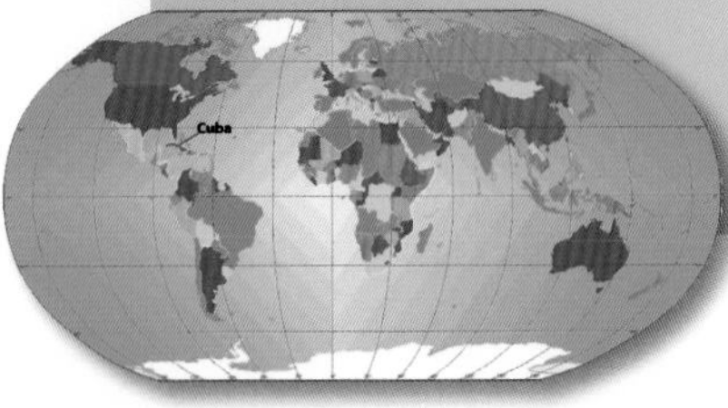

Annual average temperature: 24.6° C (76.3° F).
Annual average summer temperature: 25° C (77° F).
Annual average winter temperature: 22° C (71.6° F).
Average relative humidity: 80 %.

Seasons: Two, well-defined: dry, from November to April; and rainy from May to October. The average of precipitations in Cuba is 1,370 mm.

An overview of **THE ISLAND**

Relief

Most of Cuba's territory is flat (75%), with some low heights and mountains. Four percent of the national territory is wetlands. There are three main mountain systems: Guaniguanico in the West, formed by the Órganos and the Rosario Mountain Ranges; Guamuhaya, in Central Cuba, which includes the Trinidad, Sancti Spiritus and Escambray Mountain Ranges. The latter is erroneously believed by many to be the name of the whole Guamuhaya massif; and the Sierra Maestra, in Eastern Cuba, with the country's highest elevation, the Turquino Peak (1,974 meters above sea level), escorted by the Cuba and Suecia Peaks. The three of them form the Turquino Sierra. Farther to the East you can find the Sagua-Baracoa heights, with the Cristal Mountain Range, the Toa Ridge and others. The southern part of the island is an area particularly wealthy in small lakes and wetlands. The most important of the latter is the Zapata Swamp, in Matanzas province.

Hydrography

Because of the island's elongated and narrow configuration, rivers are short and most of them have little volume of water. The longest river in Cuba is the Cauto, 370 Km long, and the Toa is the fastest-flowing.

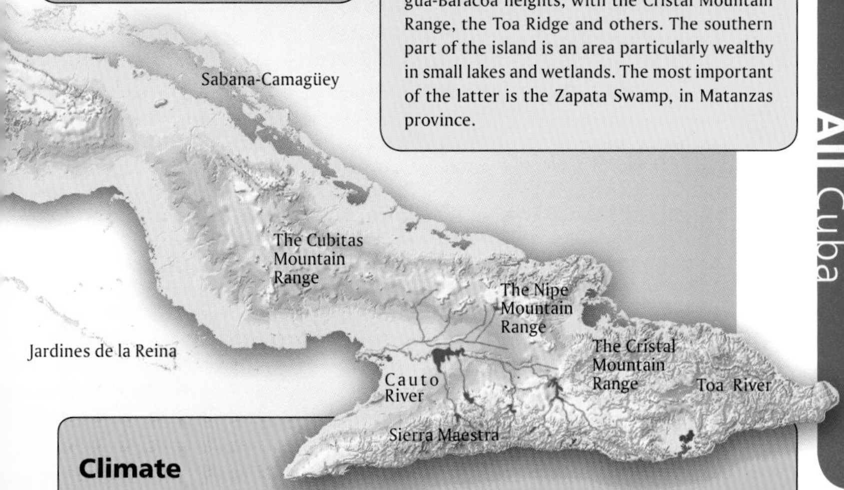

Climate

The predominant climate in most of Cuba, according to the Köppen (modified) classification, is of the tropical warm type, with a rainy season in the summer. Other climate types are reported in the higher areas of the main mountain systems. On the southern coastal area of the Santiago de Cuba and Guantánamo provinces there is a relatively dry tropical climate. The Eastern part of the country has a warmer climate that the Western zone.

Cuba lies near the Tropic of Cancer, so the values of solar radiation are high the whole year round. Also, because of its elongated and narrow shape, it is influenced by the trade winds. Being on the border of the tropical and extra tropical zones of circulation, it is influenced by both in a seasonal manner.

From November to April, variations of the weather are sharper, with sudden changes associated to the arrival of cold fronts, the anticyclonic influence from the continent and extratropical low pressure centers. In this season, cold wind masses from the North cause lower than usual temperatures. On the contrary, from May to October there is little change in the weather with a more or less marked influence of the North Atlantic anticyclone. The most important changes are linked to the presence of air masses from the East and tropical hurricanes.

Flora and wildlife

The great diversity of flora and wildlife and the high level of terrestrial endemism make Cuba a true natural paradise. The fact of being an island and the incredible geological variety contribute to a multiplicity of habitats and dissimilar life conditions. While knowledge on this particular is still incomplete, some scientists believe that there are some 32,000 living organisms; a great many of them are considered inferior. In that manner, the country offers a mosaic of plants; mammals; reptiles –none of them poisonous–, including a large population of crocodiles; birds; fish; insects; and amphibious species.

Pelican.

Hutia.

A point of interest is the absence of large terrestrial mammals, as well as the presence of some of the smallest animals in the world, such as the funnel-eared bat; the bee-hummingbird; the Monte Iberia Eleuth —the smallest frog in the world, less than 1 cm. long—; the dwarf gecko; and the pigmy scorpion. Another autochthonous species is the hutia, which served as food for Cuban independence fighters in the 19th century. There are some representatives of ancient species, such as the Cuban solenodon (almiqui), the alligator gar, and the almost extinct manatee. Also noted are the Cuban polymita snail, the exceptional glasswing (a butterfly with transparent wings), blind fish in subterranean lakes of carstic caves located at Pinar del Río, Mayabeque and Holguín, as well as a large variety of terrestrial and aquatic birds. Among the latter, migratory birds find in Cuba favorable conditions for feeding, nesting and reproducing.

One of the smallest frogs in the world.

Exploring the island's wildlife you will also find coral reefs, famous the world over and home to sponges, corals, mollusks, starfish, crustaceans, and wildly-colored fish. There are also sardine, smelt, barracuda, red snapper, pompano, mahi-mahi and turtles, that together with the brown booby, seagulls, and the double-crested cormorant, among other species, are part of the marine and terrestrial binomial that seduces visitors.

Left: Bee hummingbird; below: Hummingbird.

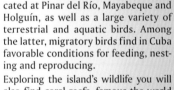

Lizard.

An overview of **THE ISLAND**

As heterogeneous as Cuban wildlife, the flora shines for its extraordinary wealth and endemism. Some claim that marine currents and migratory birds brought to this land seeds and fruits; others mention the ancient connection of Cuba to Central American territories through natural bridges, and there are also theories about different Indian migrations. In truth, the island is blessed with the presence of tropical plants that turn it into a showcase for nature-lovers. Over 6,500 species, half of them endemic, conform its wide range of flora among which there are valuable specimens, such as the cork palm, (*Microcycas calocoma*), Cuban magnolia (*Magnolia cubensis*), Cuban bottle palm (*Colpothrinax wrightii*), Moa dragon tree (*Dracaena cubensis*), Cuban pine (*Pinus cubensis*) and the butterwort, a delicate-looking carnivorous orchid (*Pinguicola lignicola*).

Alexander von Humboldt

German naturalist Alexander von Humboldt, known as Cuba's Second Discoverer, visited the island on two occasions, the first one from December 19, 1800 to March 15, 1801; and the second from April to May, 1804. His work, *A Political Essay on the Island of Cuba*, is considered the first scientific geography of this country. Von Humboldt described in his book Cuba's relief, coasts and climate, as well as a part dedicated to social and economic subjects of the time. At Old Havana, on the corner of Oficios and Muralla Streets, there is a House-Museum dedicated to von Humboldt, particularly to his Cuban sojourn.

An overview of THE ISLAND

Additional information

Official language: Spanish.

Population: Cuba has approximately 11 million people (11,241,161) characterized by the mixing of descendants of Spaniards, Africans, Chinese and some small migratory flows of French, Arabs, Haitians, Jamaicans and Italians, among others.

Male population: 50.2 %.

Female population: 49.8 %.

Urban population: 76 %.

Rural population: 25 %.

Political and administrative division

Cuba has been divided in different manners since the Spanish conquest. Preceded by other decisions, on June 9, 1878, a Royal Decree created six provinces that were named after their respective capitals: Pinar del Río, Havana, Matanzas, Santa Clara, Puerto Príncipe and Santiago de Cuba.

With great differences regarding area, population, and economic potential, when the Revolution came to power in 1959 the division was practically the same. Since then, municipalities have grown in number and the role and authority of provincial governments has been strengthened. For a time there were also regions that grouped different provinces, but they were eliminated after the new political and administrative division of the country in 1976. The six provinces became 14; the number of municipalities decreased to 169, and the Isle of Youth became a "special municipality" directly subordinated to the central government.

On August 2010, another modification was approved by the National Assembly that created two new provinces, Artemisa and Mayabeque, out of the territory of the province of Havana. Likewise some municipalities in the provinces of Matanzas and Guantanamo were reorganized, and the Province City of Havana regained its historic name of Havana. So at present Cuba is divided in 15 provinces that include 168 municipalities, plus the special municipality of Isle of Youth. The provinces are, from West to East: Pinar del Río, Artemisa, Mayabeque, Havana, Matanzas, Cienfuegos, Villa Clara, Sancti Spíritus, Ciego de Ávila, Camagüey, Las Tunas, Holguín, Granma, Santiago de Cuba, and Guantánamo.

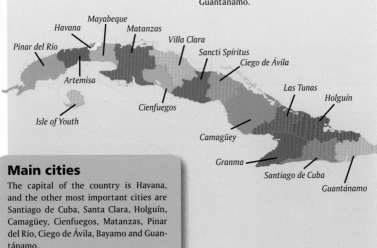

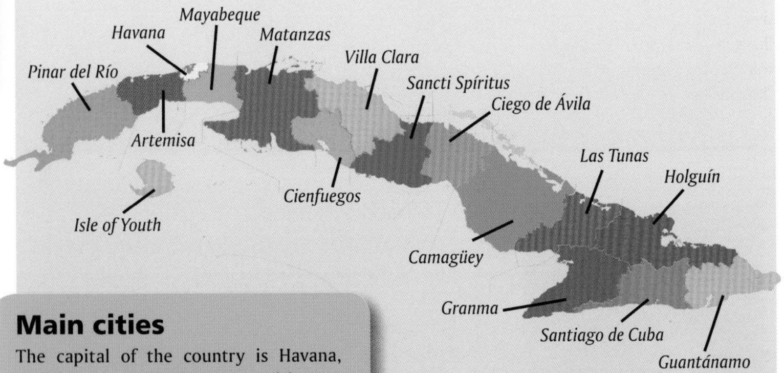

Main cities

The capital of the country is Havana, and the other most important cities are Santiago de Cuba, Santa Clara, Holguín, Camagüey, Cienfuegos, Matanzas, Pinar del Río, Ciego de Ávila, Bayamo and Guantánamo.

An overview of **THE ISLAND**

SYMBOLS

The flag

The Cuban flag, known as the "Lone Star Flag" was officially decreed on April 11, 1869 at the Guáimaro Assembly. It was raised for the first time in Cuba on May 19, 1859, the day that Venezuelan born General Narciso López occupied the city of Cárdenas, in the province of Matanzas. Its design is simple and harmonious, combining the colors red, blue and white. The three blue stripes represent the three departments in which the island was divided at the time; the two white stripes signify the strength of the independence ideal, and the equilateral red triangle is a symbol of equality among men and the blood that has been shed for freedom. The five-pointed star is a sign of absolute liberty and independence.

The other flag that presides over the Cuban National Assembly of Popular Power is the one known as "La Demajagua flag", raised by Carlos Manuel de Céspedes on October 10, 1868. It has two horizontal stripes of the same width, a lower one in blue and an upper one divided vertically in two equal parts, red and white; a star is placed on the red part with a point up. At the Guáimaro Assembly, in April 1869, it was voted that this flag would preside parliamentary sessions together with the "Lone Star Flag."

Coat of arms

It was designed by poet Miguel Teurbe Tolón following the ideas that Narciso López gave for the national flag. The present coat of arms was approved by the Guáimaro Assembly on April, 1869 and represents our island. It is shaped like a pointed leather shield, and divided into three sections. A red Phrygian cap with a white five-pointed star crowns the shield. The star points upwards and as in the flag represents the independent state. The shield is held by a *fasces* or pack of eleven rods joined by a red ribbon representing union.

In its horizontal upper part, there is a golden key between two mountains or land points, and a sun rising over the sea –which symbolizes the position of Cuba as the Key to the New World, between the two Americas. Down the right hand side, a Cuban country scene is dominated by a royal palm; on the left, the blue and white stripes with the same width are associated to the flag and represent the situation of the island, in terms of its division into states during the colonial period.

The shield is decorated by an oak branch on one side and a laurel wreath on the other. The former symbolizes the strength of the nation; and the latter, victory.

National anthem

On August 14, 1867, Perucho Figueredo wrote the music that would become the national anthem. At the time he called it "La Bayamesa", as the expression of its revolutionary character and as a reference to the city of Bayamo, where the national rebellion was born. When on October 20, 1868 the independence forces took Bayamo, Figueredo, spurred on by the jubilant crowd, crossed a leg over his horse's saddle and wrote the lyrics that were sung that day for the first time.

On to combat, people of Bayamo
For the homeland looks on you proudly
Do not fear a glorious death
Because dying for the homeland is to live
To live in chains is to live
Plunged in affront and dishonor
Hear ye the sound of the clarion:
To arms, brave people, to arms.

An overview of **THE ISLAND**

The national flower

The White ginger lily (*Hedychium coronarium*), known in Spanish as "mariposa" (butterfly) is an exquisitely perfumed flower. Leaves are large, green and lance-shaped. The flower is associated to the purity of the ideals of independence and was used by women for carrying messages during the 19th century liberation wars. It is also a symbol of the gentleness, gracefulness and slenderness of Cuban women.

The national bird

The bird that represents the country is the endemic Cuban trogon (*tocororo* in Spanish), which belongs to the quetzal family. Because its plumage mimics the colors of the national flag –red, white and blue– and cannot live in captivity, it was adopted as the national bird. The tocororo is found in the Órganos Mountain Range, the Zapata Swamp, the Escambray Mountains, the Sierra Maestra and the Isle of Youth, preferring forests and pine trees. Cuba's aborigines called it "guatani", a term that can still be heard in the Eastern region of the country.

The national tree

The royal palm tree, considered the queen of the fields, stands out for its majesty, great height, sturdiness and usefulness. Crowned by an attractive crest of leaves, it is the most abundant tree in the country and a symbol of the Cubans' indomitable character. For that reason, it is included in the country's coat of arms.

State and government

The National Assembly of Popular Power is the supreme body of the state and represents the people's sovereign will. It is the only institution in the republic with constituent and legislative powers. Its members are elected for a period of five years by free, direct and secret ballot of voters in the proportion and procedures determined by law.

After being sworn in, the Assembly elects the President, Vice President and Secretary of the body from among its members. The procedure for constituting the Assembly and that election is regulated by law. It also elects the Council of State, headed by a President, a first Vice President, other five Vice Presidents, a Secretary and 23 additional members. The President of the Council of State is the Head of the State and presides over the Government. The Council of State answers to the National Assembly of Popular Power on all its activities.

The Assembly also confirms the first vice president, the other vice presidents and the rest of the members of the Council of Ministers, nominated by the President of the Council of State. The Chief Justice and the rest of the members of the Supreme Court are nominated by the Council of State and confirmed by the Assembly.

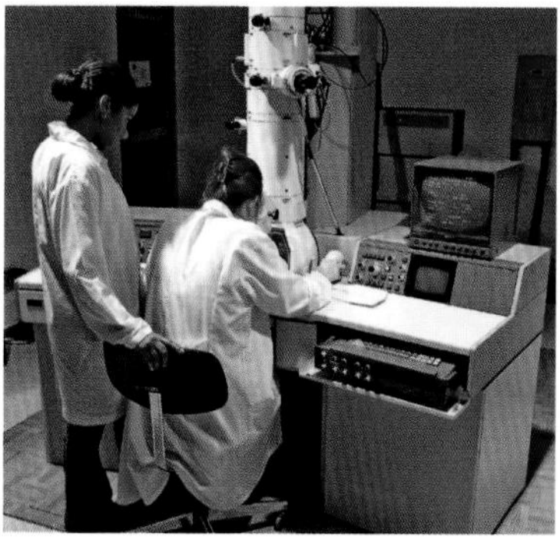

Economy

Among the main branches of the economy are tourism, nickel, tobacco, rum, coffee, and cane sugar. In recent years other sectors have gained in importance, such as pharmaceutical products, biotechnology, and special services that are exported to other countries in the fields of health care, education, sports, and culture, among others.

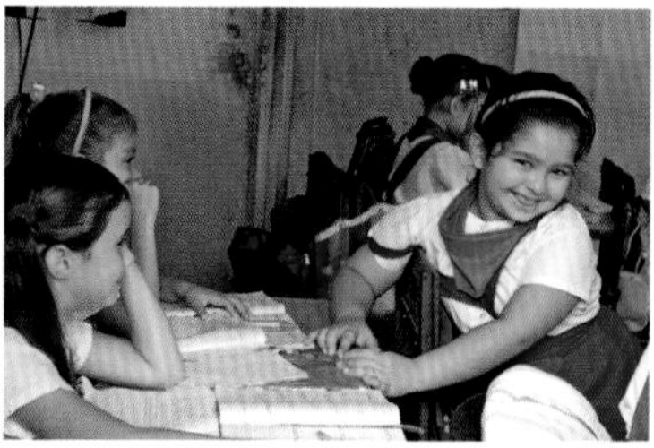

Education

In Cuba education is free and mandatory up to ninth grade. Illiteracy was eradicated in 1961. There is a high level of instruction and the population has access to a national system of education from day-care centers for the children of working mothers, to primary, secondary, technical schools and universities located all over the island. Cuba also has centers for training skilled workers and informal education up to university level for young people and workers.

Teófilo Stevenson.

Javier Sotomayor.

Sports

A far reaching program of physical education and specialized schools promote the massive practice of sports all over the country. Cuba's high sports standards have made it a steady winner of Olympics and world championship medals in several sports. Baseball is the national pastime, although boxing, volleyball, judo, athletics, wrestling and weight-lifting have won medals and championships. In the history of sports in the island there are names such as Chocolate Kid (1910-1988), a world boxing champion who reached stardom as a professional in the United States before the Revolution; middle-distance runner Alberto Juantorena, a two gold-medal winner in the 1976 Olympic Games; boxer Teófilo Stevenson, three-time Olympic boxing champion (Munich, 1972; Montreal, 1976; Moscow, 1980) and the winner of several world championships; and Pedro Pérez Dueñas, world record holder in 1971 in the hop-scotch-jump. To these sport stars other names should be added, such as Javier Sotomayor, world and Olympic champion and holder of still standing world records –outdoor (1988) and indoors (1989). Sotomayor, who was awarded by Spain the Prince of Asturias Prize, also was honored by the International Olympic Committee with the trophy "Sports: an inspiration to youth." Other outstanding world and Olympic Cuban champions are middle-distance runner Ana Fidelia Quirot, long-jumper Iván Pedroso, javelin thrower Osleidys Menéndez, judoka Legna Verdecia, baseball player Omar Linares, and volleyball players Mireya Luis and Regla Torres, the latter named Best Volleyball Player of the 20th century by the Volleyball International Federation. On the other hand, Eugenio George, head coach of the women's Cuban volleyball team, besides being the most winning coach in the world, was elected by the International Volleyball Federation as the best coach in the 20th century and a member of its Hall of Fame.

Alberto Juantorena.

An overview of **THE ISLAND**

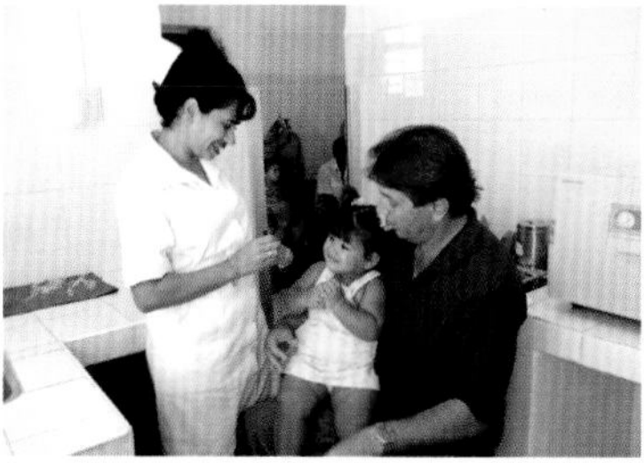

Health Care

Cuba boasts a health care system on the same level as that of advanced countries. It has one of the most comprehensive primary attention programs in the world, the lowest infant mortality rate in Latin America, high life expectancy, and universal and free health care for all. Family doctors and polyclinics in neighborhoods are part of a primary network complemented by hospitals; dental clinics; maternal, old age, and disabled persons homes, among other institutions. The high qualification of its professionals has been recognized in other countries that received the benefits of Cuban health care collaborators. The formation and education of human resources in other countries as well as in Cuba, where the Latin American School of Medicine was created, is another line of work of the sector. The country has also become a destination for health tourism where many persons from abroad receive specific attention and treatment.

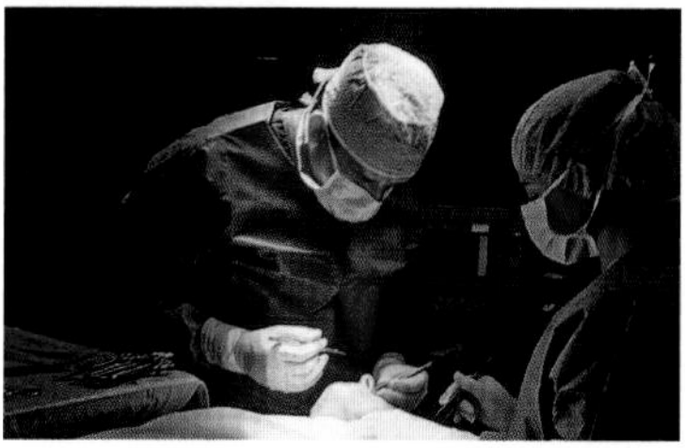

Culture

Cuba is an important cultural venue, with many artistic manifestations and national and international events. Theaters, museums, art galleries, movie theaters and public spaces are part of the infrastructure of the Cuban cultural system. Cuba is also famous for its many important performers and creators in all the arts. **See page 41.**

Religion

There is a peculiar religious diversity in the country, where the practice of Catholicism and religions that originally came from Africa predominates, although there are also other cults and beliefs. **See page 62.**

An overview of
THE ISLAND

World Heritage Sites in Cuba, according to Unesco

1982. Old Havana's Historical Center and its fortifications. **Pag. 90.**

1988. Trinidad and Sugar Mill Valley. **Pag. 182.**

1997. San Pedro de la Roca del Morro, Santiago de Cuba . **Pag. 249.**

1999. Viñales National Park (World Cultural Landscape), Pinar del Río. **Pag. 75.**

An overview of **THE ISLAND**

2005. Historical Center of Cienfuegos, the only city founded by the French in Cuba. **Pag. 159.**

2003. Tumba Francesa, Masterpiece of Oral and Immaterial World Heritage, Santiago de Cuba and Guantánamo. **Pag. 238.**

1999. Granma's Landing National Park . **Pag. 237.**

2001. Alexander von Humboldt National Park, Holguín and Guantánamo **Pag. 255.**

2000. Archeological Landscape of the First Coffee Plantations in Southeast Cuba, Santiago de Cuba . **Pag. 250.**

2008. Camagüey's Historical Center. **Pag. 200.**

History, art and **traditions**

The first settlers

When Christopher Columbus arrived to the island on October 27, 1492, Cuba had already been inhabited for 4,000 years through different migrations. The first one probably came from northern South America and the later ones from the mouth of the Orinoco River and the Lesser Antilles. At the beginning of Spanish colonization, there were notable differences among the approximately 100,000 aborigines that populated the island.

A portrait of Christopher Columbus.

The most ancient and backward groups —almost extinguished in the 15th century— were fishermen and collectors, and manufactured their tools from the shells of large mollusks. Other groups, besides using shells, also made tools of polished stone and in addition to collecting also hunted and fished.

The more developed, part of the Arawak branch, originally from South America, were farmers and mandioc was their main crop. From it they made cassava, a type of bread that they ate not only freshly baked, but that could be stored. They had different tools made from shell and polished stone, as well as ceramic objects and containers, and lived in small villages of thatched huts (bohíos) made from the wood and leaves of the royal palm tree.

Originally, Christopher Columbus christened the island as Juana, in honor of Don Juan of Aragón, heir to the crown of Spain's "Catholic Monarchs", who sponsored the voyage. Reliable evidence that Cuba was an island was found when Sebastián de Ocampo sailed around it in 1508.

The conquest

Almost two decades after Columbus' maiden voyage, Spain began the conquest of Cuba. Diego Velázquez, a rich Spanish settler in Hispaniola (present Haiti and Dominican Republic) was appointed in 1510 as "Adelantado" (governor) and charged with conquering Cuba. He fulfilled his mission with a long campaign riddled with cruel and bloody incidents, such as the one against the aborigines of Cuba's Eastern region, who led by a chieftain called Hatuey, put up a fierce resistance to the Spanish invasion. Hatuey was made a prisoner and burned at the stake as an example. Our Lady of the Assumption of Baracoa (1511) was the first of the seven towns founded by Velázquez, followed by Bayamo (1513), Trinidad (Holy Trinity), Sancti Spíritus, St. Christopher of Havana, and Camagüey (1514), and finally Santiago de Cuba (1515). Using these settlements as bases (later on most of them were moved from the original sites) the conquistadors began exploiting the island's resources using aborigines as slaves. The conquest and colonization exterminated the original population and the Spaniards began importing Africans as slave workers.

Cuba was prey to raids by corsairs and pirates in the Caribbean Sea, particularly by Jacques de Sores, Francis Drake and Henry Morgan, who kept the population on full alert for over a century. But piracy brought certain advantages to the development of the island, for in order to safeguard trade Spain decided to organize large fleets that gathered at the Port of Havana, strategically close to the Gulf Stream. Thus, the constant flow of traders and travelers, as well as resources dedicated to construction and improvement of fortifications that guarded the harbor, became a very important source of income for Cuba. Excluded from those benefits, the inhabitants of far-away areas began a lucrative illegal smuggling trade with the very pirates and corsairs that threatened the island.

On June 6, 1762, the Spanish authorities were surprised by the presence of an English fleet before Havana Bay. While the inefficiency of the Spaniards in the city's defense was obvious, the attitude of Creoles was quite the opposite. A particular example was Pepe Antonio, a brave militia Captain from the nearby town of Guanabacoa, who died in combat. During the 11 months of English occupation, Havana intensified its trade, a fact that would prove the potential of Cuban economy. Through the Treaty of Paris (1763), Great Britain returned Havana to Spain in exchange for Florida.

Slavery

After the aborigine population was decimated in the process of conquest and colonization, Spain began to introduce Africans for the purpose of using them as work force. In the first years, the conquistadors strived to attain massive extraction of gold and other minerals from Cuban soil, but later build up a plantation system of sugar cane, coffee, tobacco and other crops based on slavery. Thus Africans were responsible in great part for the development of Cuban sugar industry at the time, so much so, that many academics claim that sugar and slavery were the same thing. But slaves were also a source of social instability, not only due to the frequent manifestations of rebellion among them, but because the rejection of slavery originated conspiracies with abolitionist purposes, such as the one headed by free Black José Antonio Aponte, put down in 1812 in Havana, and the one known as Conspiracy of the Ladder (1844), which was crushed in a bloody repression. Many slaves and free Mulattoes lost their lives, including poet Gabriel de la Concepción "Plácido" Valdés.

THE STRUGGLES FOR INDEPENDENCE

1868-1879

The existing economic and political conditions in mid-19th century favored the articulation of a vast conspiratorial movement in Central and Eastern Cuba. The movement finally went public on October 10, 1868, when Bayamo lawyer Carlos Manuel de Céspedes proclaimed Cuban independence and freed his slaves at La Demajagua sugar mill. The rising, joined shortly after by co-conspirators in Camagüey and Las Villas, was able to take hold, in spite of merciless Spanish retaliation.

Months later, the independence movement voted in Guáimaro the Constitution of the Republic of Cuba in Arms. After months of hard military apprenticeship, the Liberation Army reached an offensive capacity that would be revealed in actions headed by Máximo Gómez and Ignacio Agramonte. Yet, political differences among revolutionaries, which culminated in the impeachment of President Céspedes (1873), undermined the unity of the movement, which could not reach its goal of taking the war to the East.

The unfavorable correlation of forces and the decline of the liberation movement led an important sector to accept a proposal by Spanish General Arsenio Martínez Campos. Peace without independence, signed at El Zanjón (1878), did not have consensus among the liberation forces, and was particularly rejected by General Antonio Maceo in a declaration known as the Protest of Baraguá.

After the so called Ten Year War, there was a period of great economic and social changes. Slavery, much weakened by the war, was finally abolished by Spain in 1886. Another attempt by Cubans to gain independence from colonial power was the Short War (1869), waged in the Eastern and Central regions, but crushed after a few months due to its poor organization and lack of political coherence. Expeditions, conspiracies and uprisings, almost all led by military leaders of the Ten Year War, were aborted or put down by Spanish authorities.

Carlos Manuel de Céspedes (1818-1874)

Considered by Cubans as the Founding Father of the Nation, Céspedes initiated Cuba's Independence War on October 10, 1868 after granting his slaves their freedom. He was the first President of the Republic in Arms and died when his camp was surprised by Spanish troops at San Lorenzo, in the Sierra Maestra.

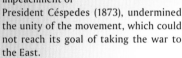

Ignacio Agramonte (1841-1873)

One of the most outstanding leaders in the Cuban revolutionary process. Known as "El Mayor", he took part in conspiratorial activities prior to the uprising in Camagüey on November 4, 1868. He was a revolutionary intellectual, and a daring and brilliant military leader forged in the practice of daily fighting.

Máximo Gómez (1836-1905)

A general in the Ten Year War and General in Chief of the Cuban Liberation Army in 1896, Dominican-born Gómez was a military genius who led important actions, such as the first machete charge on November 4, 1868. He planned and jointly executed with Maceo the invasion of Western Cuba in late 1895. Together with Martí, he played an important role in the organization of the Necessary War.

Antonio Maceo (1845-1896)

Considered a brilliant tactician, Maceo was the combatant *par excellence* and prestigious military leader. He participated in over 600 combats, including 200 of great importance for the outcome of the war. For his bravery and the color of his skin, he made history as the "Bronze Titan". The wounds he received in combat left him with 26 scars, 21 of them from the Ten Year War.

1895-1898

It was José Martí who understood that the struggle for independence should be set on new programmatic and organizational bases. His work of clarification and unification focused on communities of Cuban émigrés, particularly in the United States, but with ample repercussion in the island, crystallized in 1892 with the creation of the Cuban Revolutionary Party, which played a decisive role in the outbreak, on February 24, 1895, of what Martí called the "Necessary War". In spite of his early death in a skirmish at Dos Ríos, on May 19, 1895, the war developed in the province of Oriente, where General Antonio Maceo was in command, and later spread to Camagüey and Las Villas.

Led by Máximo Gómez as General in Chief and Antonio Maceo as second in command, the Liberation Army marched on to invade Western Cuba. The mission was completed and the devastating effects of war were felt throughout the island. Months later Maceo died in action at San Pedro and General Calixto García was appointed in his place. The war raged on decimating the Spanish Army in the different regions of the national territory. →

José Martí's death in action.

José Martí with members of the Cuban Revolutionary Party.

USS Maine, sunk in Havana Bay.

José Martí (1853-1895)

Cuba's National Hero, Martí was a man that transcended his time to become one of the greatest Spanish-American political thinkers in the 19th century. He is the author of a vast work that includes poetry, letters, essays and speeches. Martí founded the Cuban Revolutionary Party and played an essential role in the organization of the 1895 War of Independence.

Spanish colonialism in Cuba was coming to an end.

But on February, 1898, the USS battleship *Maine* exploded at Havana Bay, a fact that Washington used as a pretext for mobilizing public opinion and intervening in the Cuban War of Liberation. Although the US formally admitted Cuba's right to independence, it did not recognize its institutions. Thus the United States declared war on Spain and with the collaboration of Cuban forces landed its troops in southeastern Cuba. The Spanish fleet, bottled up in Santiago Bay, made a desperate run and was annihilated by US naval forces. After the attack on the outer defenses of the city by joint Cuban-US troops, the Spanish command surrendered. Months later, Spain signed the Treaty of Paris and ceded Cuba to the United States.

Death of Antonio Maceo.

The military occupation (1899–1902)

After the Treaty of Paris, a period of transition began under US occupation and its handling of the destiny of the island. The Cuban Revolutionary Party was dissolved and all representative institutions of Cuba's independence movement were eliminated, leaving independence forces without a viable leadership.

Annexation began to gain ground with a US military occupation that became the experimental framework for a policy regarding Cuba. Several projects came into being, but more than transforming the outdated structures of the former Spanish colony, they were designed for creating the conditions of promoting a "land market" that would facilitate the transfer of properties to the hands of US politicians and land barons. The economic situation of Cuban plantation owners was also disadvantageous and the need for a change of policy that prepared the road for annexation through the establishment of a republic with certain conditions was seen as a solution.

The Republic (1902-1958)

In 1901 US Sen. Orville Platt presented a rider to the Army Appropriations Act that ensured U.S. involvement in Cuban affairs, both foreign and domestic, and gave legal standing to U.S. claims to certain economic and military territories on the island, including Guantanamo Bay Naval Base. Its text was unacceptable for Cubans who had fought for 30 years to gain independence from Spain. On March of that same year, the US Congress gave its final approval and subsequently the bill was signed into law by President William McKinley. In spite of popular demonstrations in the country, the Cuban Constituent Assembly approved by a narrow margin the inclusion of the Platt Amendment in the Cuban Constitution, on pain of maintaining US military occupation of the country.

With such a premise, on May 20, 1902 the neocolonial republic was established with Tomás Estrada Palma as first President of Cuba. From this date up to 1909, several treaties that strengthened Cuba's dependence to the United States were signed between the two countries. Subsequently almost all of the island's successive governments were marked by corruption, economic inefficiency, repression and political conflict.

There were several periods of national crisis and social unrest in which actions by student and labor movements stood out, and leaders such as Julio Antonio Mella, Antonio Guiteras, Rubén Martínez Villena, Lázaro Peña, Jesús Menéndez and others excelled. Prior to 1959, the country suffered bloody dictatorships such as the ones presided by Gerardo Machado (1925-1933) and Fulgencio Batista (1940-1944 and 1952-1959). The latter's regime was opposed by a new generation, led by a young lawyer named Fidel Castro, who began organizing a movement to attack simultaneously the Moncada Barracks in Santiago de Cuba, and the Carlos Manuel de Céspedes in Bayamo, as detonators of a popular insurrection. The attacks (July 26, 1953) failed and dozens of the revolutionaries were murdered after being taken prisoners. The survivors, including Fidel Castro, were tried and sentenced to harsh prison penalties. In 1955 a nation-wide popular movement forced →

Photo: From the media at the period

Moncada Barracks in Santiago de Cuba.

Photo: OAH

Moncada Barracks assailants are freed from the Model Prison, at former Isle of Pines, now Isle of Youth.

Julio Antonio Mella (1903-1929)

Cuban revolutionary, co-founder of the first Communist Party of Cuba and of the Federation of University Students, among other organizations. In his brief life he carried out a feverish political and revolutionary activity that made him a leader of international stature.

Abel Santamaría (1927-1953)

A young Cuban revolutionary appointed as second in command of the movement that started the revolution on July 26, 1953, led by young lawyer Fidel Castro. He was taken prisoner during the attack on the Moncada Barracks in Santiago de Cuba and murdered shortly after.

The Granma.

Photo: From the media at the period

Haydée Santamaría and Celia Sánchez, guerrillas at the Sierra Maestra.

Photo: Andrew St.George

the government to pardon these political prisoners. On leaving prison, Fidel Castro and his comrades founded the 26th of July Movement. A year later, the most combative elements of University of Havana's students created the Revolutionary Directorate.

With the purpose of organizing an armed expedition and launch the revolutionary war, Fidel Castro left for Mexico. From that country the expedition sailed in a small yacht, the *Granma*, which reached Cuba at Las Coloradas, in the former eastern province of Oriente, on December 2, 1956. After an initial defeat, in which most of the revolutionaries were killed or captured, a dozen survivors regrouped to restart the struggle in the Sierra Maestra mountains. Led by Fidel and Raúl Castro, Ernesto Che Guevara, Camilo Cienfuegos, Juan Almeida and others, the guerrilla force soon expanded the operations theater and organized its men in columns. In less than two years they took small towns and defeated regular army units. At the same time, in the larger cities there was a climate of terror and repression while the underground grew stronger and carried out actions of great importance. →

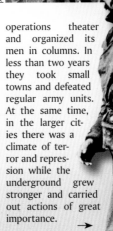

Fidel Castro at the Sierra Maestra.

Photo: Enrique Meneses

Photo: Robert Tabern

In December, 1958, the situation was grim for the Batista regime. The Rebel Army was advancing on all fronts. Columns from the Second and Third Fronts took the towns that opened the way for the siege of Santiago de Cuba. Commanders Camilo Cienfuegos and Che Guevara advanced towards the province of Las Villas. Cienfuegos, after a fierce combat, took the city of Yaguajay, while Guevara took one town after another along the Central Highway and launched the attack on the city of Santa Clara, the provincial capital. In view of the situation, Fulgencio Batista fled the country in the early morning of January 1, 1959. In a last ditch maneuver, General Eulogio Cantillo attempted to create a civic-military junta. Fidel Castro demanded the surrender of Santiago de Cuba's garrison and called on the people for a general strike that was answered massively. Both actions assured the triumph of the revolution.

Photo: From the media at the period

Camilo Cienfuegos (1932-1959)

Cuban guerrilla and revolutionary, a member of the *Granma* expedition and one of the main military chiefs of the war that toppled the Batista tyranny. Known as the "Hero of Yaguajay" and "Lord of the Vanguard", he headed important armed actions in the Sierra Maestra and led the battle of Yaguajay as part of the invasion of Central Cuba in 1958. He died in an airplane accident in 1959.

Photo: Osvaldo Salas

Ernesto Guevara (1928-1967)

Universally known as Che Guevara, or just Che, the Argentine-Cuban was an exceptional revolutionary guerrilla leader, statesman, author and medical doctor. A participant of the *Granma* expedition that reached Cuba on December 2, 1956, he was one of the first Sierra Maestra Commanders and led the successful Las Villas campaign. After the triumph of the Revolution he held important government posts.

Photo: José Agráz

The explosion of the SS La Coubre.

Photo: Raúl Corrales

Fidel signs the Agrarian Reform Law.

The revolutionary period

Once in power, the revolutionary government began dismantling the neocolonial political system. Shortly after, Fidel Castro was appointed Prime Minister and took a number of measures for the benefit of the people, including the first Agrarian Reform Law, in force on May 17, 1959. The law immediately polarized the public: on one side, those who backed the measures, and on the other those who opposed anything that would mean a change on the economy and the social and political status quo. Because of the obstruction of President Manuel Urrutia to revolutionary transformations, Fidel Castro resigned from his post. A few days later he was back in office as Prime Minister in the wake of massive demonstrations of support to his policies. President Urrutia resigned and Osvaldo Dorticós was sworn in as President of Cuba.

The first years were characterized by the occurrence of dramatic events, including acts of sabotage and the creation of different popular organizations. Thus began a long period of radical transformations of the economy and Cuban society that would finally end in the transition from capitalism to a government that nationalized foreign properties and placed private industries, services and trade under government administration. →

Photo: Osvaldo Salas

Fidel, Raúl and Che.

Fidel and Camilo making their entrance in Havana with the Rebel Army on January 8, 1959.

Photo: Luis Korda

Photo: Mario Collado

Fidel Castro at the front line at Bay of Pigs, April, 1961.

Photo: Mario García Joya

Literacy Campaign.

Counterrevolutionary activities were not limited to the economy, and soon organizations and bandits appeared in several regions of the country. Meanwhile the Eisenhower administration, which severed diplomatic relations with Cuba on 1960, began preparing the invasion of Cuba.

On April 17, after a surprise attack by bomber planes based in Central America, the invasion was launched at Bay of Pigs. In the burial of the victims of the bombing attack, Fidel Castro proclaimed the socialist character of the Revolution, a fact perceived from the measures taken in the final months of 1960. The invasion force, recruited, armed and trained by the United States, was defeated in less than 72 hours by the Cuban Army and the National Revolutionary Militia. The year 1961 was also the date of the Literacy Campaign, one of the most outstanding deeds of the social project applied in the fields of education, public health, culture, science, and social security. One year later, on October, the so-called Cuban Missile Crisis was triggered off and placed the world on the brink of nuclear war.

The following decades witnessed relevant events, including the election of the Central Committee of the Cuban Communist Party in 1965 as the country's highest political instance, the meeting

Photo: Alberto Korda

Anti-aircraft artillery pieces at Havana's Malecón.

Photo: Estudios Revolución

Fidel Castro

(August 13, 1926)
The historical leader of the Cuban Revolution has led the struggle for the consolidation of the revolutionary process, as well as the country's economic and social transformations, confrontations with aggression from abroad, foreign policy, solidarity actions and the strengthening of revolutionary and internationalist conscience of the people.

Raúl Castro

(June 3, 1931)
General of the Army and President of the Council of State and the Council of Ministers of the Republic of Cuba, General Castro was one of the assailants of the Moncada Barracks in 1953, member of the Granma's expedition and a guerrilla leader in the war against Batista's dictatorship, where he headed the Frank País II Front.

of the first congress of the Party in 1975, the constitution of the National Assembly, the Council of State and the renewed Council of Ministers, Fidel Castro's election as President of the Council of State, and the country's new political and administrative division.

In the late 1970s and early 1980s there were mutually beneficial agreements for cooperation and exchange with the socialist countries. In the midst of this process, the socialist block collapsed and the Soviet Union disintegrated –events that had a dramatic effect in Cuban society. In 1990, the Cuban government took a number of steps to confront what would be known as the Special Period, a time of great shortage of food and fuel in the country, and the almost complete standstill of industries. Drastic measures had to be applied in the economy, transportation, electric power and social life; also the country had to search for solutions to strengthen Cuban government companies and promote foreign investments, as well as the development of tourism.

Little by little the country advanced until the mid-2000s, when on July 31, 2006 Fidel Castro left temporarily his posts due to ill health. The leader of the Cuban revolution temporarily delegated his responsibilities and office to Army General Raúl Castro Ruz and other top officials. On February 24, 2008, Raúl Castro was elected President of the Council of State and the Council of Ministers, posts he currently holds.

Hit by three consecutive hurricanes in 2008 that caused severe losses to the economy, the island is facing reorganization in several sectors such as transportation and agriculture, among others. The 6th Congress of the Communist Party of Cuba, held on April, 2011, discussed and voted the Guidelines of Economic and Social Policies for the Party and the revolution. These Guidelines propose an economic model that besides maintaining the government socialist enterprise as the basis of the national economy, recognize and promote foreign investment, cooperatives, small landowners, usufructuaries of land leasing, self-employment and other forms that could emerge for contributing to raise efficiency. At present the country is implementing and developing those Guidelines.

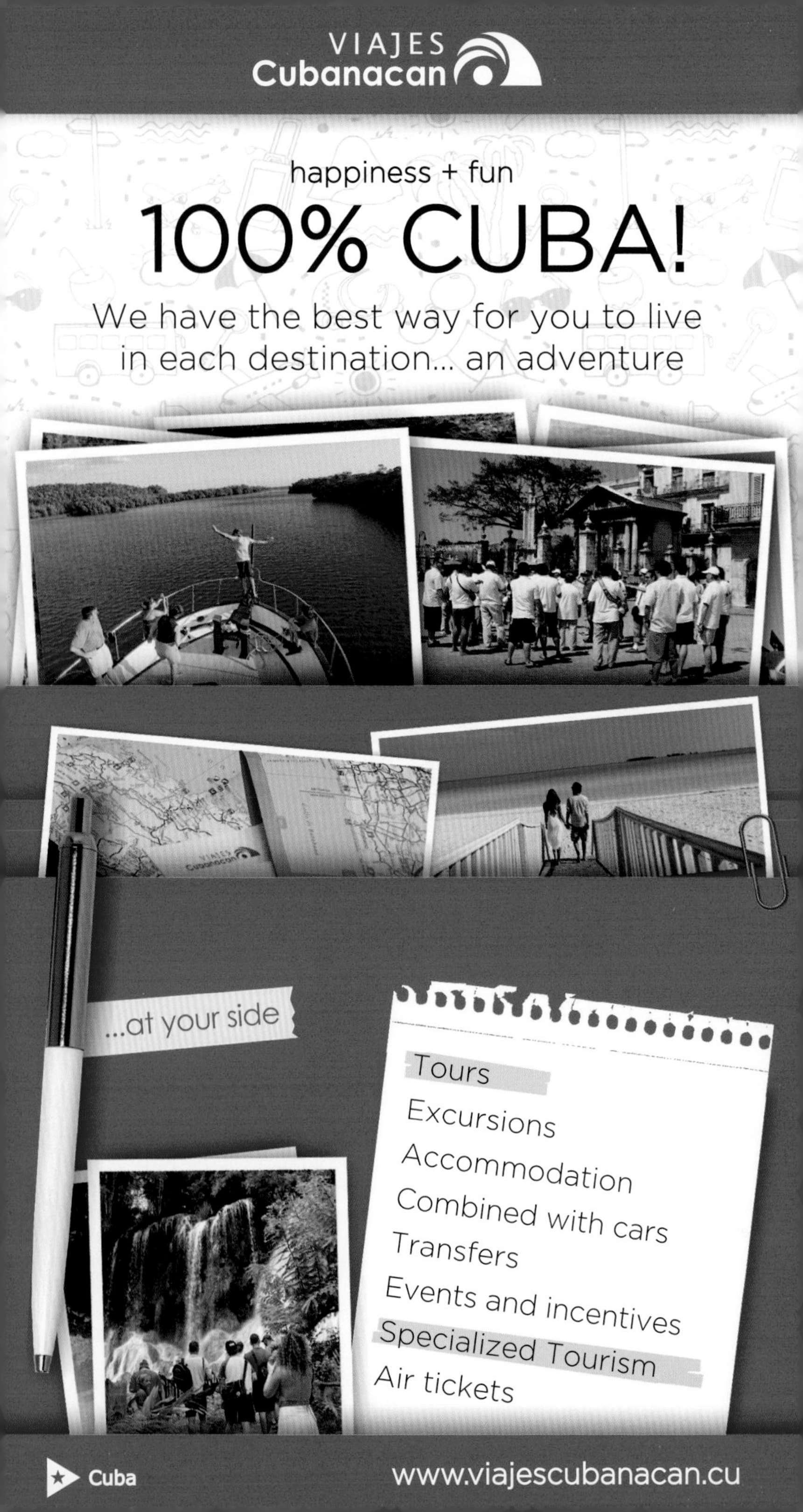
VIAJES Cubanacan
happiness + fun
100% CUBA!
We have the best way for you to live in each destination... an adventure
...at your side
Tours
Excursions
Accommodation
Combined with cars
Transfers
Events and incentives
Specialized Tourism
Air tickets
Cuba
www.viajescubanacan.cu

MUSIC

Los Van Van, founded by Juan Formell.

No wonder Cuba is called the "Island of Music", for the country's heart beats to many rhythms on streets, homes and public places. To make music heard throughout the island, Cubans just need a piece of wood or metal, or even an empty box. This mosaic ranges from the symphony to the street vendor's cry, for which there are excellent composers and performers, famous both at home and abroad.

Cuban music is the expression of the cultures brought to the island particularly by Spanish settlers and African black slaves. But beyond this simplification, it is the rich and complex result of the creative fusion of those two sources, to which influences from many cultures and musical tendencies have been added.

Cuba offers a wide array of genres that includes the *habanera*, *contradanza*, *danzón*, *rumba*, *guajira*, *son*, bolero, traditional and new *trova*, *changüí*, jazz, salsa, *timba*, rock, hip hop, rap, and concert music in all its variables.

Dancing is also a very important part in the life of Cubans. Bands such as Los Van Van, La Charanga Habanera, NG La Banda, Adalberto Álvarez y su Son, and many others make the most timid shake and rattle. You can see it at disco clubs, music houses and at the so called "cathedral of dancers", Jardines de la Tropical, in Havana.

Trumpet jazz player Yasek Manzano.

MUSIC

Ernesto Lecuona.

Benny Moré and Roberto Faz.

Trío Matamoros.

Composers and performers

A comprehensive list would be endless, but a few of the best known names from the 19th century to the present are Ignacio Cervantes, Manuel Saumell, Amadeo Roldán, Alejandro García Caturla, Sindo Garay, the Matamoros Trio, Antonio María Romeu, Ñico Saquito, María Teresa Vera, Ernesto Lecuona, Ignacio "Bola de Nieve" Villa, Rita Montaner, Benny Moré, Isolina Carrillo, Arsenio Rodríguez, Chano Pozo, Harold Gramatges, Miguelito Cuní, Roberto Faz, Elio Revé, Pacho Alonso, Enrique Jorrín, Rafael Lay, Compay Segundo, José Antonio Méndez, Bebo Valdés y su hijo Chucho Valdés, Juan Formell, Adalberto Álvarez, Leo Brouwer, Noel Nicola, Silvio Rodríguez, Pablo Milanés, José María Vitier, Elena Burke, Omara Portuondo, Ibrahim Ferrer, Pío Leyva, Rubén González, Eliades Ochoa and many more.

From left to right: Silvio Rodríguez, Leo Brouwer, Omara Portuondo and Arsenio Rodríguez.

Typical musical instruments

Some of the instruments that give Cuban music its unique sounds are the *tres* (Spanish for three), a smaller-than-usual guitar with three pairs of metal strings; conga drums; bongo, two small round drums with different pitch struck with the hands; *clave*, two wooden cylinders struck against each other; and the *güiro* (gourd), made from the dried fruit of the *güira* tree.

Celina and Reutilio, Cuban country music stars.

José Antonio Méndez.

MUSIC

Buena Vista Social Club

Buena Vista was a famous club in Havana that in the 90s inspired a recording by Cuban musician Juan de Marcos González and US guitar player Ry Cooder together with traditional Cuban musicians, many of them former members of the club who performed there when their popularity was strong. The recording, named after the club, became a worldwide hit. Several musicians over 70 years old joined the project that brought many of them back from oblivion. The band performed with its full cast in Amsterdam in 1998 and its presentation was filmed by German filmmaker Win Wenders. The documentary, also named *Buena Vista Social Club*, was nominated for an Oscar as best long-feature documentary and won in the same category at the European Film Awards. Thanks to its success, traditional Cuban music was once again placed on the world stage. The new success was short-lived for most members of the group. Compay Segundo died in 2003 at 95, Rubén González in 2003 at 84, and Ibrahim Ferrer in 2005 at 78. But Omara Portuondo and Eliades Ochoa keep on going strong with the Buena Vista Social Club band.

Compay Segundo.

Chucho Valdés.

Granmmy Latino

Several Cuban musicians have won the Latin Grammy, among them Chucho Valdés, Juan Formell, Los Van Van, Buena Vista Social Club and Leo Brouwer, as well as the CD *La rumba soy yo* (Bis Music).

Pedrito Calvo.

Kelvis Ochoa.

Benny Moré.

FILMS

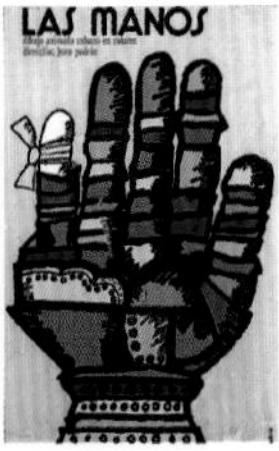

Although films were made in Cuba before the Revolution, Cuban cinema did not really take off until 1959 with the creation of the Cuban Institute of Cinematographic Art and Industry (ICAIC, for its acronym in Spanish). The institution, headed since its inception by Alfredo Guevara, disseminated cinema culture all through the country and promoted the formation of Cuban film directors. The first years witnessed the production of fiction films, documentaries, newsreels and animated films. Cuban cinema began to attract attention at European festivals, particularly through its documentaries and the influence of Italian Neo-realism in its works.

Tomás Gutiérrez Alea.

Alfredo Guevara.

Documentary films were the most novel, and Santiago Álvarez was its star renovating the genre and directing for more than 30 years the weekly ICAIC Latin American Newsreel that reflected the most important Cuban events. Havana also became the capital of Latin American New Cinema thanks to the celebration of a prestigious festival that since 1979 floods the city in December with fans and movie people.

Many are the Cuban film directors that have shined (among them Julio García Espinosa, Manuel Octavio Gómez, Pastor Vega, Manuel Pérez, Fernando Pérez, Arturo Soto, Daniel Díaz Torres), but undoubtedly, besides Santiago Álvarez, two other name excel over the rest: Humberto Solás, director of the classic *Lucía* and *Cecilia*, and Tomás Gutiérrez Alea, director of *Memories of Underdevelopment*, and co-director with Juan Carlos Tabío of the outstanding *Strawberry and Chocolate*, nominated to the Oscars as best foreign film.

Cuba is also home to the San Antonio de los Baños International Cinema School, where many filmmakers from Latin America and elsewhere have learned their trade.

ICAIC also promotes several events, such as the Festival of Young Filmmakers that give many talented young people a chance to show their work.

Some of the latest Cuban films

The Broken Gods, by Ernesto Daranas (2009).
City in Red, by Rebeca Chávez (2009).
The Cornucopia, by Juan Carlos Tabío (2009).
José Martí: The Eye of the Canary, by Fernando Pérez (2010).
Memories of development, by Miguel Coyula (2010).
Lisanka, by Daniel Díaz Torres (2010).
Affinities, by Vladimir Cruz and Jorge Perogurría (2010).
Old House, by Léster Hamlet (2010).
Ticket to Paradise, by Gerardo Chijona (2010).
The Gaze, by Alfredo Ureta (2011).
Habanastation, by Ian Padrón (2011).

LITERATURE

Cuba boasts one of the best literatures in Latin America. This is confirmed by its long history that goes back to early 17th century when Spanish born Silvestre de Balboa wrote what is considered Cuba's first work of literature, the epic poem *Mirror of Patience*. But it would not be until the 19th century, at the time of the struggle for the abolition of slavery and independence from Spain, that a truly national literature emerged. There are great names from those times, such as Romantic poet José María Heredia, poetess Gertrudis Gómez de Avellaneda, and Cirilo Villaverde, the author of the first great Cuban novel *Cecilia Valdés*. Other unforgettable names are poets Julián del Casal, Gabriel de la Concepción "Plácido" Valdés, Juan Cristóbal "El Cucalambé" Nápoles Fajardo, Juan Clemente Zenea, Juana Borrero, José Jacinto Milanés and Luisa Pérez de Zambrana. But undoubtedly the 19th century's most outstanding figure was José Martí, poet, essayist and journalist that expressed in his works the ideals of independence and became a paradigm of Latin American Modernism, a movement that also includes Julián del Casal.

José Martí.

One century later other authors and styles continued to excel. Some of the poets that have won prestige for the island are Regino Botti, Emilio Ballagas, Nicolás Guillén, Carilda Oliver, Virgilio Piñera, José Lezama Lima, Roberto Fernández Retamar, Gastón Baquero, Nancy Morejón, Antón Arrufat, Eliseo Diego (winner of the Juan Rulfo Prize), Cintio Vitier (also a Juan Rulfo Prize winner), Fina García Marruz (Queen Sofía Poetry Prize), Mirta Aguirre, Pablo Armando Fernández, Jesús Orta Ruiz, Fayad Jamís, Ángel Augier and Dulce María Loynaz (winner of the Cervantes Prize of Literature), among many others.

Fiction has also attained an outstanding height in the 20th century in the works of novelist Alejo Carpentier (Cervantes Prize of Literature) and once again José Lezama Lima, to name just two of most famous Cuban writers. Also worth mentioning are Eduardo Heras León, Senel Paz, Francisco López Sacha, Leonardo Padura, Reinaldo Montero and other younger writers like Daniel Díaz Mantilla and Ana Lidia Vera Serova, who bring new vitality to the island's letters.

José Lezama Lima.

Alejo Carpentier.

Dulce María Loynaz.

THE FINE ARTS

Since 1818, when the San Alejandro Academy of Fine Arts was founded and French painter Jean-Baptiste Vermay was appointed as its first Director, there have been several great moments for art in Cuba. Great painters such as Wifredo Lam, René Portocarrero, Amelia Peláez, Víctor Manuel, Mariano Rodríguez, Carlos Enríquez, Fidelio Ponce and Eduardo Abela revolutionized Cuban art from the 1920s with a far-reaching universal language.

The so-called vanguard was followed by other stages, such as abstractionism, pop art and other movements backed by the development of an ample program of artistic education promoted by the Cuban Revolution. The 1970s brought to Cuban art names like Roberto Fabelo, Pedro Pablo Oliva, Nelson Domínguez, Zaida del Río, Eduardo "Choco" Roca, and Flora Fong. Ten years later, in the 1980s, one of the most transcendental events of Cuban art took place with the exhibit *Volume I*, considered by critics as the starting point of another renovation of art in the island.

The 90s would bring a fresh air to Cuban visual arts with a generation of artists, most of them from art schools and the Higher Institute of the Arts, who were the protagonists of a stage that would be marked by the interest of international markets in Cuban artists. Little by little easel painting and sculpture are left behind and other more contemporary tendencies become the center of the limelight with installations,

Still Life with Pineapples, 1967, by Amelia Peláez.

The Third World, 1965-1966, by Wifredo Lam.

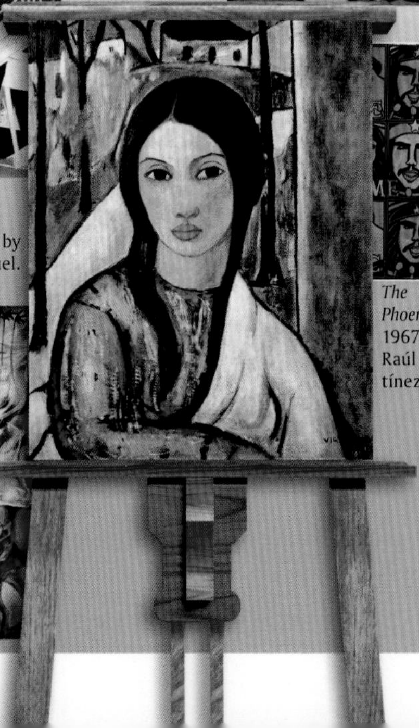

Tropical Gypsy, 1929, by Víctor Manuel.

The Phoenix, 1967, by Raúl Martínez.

The Rape of the Mulatto Women, 1938, by Carlos Enríquez.

THE FINE ARTS

Interior in El Cerro, 1948, by René Portocarrero.

Peasants, 1938, by Eduardo Abela.

video art, performances, postmodern use of photography and any combination of the previous ones. New names reach success abroad: Alexis "Kcho" Leyva, Carlos Garaicoa, Los Carpinteros, Agustín Bejarano, Esterio Segura, José Ángel Toirac and Tania Brugueras, among others.

At present, Cuban fine arts are also marked by the use of new technologies and a strong presence of more contemporary concepts of design. Many Cuban artists are internationally recognized and part of their success has been due to events such as the Havana Biennial.

Havana Biennial at San Carlos de la Cabaña Fortress.

El sueño, 1959, by Raúl Corrales

Photography

Before 1959 there were relevant photographers such as Constantino Arias, Tito Álvarez and José Manuel Acosta; but it is with the triumph of the Revolution that Cuban photography gets the attention of critics abroad, first with the so called "epic photography", with names such as Raúl Corrales, Alberto "Korda" Díaz, Ernesto Fernández, Liborio Noval, Osvaldo and Roberto Salas, who documented with their images the essence of a process that changed the life of the country and of the world. Militiamen, great demonstrations, and volunteer cane cutters, among other scenes, were recorded in the photographic memory of that first stage.

Years later artists would keep taking everyday life on the island as an inspiring motive, but images with intentions more artistic than documentary began to appear. Many joined contemporary tendencies and others centered on the body, customs and religious subjects, abstraction and Nature, even underwater images, Relevant names of this transformation are those of Rogelio "Gory" López Marín, Ramón Grandal, José Manuel Fors, Marta María Pérez, Juan Carlos Alom, René Peña and Cirenaica Moreira, among others.

THE FINE ARTS

National Museum of Contemporary Cuban Ceramics, at Old Havana.

Ceramics

It was the Santiago de las Vegas workshop that welcomed first class artists such as Wifredo Lam, René Portocarrero and Amelia Peláez, thus becoming the driving force of ceramics in Cuba. Since then new ceramists that not only make utilitarian objects, but also have made incursions into statues, murals and installations of artistic values have emerged. A great contribution has been made by the National Museum of Contemporary Cuban Ceramics, located at present in an old mansion on Mercaderes and Amargura Streets, Old Havana. Besides treasuring a valuable collection, the institution also promotes events such as the Amelia Peláez Biennial and others dedicated to vase modeling.

Graphic Arts

Graphic arts in Cuba have at present a promising development, anteceded by exceptional examples related to the tobacco industry since colonial times and the poster movement of the 1960s that became the backbone of political and cultural campaigns. Particularly the 1960s was a decade that launched Cuban graphic arts internationally. Designers like Alfredo Rostgaard, Eduardo Muñoz Bach, José Gómez Fresquet (*Frémez*) and Félix Beltrán, to name just a few, opened new roads both in film and political posters. At present, young designers have continued expanding the horizons of the art in Cuba.

Craftworks

Cuban artisans use a variety of materials, ranging from precious woods to fiber as well as metal, ceramics, fabric, thread, leather, seeds and shells. Different works are born from their hands and can be found at markets all over the island, stores, and public spaces, and in points of sales at the main tourist destinations. But the most important of these markets is the Former San José Warehouse Cultural Center, on the waterfront of the Port of Havana, where the largest concentration of artisans can be found.

Cultural events

Cuba is also the venue of important cultural events. Some of them are: the International Book Fair (February), the Havana Biennial (March), The International Havana Theater Festival (September), the Camagüey Biennial Theater Festival (Oct.-Nov.), the Havana Contemporary Music Festival (October), San Cristóbal de La Habana Festivities (November), the International Festival of New Latin American Cinema (December) and the International Craftworks Fair (December).

THE STAGE

At present, Cuban theater is in search of concepts for the stage with a fusion of different genres: ballet-drama, drama, dance, musicals. There is also an effort to increase the production of operettas. Comedy groups have also been widely promoted, with the celebration of their annual festival, as well as projects that are dedicated to the great universal classic works of all times. Dance also has a wide array, from classic ballet to contemporary dance, and sometimes troupes take to the streets as its main stage.

National Ballet of Cuba

Alicia Alonso dances *Swan Lake* and *Carmen.*

On October 28, 1948, Alicia, Fernando and Alberto Alonso founded the Alicia Alonso Ballet. Fernando was a renowned maitre de ballet and his brother Alberto a choreographer. After the Revolution in 1959, the company would be renamed as National Ballet of Cuba (BNC), and in a short time critics would begin to mention the existence of a Cuban ballet school. The BNC hosts the prestigious Havana's International Ballet Festival, which attracts renowned dancers and ballet companies. *Prima ballerina assoluta* Alicia Alonso, choreographer and General Director, is the BNC's soul. Many generations of dancers have followed in the steps of Ms. Alonso. Another prestigious company is the Camagüey Ballet, which has gained world recognition.

Cuban Carlos Acosta, a principal guest dancer at the Royal Ballet Theatre, and winner of Cuba's National Prize of Dance.

ARCHITECTURAL DETAILS AND STYLES

A detail of the balcony at Lombillo Palace.

Façade of the Archeology Department.

Cuban architecture was born out of the fusion of styles, and its development was influenced by the warm and rainy tropical weather of the island. In the 16th and 17th century, the privileged geographic location of Cuba and the fact that Havana was the hub for trade between Spain and its possessions favored the wealth of important segments of its population. On the other hand, because it had become a coveted prey for pirates, corsairs and filibusters, the city had to be fortified and confined to a restricted walled space. Several fortresses were built, great examples of military architecture, and dwellings were raised wall to wall, patio besides patio, leaving the shortest side for the front of the homes that looked on narrow streets or small plazas on an almost domestic scale. Thus neighbors and lifestyles were also mixed in this great Creole fusion that became the Cubans.

To the insular heterogeneity we must add the influence of Mudejar art that arrived from Granada and other regions of South Spain. Soon buildings were showing semicircular, ogee, horseshoe or lobed arches, as well as gabled roofs held by wainscoting, usually decorated. Local materials were used to build a functional scheme of one story homes with an inner patio through which the house breathed. Subsequently the mezzanine and a second story were added. The inner patio was maintained, but now surrounded by a gallery at each different levels.

Judging by the examples that still exist, the 18th century may be considered the most prolific and peculiar

ARCHITECTURAL DETAILS AND STYLES

A view of the convent of St. Francis of Assisi.

of home architecture and Cuban urban development. During the last quarter there was an economic flourishing that permitted the expansion of solid and attractive facilities, particularly government, religious or public building with a strong influence of the Spanish Baroque.

Such features, plus the presence of military engineers and master craftsmen at construction sites, modeled Cuban colonial architecture that evolved up to the 19th century influenced by Baroque and Neoclassic styles. Later on, the eclectic condition of Cuban architecture became more obvious with the 20th century's modern styles. Several Cuban colonial historic centers are proud bearers of cultural and functional values that have been granted the condition of World Heritage Sites by UNESCO. Likewise, Cuba's modern cities show the influence of the most important architectural trends in the world.

The balcony at Aguilera House.

A detail of the façade of Havana's Cathedral.

cubatur

580
transtur

Cubans

The result of the fusion of Spanish and African cultures, and also influenced by the French, Italians, Arabs, Chinese and others, Cubans are the result of a five century process. Different cultures were integrated for shaping national identity, marked by the arrival of traditions and customs so rooted here that sometimes it is difficult to trace their origins. Heterogeneity is clear not only in the architectural uniqueness of the island, but also in the character itself of Cubans, recognizable everywhere because of their joy, liveliness, emotion, a great sense of humor and hospitality. For Cubans there is no unsolvable situation, and they even joke about the most serious matters. They also are communicative, unselfish and rhythmic, while also heirs of a great source of education that allow them to enjoy different manifestations of art and culture.

GROWING THE TOBACCO

Christopher Columbus wrote in his diary that Cuban tobacco is a mystery. Maybe it is so for being the result of a long process where nothing is left to chance. In Cuba, the best regions for tobacco growing are Vuelta Abajo, in Pinar del Río, and Vuelta Arriba, in North Villa Clara although at the latter the crops are smaller. It all begins in the fields with the intervention of the grower, a persona with a special talent and a gift for communicating with the soil and the seed.

In Cuba, the process of tobacco **growing** has a long tradition, enriched during centuries, which is part of the country's culture. The task of the Cuban *veguero* -tobacco farmer requires passion for his work, experience and working capacity in extreme conditions.

There are two different ways to cultivate the Cuban tobacco depending on the function that each leaf will have in the making of the Habano. In order to understand well this process it is necessary to define previously the three parts that make up a Habano: the *filler,* which contains up to 4 different leaves (*Volado, Seco, Ligero* and *Medio Tiempo*), the *binder,* whose function is to wrap the *filler*; and the *wrapper*, on which the finishing touch and final appearance of the Habano depend.

Open air **maturing** is another one of the stages in this long process. Picked leaves are taken to the tobacco house, its first laboratory after being harvested. This moment requires extreme watchfulness and temperature, humidity and light must be in check. Then there is the first fermentation: the mature dehydrated leaves are bound in "mazos" (rolls) and taken to the fermentation house. There they are piled in large bundles half a meter high and stored for 30 days.

CREATING A HABANO

The Habanos are the only cigars that continue to be made *Totalmente a Mano* -Totally hand made for now more than 200 years. At the factory, the first step is the reception and conditioning of the tobacco leaves. In the case of the *wrappers*, they receive a much more careful treatment. These delicate leaves are prepared for their final function in the department known as *Moja* –Moistening.

Here, the 40 or 50 leaf bunches are moistened with a fine spray of water in order to restore the silky, uniform aspect of the leaves, as well as their elasticity.

Subsequently, they pass to the *despalilladoras* -strippers- in order to withdraw the central vein or stem of the leaf, thus dividing it into two halves and leaving it ready for the *grading*. The *escogedor* –grader– puts the wrappers together in 25 *vitolas* and shades, classifying them according to their colour, *vitola* and texture.

The *Ligador* -master blender- is the key person at the time of keeping the consistency of a *blend*. His task is to maintain the stay of continuity concerning the aroma, flavour and strength of each *vitola* and brand.

The *galera* or rolling room is the heart of the factory. Here the *torcedores* –cigar rollers– make different *vitolas*. Their only tools are the wooden board, two cutters: the flat-bladed chaveta and the little disccutting, the guillotine, vegetal glue (tasteless and odorless), the template, the press, the molds and, above all, the hands of the *torcedores*, their ability and experience. With the leaves in their hands, the *torcedores* begin roll the leaves: first, they place them properly to form the *filler* that is covered with the binder and placed into the mold. This compound of *filler* and *binder* is called *bonche* –bunch-. The molds are closed and placed in the press for about 15 minutes for each side. Subsequently, the *bunch* is passed through the drawing machine to check the draw. If everything is in order, the *wrapper* is passed to the *torcedores* for cutting the leaf to the size required with the *chaveta* blade, stretching it carefully to wrap the Habano with its gala dress.

After being made and before moving them to the boxes, the Habanos are placed in roderos at the *Escaparate* –Conditioning Room– where they are left to rest in cedar-lined cabinets in order to shed the excess of moisture that was gained in the rolling process. The *Escaparate* is often referred to as the "treasury" because it is here where the true wealth of the factory is stored.

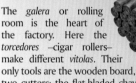

HABANO

Although all Havana cigars are only Cuban, not all Cuban cigars are Havana. The name is reserved for the selections of the most prominent brands and are made according to most rigorous standards from leaves grown in certain areas called "vegas finas de primera" (first-class fine meadows). Havana cigars are classified by color: light, red, light red, green red and ripe red.

Its fame gave birth to points of sale especially designed for the conservation and enjoyment of a fine cigar in ideal conditions. *Casas del Habano* (Havana Cigar Houses), authorized dealers all over the country and abroad, also have hand-carved humidors made from precious woods, true works of art for keeping Havana cigars in a proper environment and maintaining its original taste and aroma.

Every February Cuba is the venue of the largest international meeting of the best cigar in the world, the Havana Cigar Festival.

FESTIVAL HABANO

Few things in the world leave no doubt about being the best in their class. One of them is the Havana Cigar. Not surprisingly, unscrupulous persons attempt to imitate the product and its presentation.

Whenever you buy Havana Cigars, check each sign of distinction that identify them. It is important to buy your Havana cigars only at authorized dealers.

D.O.P. Seal

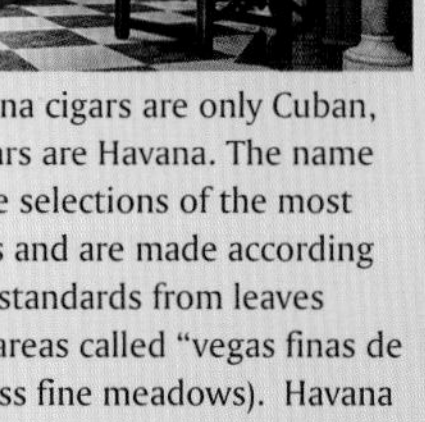

"Havana Cigar" is a Denominación de Origen Protegida (Protected Designation of Origin), a distinction granted by the Havana Cigars of Cuba Regulating Council of Designation of Origin. The seal D.O.P. is seen on the right upper corner of every Havana Cigars box.

Institutional Block

Since 1994, all the boxes have also been hot stamped with the words "Habanos s.a." as an indicator of the Protected Denomination of Origin which covers these cigars. No box of Habanos leaves Cuba without this seal, which contains the company name that commercializes the Habanos worldwide. Since 1989, the boxes of classic *long filler* Habanos have another seal with the words "Totalmente a mano". The boxes of *short filler* Habanos have, besides this mark, the letters "TC" (Tripa Corta) indicating the consumer the way of manufacturing each box.

Habanos s.a.
HECHO EN CUBA
Totalmente a mano

New Warranty Seal of the Republic of Cuba

This warranty seal appears in all tobacco products made in Cuba.

The Warranty Seal was first used in 1889, following a Royal Decree issued by the King of Spain. Later, in 1912, the independent government of Cuba passed a law authorizing the use of a new design, which is similar to the one used at present.

In 2009 a new seal was introduced that differs from the former one by incorporating two new elements: a holographic band on the right end and a bar code on the left side, next to the Coat of Arms of the Republic of Cuba, wich personalizes each packing and allows to monitor all the stages of its commercialization after the departure from Cuba.

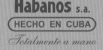

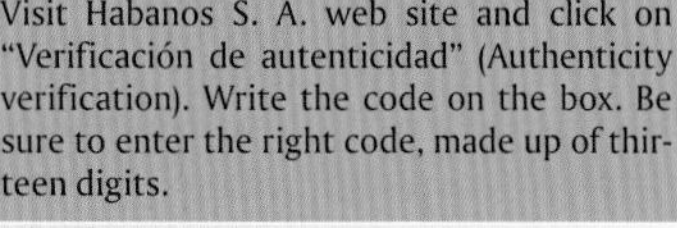

How to verify your Havana Cigar at www.habanos.com

Visit Habanos S. A. web site and click on "Verificación de autenticidad" (Authenticity verification). Write the code on the box. Be sure to enter the right code, made up of thirteen digits.

LA CASA DEL HABANO
International franchise of luxury shops for the good taste and comfort of the art of selling Habanos and another Cuban tobacco products under Corporacion Habanos S.A. license.
Professional and personalized customer care, widest assortment of Habanos in optimum conservation conditions.
LA CASA DEL HABANO: our Worldwide Presentation Card.
Habanos
Unique since 1492
www.lacasadelhabano.com

RUM

Rum is linked to the introduction of sugar cane in Cuba. Its origins go way back to the spirits made from sugar molasses and at first used by slaves in their rituals. Since the second half of the 19th century it became the genuine Cuban rum, the light rum that later conquered the world.

The perfect combination of sugar molasses from Cuba's fertile lands, natural ageing in ancient barrels, and the cultural heritage transmitted from one generation of master blenders to the next one are the main ingredients of this unique product tasted as part of a Mojito, a Daiquirí, a Cuba Libre, or simply on the rocks or neat. Many like to sip it while smoking a Havana cigar.

Each maker gives peculiar aroma, taste and color to their brands in order to create its own faithful followers. The best known in Cuba and abroad is Havana Club, founded by the Arechabala family, owners in the late 19th century of one of the largest Cuban distilleries in the city of Cárdenas. Havana Club, Cuba's iconic brand and the flagship of the Cuban rum industry, is outstanding for the perfect balance between taste and aroma. At present, Havana Club dark rums are made in one of the largest and most modern distilleries in the world, located at San José de las Lajas, southwest of Havana.

Here the traditional techniques of rum-making are zealously guarded, from the selection of the best molasses and the resulting spirits to the patient art of ageing, blending, and ageing again.

The quality of the renowned Havana Club family of products, guaranteed by the *know-how* of its master rum-makers, has been recognized by the best experts and liquor tasters in the world, as well as by the public that in 2010 bought 45 millions of Havana Club bottles; that means over 20 drinks per second.

Besides Havana Club, there are other rums in Cuba, such as those that reach consumers from Santiago de Cuba, among which are Santiago, Paticruzado, Caribbean Club, Caney, Varadero and Caribe; while Villa Clara contributes to that great community with Decano, Siboney and Mulata. Havana's brands are Legendario, Bocoy, Bucanero and Antillano.

At Old Havana, in an 18th century palace on the Avenida del Puerto (Port Avenue) stands the Havana Club Rum Museum. Its goal is to expand the knowledge of rum and its natural bond with Cuban culture. Among its attractions, the place includes a live exhibit that reproduces the traditional process for making rum, ending with a tasting of Havana Club. It also has an art gallery, a shop, and a bar-restaurant operated by Habaguanex Tourism Co., as well as other attractions.

A model that reproduces traditional rum making.

Interior patio at the Rum Museum.

COFFEE

Many are the legends about the origin of coffee, the stimulating drink consumed the world over. Coffee was introduced in Cuba by José Gelabert, who in 1748 inaugurated the first plantation with seeds from Santo Domingo, the present Dominican Republic. But its generalization occurred in 1791, when plantations mushroomed in Cuba with the arrival of French colonists from Haiti fleeing from the revolution.

At present it is an indissoluble part of everyday life, for Cubans cannot start their journey without their aromatic coffee, for most very strong and with little sugar. It is one of the country's exports and is grown mainly in mountain areas. The quality of Cuban coffee is internationally recognized due to brands such as Cubita, Turquino and Serrano, among others. Together with rum and tobacco, coffee is included in this triad of aroma and taste that has become a wonderful treat for locals and foreigners alike.

THE TASTE OF CUBAN CUISINE

Cuba offers a wide mosaic of dishes, the result of the confluence of aboriginal products and Spanish and African components, to which later were added elements from Asian –particularly Chinese– cuisine. Typical Cuban gastronomy came into being through the fusion of all these ingredients, represented by traditional staples, such as rice and beans. Creole cooking soon began to steer away from the Spanish and acquired its own taste in dishes such as chicken and rice, rice and black beans (also called "moros y cristianos", or Moors and Christians), and "congrí" (rice and red beans)

But the true King of the Cuban Table is "ajiaco". This combination of tubers, vegetables and meats, cooked together in a pot as a combination between a thick soup and a stew, varies according to spices and ingredients in different parts of the country. An offspring of the Spanish "olla" and brother to several Latin American "sancochos", it is a symbol of Cuban nationality due to its fusion of ingredients.

Another national specialty is "tamal" (Spanish for tamale), made with cornmeal, first cooked for a short time in a spiced salsa and with some kind of meat (cracklings, pork meat or even chicken). The mixture is packed into corn or banana leaves and later boiled in water. Tamal is eaten as an appetizer and tapas, cut in small pieces, or whole as a main course. There is also "tamale in the pot", which is practically the same recipe, but served in a soup dish, not in leaves. From corn Cubans also make the tasty "guiso de maíz" (corn stew), which together with rice substitutes beans as a staple.

The *piece de resistance* on the island is undoubtedly rice, indispensable for most Cubans. It must be served with every meal, whether plain white rice to accompany another dish, with beans, or cooked with meats, vegetables and seafood. Besides these combinations, a menu preferred by Cubans, especially at a celebration, is roast or fried pork, accompanied by Moors and Christians and boiled cassava with mojo.

"Tostones" (also called "chatinos") are chunks of crushed and fried green plantain; "mariquitas" (wafer-thin fried plantain); pork crackling; and minced beef, particularly Havana style. All are part of the wide culinary array of the country that strives to renovate traditional recipes with new approaches, and adopts the influence of contemporary international trends.

RELIGIONS

According to the Constitution, Cuba is a lay state that guarantees equality before the law for all religious manifestations, as well as the right of every citizen to practice his or her religion of choice, to convert to another, to practice more than one (a characteristic of religious practice in the country), or none at all.

A distinctive feature of religious belief in Cuba is the mixture of several creeds and manifestations. This mixture, called "transculturation" by Cuban ethnologist Fernando Ortiz (1881-1969), was formed mainly by the juxtaposition of elements of Catholicism, introduced by Spanish colonists, and of African religions brought by the slaves brutally torn away from their cultures, to which later were added elements of spiritualism.

RELIGIONS

The conquest and colonization of Cuba by Spain brought with it not only transculturation, but also a new religious belief, Catholicism. For nearly five centuries it held the hegemony as official religion of the colonial regime and subsequently was the dominant one in the republic (1902-1959). At present, although still the most practiced, it increasingly shares the preference of Cubans with Protestant denominations that began their missionary work in 1899, with US military occupation of Cuba. Hundreds of churches and houses of worship –Baptist, Episcopal, Methodist, Presbyterian and other denominations– are found all over the country. On its part, the Catholic Church has 11 dioceses, three of them with the rank of archdioceses. The highest rank is held by the Archbishop of Havana Jaime Ortega Alamino, who was appointed Cardinal in 1994.

Santería, the popular name for Regla de Ocha (Rule of Ocha [ochá-orisha: saint or deity]) came to the island in the minds of Africans brought to Cuba as slaves. In the mid-18th century, slaves worshipped particular deities that ruled their respective tribes. For example: the Oyo worshipped Shango; the Egba, Yemaya; the Ekiti and Ondo, Oggun: the Iyesa and Ijebu, Oshun. Each one of these deities had its own characteristics that set them apart from the others, but they nevertheless had two common denominators: the stone and the shell. Besides, they also had in common the chants and drum beats or secret callings to their orishas. The originality of the Yoruba or Lukumi religion is closely associated to Catholicism and its best known virgins and saints.

At present Santeria is one of the most popular beliefs, together with Regla de Palo and the Abakua secret society. The internal migration from other provinces to Havana, particularly from East Cuba, influenced Regla de Ocha with the so called *espiritismo cruzado* (a kind of spiritualism), a religious belief brought by temporary Haitian immigrants that came to Cuba to work in the sugar cane harvest eventually and settled in that part of the country. In this period that registers a third evolutionary stage of the Regla de Ocha, it is introduced also divination with a glass of water and the use of playing cards in the religious systems, as well as elements with injections from different manifestations in Regla de Ocha's believers.

OFICINAS DE VENTAS

CIUDAD DE LA HABANA

BOYEROS

Aeropuerto Internacional José Martí, Terminal 3.
Telf: (537) 649 0410
E-mail: ventat3@hav.cubana.avianet.cu
Aeropuerto Internacional José Martí, Terminal 1.
Telf: (537) 266 4732

LA HABANA VIEJA

Representada por: Paradiso
Telf: (537) 8615845

MIRAMAR

5ta. avenida Esq. 110, Playa.
Telf: (537) 202 9367
E-mail: cubana.5y110@cubana.avianet.cu
Representada por: ENRIDAN
5ta. Avenida entre 76 y 78, edificio Barcelona, Playa.
Telf: (537) 204 0171
E-mail: cubanaenridan@miramar.co.cu

VEDADO

Calle 23 No. 64 esq. Infanta. Vedado.
Telf: (537) 8344446 - 49
E-mail: informacion.cliente@cubana.avianet.cu

BARACOA: Calle Martí No. 181. Telf: (5321) 4 2171
BAYAMO: Calle Martí No. 58 e/ Parada y Rojas. Telf: (5323) 42 7514 / 427507
CAMAGUEY: Calle República No. 400, esq. Correa. Telf: (5332) 29 1338 / 29 2156, E-mail: cubana.cmw@enet.cu
CIEGO DE AVILA: Calle Chicho Valdes No. 83, Carretera Central. e/ Maceo y Honorato Castillo. Telf: (5351) 30 9161 al 69 / 20 1117
CIENFUEGOS: Telf: (5343) 528048
GUANTANAMO: Calle Calixto García No. 817 e/ Prado y Aguilera. Telf: (5321) 35 5453
HOLGUIN: Edificio Pico de Cristal, calle Libertad esq. Martí. 2do. Piso Policentro. Telf: (5324) 46 1610 E-mail: cubanahg@enet.cu
LAS TUNAS: Calle Lucas Ortíz esq. 24 de Febrero. Telf: (5331) 4 6873 / 4 6872
ISLA DE LA JUVENTUD: Telf: (5346) 32 4259 Aeropuerto: (5346) 32 2531
MANZANILLO: Calle Maceo No. 70 e/ Marchan y Villuenda. Telf: (5323) 5 7558 / 5 7401
MOA: Ave. del Puerto. Rolo Monterrey. Telf: (5346) 6 7012 / 6 7916
NUEVA GERONA: Calle 39 No. 1415 e/ 16 y 18. Telf: (5361) 32 4259 / 32 2531
SANTA CLARA: Telf: (5343) 52 8048
SANTIAGO DE CUBA: Calle Enramada esq. a San Pedro. Telf: (5322) 65 1577 al 79 E-mail: mmilan@cubanascu.co.cu
VARADERO: 1ra Ave. entre 54 y 55,Varadero, CP 42200. Telf: (5345) 61 1823, 24, E-mail: vra@enet.cu

www.cubana.cu

CUBANA

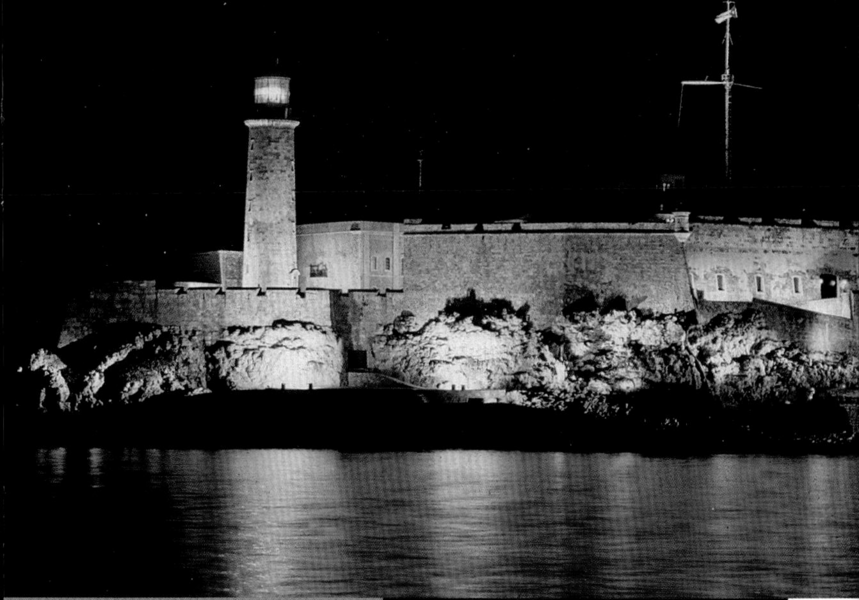

Regions of **Cuba**

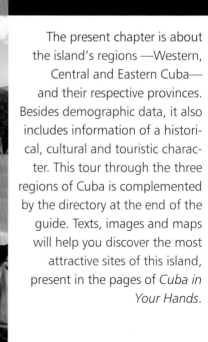

The present chapter is about the island's regions —Western, Central and Eastern Cuba— and their respective provinces. Besides demographic data, it also includes information of a historical, cultural and touristic character. This tour through the three regions of Cuba is complemented by the directory at the end of the guide. Texts, images and maps will help you discover the most attractive sites of this island, present in the pages of *Cuba in Your Hands*.

A Journey Through
Western
Cuba

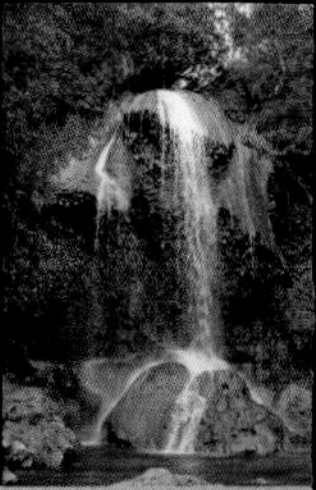

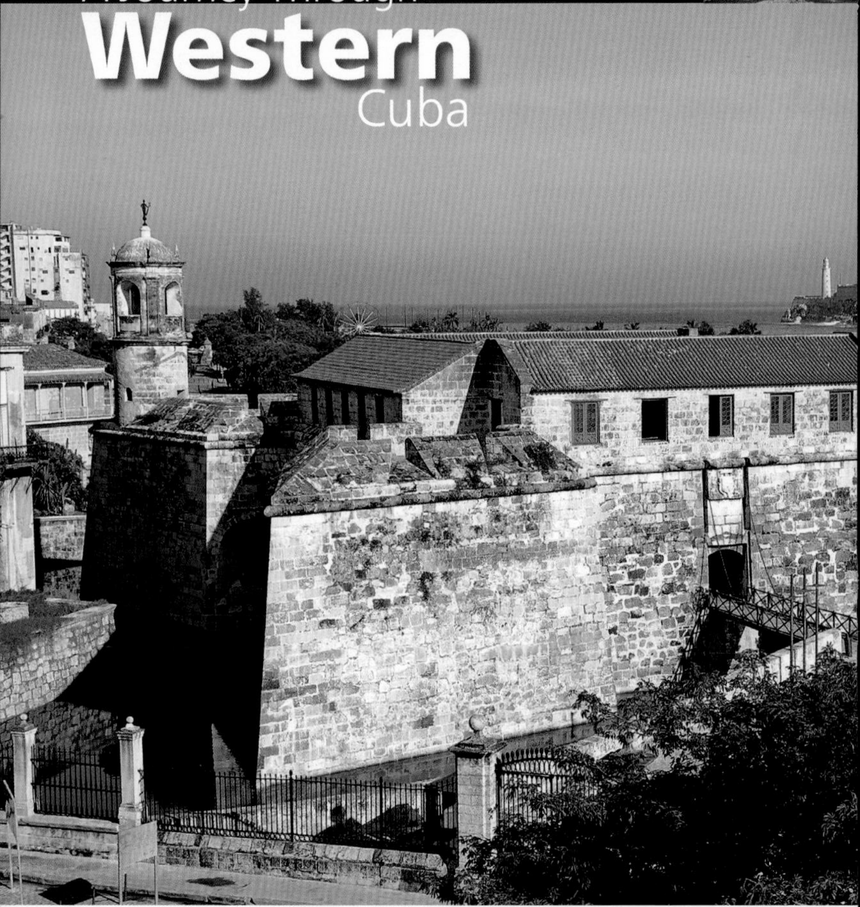

HABANA
CUBA

western
Cuba

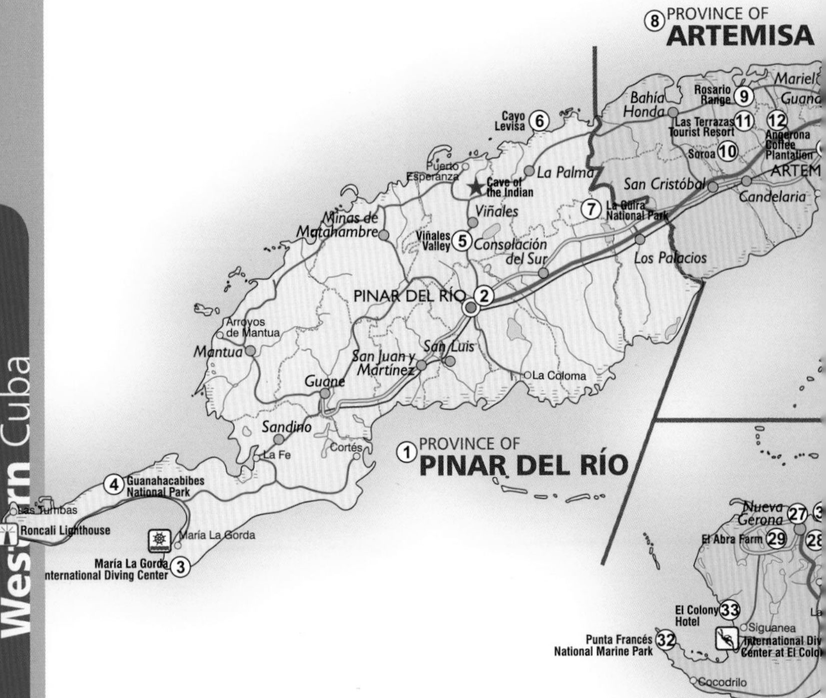

Western Cuba, which includes the two tourist destinations of greatest importance in the island –Havana, the country's capital, and Varadero, one of the world's best resorts– is of great significance. The former has the main political, economic, social, and cultural institutions, while the latter, a most beautiful beach, is the venue of a great network of hotels, restaurants and other facilities.

Another attraction of the capital is Old Havana's Historical Center and its system of fortifications, declared a World Heritage Site by Unesco in 1982. A place of relevant historical and cultural values, the old sector of the city is recovering its splendor thanks to architectural conservation by the Office of the City's Historian, headed by Eusebio Leal Spengler.

Although the western region is mostly plains, Pinar del Río has the Guaniguanico Range, where the rare beauty of Viñales Valley's *mogotes* (rocky hillocks) greets visitors. The province is also famous for the territory of Vuelta Abajo, the land where the best tobacco in the world is grown. Matanzas, with its "City of Bridges" and the Hicacos and Zapata peninsulas, also offers the majesty of Yumurí Valley. On its part, the Isle of Youth, the second largest in the Cuban archipelago, invites visitor to Bibijagua Beach, (famous for its black sand), the International Diving Center, and the tourist destination of Cayo Largo del Sur.

Two new provinces have been recently added to this region, Mayabeque and Artemisa, born out of a modification in 2010 that changed the political and

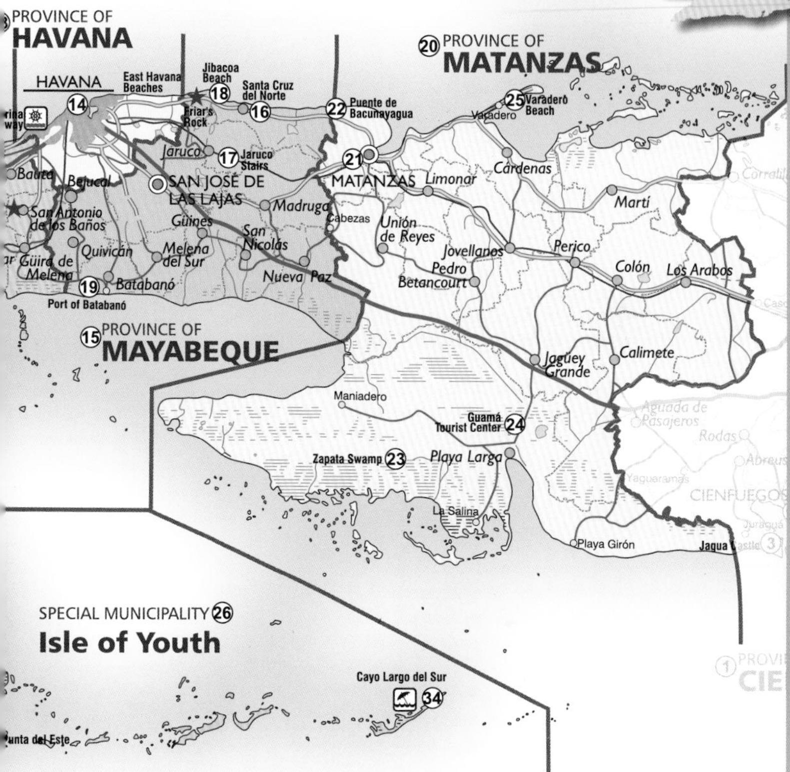

administrative division in the island since 1976. With its aboriginal name, Mayabeque has 11 municipalities carved out from the former province of Havana. Among its main attractions are the facilities on its northern shore and the hills called Escaleras de Jaruco (Jaruco Stairs). On its part, of the 11 municipalities of Artemisa 8 were part of Havana, while the other three belonged to Pinar del Río. The province harbors the Museum of Humor and the International School of Film and Television, both at San Antonio de los Baños, as well as Soroa Park, with its famous Orchid Garden, and Las Terrazas, an ecological community, home to deceased Polo Montañez, a popular country music singer and songwriter.

Index

In this section you will find general data and references on historical and tourist sites on the five Western provinces and the Isle of Youth special municipality, as well as curious facts and the region's characters.

① province of
Pinar del Río

A tobacco field

Westernmost of Cuban provinces, its main attraction for tourists is its natural beauty. The territory includes two areas that have been declared Reserves of the Biosphere by Unesco –the Rosario Mountain Range and the Guanahacabibes Peninsula. Called by some Cuba's "natural cathedral", Pinar del Río is not only famous for the Viñales Valley, a Unesco World Cultural Landscape, but also for growing the best tobacco in the world.

Crossed almost completely by the Guaniguanico Mountain Range, the province also offers the possibility of exploring magnificent caves and visiting important medicinal water springs, a collection of several virgin keys and islets and other ideal diving and sailing sites, as well as small lakes and reservoirs where fishing with light tackle is allowed.

Capital: Pinar del Río.

Area: 8,884. 51 Km^2.

Municipalities: Pinar del Río, Consolación del Sur, Los Palacios, La Palma, Minas de Matahambre, Viñales, San Luis, San Juan y Martínez, Guane, Mantua and Sandino.

Population: 590,000.

Boundaries: To the North, the Gulf of Mexico; to the East, the province of Artemisa; to the South, the Caribbean Sea; and to the West, the Yucatan Channel.

Economy: Industrial-agrarian.

Main products: Tobacco, cane sugar, fish and shellfish, among others.

Relief: Varied, The main geographic accident is the Guaniguanico Mountain Range, formed by the Órganos Range to the West, and the Rosario Range to the East. Its longest river is the Cuayaguateje, 112 Km long and with an area of 723 Km^2.

Access: The main gateway to the province from Havana is the National Expressway. You can also access by sea through the María La Gorda Marina, at the Guanahacabibes Peninsula.

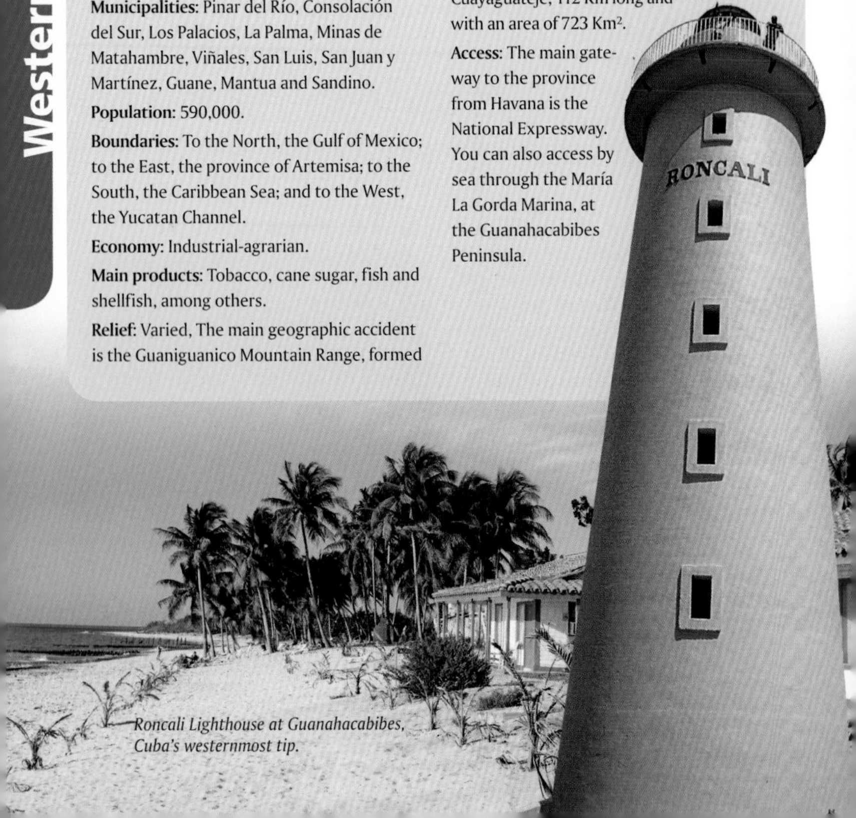

Roncali Lighthouse at Guanahacabibes, Cuba's westernmost tip.

② A map of the city of **Pinar del Río**

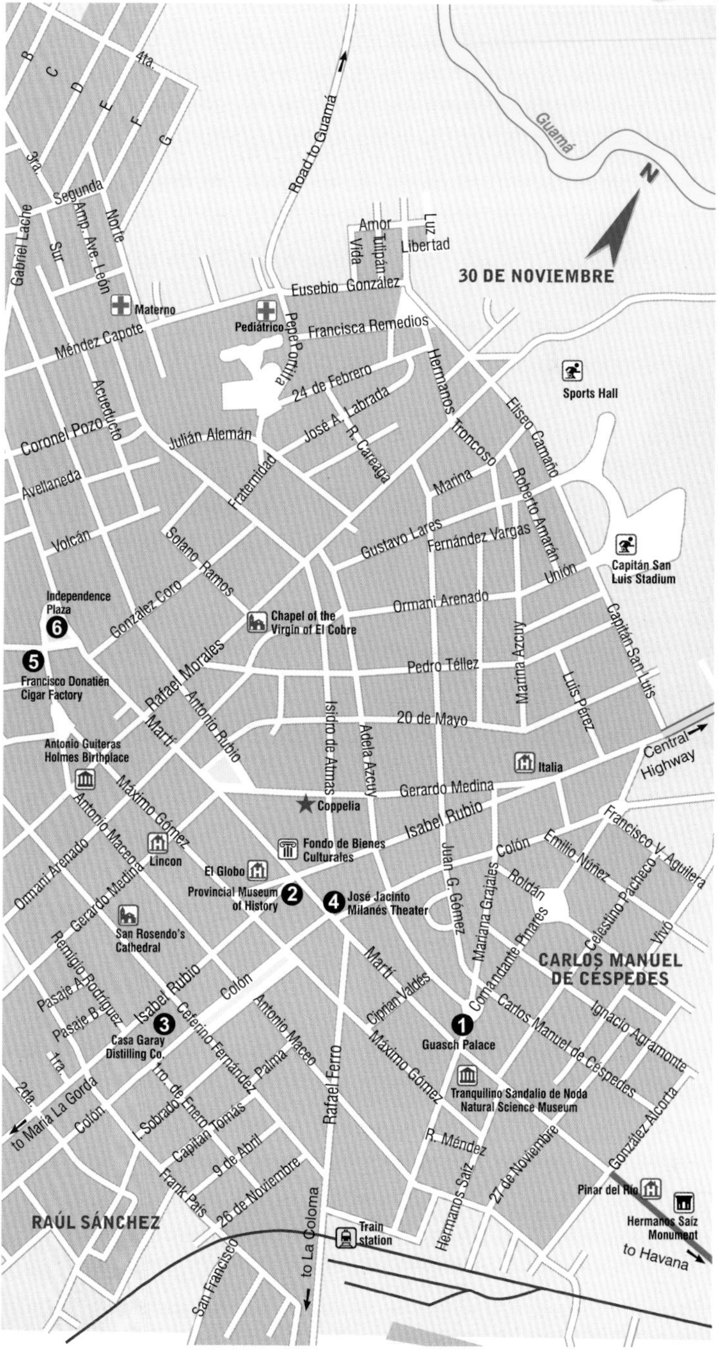

Pinar del Río

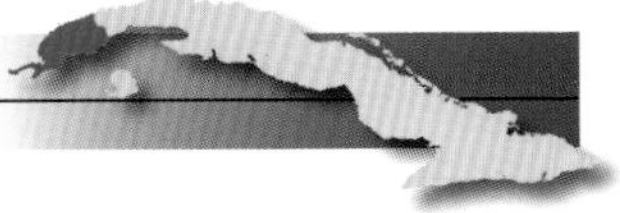

Sites of interest

❶ Guasch Palace

202, Martí Este St., Comandante Pinares.

From the patrimonial point of view, the facility is the most relevant in the city of Pinar del Río. It was designed and built by Francisco Guasch, from the foundations up, plinths, columns and capitals, coffering, friezes on the façade, as well as mosaics and the stained-glass windows. It is said that he even painted frescoes on the walls, designed most of the furniture and the lamps that were made in Europe. According to experts the building's style can only be described as eclectic *a la* Guasch, who took, reinterpreted and used elements from the different cultures he knew. At present, it houses the Tranquilino Sandalio de Noda Natural Science Museum.

❷ Provincial Museum of History

56 Martí Este St., between Colón and Isabel Rubio. Tel (5348) 754300.

Close to the Tranquilino Sandalio de Noda Natural Science Museum, it exhibits documents from the pre-Columbus era to the present. The museum was inaugurated on December 14, 1979 with a single exhibition room. Two years later it grew to the present number of five.

❸ Casa Garay Distilling Co.

189, Isabel Rubio Sur St., between Fernández and Frank País. Tel.: (5348) 752966.

Founded in 1892, this is the only place where the unique liqueur Guayabita del Pinar is made. For many, it is the seal of identity of the province, combining the best traditions of Spanish liqueurs and the delights of a local fruit that only grows here. Because of the traditional arts and techniques used in its production and packing, the Guayabita del Pinar has maintained its authenticity for over one hundred years.

Pinar del Río

Sites of interest

❹ José Jacinto Milanés Theater

60 José Martí St., between Recreo and Colón. Tel.: (5348) 753871.

On November 28, 1898, the former Lope de Vega Theater changed its name to the present one. On that day a banquet and ball were held at the theater in honor of Generals of the Independence Army Juan Lorente de la Rosa and Antonio Varona. In his speech, the theater's owner Félix del Pino Díaz said that once the War for Independence had ended, he would like to give the facility the name of Cuban poet and playwright José Jacinto Milanés, one of his favorites, born in the province of Matanzas.

❺ Francisco Donatién Cigar Factory

Máximo Gómez St. Tel.: (5348) 773069.

Located in a building that is an emblematic example of 19th century architecture in Pinar del Río, authentic Havana cigars are hand-rolled here in this factory with centuries-old traditional methods. At the entrance of the factory there is a store, and just facing it, a Casa del Habano with a wide selection of the best brands.

❻ Parque de la Independencia (Independence Plaza)

Ending of Martí on Real St.

Initially it was the Main Square, and like in the rest of the country, official buildings sprung up around it. In 1917 the Independence Plaza was built on it, with its concrete benches and gazebo. But during President Carlos Prío Socarrás (1948-1952) administration, it was demolished to substitute it with a parking lot. After the Cuban Revolution, the park was rebuilt and at present a new gazebo is rising up.

③ María La Gorda International Diving Center

Guanahacabibes Peninsula, Sandino.

One of the most spectacular diving sites on the island, harboring the largest population of black coral in the whole archipelago. It is named after the legend of María La Gorda (Fat Maria), who together with other women hid their treasure in these parts. In time, and overweight, she headed the brothel that catered to the crew of the ships that touched land in these parts. At present it is an ideal place for resting or diving, serviced by World Confederation of Sub-Aquatic Activities-certified equipment and instructors. Its sea bottom offers vivid colored contrasts and crystal-clear water for practicing underwater photography.

④ Guanahacabibes National Park

Guanahacabibes Peninsula, Sandino.

Recognized by Unesco in 1987 as a Reserve of the Biosphere, at the park you will find coral reefs and several endemic species. The Guanahacabibes Peninsula was one of the havens of aborigines that fled from Spanish conquistadors. It holds 140 archeological sites linked to the life of these aborigines, known as *Guanahatabeyes*. Located in the westernmost part of Sandino municipality, in the peninsula's south coast from Corrientes Cape to El Cajón, there are great sandy beaches where every year loggerhead and green sea turtles come to lay their eggs. The park's forests are home to thousands of hutias, iguanas, wild pigs and deer. Hunting and fishing are not allowed in most of the park, but lately a very special infrastructure has been developed for ecological tourism, where planned catch-and-release fishing is allowed, thus preserving marine species.

⑤ Viñales Valley

Los Jazmines Hotel.

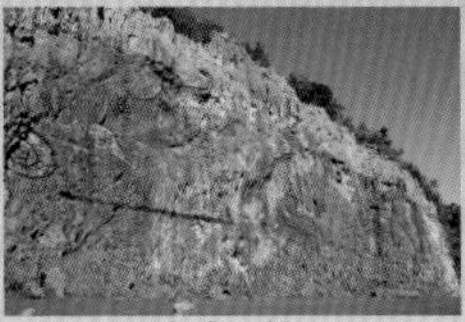
Mural of Prehistory.

Cave of the Indian.

Located at the Órganos Mountain Range, in the Guaniguanico Range, the valley and a large part of the range became in 1999 a national park, In December of that same year, Unesco declared it a World Heritage Site in the category of Cultural Landscape. Typical of the site are the unique *mogotes*, hillocks of limestone, honeycombed with cavities and with a nearly flat top. Seventeen endemic botanical species thrive in the valley, the most peculiar the cork palm (*Microcycas calocoma*), a 150 million years living fossil. There are 47 archeological sites in Viñales, and 19 of them are related to aborigine communities previous to the Spanish colonization, with evidence of funeral rites. Twenty of the sites are linked to runaway African slaves. Among Viñales' attractions are the Cave of the Indian, the Mural of Prehistory, the great Santo Tomás Cave, San Vicente Ranch and Los Jazmines Lookout

Mural of Prehistory: Located at Dos Hermanas Valley, the spectacular mural (120 meters high and 160 meters long) was painted on the Pita mogote by Leovigildo González Morillo, already deceased, who was Cuban Academy of Science's Chief Cartographer. You will find on the mural Guanahatabey aborigines, mammals, gigantic animals and mollusks. In 12 pieces, the evolution process of humans and that of animals can be appreciated.

Cave of the Indian: Two subterranean rivers flow through this 300-meter long cave. Stalactites and stalagmites make different forms and figures, and in its interior cave paintings and fragments of utensils have been found, as well as aborigine' burial sites. The biggest attraction for tourists is the boat ride through the subterranean San Vicente River. The Cave of the Indian is close to the Viñales-San Cayetano highway, about 5 kilometers from the town of Viñales.

A landscape of Viñales with "mogotes" in the background.

Pinar del Río

Sites of interest

⑥ Cayo Levisa

Located in La Palma municipality, in North Pinar del Río, it is part of Las Coloradas archipelago. There is a concrete-built hotel, but with a typical thatched roof. There are also log cabañas built on stilts and covered with tiles similar to typical Cuban roofing.

⑦ La Güira National Park

The park is situated in the midst of a colorful landscape with distinctive architectural, sculptural, and cultural elements. It is part of the former Cortina Hacienda, founded in 1920, the property of absentee large landowner José Manuel Cortina.

The Best Tobacco in the World

Experts consider Cuban tobacco the best in the world. Its quality is born at the field, where farmers transmit their secrets from fathers to sons. This is the beginning of a process that goes through the factory and ends with marketing and distribution. Only some lands called "vegas" (meadows) are considered fit for making a Havana cigar. There are four tobacco regions in Cuba: Vuelta Abajo (Pinar del Río), Semi Vuelta (Consolación del Sur), Partido (San Antonio de los Baños), Vuelta Arriba (Remedios, in Central Cuba), and Bariay (Eastern Cuba).

But the best of all is Vuelta Abajo, the only region that produces all kinds of leaves. Even here, only a small number of plots are rated as Vegas Finas de Primera, where the tobacco grown is used for Havana cigars. Some of the most famous are Vizcaíno, East of the city of Pinar del Río; El Corojo and Cuchillas de Baracoa, at San Luis; and Hoyo de Monterrey, at San Juan y Martínez.

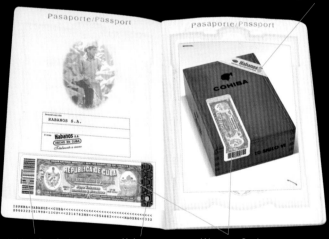

Artemisa

The lake at Las Terrazas community.

Artemisa is one of two new Cuban provinces voted by the National Assembly on August 2010, and in force since January 1, 2011. Eight of its municipalities were part of the former province of Habana, and the other three belonged to Pinar Río. During the War of Independence of 1895, as part of the so called "Invasion to the West", Cuban troops led by General Antonio Maceo held several battles in the territory. Years later most of the participants in the attack to the Moncada Barracks on July 26, 1953 came from Artemisa. Important figures of Cuban culture are native to this province, such as Cirilo Villaverde, the first important Cuban novelist and author of *Cecilia Valdés*; singer/songwriter María Teresa Vera; Silvio Rodríguez, the most famous member of the Nueva Trova Movement; and Polo Montañez, country music singer/songwriter, born in the Rosario Range. There are two outstanding institutions in the province, the Museum of Humor and the Film and TV International School, both at San Antonio de los Baños. Among the school's founders are Colombian Nobel Prize winner Gabriel García Márquez, Argentinean Fernando Birri and Cuban Julio García Espinosa, both filmmakers.

On nature, Artemisa has much to offer, including the beauty of the famous orchid garden at Soroa and the rural experience of Las Terrazas community, both part of the Rosario Range Reserve of the Biosphere. Another one of its attractions is the visit to the Angerona ruins, evidence of the times when coffee plantations reigned in the region in the 19th century and gave Artemisa the nickname of the Garden of Cuba. It also has El Salado Beach, with different tourist facilities.

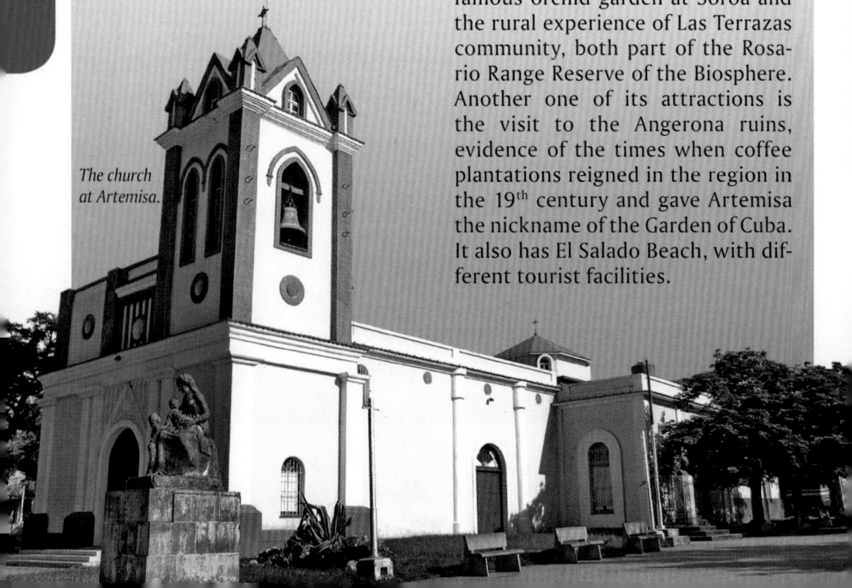
The church at Artemisa.

Artemisa

Sites of interest

Capital: Artemisa.

Area: 4,004.27 Km².

Municipalities: Mariel, Guanajay, Caimito, Bauta, San Antonio de los Baños, Güira de Melena, Alquízar, Artemisa, Bahía Honda, Candelaria and San Cristóbal.

Population: 500,000.

Boundaries: To the North with the Florida Straits and the Gulf of Mexico; to the East with the provinces of Havana and Mayabeque; to the South with the Batabanó Gulf; and to the West with the province of Pinar del Río.

Economy: Agriculture, cattle raising, sugar cane growing. Its large agricultural areas (68.1 % of the territory) satisfy local demand and the produce is also marketed in Havana. It also includes Mariel, where great plans are in motion for developing its high potential as a port and industrial zone.

Main products: Tubers, vegetables, citrus, fruits and tobacco (the latter in the vicinity of San Antonio de los Baños), as well as cement, roof tiles, carbide, acetylene, electric power, light, mechanical, food and sugar industries.

Relief: Predominantly plain, although it includes the Rosario Range, part of the Guaniguanico Mountain Range. The highest elevation of the territory is the Pan de Guajaibón (699 meters), in the municipality of Bahía Honda. Here is also the shortest distance between the North and South coasts of the island (31 Km), between Mariel Bay and Majana Cove, municipality of Artemisa.

Access: Mainly by land (highways and railroad).

(9) Rosario Range

The Rosario Range, the first in Cuba to be awarded the condition of Reserve of the Biosphere, lies at the Eastern limit of the Guaniguanico Mountain Range. It has some 800 plant species, 34 percent of which are endemic, together with most of the wildlife present in the country, particularly the bee hummingbird (*Mellisuga helenae*), the smallest bird on the planet, the Cuban trogon and several species of woodpeckers. The province is also proud of the Soroa Resort, home to the largest orchid garden in Cuba, and Las Terrazas tourist resort.

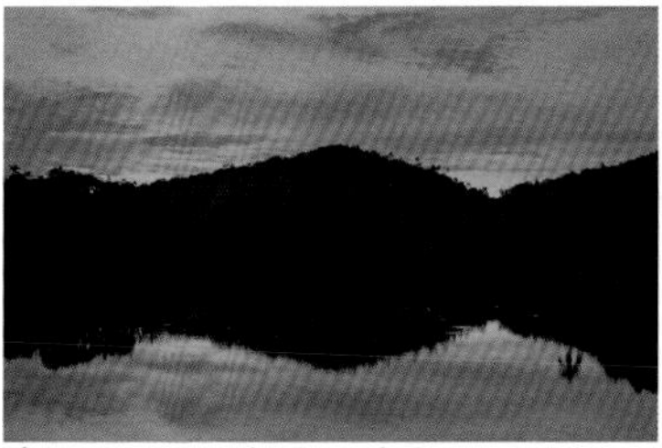

The sunset at Rosario Mountain Range.

Las Terrazas community.

Artemisa

Sites of interest

The pool at Soroa Villa.

⑩ Soroa

Soroa Highway, Km 8, Candelaria.

This beautiful and most varied spot attracts visitors from all over the world. It was named after two Spanish immigrants, the Lorenzo and Antonio Soroa brothers, who arrived to the area in 1856 dreaming of making a fortune. The Soroas bought several coffee plantations and in time the area took their name. Located at the limits of the Rosario Range's heights, it includes several attractions.

El Castillo en las Nubes (Castle in the Clouds): The construction, commissioned in 1940 by plantation owner Antonio Arturo Sánchez Bustamante and located on El Fuerte Hill, includes elements of medieval architecture. It has an exhibit of pieces from real medieval castles, bought by its former owner in European auctions. At present it is a restaurant.

El Mirador (The Lookout): At 250 meters above sea level, it offers one of the best views of the Rosario and Órganos mountain ranges.

Soroa Orchid and Botanical Garden: In 1952, Spanish lawyer Tomás Felipe Camacho, famous for his large orchid collection, began to build a garden near his Pinilla Ranch, in honor of his wife and daughter. Exotic species of Asian, Central and South American orchids, as well as many local ones, fill this garden that kept growing with the years. Today it is the largest orchid garden in the country and one of the most important in the world, with over 20,000 specimens of 700 species in an area of 35,000 square meters. On the

The entrance to Soroa Villa.

Artemisa
Sites of interest

Soroa Waterfall.

premises you will find a library specialized in orchids.

Soroa Waterfall: The Manantiales River and its small waterfall (22 meters high) is one of the site's wonders, also known as Cuba's Rainbow. There are paths by the river that go down to a natural pool formed by the waterfall where visitors take a dip and enjoy the splendid surroundings.

Castle in the Clouds.

Restaurante El Cafetal.

Río y baños del San Juan.

⑪ Las Terrazas Tourist Resort

Havana-Pinar del Río Highway, Km 51, Las Terrazas Community, Candelaria.

Las Terrazas Tourist Resort is a rural experiment of sustainable development located at the Rosario Reserve of the Biosphere, 60 Km west of Havana. It has a small town by a small lake, with an architecture that is a model of integration with the surroundings. There are several facilities offering services, as well as the Moka Hotel. You can also stay at private homes. If you want to live in direct contact with Nature, you can camp by the San Juan River or by the San Claudio Waterfalls.

Moka Hotel at Las Terrazas.

Rancho Curujey: A bar and lookout with a wonderful view.

Water Activities Center: At the lake, by the town's entrance, you can rent rowing boats and watercycles. Trout fishing is allowed, but only in the catch and release modality.

Unión Hacienda: A country estate near the ruins of La Unión coffee plantation (early 19th century), with services by a local family. It has a restaurant and La Unión tropical garden.

Ruins of the Buena Vista Coffee Plantation: There is a restaurant with a lookout at 240 meters above sea level.

Polo Montañez's Home: A museum to honor Polo Montañez (June 5, 1955-November 26, 2002), a local singer/songwriter that in his short career gained national and international recognition thanks to his unique style and songs.

San Juan River's Baths: A spa on the San Juan River with natural pools of crystal clear medicinal waters, some of them deep.

Routes and Paths: There are several paths with different degrees of difficulty, although apt for most tourists: *Ruta de la Cañada del Infierno* (Hell's Ravine Route), *Las Delicias* (The Delights), *La Serafina*, *El Terraceo* (Terracing), *El placer de caminar* (The Pleasure of Trekking), *El Taburete* (The Stool), and *El canto del tocororo* (The Trogon's Song).

⑫ Angerona Coffee Plantation

Artemisa-Cayajabos Highway, Km. 5.

A symbol of the splendor and wealth of coffee plantations in Western Cuba in colonial times, the ruins of the former Angerona coffee plantation are today a site of great value due to its history and exceptional architecture. In the first quarter of the 19th century it was recognized as the most important coffee plantation in West Cuba and the second of the island. Its history is linked to German immigrant Cornelius Souchay, who bought the land in 1813, and Ursula Lambert, a free black woman born in Haiti who came to Cuba fleeing from the revolutionary war. People say that in spite of social and racial prejudices of the time, they lived an intense love affair. The story inspired the film *Roble de Olor*, by Cuban director Rigoberto López.

All that remains of the former coffee plantation, a National Monument since 1989, is a fragment of the owner's manor, the farm manager's home, the water storage system, the confinement walls for slaves and the watchtower. At the plantation's entrance there was a Carrara marble statue of the Roman goddess Angerona. At present, the figure can be seen at Artemisa's Municipal Museum.

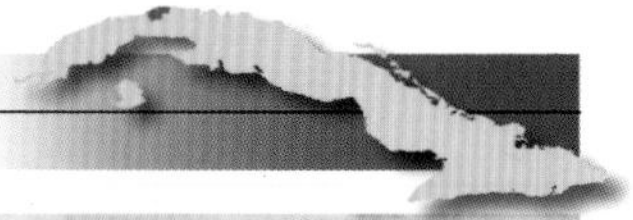

(13) province of

Havana

The Three Kings of El Morro Castle.

As restless as the rest of the first Cuban towns, St. Christopher of Havana was founded in 1514 at a site on the South coast, on a low and unhealthy land that forced the early migration of its neighbors to the North. The pilgrimage of the fifth and westernmost of the first towns ended five years later at the Port of Careening. The story goes that founding festivities at St. Christopher were on the same day that those of St. James the Greater, on July 25, and the bishop could not attend the Havana celebrations. So on an undetermined good day, the city ruled that the festivities would take place on November 16. Traditionally, on that date Havana citizens flock to the Templete (the Small Temple), site of the foundation, and circle a legendary silk-cotton tree three times and ask the patron saint for the same number of wishes.

At this point, a tour can be made of Havana's oldest section, declared a World Heritage Site in 1982 by Unesco. The Historical Center, in the midst of a restoration process by the Office of the City's Historian, headed by Eusebio Leal, is an invitation to breathe in the past and modernity in its streets and buildings, many of them restored to serve as museums, art galleries, hotels, restaurants and facilities for social and community services.

Diverse in its architecture and details, the city invites visitors to expand their experience into other very attractive areas. Across the bay you will find the towns of Regla and Casablanca, with their picturesque sites; to the East lies Guanabacoa, which seduces for its Afro Cuban traditions; the beaches of this area are an invitation to the immensity of the sea. More to the center of the city, you can discover the beat of urban life in Old Havana, Cerro and Centro Habana. The capital of Cuba changes its look until it surprises visitors with residential neighborhoods like El Vedado and Miramar, the latter more to the West, part of the municipality of Playa. In the outskirts, Nature reigns at places like Lenin Park and the National Botanical Garden.

Havana is also the nation's cultural capital, for it is the venue of the most important events held in the country, such as the International Ballet Festival, the Latin American New Cinema Festival, Jazz Plaza Festival, the Havana Biennale of Visual Arts, and the International Book Fair, It also has a wide network of art galleries, movies and theaters, such as the García Lorca, Bertold Brecht, Hubert de Blanck, Nacional, Mella, Karl Marx, and also concert halls such as St. Francis of Assisi Lesser Basilica, Paula Church, and San Felipe Neri Oratorio, the last three at the Historical Center.

Many nightclubs and discos liven up Havana nights all over the city, particularly at El Vedado and Playa. The most famous place is the fabulous Tropicana, the legendary Gato Tuerto –a night spot from the 1960s where you can enjoy *feeling*, a musical style born in the 1940s and still much alive–; and La Zorra y el Cuervo for jazz fans.

A view of the city from San Carlos de la Cabaña.

José Martí Revolution Square

Above: A view of the city; below: Nacional Hotel

Capital: Havana.

Area: 721.01 Km^2.

Municipalities: Arroyo Naranjo, Boyeros, Centro Habana, Cerro, Cotorro, Diez de Octubre, Guanabacoa, Habana del Este, Habana Vieja, La Lisa, Marianao, Playa, Plaza de la Revolución, Regla and San Miguel del Padrón.

Population: Over 2,100,000.

Boundaries: To the North with the Florida Straits; to the East with Mayabeque province; to the South with Mayabeque and Artemisa; and to the West with Artemisa.

Economy: Havana is the center of Cuban industries, but tourism is its main source of income. There is a science park west of the city, home to Cuba's biotechnology companies that export medical products, equipments, and vaccines that compete with its counterparts in more developed countries. At present, Havana is the country's main port of entry.

Main Products: Electric power, steel and metallurgical production, oil derivatives, glass, pharmaceutical and biotechnology products, food industry, textiles, perfumes, cosmetics, cigars and cigarettes, liquor distilleries.

Relief: The territory of the province consists of the Havana Plains and the Havana-Matanzas Heights. Its greatest elevation is Tetas de Managua (210 m) and the longest river the Almendares (49.8 Km).

Access: Its main access is by air, with three international terminals and one national airport. There is also access by sea through the Hemingway and Tarará marinas, as well as through the Cruiser Terminal at Havana Bay. The capital is connected to the rest of the country by the National Expressway and the railway network.

Additional information: Havana is the capital of the Republic of Cuba. From 1976 to the 2010 its official name was City of Havana. With the new political and administrative division of the country, in August 2010 the National Assembly of Popular Power voted to restore Havana's original name. This is the seat of the country's main institutions, such as the Council of State, the National Assembly and the Council of Ministers. At Havana are also located the greater part of entities, enterprises, both local and foreign. It is the main tourist destination and has the largest hotel infrastructure, many of them 5 stars, like the Nacional de Cuba Hotel.

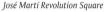

The Giraldilla, the city's symbol.

⑭ A map of the city of **Havana**

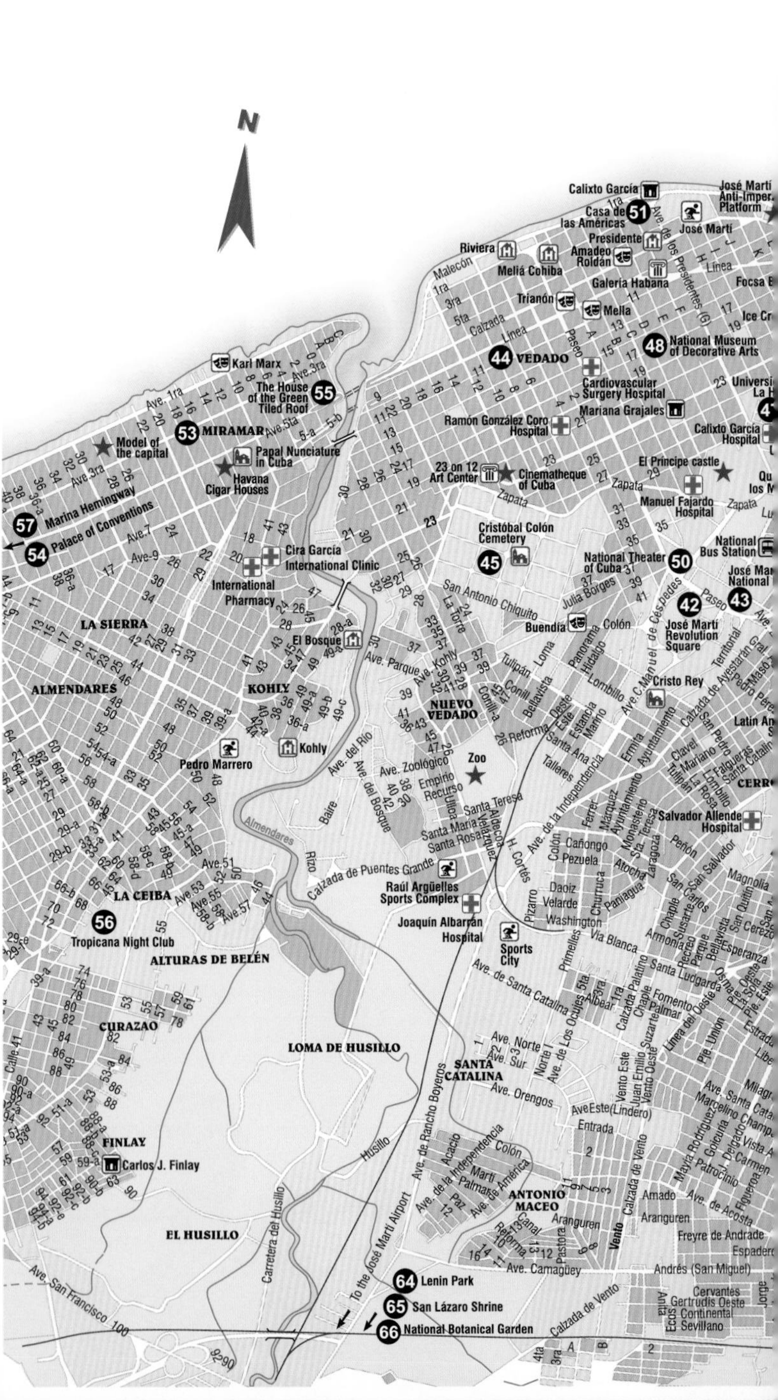

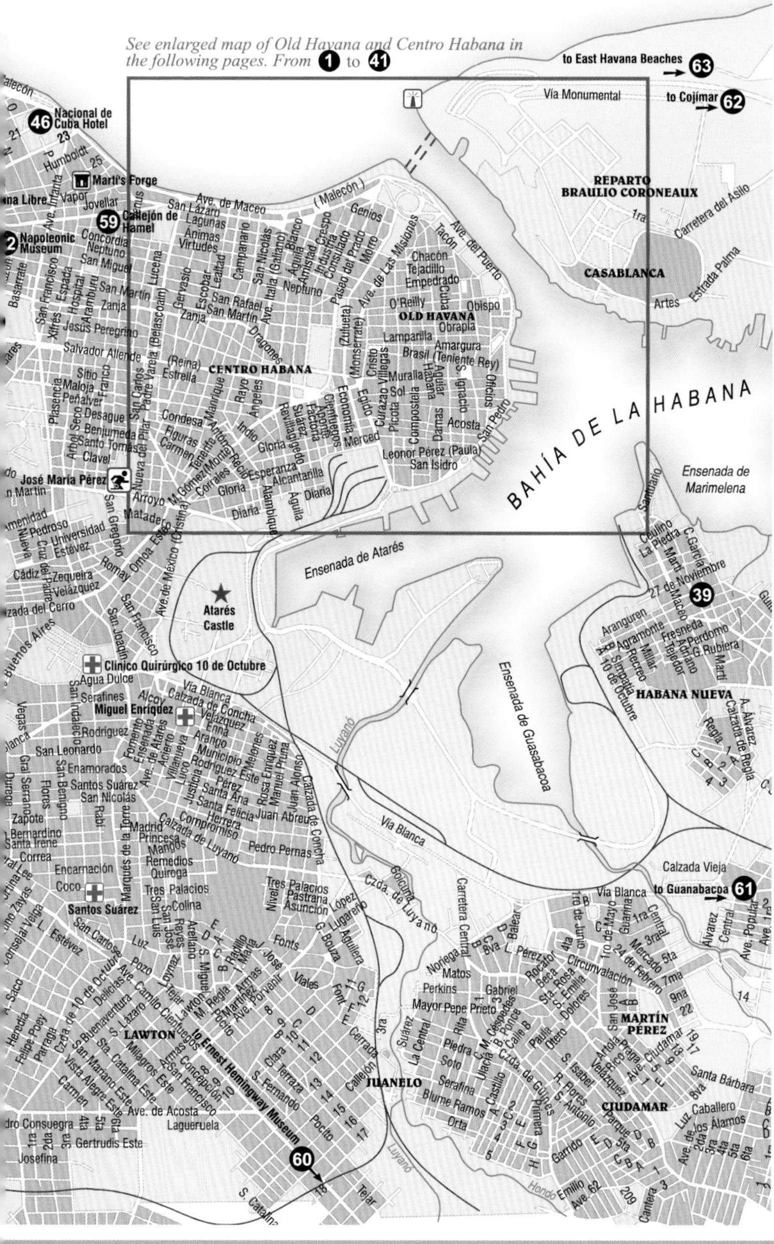
See enlarged map of Old Havana and Centro Habana in the following pages. From 1 to 41
to East Havana Beaches 63
to Cojímar 62
Vía Monumental
REPARTO BRAULIO CORONEAUX
CASABLANCA
Carretera del Asilo
Estrada Palma
Artes
46 Nacional de Cuba Hotel
Martí's Forge
59 Callejón de Hamel
2 Napoleonic Museum
Ave. de Maceo
(Malecón)
OLD HAVANA
CENTRO HABANA
BAHÍA DE LA HABANA
Ensenada de Marimelena
Ensenada de Atarés
Atarés Castle
39
José María Pérez
Clínico Quirúrgico 10 de Octubre
Miguel Enríquez
HABANA NUEVA
Ensenada de Guasabacoa
Vía Blanca
Calzada Vieja
to Guanabacoa 61
Santos Suárez
LAWTON
to Ernest Hemingway Museum
60
JUANELO
MARTÍN PÉREZ
CIUDAMAR
Luyanó

A map of **Old Havana and Centro Habana**

N
San Salv
La Punta
Ave. de Maceo
(Malecón)
San Lázaro Cove
Chapel of the Immaculate Virgin
Hermanos Ameijeiras
San Lázaro
Lagunas
Ánimas
Virtudes
Concordia
Neptuno
Genios
Refugio
Colón
Trocadero
Blanco
Águila
Amistad
Crespo
Industria
Consulado
Paseo del Prado (The Prado Promenade)
Sevilla
National Museum of Fine Arts
24
Plaza
29
Venus
M. González
Lucena
Escobar
Lealtad
Perseverancia
Campanario
San Nicolás
CENTRO HABANA
San Miguel
San Rafael
San Martín
Zanja
Ave. Italia (Galiano)
Inglaterra Hotel
26
27
Parque Central
José Martí
Grand Theater of Havana
25
34
Payret
Bernaza
(Belascoaín)
Gervasio
Pacífico Restaurant
La Muralla Restaurant
30
Havana's Chinatown
J.Peregrino
Salud
28
The Capitol
Havana Cigar Houses
Agramonte
(Zulueta)
(Monserrate)
Church of the Sacred Heart of Jesus
Carlos III
Padre Varela
Manrique
Salvador Allende
(Reina)
Dragones
Fraternity Plaza
32
The Fountain of the Indian Woman
Estrella
Maloja
Sitio
Peñalver
Condesa
Concepción de la Valla
Figuras
Carmen
San Carlos
Rayo
Ángeles
Indio
Revillagigedo
Suárez
Factoría
Aponte
Cienfuegos
Economía
Egido
Gloria
Misión
Esperanza
Alcantarilla
Central train station
Nueva del Pilar
Lindero
Tenerife
Máximo Gómez(Monte)
Antón Recio
Corrales
Alambique
Águila
Diaria
Arroyo
Matadero
Puerta Cerrada

37 Three Kings Castle of El Morro
62
39
63
to Cojímar
to Regla
to East Havana Beaches
REPARTO BRAULIO CORONEAUX
Monument to Medical Students
Máximo Gómez
40 The Havana tunnel
Chapel
Main Square
Fortifications and Weapons
38 San Carlos de la Cabaña Fortress
Cannon Shot 9 O'clock Ceremony
1ra
National Museum of Music
Historical Center's Amphitheater
Ave. del Puerto
Remains of the Old City Walls
Cuarteles
Tacón
Chacón
31 Church of the Holy Custodian Angel
Street Los Cocos
The Christ of Havana 41
CASABLANCA
Tejadillo
La Bodeguita del Medio 10
9 Havana Cathedral
Cathedral Square 8
4 Castle of the Royal Force
Empedrado
San Juan de Dios
Colonial Art Museum 11
Aries
Museum of the City 3
1 Main Square
2 El Templete
Santa Isabel
O'Reilly
Aguiar
Cuba
San Ignacio
Obispo
Ambos Mundos
OLD HAVANA
Mercaderes
Obrapía
BAHÍA DE LA HABANA
Lamparilla
Stock Exchange 7
the Christ
Amargura
5 San Francisco Square
6 Convent of San Francisco de Asís
Oficios
Museum of Havana's Pharmacies
Brasil (Teniente Rey)
16
12 14 Camera Obscura
Rene Portocarrero Serigraphy Workshop
The Old Square 13 Planetarium
Muralla
Alejandro de Humboldt
Rum Museum
Aguacate
Compostela
Habana
Sol
22 Santa Clara Convent
Santa Clara
Luz
Ferry to Regla
Jesús María
Damas
23 Church of the Holy Spirit
San Pedro
Merced
21 Our Lady of Mercy Church
Poplar Grove Avenue 18
José Martí's Birthplace and Museum
Leonor Pérez (Paula)
Paula Church
San Isidro
19 San José Arts and crafts fair
Havana's Defense System
Regla 39

OLD HAVANA'S HISTORICAL CENTER

On December 14, 1982, Old Havana's Historical Center and its colonial fortification system were included by Unesco in its list of World Heritage Sites. From that moment on restoring efforts on the old part of the city by several Cuban institutions were intensified. For the Office of the City's Historian, the agency charged with the task of heading the area's restoration, saving the original core of the city became its top priority.

Attracted by this preserved site, travelers walk the streets that once upon a time captivated traders, seamen and illustrious people. Visitors are surprised by the majesty of the 100-plus year old Santa Isabel Hotel, by the originality of hostels that recapture medieval atmospheres, pubs and taverns in the old Spanish tradition, intimate moods and other places catering to the most demanding of tastes.

The setting at Main Square

1 Main Square

A few steps away from where the town of St. Christopher of Havana was founded, the Main Square marked the development of a city that grew around its most important plazas. The square was built between the Greater Parochial Church and the Castle of the Royal Force, a spot that grouped the political, military, religious and civil functions of a growing population. Although its existence is documented since 1559, its space was demarcated in 1582 and seven years later achieved its definite profile. At present it is surrounded by two of the most important public buildings of the time –the Royal Post Office (1772-1790), subsequently the Lieutenant Governor's Palace, and the Captain General's (Governor) Palace, since 1968 the City Museum. Other constructions, such as the Count of Santovenia's Palace (today Santa Isabel Hotel), and El Templete (Spanish for small temple), a memento of the city's foundation, were also built around the Main Square.

At present it is the venue of important official celebrations and one of its streets, paved with wooden blocks, where the National Concert Band routinely performs, has become also the stage for dancers, actors and music performers. Around the Square you will find Old Havana's booksellers, who exhibit their old and second-hand books lending additional charm to the site.

La Habana

Sites of interest

❷ El Templete

Baratillo and O'Reilly, Main Square.

El Templete, inaugurated on March 19, 1828, was built according to the design of Antonio María de la Torre as a remembrance of the town's foundation. Its Neo-Classic style reproduces a Greek-Roman temple in smaller dimensions. Bishop Juan José Díaz de Espada presided over the inaugural act and French painter Jean-Baptiste Vermay reproduced the moment in canvas. The painting can be seen inside the Templete, together with two others that represent the first mass and the first town council meeting.

Every year, on November 16, Havanians come to this place to commemorate the founding of the city and for taking part in a ceremony transmitted from one century to the other. They circle the silk-cotton tree three times, ask for their wishes and subsequently make a pilgrimage to the Cathedral, where the image of the city's patron saint St. Christopher is worshipped.

❸ Museum of the City

1 Tacón St., between Obispo and O'Reilly.

Inaugurated on 1791 by Captain General Don Luis de las Casas Arragorri, the buildinghoused the heads of three different types of governments –the Spanish governor, the US military governor, and the President of Cuba up to 1920. It was also the City Jail, seat of the Office of the City Historian since 1938, under the aegis of Dr. Emilio Roig de Leuchsenring (1889-1964), and also City Hall until 1967, when restoration work began. A year later it became the Museum of the City. The institution has several rooms for permanent exhibits dedicated to the history of the Cuban nation. Its atmosphere is a reminder of colonial times and in its interior notable collections that extol the national patrimony can be found.

❹ Museum Castle of the Royal Force

Main Square, Tel.: (537) 8644488.

Considered the most important example of Renaissance architecture in Cuba, according to experts, the Castle of the Royal Force was a paradigm for the building of other fortifications in the American continent between the 16th and 18th centuries. Besides the royal coat of arms of the House of Austria that appears over its main gate, the fortress has among its attributes the Giraldilla, a sculpture cast in bronze by Havana artist Jerónimo Martínez Pinzón and placed as a weather vane on top of the northwest tower at the time of Governor Juan Vitrián Viamonte, between 1630 and 1634. The original sculpture is on display inside the Museum Castle of the Royal Force, while the one crowning the castle is a replica.

The setting at San Francisco Square

5 San Francisco Square

San Francisco Square, by Havana Bay, played an essential role in the development of the city. Its position made it the center of business activities in relation to exports and imports, as well as for disembarking troops and seamen. The construction of a simple Franciscan convent, transformed later in one of the most beautiful buildings of the area, was the reason for its name. Around it began to spring up docks, scriveners, residences of notables, and until 1792 government institutions, as well as the city hall, the governor's mansion and the jail, all which moved subsequently to the Main Square.

A distinguishing trait is the Fountain of the Lions, by Italian sculptor Giuseppe Gaggini at the time of Captain General Miguel Tacón. It was built of white marble and bears, sculpted allegories of the city and commerce. In the 20th century (1909), the square welcomed a new addition, the Stock Exchange, a massive building crowned with the statue of Mercury.

Culture, commerce and real estate converge today at San Francisco Square. The convent itself has become an emporium of the arts; the Stock Exchange is the seat of Áurea Real Estate Company; and several artists have their studios and galleries near the square, where the Marquis of San Felipe and Santiago Hotel is one of the latest facilities.

6 Convent of San Francisco de Asís

Oficios between Amargura and Churruca.

At present it is a cultural complex that boasts one of the city's best concert halls, the Lesser Basilica of St. Francis of Assisi, dedicated to choral and chamber music, and the only Museum of Sacred Art in the country. It also has three areas for exhibits and different events. From its tower, one of the highest in colonial times (42 m), a great panorama of the city can be admired.

Havana's Defense System

Due to the constant threat of pirates and corsairs in the early 16th century, the Spanish Crown decided to strengthen the city's defenses. The first fort, built around 1510, was known as the Old Force. This original fortress, after French pirate Jacques de Sores torched it down, ceded its space to the Castle of the Royal Force (1558-1576), which can be seen at the Main Square. From that moment on there were watch towers at the bay's entrance, at San Lázaro Cove and at the Morro; trenches were dug in La Punta and a platform with two guns was built. This system of defense, declared by Unesco a World Heritage Site in 1982, also has the fort of La Chorrera, the San Lázaro watchtower, La Punta and Morro castles, the San Carlos de la Cabaña Fortress, El Príncipe and Atarés castles, and the land and sea walls that divided Havana into the outer and inner city.

7 Stock Exchange *2 Lamparilla St., San Francisco Square.*

Since 1996, after a thorough remodeling by the Office of the City's Historian and the Spanish banking group Argentaria, the Stock Exchange was inaugurated as an office building. It has six floors divided into 74 modules, which can be redesigned into sub-modules. With a usable area of over 9,000 square meters, it has the characteristic of an "intelligent" building, for its functions are computer-controlled. The building is managed by Áurea Real Estate Co.

The setting at Cathedral Square

8 Cathedral Square

Originally it was Swamp Square, because of the marshy land due to subterranean springs where it stood. At its mouth, the Díaz Pimienta family set up house and under their sponsorship the first Havana ships were built in the late 17th century. One hundred years later some manors began to appear, such as Luis Chacón's, the first Havana-born governor of the island in the early 18th century, and other edifications –the Lombillo Palace, and mansions belonging to the Marquis de Arcos, the Count of Peñalver, and the Marquis of Aguas Claras. In the late 18th century, a church built by the Jesuit order was promoted to the status of cathedral. Thus the original plaza became Cathedral Square.

At present it is one of the most photographed spots in Havana, and also the stage for official gala dinners and cultural presentations. Dominated by the majesty of the church, there are several cultural and recreational facilities, such as the Colonial Art Museum, El Patio restaurant, the Víctor Manuel Art Gallery, and the Experimental Graphic Workshop of Havana, at the Chorro Alley (Callejón del Chorro). In its surroundings you will find the Alejo Carpentier Foundation, the Wifredo Lam Contemporary Art Center and the famous La Bodeguita del Medio Restaurant.

9 Havana Cathedral *156 Empedrado St.*

Although the Jesuit order was expelled in 1767 and its properties confiscated, the construction of the church that the Company of Jesus had planned at Swamp Square was not halted. In 1773 the Greater Parochial Church was moved here and in 1789 the temple with its Baroque façade was given the status of cathedral. Bishop Juan J. Díaz de Espada modified the interior in the Neoclassical style, a symbol of progress at the time. He also commissioned frescoes from Italian Giovanni Perovani, which were later restored by Jean-Baptiste Vermay. Christopher Columbus remains allegedly were brought here from Hispaniola in 1796 and were kept in the Cathedral until 1898, when they were taken to Spain. The main image of St. Christopher, the city's patron saint and protector of travelers, is found at the church.

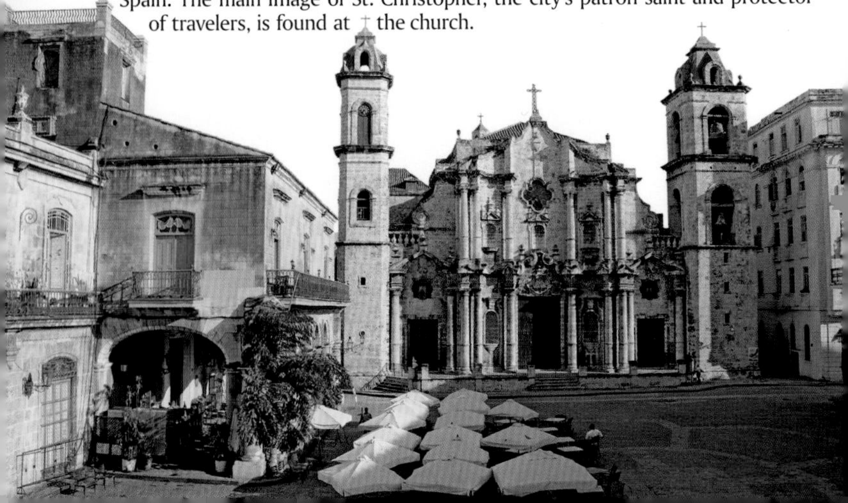

⑩ La Bodeguita del Medio

206 Empedrado St., between San Ignacio and Cuba. Tel.:(537) 8671374.

A very well-known restaurant and one of the city's great tourist attractions, where countless visitors have left their imprint in a souvenir, a photo or on its graffiti covered walls. Here you will find signatures by Errol Flynn, Nat King Cole, Ernest Hemingway, Pablo Neruda, Gabriel García Márquez, Alejo Carpentier and Nicolás Guillén, among many others.

⑪ Colonial Art Museum

61 San Ignacio. Tel.: (537) 8664458.

The Colonial Art Museum, housed in a typical example of 18th century domestic architecture at Cathedral Square, exhibits decorative art of a transcendental era in the formation of Cuban identity. There are several collections, from furniture to glassware, chinaware, textiles, paintings, carriages and gold and silver articles that reveal the dominant tastes and customs of that bygone time.

The setting at The Old Square

12 The Old Square

The hustle and bustle of life at San Francisco Square, livened by the harking of street vendors, bothered the hush and quiet of religious services at the Basilica. For that reason, the Franciscan fathers requested the creation of a square for commerce and trade, which finally came into being in the late 17th century under the name of Plaza Nueva (Spanish for New Square). In the 19th century it lost its original name and became the Plaza Vieja (Old Square), limited by Mercaderes, Muralla, Teniente Rey (aka Brasil) and San Ignacio streets. In honor of the Queen, Cristina Market was built on the center of the square. In 1908, it was demolished and the Juan Bruno Zayas Plaza was constructed. Other transformations came with the 20th century: manors became administrative and business offices, tenement buildings sprang up, and in 1952 an underground parking lot was built beneath the square.

After the declaration of the Historical Center as a World Heritage Site, architects and restorers insisted on saving the Old Square. At present it is one of the most beautiful public spaces in the city, surrounded by businesses, as well as real estate companies, private homes and educational and cultural centers.

13 Planetarium

Old Square. Tel.: 864 9544.

The result of an ambitious project by the Office of the City's Historian, it is located in the building where the Habana Movie Theater once stood, very close to the unique Camera Obscura lookout. In the space theater with a seating capacity of 65, there is a projector of 6,500 stars, and a huge sphere representing the sun. The equipment and accessories, donated by the Government of Japan, give visitors a view of the origins of the Universe in a tour through several rooms and galleries.

14 Camera Obscura

Teniente Rey and Mercaderes. Tel.: 8621801.

On the last floor of the Gómez Vila building, at Old Square, you can witness the wonderful view of a living city. It is based on an optical effect that reflects on a white concave screen the scenes of everyday life taking place at that same instant. A twin of the Tavira Tower in Cádiz, Spain, the Havana Camera Obscura is the only one in Latin America and one of the six existing in the world –two others in the UK, two in Spain, and one in Portugal.

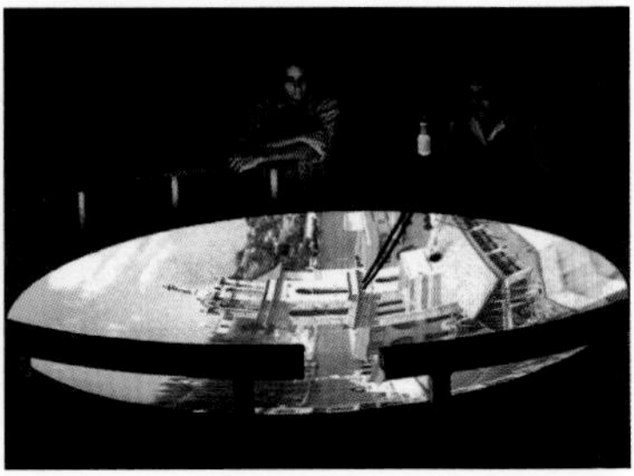

The setting at Square of the Christ

⓯ Plaza del Cristo (Square of the Christ)

The Square of the Christ of the Good Voyage sprang up in 1640 besides its namesake Church, also called "the humiliating place", for it was the final station of the Via Crucis procession that went down Amarguras St. The place was known by several names, one of them "Washerwomen Square", because of the great number of African slaves of that trade that gathered there before hearing Mass. In the 19th century the market stalls that were at the then New Square were moved here. Later on the wooden stalls were removed and the space became Michelena Plaza, which lasted until the 20th century. From that moment on the Square of the Christ –limited by Teniente Rey (Brasil), Bernaza, Lamparilla and Villegas streets–, as well as the pavement and buildings around it, were transformed. After a period of neglect, in the 1980s restoration work was undertaken at the square. Several neoclassic buildings surround the square, except on the corner of Bernaza and Teniente Rey, where a 17th century property known as Casa de la Parra (Home of the Vine) still stands. At present a restaurant by the same name is located there.

⓰ Museum of Havana's Pharmacies

Teniente Rey St., between Habana and Compostela.

Located at the former La Reunión (The Meeting) Drugstore, thus named by its owners, the Catalá, Sarrá Co., the Museum was inaugurated on July 30, 2004. The institution presents the history of this science in Cuba through permanent exhibits distributed in three large rooms. The furniture of the old drugstore is still present, besides a collection of medicine bottles and other items related to the art of curing and prescribing, a result of the archeological excavations made at the Historical Center. One of the rooms is dedicated to the sale of spices and medicinal plants.

⓱ Church of the Christ

Of the original 17th century edification all that is left is the premise and the coffering covering of the central nave. In 1775 it was restored with the important present façade, the side towers, the splayed doorway and the blind oculus of the upper part. In 1932, two lateral naves were added.

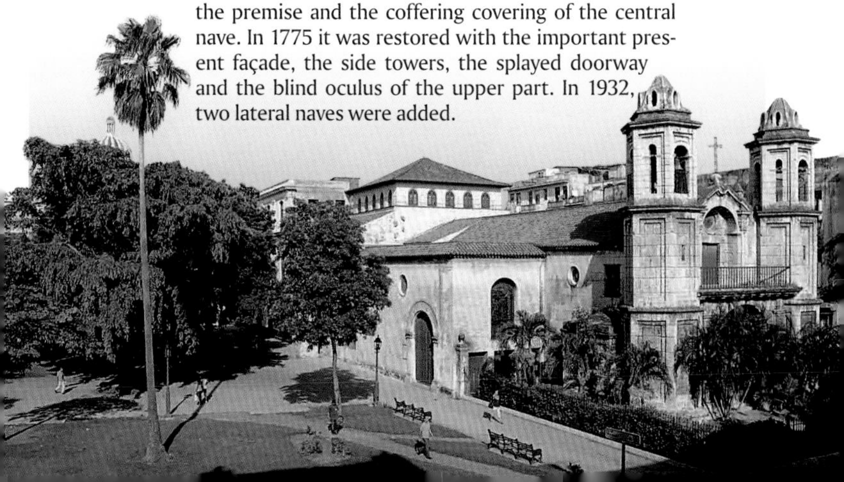

South of the Historical Center

⓲ Paula Church and Poplar Grove Avenue

Leonor Pérez y Ave. del Puerto.

By order of Captain General Felipe de Fondesviela, Marquis de la Torre, the first seaside promenade in Havana was built in 1777 by Antonio Fernández Trevejos. The Avenue comes out onto Paula Church, which after been restored in 2000 was converted into a concert hall dedicated to ancient music *cum* art gallery where well known Cuban artists exhibit their work. This is the seat of the Ars Longa Ensemble of Ancient Music, which sponsors several events dedicated to Baroque and Renaissance music, Very close by are the San José Cultural Center (a handicrafts fair), and Our Lady of Kazan Russian Orthodox Sacred Cathedral, a solid but slender building and a fine example of Russian traditional architecture.

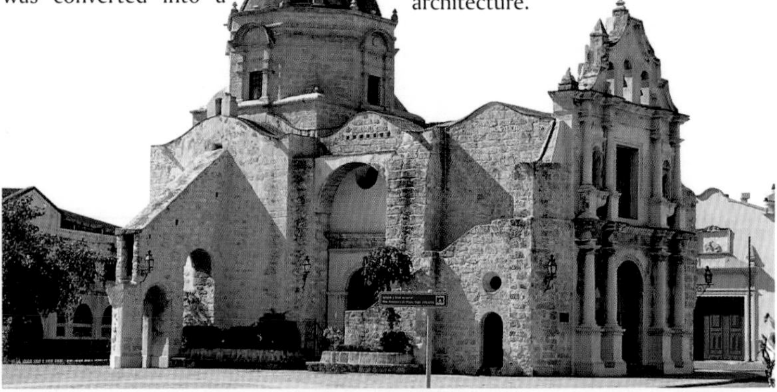

⓳ San José Arts and crafts fair

Port Avenue and Desamparados, at the end of Poplar Grove Avenue.

Former San José In-Bond Warehouses Cultural Center, by Havana Bay, has reborn thanks to its restoration by the Office of the City's Historian, and turned now into a cultural and commercial center for the sale of Cuban handicrafts. An example of the historic and industrial patrimony, it houses the largest arts and crafts fair of the city. It also has a currency exchange, restrooms, coffee shops and telephones. In the near future it will also have stores and a restaurant.

20 José Martí's Birthplace and Museum

314 Leonor Pérez St., between Picota and Egido.

Founded on January 28, 1925 at the house where Cuba's National Hero was born, it is Havana's oldest museum. There are exhibits from Martí's childhood, adolescence and youth (1853-1870), as well as rooms with references to several events linked to his life.

21 Our Lady of Mercy Church

Cuba between Merced and Paula, Old Havana.

Built between 1865 and 1867, the temple is one of Havana's most luxurious. It is located by a small square that allows the appreciation of its towerless Baroque façade on which the main entrance and a central niche stand out. The church's greatest attraction is the mural paintings in its interior made by renowned Cuban artists.

22 Santa Clara Convent

602 Cuba St., between Sol and Luz, Old Havana.

The Seraphic Virgin St. Clara of Assisi Convent, inaugurated in 1644, was the first one dedicated to women in Havana. The main church of the order was in Cartagena de Indias. In its interior are found small streets, lodgings and a public fountain. Abandoned by the nuns in 1922, the following year it was the centerpiece of a great scandal due to its fraudulent sale by the government. At present it is the seat of the National Center for Conservation, Restoration and Museology (CENCREM).

23 Church of the Holy Spirit

Cuba, between Acosta and Jesús María, Old Havana.

An outstanding feature is the stone vault above the altar, while the rest of the ceiling is made of wood. There is a great archeological wealth in the church's catacombs. It is also the final resting place of Bishop Jerónimo Valdés, the city's benefactor in the 18th century. Services are still held at the church.

El Prado and its Surroundings

㉔ The Prado Promenade

Built in 1772 by order of Captain General the Marquis de la Torre, was a consequence of Havana's development, which had outgrown the limits imposed by the city walls. Almost one kilometer long, the Nuevo Prado (New Prado), as it was called then, became the center of the city's social life. In time, elegant mansions, clubs, hotels and theaters were built along the avenue. The Prado flows from the Fountain of the Indian Woman and Fraternity Square down to the Malecón, bordered by trees, stone and marble seats, artistic iron-cast lamp posts and bronze lions. It has three well defined sections: the tree-lined central promenade section between the traffic lanes, from Neptuno St. to Malecón; the area linked to Central Plaza; and a traffic area with a parking lot in the middle and the Fountain of the Indian Woman at the end.

㉕ Grand Theater of Havana

Prado on San Rafael.

Its most important hall is the García Lorca, originally named Grand Tacón Theater, which witnessed the first performances on November 1837 but was officially inaugurated in April, 1839. Active since then, through its stage great troupes and soloists have paraded. Built in a grand Baroque style, it was designed by Belgian architect Paul Belau as the venue for the Galician Center social events. At present it is the seat of Cuba's National Ballet. At the theater there are also opera and operetta performances as well as concerts by the Pro Lyrical Art Center, the Spanish Ballet Cuba, and the Center for the Promotion of Dance (PRODANZA).

㉖ Inglaterra Hotel

416 Paseo del Prado on San Rafael.

Behind the neoclassic façade of this 19th century hotel there are Mudejar interiors. It was inaugurated on December 23, 1875, and its sidewalk, known as the Louvre Sidewalk, was a meeting point for Havana liberals of the time. At the hotel, great French actress Sarah Bernhardt and Russian ballerina Anna Pavlova were among its most illustrious guests. At present, the hotel is a second home for many outstanding Cuban artists, writers and musicians.

27 Parque Central (Central Plaza) *Prado, Zulueta, Neptuno and San José streets.*

Built in 1877, the Central Plaza occupied the space of three small colonial squares and the former Isabel II Plaza. It is a tree-shadowed place conceived as a site for entertainment and relaxation. Since February 1905, its large esplanade is presided by the first statue of José Martí, placed on the same site previously occupied for years by the marble statue of Isabel II of Spain, lowered from its pedestal on March 12, 1899, shortly after the ending of the War of Independence. A meeting place and point of reference in the city, the Central Plaza is surrounded by significant buildings, such as the Grand Theater of Havana; the Inglaterra, Telégrafo, Plaza and Parque Central Hotels, the old Manzana de Gómez mall, the National Museum of Fine Arts' Universal Art Building, and the Payret Movie Theater.

28 The Capitol

Prado, Industria, Dragones and San José.

Inaugurated on May 20, 1929, this architectural icon of Havana marks the Kilometer 0 of Cuba's highways system. The building's majesty is enhanced by its cupola, 92 meters high, which because of its proportions and outline resembles the St. Peter Basilica in Rome. Among its many attractions, you will find the gigantic statue of the Republic of Cuba, made by Italian artist Angelo Zanelli and the third largest indoor sculpture in the world.

The Cuban Capitol, with a striking similarity to the one at Washington, was the seat of the House of Representatives and the Senate until 1959. In its chambers the Constituent Assembly held its sessions in 1940, and the Constitution of the Republic was promulgated there on that same year. Since 1960 and until recently it housed the Ministry of Science, Technology and the Environment (CITMA).

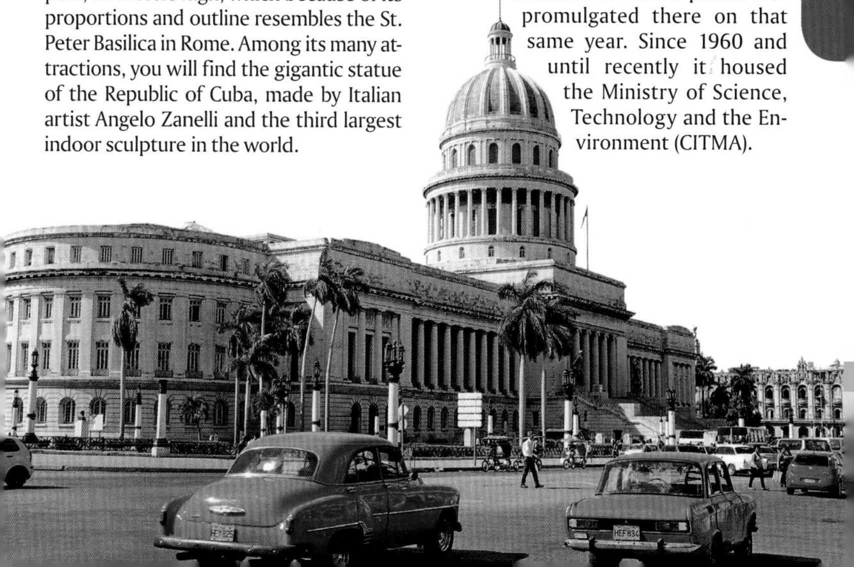

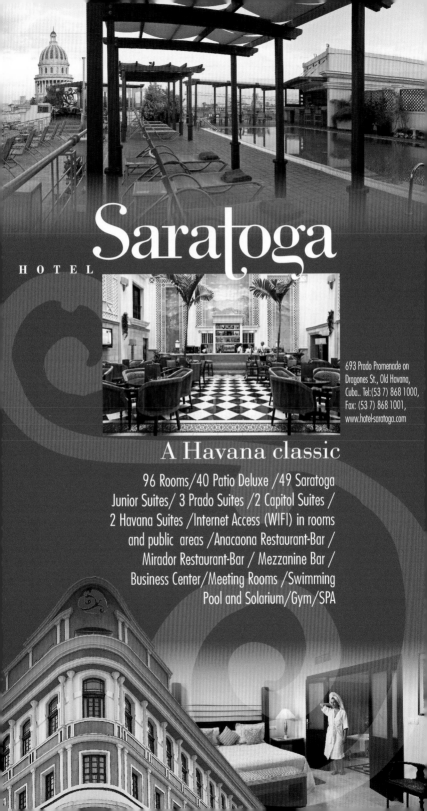

㉙ Bacardi Building

261 Monserrate, between Empedrado and San Juan de Dios.

Havana's first *art deco* building goes back to 1930 and was built to house the headquarters of the Bacardi Rum Company. At the time of its inauguration it was the country's tallest structure. The façade is dressed in red granite and on the top there is the Bacardi bat symbol. Both the interior and the exterior have kept the original décor. At present it is an office building for local and foreign companies.

㉚ Havana's Chinatown

From Amistad to Dragones St., Centro Habana.

Havana's Chinatown, a few steps away from the National Capitol building, is not the bustling place it once was, but subsists thanks to the spirit of Chinese seniors still living there. According to historian Julio Le Riverend, 150,000 Chinese nationals, almost all men, arrived in Havana between 1847 and 1874. In the early 20th century, 10,000 Chinese lived in an area from Galiano St. to Lealtad, and from Reina to Belascoaín. If the heart of Chinatown is Zanja St., Dragones is the most typically Chinese, for it is there that you can find the majority of the social clubs. At present, the neighborhood harbors the Chinese societies (clubs), small restaurant-bars, the Cuban School of Wushu, the Chinese Popular Daily, and the House of Chinese Art and Traditions (313 Salud St.) that promotes the celebration of the Chinese (lunar) New Year and commemorates the arrival of the Chinese to Cuba.

㉛ Church of the Holy Custodian Angel

Compostela, between Cuarteles and Chacón.

The original 17th century church was razed by a hurricane in 1846, but shortly after it was reconstructed in a Neo-Gothic style. The then famous St. Raphael Fairs, mentioned by Cirilo Villaverde in his novel *Cecilia Valdés or Angel's Hill*, were held there. Two of Cuba's most illustrious patriots, Father Félix Varela and José Martí, were baptized in this church.

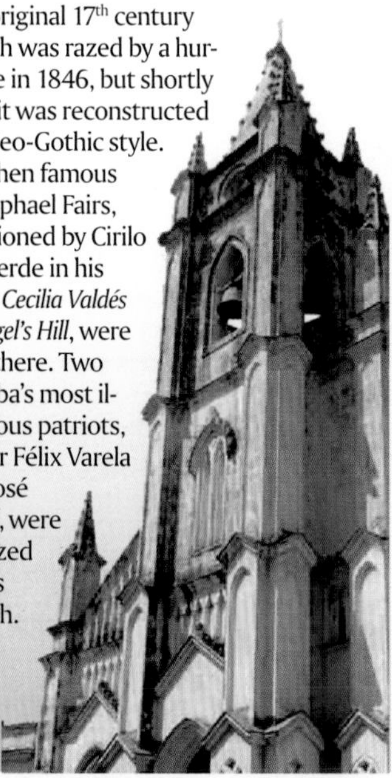

㉜ The Fountain of the Indian Woman

Also known as the Noble Havana, it is a representation of a mythical Indian woman by that name, the wife of aboriginal chieftain Habaguanex before the arrival of Columbus. According to legend, Cuba's capital was named after him. Located at the South side of the Prado Promenade, close to the National Capitol, the fountain was designed by architect Giuseppe Gaggini in the Neoclassical style at the time of Governor Claudio Martínez de Pinillos, Count of Villanueva. It is 3 meters high and built entirely of Carrara white marble.

㉝ San Salvador de La Punta Castle

Port Avenue and Prado Promenade.

Built by Bautista Antonelli *circa* 1593 as part of Havana's first defense system, since 2002 the castle housed in its former military supplies warehouse the underwater archeological findings recovered for the national patrimony in 1970-1990. The exhibits came from shipwrecks north of Pinar del Río and Havana found by Carisub Enterprise. Due to damage caused by powerful Hurricane Wilma, since October 2005 the castle is undergoing restoration with the purpose of transforming the building into a Museum of Siege or an Archeological Museum. In June, 2008, the underwater archeological findings and the ship models were transferred to the Castle of the Royal Force Museum's collections.

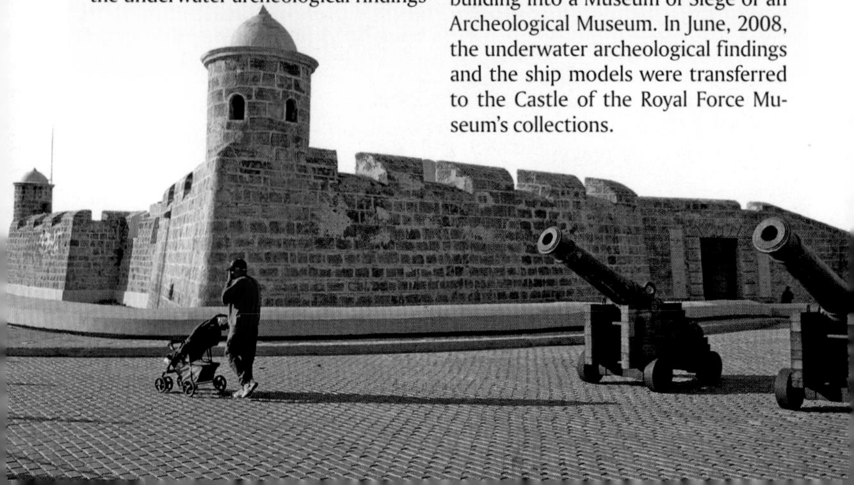

A Bird's Eye-View of the Prado Promenade's Last Stretch.

34 El Floridita Bar-Restaurant

557 Obispo St., on Monserrate.

On 1817 La Piña de Plata was inaugurated on that same block, but later moved to the corner and changed its name to La Florida. Subsequently, patrons used the diminutive Floridita as a term of endearment. Known as the "cradle of the Daiquiri," it maintains its original Regency décor from the 1950s. Many distinguished visitors are remembered as patrons, but the most famous of all was US writer Ernest Hemingway, an almost every day presence. They say that the Nobel Prize winner spent hours at the bar listening to the regulars or thinking about one of his plots, always with one of his two favorite drinks, a Daiquiri or a Papa's, the latter a variant of his own invention of the former.

The Floridita, recognized in 1992 as Best of the Best Five Star Diamond and King of the Daiquiri by the American Academy of Gastronomical Science, is a restaurant specialized in fish and shellfish. Its famous bar also serves other popular cocktails, and its *cuisine d'auteur* by well-known master chefs is outstanding.

35 Museum of the Revolution and Granma Memorial

1 Refugio St., between Zulueta and Monserrate.

Located in what used to be the Republic of Cuba's Presidential Palace, it is an exhibition of the most important events and historical processes in Cuba, from the first aboriginal settlers to the present, The main entrance is flanked by two emblematic elements –the ruins of the Angel's Sentry Box, a part of the city wall in colonial times; and the SAU-100 self-propelled gun that Fidel Castro himself fired against the Bay of Pigs invaders, on April, 1961. In front of the Museum's back entrance is the Granma Memorial, which exhibits valuable historical pieces related to the war of liberation and subsequent battles of the Cuban people in defense of its sovereignty and independence. The most valuable exhibit is the Granma, the yacht in which Fidel Castro and his comrades came to Cuba from Mexico on December, 1956 to renew the war against the Batista dictatorship.

36 National Museum of Fine Arts

Trocadero between Zulueta and Monserrate.

The National Museum, founded in 1913, did not have its own building until 1954, when the facility known then as Palace of Fine Arts was built to replace the old one at Colón Market (1884). Since then its collections have outgrown the premises and the institution underwent a comprehensive process of renovation and updating. At present it is located in two buildings for exhibitions and a third one for administrative work and logistics. The former Palace of Fine Arts was transformed for exhibiting only Cuban art, while the former Asturias Center, in front of the Central Plaza, is home to collections of universal art. The exhibit rooms have been renovated to fulfill the demands of a modern museum, and state-of-the-art systems of lighting, air-conditioning, environment control and security have been installed. The exhibits can be visited in a sequential manner or at random.

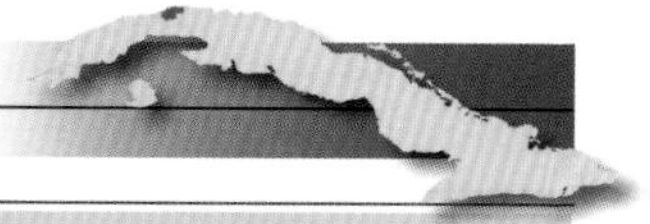

Across the Bay

37 Three Kings Castle of El Morro

Historical and Military Morro-Cabaña Park, Habana del Este.

Together with the National Capitol and La Giraldilla, the Park forms a trilogy of Havana iconic symbols. Part of the city's defense system, the castle was designed by Bautista Antonelli and built between 1589 and 1630. Since the 1990s it leads an active life, exhibiting art works and having a very much animated cultural life. At present, at the site of two of the castle's old batteries, called Los Doce Apóstoles (The Twelve Apostles) and La Divina Pastora (The Divine Shepherdess) there are two restaurants, namesakes of the former emplacements.

38 San Carlos de la Cabaña Fortress

Historical and Military Morro-Cabaña Park, Habana del Este.

When the occupation of Havana by the English in 1762 proved how vulnerable the city was, the need to fortify the heights of La Cabaña became obvious. This was a strategic terrain through which enemy troops had advanced and besieged Morro Castle. Subsequently, in 1763 work began, and once ended in 1774 La Cabaña became Cuba's largest fortress. Today it is the stage of one of the city's traditional ceremonies, the famous 9 o'clock shooting of the cannon, which attracts hundreds of visitors. Because of its position across the bay, it serves as a backdrop to a sizable part of the inner city, as well as a marvelous lookout on Havana.

39 Regla

This municipality across the bay, formed by the towns of Regla and Casablanca, is set on lands that the aborigines called Guaicanamar, which means "in front of the sea", part of the chieftainship of Guanabacoa ("place of the waters"). It takes its present name from Our Lady of Regla, holy patron of the bay and a symbol of the town, which attracts the faithful who come from all over the country and abroad to pay homage. The town is also home to a famous Cuban carnival parade, "Los Guaracheros de Regla", created in 1959. Regla can be reached by boats that ferry passengers from one of the docks at Port Avenue, although it can also be accessed by land.

40 The Havana tunnel

The Havana tunnel, which runs 733 meters under Havana Bay, was laid in 1957-58 by the French company Societé de Grand Travaux de Marseille and is considered one of Cuba's seven wonders of civil engineering. Of the capital's three tunnels this is the most important with four lanes –two into the city and two to the East, where Havana's most beautiful beaches make the delight of locals and visitors.

41 The Christ of Havana

A majestic and colossal statue placed to the left and above the entrance to Havana Bay, halfway between the old San Carlos de la Cabaña Fortress and the town of Casablanca. Inaugurated on December 25, 1958, the Christ of Havana was sculpted in Italy by Cuban artist Gilma Madera who designed it according to her idea of masculine beauty –a sidelong look and full lips, a representation of the racial fusion of the Cuban people. This statue that can be seen from different points of the city is 15 meters tall with a 3 meter high pedestal. It is placed on an esplanade on top of a hill, from which great views of Havana can be seen, particularly of the old quarter and the bay.

Plaza de la Revolución and El Vedado

42 José Martí Revolution Square

Independencia Ave. and 20 de Mayo.

The idea for building the square is from the early 1940s, but it was not finished until after the triumph of the Cuban revolution in 1959. Since then, it became the stage for the main ceremonies of the country. It is presided by the monument to Cuban hero José Martí, Havana's tallest structure, 113 m including the closing tower, and 142 to the tip of the beacons and flag posts. At the monument's base in the shape of a star is the José Martí Memorial, a historic and cultural center, inaugurated on January 27, 1996, and where texts and images about Martí can be found, as well as others about the construction of the square.

43 José Martí National Library

Independencia Ave. on 20 de Mayo, Plaza de la Revolución.

Across the square's east side stands the National Library, founded in 1901 before moving to its present location. The library is the depository of the nation's documental, bibliographic and sound patrimony, as well as representations of the world's culture.

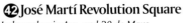

44 El Vedado

Developed mainly as a residential sector that began in the second half of the 19th century, El Vedado neighborhood at Plaza de la Revolución Municipality has a treasure of constructions from different eras and architectural styles, from old wooden homes, Neoclassic and eclectic villas and mansions, examples of *art décor*, and high rise buildings; two of the latter, the FOCSA apartment building and the Habana Libre Hotel, are the country's tallest edifices. Numbered streets and others identified by letters, many plazas, ironwork grills and gardens characterize this neighborhood, considered the economic and financial center of the Cuban capital, besides being the most touristic part of the city.

㊺ Cristóbal Colón Cemetery

Zapata Ave. on 12 St., El Vedado.

Declared a National Monument in 1987, the cemetery shows in its 57 hectares a display of a great number of sculptures and architectural works. For that reason it is considered by experts the third most important in the world, after the Staglieno in Genoa, Italy, and the Montjuic in Barcelona, Spain. The Colón Cemetery's cornerstone was laid on October 30, 1871 and its construction took almost 15 years, until July 2, 1886. The burial grounds, the largest in the Americas, has a rectangular design, like a Roman military camp in the Romanesque-Byzantine style, with the addition of sidewalks, streets and avenues, the latter two numbered for easier access. The front gate is the work of Spanish architect Calixto de Loira, and the reliefs and sculptures in Carrara marble that crown the gate are by Cuban artist José Villalta de Saavedra. The most visited tomb is the one belonging to Amelia Goire de la Hoz, a high society lady that at present is popularly known as "The Miraculous One."

㊻ Nacional de Cuba Hotel *0 and 21 St., El Vedado.*

Cuba's flagship hotel, inaugurated in 1930, is famous for its eclectic architecture, an excellent service, and a long list of illustrious and famous guests. A National Monument since 1998, it is located at the Punta Brava salient, on top of Taganana Hill, at the end of San Lázaro Cove, a privileged position that allows a great view of the Havana Malecón. The site where the hotel stands today is the same where in the 18th century the Santa Clara Battery was emplaced, part of the old city's original defense system, and of which two cannons remain in the hotel's garden. In 2009, World Travel Group named it Cuban tourism's leading hotel.

㊼ Universidad de La Habana

Colina de Aróstegui, El Vedado.

On January 5, 1728, the Dominican friars founded in Old Havana the Royal and Pontifical St. Hieronymus University of Havana, at the San Juan de Letrán Convent. In 1850 it changed its name to Royal and Literary University of Havana. On May, 1902, the University began its transfer to Aróstegui Hill, also known as Pyrotechnic Hill, in El Vedado. Cuba's oldest higher learning center is also related to important historical events, such as the creation of the Federation of University Students and its struggle against dictatorships. Important facilities of the University are its Central Library, and the Felipe Poey Museum of Natural History, among other institutions.

㊽ National Museum of Decorative Arts

502, 17 St. on D St., El Vedado.

Inaugurated on July 24 1964 at the former mansion of the Countess of Revilla-Camargo, it has a collection of over 33,000 works of extraordinary artistic and historic value from the Louis XV, Louis XVI and Napoleon III periods, as well as oriental pieces from the 16th to the 20th century. Also on exhibit are important Sèvres, París, Chantilly and Limoges French chinaware, and Derby, Chelsea, Wedgwood, Worcester and Staffordshire in England.

㊾ Focsa Building

17 St. on M El Vedado.

Inaugurated in 1956 and considered one of the seven wonders of Cuban civil engineering, its construction took two years and four months. Its design was a sensation because of its technological novelty and marked the beginning of the era of tall buildings in Havana. At a time that concrete constructions of more than 18 floors were considered unaffordable, the FOCSA became the second of its kind in the world. Located near the Havana Malecón, it is 121 meters high, and has 39 floors and 373 apartments. There are also several underground parking levels, offices, TV studios, a mall, La Torre (33th floor) and El Emperador restaurants, and radio stations COCO and Metropolitana.

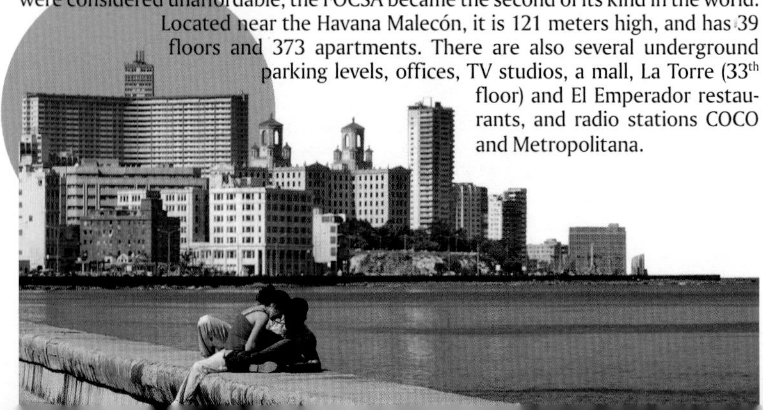

50 National Theater of Cuba

Zapata and 39th St., Plaza de la Revolución.

The theater has two halls, Covarrubias, thus named to honor Francisco Covarrubias (1775-1850), a playwright considered the founder of Cuban theater, and Avellaneda, the name of the foremost woman author of Cuban Romantic literature in the 19th century: Gertrudis Gómez de Avellaneda. This is one of the few theaters in the continent that has a collection of art works, among which there are pieces of important Cuban vanguard artists. The gardens exhibit statues and ceramics of important Cuban authors. The Mi Habana nightclub and the Delirio Habanero piano bar are also part of the theater.

51 Casa de las Américas

3ra. and G streets, El Vedado.

Founded in 1959 by Haydée Santamaría and headed at present by poet and essayist Roberto Fernández Retamar, Casa de las Américas promotes, researches, gives prizes and publishes Latin American and Caribbean literature, arts, and the social sciences. Besides organizing the prestigious Casa de las Américas Literary Prize, the institution also has a Center for Literary Research, the José Antonio Echeverría Library, the Center for Caribbean Studies, the *Casa de las Américas* magazine and a publishing house.

52 Napoleonic Museum

1159 San Miguel St., between Ronda and Masón streets, Centro Habana.

Havana's Napoleonic Museum harbors a surprising collection, most of it the former property of Cuban sugar baron Julio Lobo. The exhibits are representative of the time between the French revolution up to the Second Empire, basically related to Napoleon. The collection is housed in a very valuable mansion inspired by a Florentine palace of the Renaissance, christened as La Dolce Dimora by its former owner, Cuban Italian politician Orestes Ferrara, who commissioned its construction to architects Evelio Govantes and Félix Cabarrocas.

Miramar and its Surroundings

53 Miramar

For many years Havana most elegant neighborhood, its life develops around Fifth Avenue, a wide and tree-shaded boulevard surrounded by beautiful early 20th century houses and de luxe hotels. Most of the embassies from foreign countries are at Miramar, besides attractions such as the Model of Havana and the National Aquarium. It is part of Playa Municipality, the same as Cubanacán, a neighboring residential area.

54 Palace of Conventions

146 St, between 11 and 13 Sts., Cubanacán, Playa.

Cuba's main convention center inaugurated in 1979 has an area of 60,000 m². It is equipped with several air-conditioned rooms with state-of-the-art sound and audiovisual equipment, and simultaneous translations. It also has several multipurpose rooms and office for guaranteeing any meeting. Located in one of the most beautiful residential neighborhoods, it also has the adjoining Palco Executive 4 Star Hotel.

55 The House of the Green Tiled Roof *2nd., between 3rd. y 5th Ave., Miramar.*

At the beginning of Fifth Avenue lies this recently restored house, turned into a center for the promotion of modern and contemporary architecture, urban development and interior design. An example of domestic architecture in the style of early 20th century chalets, greatly influenced by the American cottage, the house is surprising because of the geometric shapes in its façade crowned by a tilted cover with gabled windows and a small cone-shaped tower that contribute to the building's beauty. Precisely its sharply-sloped roofs covered with green tiles are the most striking elements that make it stand out in an environment of great mansions.

56 Tropicana Night Club *72 between 41 y 45, Marianao.*

Identified by a large arch and known as *A Paradise Under the Stars*, the most famous of Cuban night clubs was built in 1939 in the open on a wooded area of Marianao, a complete breakaway from traditional night spots. The stage where great stars have performed, including Josephine Baker, Nat King Cole, Bola de Nieve and Rita Montaner, has among its symbols the sculpture of a ballerina, made by Cuban artist Rita Longa in 1959, and the Fountain of the Muses, by Italian sculptor Aldo Gamba, transferred here in 1952 from its original place to the night club's entrance. In 1992, The American Academy of the Restaurant Industry chose Tropicana as the Best of Five Stars Diamond Award for the greatest night club in the Americas.

57 Marina Hemingway

Calle 248 y 5ta Av. Santa Fe, Playa.

In 1956-57, some 600,000 m^2 were recovered from the sea to lay out the marina with four 5 meter-deep traffic canals. Conceived for catering to sport fishing boats, Cuba's No. 1 marina can service simultaneously up to 400 boats, of which 200 can be fitted for life-on-board. For those who prefer it, there are several lodging facilities. Only minutes away from downtown Havana, the marina is the venue of the world famous Ernest Hemingway Fishing Tournament and of international regattas.

Other Areas in the Capital

58 Quinta de los Molinos (Mills Estate) *Salvador Allende and Infanta Avenues.*

With an area of almost 5 hectares, there are some 170 vegetable species in its premises, most of them trees. The estate owes its name to the former existence of two mills that were used for grinding tobacco for snuff, which was much in demand in all of Europe during the 18th century. Subsequently it was the summer home of the Spanish governor in colonial times, and years later the residence of Generalissimo Máximo Gómez, commander in chief of the Cuban Liberation Army.

59 Callejón de Hammel (Hamel Alley)

Hamel Alley, between Espada and Aramburu, Centro Habana.

A community project led by artist Salvador González, who created this public space of the Cayo Hueso neighborhood in Centro Habana Municipality. The small street is a kind of open air art gallery with murals dedicated to Santería. There are also music and dance performances.

60 Ernest Hemingway Museum

Vigía and Steinhart St., Finca Vigía, San Francisco de Paula.

From 1940 to 1960, a year before his death, this was Cuba's place of residence of the famous US novelist. Known as Finca Vigía (Vigía Estate), the property is located at San Francisco de Paula, some 15 Km from downtown Havana. The house was inaugurated as a museum on July 21, 1962 and is considered the first institution created for the study of the life and work of the 1954 Nobel Prize of Literature. This sort of small ecological reserve because of its abundant vegetation consists of the house, a bungalow, a tower, a swimming pool and Hemingway's yacht "Pilar". The house is divided into living room, library, dining room, guest room, Mary Welsh's room, Hemingway's work room, bathroom and kitchen.

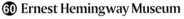

61 Guanabacoa

One of the province's oldest territories, it boasts strong traditions, such as the Afro Cuban festivities held informally by followers of Santería, Palo Monte and Abakuá secret societies in the municipality. These and rumba are indissoluble elements of the town's culture, as well as the Wemilere, a festival for celebrating African roots. Guanabacoa is also the hometown of three important Cuban 20th century musicians: pianist and composer Ernesto Lecuona, singer Rita Montaner and pianist, composer and singer Ignacio "Bola de Nieve" Villa. The Guanabacoa Municipal Museum exhibits the history of the town's heroes, such as Pepe Antonio, who fought against the English invasion in the 18th century.

62 Cojímar

With an architectural and natural combination that represents the life style of fishermen, this small town east of the capital emerged in the vicinity of the Cojímar watchtower in mid 16th century. This was the place where US writer Ernest Hemingway satisfied his love for fishing, and the setting for his novel *The Old Man and the Sea*. Hemingway was a regular at Las Terrazas Restaurant, where he sometimes ate together with local fishermen, particularly his friend and skipper of the writer's yacht, the Pilar. The Cojímar watchtower, one of the local attractions, was a small Spanish fort built around 1649 as an extension of Havana's defenses.

63 East Havana Beaches

Only 20 minutes away from the capital city there is a long string of beaches 50 Km long with crystal clear waters and fine sand, hotels, small towns and tourist facilities of all types. Particularly attractive are Santa María del Mar and Guanabo beaches, but a visit to the Bellomonte lookout is a must for enjoying wonderful views.

64 Lenin Park

100 St. and Cortina de la Presa, Arroyo Naranjo.

Aptly called Havana's lung, it was inaugurated on April 22, 1972 by then President of Cuba Fidel Castro, under the inspiring force of Celia Sánchez. This formidable green area, located some 25 Km south of Havana, has an amusement park, swimming pools, restaurants and coffee shops, as well as other attractions, such as a Cuban rodeo, boating in its small lake, water-cycling, horse-riding or simply enjoying a family picnic in contact with Nature.

65 San Lázaro Shrine

Calzada de San Antonio, Km. 23, Santiago de las Vegas.

Every December 17, believers make their pilgrimage from all over Cuba to the San Lázaro Shrine at El Rincón, in the outskirts of Havana. According to estimates, pilgrims number up to 15,000, so in order to allow their access to the shrine, motor traffic is closed. According to observers, many families save during the whole year in order to make offers to Saint Lazarus, while others go to pray and meditate on their sorrow at the feet of the statue of the saint.

66 National Botanical Garden

Rocío Highway, Km. 3,5, Calabazar, Arroyo Naranjo.

Some 25 Km away from Havana you will find this natural environment where some 400 vegetable species are on display in an area of 600 hectares. The garden was conceived with the objectives of a modern institution aimed at public use, where a great collection of live plants is exhibited –scientifically classified and ordered, with educational, scientific, recreational and conservation purposes.

Inaugurated in 1984, the Garden is a point of reference regarding ecological eating habits. It has a herbarium (the second largest in the country) with over 100,000 specimens of Cuban flora, a specialized library, and the eco-restaurant El Bambú.

⑮ province of

Mayabeque

Mayabeque is the other new Cuban province approved by the National Assembly on August 2011 and in force since January 1, 2011. Named after the river that flows in a fertile valley that stretches through several of its municipalities, the Siboney aborigines called it Güinicajinal.

A characteristic of the province's beaches is the fact of being located on a broken coast, thus they are small and usually found in coves surrounded by heights and cliffs of great beauty. They are great for diving because of its warm and crystal clear waters practically all year round. The Vía Blanca, a 4-lane highway between Havana and Matanzas, is the best access to this area with beaches such as Jibacoa (with a hotel infrastructure), Arroyo Bermejo, Boca de Jaruco, El Peñón del Fraile, Puerto Escondido and El Abra, these last two fitted for camping and with two diving centers.

Jibacoa Beach.

Capital: San José de las Lajas.

Area: 3,732.73 Km².

Municipalities: Bejucal, San José de las Lajas, Jaruco, Santa Cruz del Norte, Madruga, Nueva Paz, San Nicolás de Bari, Güines, Melena del Sur, Batabanó and Quivicán.

Population: 380,000 plus.

Boundaries: To the North with the province of Havana, capital of Cuba, and the Florida Straits; to the East with the province of Matanzas; to the South with the Batabanó Gulf, and to the West with the province of Artemisa.

Economy: Industrial-agrarian, with a great potential for cattle raising and dairy products.

Main products: Sugar cane, tubers, vegetables, and lobster –the latter its main export product–; construction materials, chemical products, food industry, metallurgy and electromechanical plants, pharmaceutical and textile production, furniture and paper products. One of the province's main assets is oil and gas production along its North coast, as well as electric power generation at Santa Cruz del Norte.

Relief: Its main feature is the Havana-Matanzas Plain, with its southern part belonging to Mayabeque. There are also the Bejucal and Madruga Heights, part of the Bejucal-Madruga-Coliseo Heights, the latter part in Matanzas. At Bejucal and Madruga is the province's most prominent elevation, called Palenque, 330 meters high.

Accesses: Mainly through the Central Highway and the National Expressway, although there is an extensive network that links the territory with the country's capital and other provinces. The railway connects different towns among themselves and Havana.

Mayabeque

Sites of interest

⑯ Santa Cruz del Norte

Located to the North of Mayabeque, one of the characteristics of this municipality is its beaches. Along the coast are camping facilities such as Los Cocos, Peñas Blancas and Las Caletas, among others. Inaugurated here on September 30, 1919, the Santa Cruz distillery makes since 1975 the famous Havana Club rum, a brand first bottled in Cárdenas in 1878.

⑰ Escaleras de Jaruco (Jaruco Stairs)

Forty kilometers east of Havana, Jaruco.

With heights under 350 meters and dense vegetation, the Escaleras de Jaruco Tourist Center is outstanding for the beauty of its surroundings, as well as for the diversity of its wildlife and flora. There are many caves around. and other attractions such as its lookout, restaurants, amusement park and a hotel. A must-see place is Cueva del Águila (Eagle's Cave), where artist Ana Mendieta carved the sculptures known as The Stone Women.

⑱ Jibacoa

A well-liked beach for its privacy, warm and tranquil waters, halfway between Havana and Varadero. There are several facilities, such as Breezes Jibacoa Hotels, cabanas, restaurants, coffee shop and parks for horse riding.

⑲ Surgidero de Batabanó (Port of Batabanó)

South Mayabeque, 4 Km from Batabanó.

A well known fishing port, located on Mayabeque's south coast, it is also where ferries sail to and fro the Isle of Youth, the Cuban archipelago's second largest island.

Charangas de Bejucal (Bejucal Carnival)

The Charangas de Bejucal, like its famous counterparts Parrandas de Remedios and Santiago de Cuba's Carnival, is a popular festivity of long tradition. Its origin is related to the Christmas Eve mass, the date when slaves were given the day off, on which they danced around the town's church. In time, the townspeople formed two groups: La Musicanga, with Creoles, Mulattos and slaves as members, and Malayos, formed by Spaniards and Creoles loyal to Spain. In spite of its origins, the festivities never had a religious character.

Peñón del Fraile (Friar's Rock).

Nestlé
Pureza Vital
agua mineral natural
www.losportales.cu

20 province of

Matanzas

La Concordia Bridge.

No wonder the province of Matanzas is considered a great tourist destination. This is due to three elements of excellence: the great resort of Varadero, located on the Hicacos Peninsula; the extraordinary ecology of the Zapata Peninsula, in South Matanzas, and the capital of the same name, known in the 1860s as the "Athens of Cuba".

The city of Matanzas grew on the shores of a very large bay and is crossed by four rivers. Its 29 bridges, four of them more than centenary and still in use, made it deserving of the title of "City of Bridges." It is considered Cuba's quintessential neoclassical city, with architecture of a strong personality and of high national values. In the late 19th century it was the most modern and best built city on the island, and even today it maintains its peculiar elegance.

Matanzas has always been famous for an intense cultural life. Land of poets and musicians, it is the cradle of the danzón, the national dance, and boasts of famous poets such as José Jacinto Milanés, Bonifacio Byrne and Carilda Oliver Labra.

Matanzas also treasures one of the most picturesque landscapes of Cuba, Yumurí Valley, whose full view can be appreciated from a lookout at Bacunayagua Bridge. The valley is bathed by the Yumurí and Bacunayagua rivers that flow into Matanzas North coast. Other attractions of the province are the Bellamar Caves and Guamá Tourist Center.

A view of the city.

A statue of the Roman goddess Minerva at Matanzas Bus Terminal.

Cathedral of Matanzas.

The Bus Terminal.

An overview of the bay.

Capital: Matanzas.
Area: 11,798 Km².
Municipalities: Matanzas, Unión de Reyes, Martí, Pedro Betancourt, Jovellanos, Jagüey Grande, Los Arabos, Perico, Colón, Cárdenas, Limonar, Calimete and Ciénaga de Zapata (Zapata Swamp).
Population: 690,000 plus.
Boundaries: To the North with the Florida Straits, to the Northeast with the province of Villa Clara: to the Southeast with the province of Cienfuegos; to the South with the Caribbean Sea; and to the West with the province of Mayabeque.
Economy: Industrial-agrarian.
Main products: Cane sugar, citrus fruits, electric power, oil and natural gas, fertilizers, textiles and food products.
Relief: Mainly flat, part of the Havana Matanzas Plains. Most of the heights are to the Northwest and Midwest of the province. On the Havana-Matanzas Heights is the greatest elevation, the Pan de Matanzas, 380 meters high. The territory has two peninsulas, Hicacos and Zapata, as well as several bays.
Access: By land from Havana through the Vía Blanca Expressway. The Juan Gualberto Gómez International Airport, 20 Km. from Varadero, welcomes national and international flights, both regular and charter. It is linked to other regions of the country through the Central Highway and the National Expressway. There is also access by sea through several marinas.

Yumurí Valley.

㉑ A map of the city of **Matanzas**

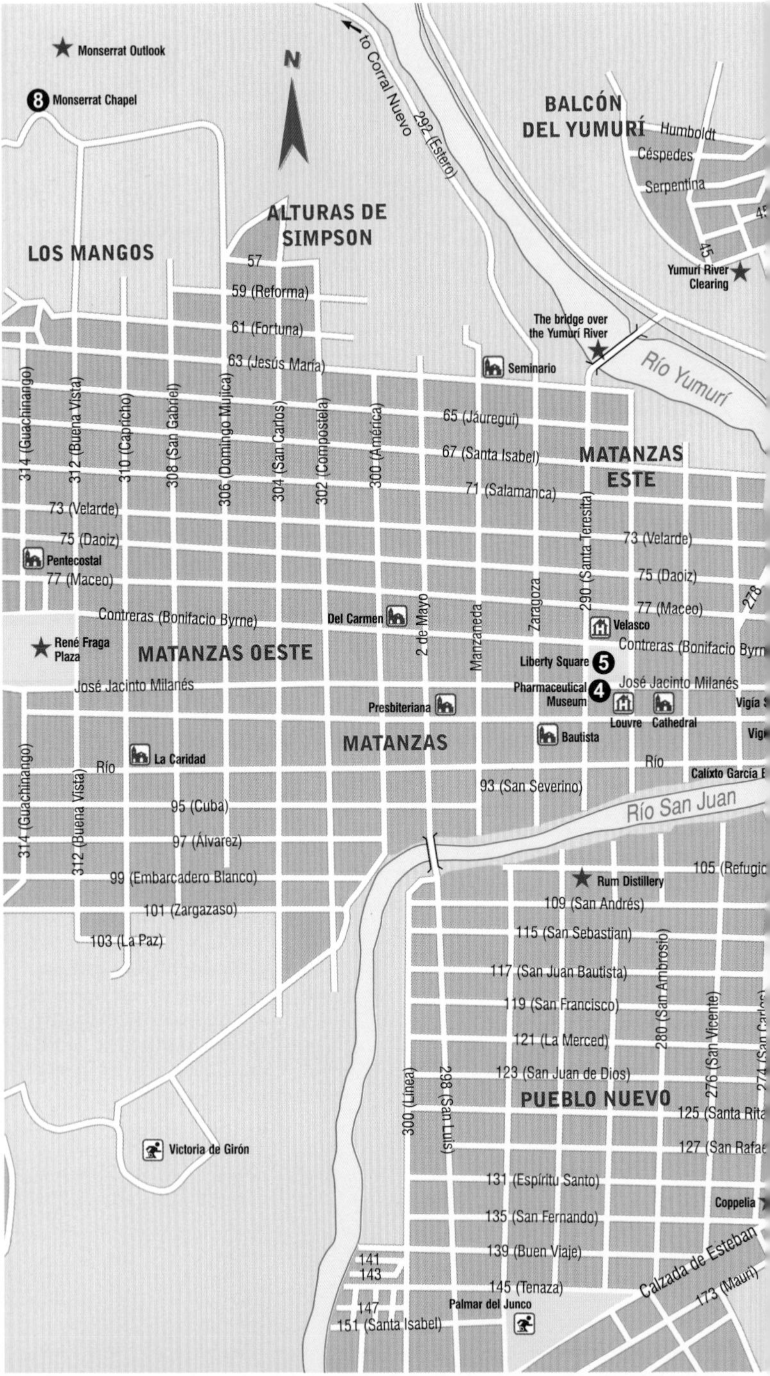

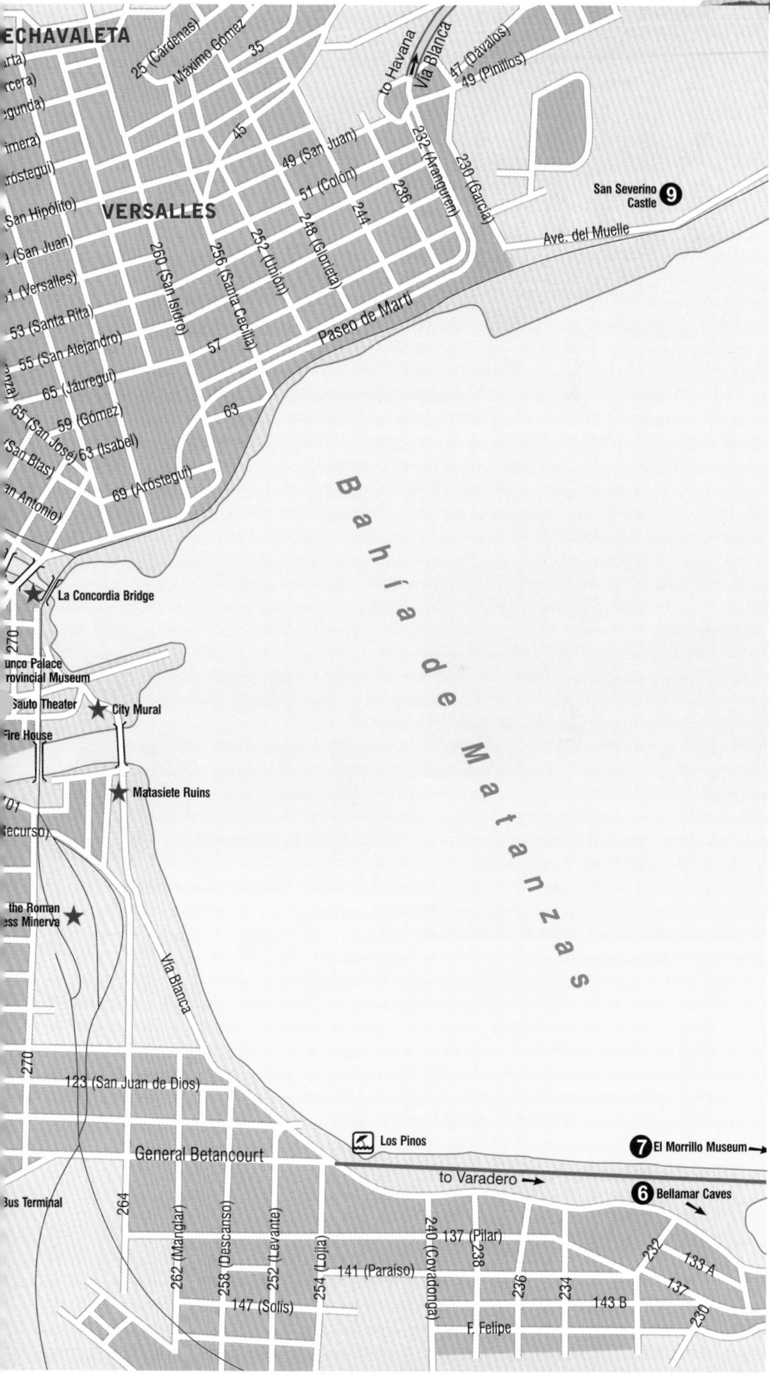
VERSALLES
25 (Cárdenas)
Máximo Gómez
35
45
to Havana
Vía Blanca
47 (Dávalos)
49 (Pinillos)
49 (San Juan)
51 (Colón)
232 (Aranguren)
230 (García)
236
244
248 (Glorieta)
252 (Unión)
256 (Santa Cecilia)
260 (San Isidro)
San Severino Castle
Ave. del Muelle
Paseo de Martí
53 (Santa Rita)
55 (San Alejandro)
57
65 (Jáuregui)
59 (Gómez)
63
63 (Isabel)
69 (Aróstegui)
Bahía de Matanzas
La Concordia Bridge
270
City Mural
Matasiete Ruins
Vía Blanca
123 (San Juan de Dios)
General Betancourt
Los Pinos
El Morrillo Museum
to Varadero
Bellamar Caves
264
262 (Manglar)
258 (Descanso)
252 (Levante)
254 (Lojía)
141 (Paraíso)
147 (Solís)
240 (Covadonga)
137 (Pilar)
238
236
234
143 B
F. Felipe
232
133 A
137
230

Matanzas

Sites of interest

❶ Vigía Square *Magdalena St., between Milanés and Río, Matanzas.*

This is the foundational core of the city of Matanzas, from where the layout of the main streets of the future town began. Linked to the outskirts by the Concordia and Calixto García bridges, important buildings are located around the square, such as the Provincial Museum, the Sauto Theater and Vigía Publishing House, a unique institution where all the publishing process is made by hand, from the printing to the book binding.

❷ Sauto Theater

Magdalena St., between Milanés and Medio, Vigía Square. Tel.: (5345) 242721.

The Sauto, located at Vigía Square is one of the country's most important theaters. Its neoclassic design was due to the efforts of Matanzas pharmacist, Ambrosio de la Concepción Sauto Noda. Great music, dance and drama performers have parade through its stage since its inauguration on April 6, 1863, when it was still named Esteban Theater, in honor of Governor Pedro Esteban Arranz. There was a time when Italian, French and Spanish opera companies made their Cuban debut in this building of unusual dimensions and beauty before performing at Tacón Theater in Havana.

❸ Junco Palace Provincial Museum

Milanés St., between Magdalena and Ayllon, Matanzas. Tel.: (5345)243195.

Built in 1838, the facility that houses the museum belonged to one of the richest men in Matanzas, Vicente del Junco Sardiñas, the owner of large plantations, sugar mills and a great number of slaves. Since 1980 it was transformed into a museum located in the vicinity of Vigía Square. It exhibits valuable objects, including the largest stone piece of Matanzas, the crowbar with which the Bellamar Caves were discovered, the notebooks of great Cuban malacologist Carlos de la Torre, several pieces that belonged to poet Bonifacio Byrne, and the only existing mummy exhibited in a Cuban museum.

Matanzas

Sites of interest

❹ Pharmaceutical Museum

49 and 51 Milanés St., betweeen Ayuntamiento and Santa Teresa, Matanzas. Tel.: (5345) 243179.

Built as a drugstore and inaugurated in 1882, it was the property of Dr. Ernesto Triolet until January, 1964. In May of that same year it was reopened as the first Pharmaceutical Museum in Latin America. It maintains the atmosphere of a 19th century drugstore due to its original shelves, flasks, utensils, books and instruments, in the very manner its founders placed them. Its collection of decorative art, one of the most distinctive of the museum, is formed by porcelain jars of the kind used in pharmacies for storing medical products or the raw materials for their production.

❺ Liberty Square

Contreras on Santa Teresa, Matanzas.

Formerly known as Main Square, at present it is a place for meeting, relaxing or recreation. At the center of the square there is a group of sculptures with the statue of liberty in the shape of a woman holding broken chains in her hands. Crowning the group, at a height of 4 meters, there is the figure of José Martí, the Apostle of Cuban Independence.

❻ Bellamar Caves

Northeast of the city.

This is a number of caverns with more than 20 Km of galleries, discovered by chance when a slave lost his crowbar through a hole that he accidentally made trying to move a limestone. Originally known as Parga's Cave after the owner of the farm where the discovery was made, later on it adopted its present name of Bellamar Caves (in plural) after a namesake beach in West Matanzas. At the entrance there is a 32 century-old stalactite called Columbus Cloak, the largest and oldest formation, shown in a shape that mimics a 12 meter high waterfall. With an uncommon beauty among the caves of the world, due to the resplendent formations covered by a layer of crystals, Bellamar Caves have a great scientific interest, for speleologists have made here several discoveries of importance.

Matanzas

Sites of interest

❼ El Morrillo Museum

Entrance to Matanzas Bay, a few meters from the mouth of the Canímar River.

This former fort was part of the defense system of Matanzas Bay for the purpose of protecting it from the attacks of pirates and corsairs. It was built on the west bank of the Canímar River's mouth and initially had a battery emplacement in the shape of a horseshoe, a lookout tower and loopholes all around.

❽ Monserrat Chapel

Alturas de Simpson, Yumurí Valley.

Built with the collaboration of Catalonian residents of Matanzas, the origins of the chapel go way back to the second half of the 19th century. In 1939, this uppermost point of Alturas de Simpson (Simpson's Heights), was visited by Spanish poet Federico García Lorca. He was photographed there with several local children.

❾ San Severino Castle *Industrial Park, Dubrocq, Matanzas.*

The first and most important edification of the city of Matanzas, it is a typical military construction of Renaissance style, an example of assimilation of the system spread by the French and the Italians in the 16th and 17th centuries. Because of its historical, architectural and functional values the castle became a National Monument in 1978. On June 16, 2009, a museum that pictures the life and history of the fortress, as well the legacy of slavery in the province of Matanzas, was inaugurated on the premises. It is also the seat of the Museum of the Slave Route, a project with the participation of Unesco.

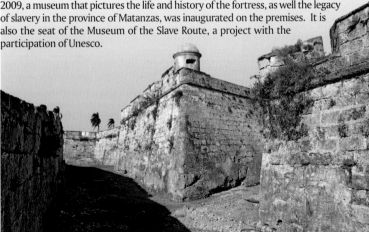

Matanzas

Sites of interest

(22) Puente de Bacunayagua

An impressive pass on the boundary with Mayabeque province, the Bacunayagua Bridge was inaugurated on September 26, 1959 and at present it is considered one of the seven wonders of Cuban engineering. On crossing it, travelers can admire one of the most beautiful sceneries of the island, both to the North and to the South. Driving to Matanzas, the dry bed and flow of what was once a river is seen on the left side; on the right, part of the exuberant Yumurí Valley. The bridge has a height of 110 meters from its bases up, 314 m. long and 16 m. wide.

The bridge Calixto García.

The bridge over the Canímar River.

City of Bridges

Matanzas was built by the namesake bay, where four rivers flow. Due to the several engineering works done over time to span these rivers, the oldest nickname of Matanzas was born –"city of bridges"– even before it was called "Athens of Cuba" in the 1860s. Back in 1772, a bridge spawned over the San Juan River. Economic development, mainly in relation with the sugar industry, caused the creation of several neighborhoods such as Versalles, Pueblo Nuevo and later on La Playa, thus demanding new crossings over beaches and the sea. Among those bridges, to mention just a few, there is La Concordia, over the Yumurí River, inaugurated on November 4, 1878; the Calixto García Bridge that since 1897 opened up the possibility at the time of a more secure traffic over the San Juan River; and the San Luis Bridge, one of the busiest in the city's center.

Western Cuba

㉓ Zapata Swamp

Located to the South of Matanzas province, it is one of Cuba's most unique spots where several types of ecosystems can be found, little or fairly modified by the actions of humans. The largest wetlands of the Caribbean islands, in Zapata live several species of plants, birds and other wildlife, some of them endemic to the area. Among its attractions are Laguna del Tesoro (Treasure Lake), the Hatiguanico River basin, the Montemar Great National Park, the Playa Girón Museum and a crocodile farm.

Playa Larga: One of the spots where Cuban militiamen and the people were mobilized during the historical events of April, 1961. Located at the end of Bay of Pigs, it is one of the best beaches on this part of the Caribbean. There is a hotel from which the swamp can be toured.

Playa Girón: A most transcendental site in Cuban history, world-wide renowned because of the Bay of Pigs invasion in April, 1961 that led to the first US military defeat in Latin America. Along the road there are signs and plaques where Cuban combatants died in action on April 17 to 19, 1961. Located on the East side of Bay of Pigs is the last sandy beach of the area, ideal for fishing and diving.

The Zapata rail and the Zapata wren are birds exclusive to the area and considered the ones with the most restricted habitat. In all, over 100 species of birds have been observed, among them the bee hummingbird (the smallest in the world), the Zapata sparrow, Gundlach's hawk, Cuban conure, Cuban Amazon parrot, and the Blue-headed Quail-dove. The Zapata Swamp is also a natural refuge for thousands of migratory birds from North America. There are also 16 species of reptiles, particularly the Cuban and American crocodiles, and in its estuaries and lakes two species of aquatic vertebrates in danger of extinction can be found: the manatee and the alligator gar, the former a marine mammal, and the latter a fish that in Cuba is found only in this region and other southern areas of the Western provinces and the Isle of Youth.

(24) Guamá Tourist Center

Located at Zapata Peninsula, declared by Unesco a Reserve of the Biosphere, and only 90 Km away from Varadero, one of the attractions of the center is a replica of a Taíno village that shows the life style of Cuba's original inhabitants. The tourist center with restaurant, bar and 47 independent wooden and thatch-roofed cabanas on an islet on Treasure Lake, is ideal for enjoying an adjacent natural park where terrestrial and aquatic animals can be observed, as well as a crocodile breeding center. On the lake there is a 25-piece sculptural group called Batey Aborigen (Aborigine Village), part of the Taíno village, and the work of Cuban sculptor Rita Longa. The tourist center is accessed by a 20 minute boat ride from Boca de Guamá to the lake, through a canal bordered with exuberant vegetation.

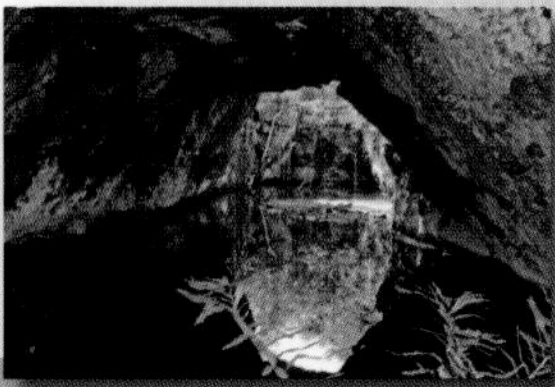

Allegro
VARADERO
EXPERIENCIAS
OCCIDENTAL
OCCIDENTAL
HOTELS & RESORTS
Autopista Sur, Km. 11 Varadero, Matanzas, Cuba.
Tel.: (53 45) 66 8288, Fax: (53 45) 66 8414
www.occidentalhotels.com

(25) A map of **Varadero**

Hicacos Peninsula

Hicacos Peninsula, which includes the world famous resort of Varadero, is 22 Km long and located between Cárdenas Bay and the Florida Straits. The peninsula tapers to Hicacos Point, Cuba's most northern land, a protected natural park with beautiful white sand and warm and transparent waters, lots of vegetation, and several caverns (like the one named Ambrosio), where cave paintings have been found. Hicacos Point is a fine place for diving and like in the rest of Varadero there are several hotels.

Cueva del Pirata Night Club
Allegro Varadero
Meliá Varadero
Sol Palmeras
Meliá Las Américas
Xanadú Mansion
Centro de Convenciones Plaza América
AUTOPISTA SUR
Iberostar Bella Costa
Tuxpan
Breezes Varadero
Complejo Sol Sirenas-Coral Resort
Varadero Golf Club
Varadero Internacional
Villa Cuba Resort
Las Morlas
Coralia Cuatro Palmas
Hotel y Bungalow Solymar
adero's Museum
Arenas Blancas
Hotetur Palma Real
Barracuda Diving Center
Dos Mares
Josone Retreat Park
an
CACOS
Bahía de Cárdenas
cho
Punta Hicacos
Punta Rincón Francés
Cactus El Patriarca
Paradisus Varadero
Varahicacos Ecological Reserve
Iberostar Alameda Varadero
Musulmanes Cave
Paradisus Princesa del Mar
Sandals Royal Hicacos
Memories Varadero
Marina Gaviota
Blau Varadero
Meliá Península Varadero
Ambrosio's Cave
Vizcaino Cave
Blau Marina Varadero
Club Amigo Gran Hotel
Meliá Las Antillas
de Oro
Turquesa
Ensenada de Marín
Dolphinarium
Cubanacán Náutica
Cayo Libertad
Cayo Buba
Ensenada Punta Hicacos
Punta Gorda del Este
da del Oeste

㉕ Varadero

Varadero's first settlers in 1887 probably never dreamed that the place would become one of the best resorts in the world. The so called "Blue Beach of Cuba" is a city almost surrounded by water located at Hicacos Peninsula, only a two-hour drive away from Havana. With over fifty hotels managed by Cuban and foreign chains such as Gran Caribe, Gaviota, Cubanacán, Sol Meliá, Barceló and many others, Varadero is still expanding. At present the resort has 15,000 available rooms, but it could hold as many as 25,300. This tourist destination is one of the most important in the country, for it has the greatest number of first class facilities right on the beach or nearby and a powerful infrastructure of specialized restaurants, snack bars, stores and malls, marinas and diving centers, the former both at hotels and away.

According to the recent modifications of the political and administrative division of the country, Varadero is at present a special territory, part of the Cárdenas Municipality. Besides its 22 Km of white powder-fine beaches, it has other natural attractions such as escarpments, caves, virgin keys and incredible seascapes in its western part. Among its wealth, visitors will find at Punta Hicacos aborigine pictographies in the Ambrosio Cave, and the ruins of La Calavera Saltworks, known to be the first exploited by the Spanish in America during colonial times.

Varadero also reveals itself a destination for business people, congresses and incentive trips, with the well equipped Plaza America Conventions Center. The resort offers excellent conditions for nautical sports of all kinds, among them deep-sea fishing. Its sea bottoms are ideal for diving, for there are over 40 different types of coral, several marine species including fish, lobster, shrimp, crab, turtles and about 60 types of mollusks.

Varadero

1 Josone Retreat Park *1st. Ave. and 56 St., Varadero.*

The park was the idea of a married couple that in 1942 dreamed of a place where their love would live on. José Iturrioz and Onelia Méndez joined the first three letters of their first names and Josone was born, a marvelous garden which took three years to build. Until 1963, the beautiful and large house was the residence of the Iturrioz family. Years later, Josone Retreat, with several restaurants and bars, was made available to tourists, and at present it is one of Varadero's most visited spots. The tunnel from the facility to the beach that the millionaire owner ordered dug under 1st. Avenue is still in use.

2 Xanadu Mansion *Las Américas Highway, Km. 8 ½, Varadero.*

Xanadu rises over the San Bernardino Crag and is a customary meeting point for players at the Varadero Golf Club. The mansion was designed in 1927 by Cuban architects Evelio Govantes and Félix Cabarrocas, and named by its owner after Coleridge's famous poem *Kublai Khan* describing the emperor's "pleasure dome". Its construction was commissioned by US multimillionaire Alfred Irénée Dupont de Nemours, who between 1920 and 1950 spent a great deal of money to buy almost all of Hicacos Peninsula from the heirs of the original Spanish owners. At present it houses the Las Américas Restaurant, with excellent cuisine and a great view of the beach.

Varadero

❸ Varadero Golf Club

Las Américas Highway, Km 8 ½.

This is the first 18-hole, par 72 golf course in Cuba, by the San Bernardino Crags, at the same place where US millionaire Dupont had its own 9-hole course in an exclusive area of 180 hectares, a few meters from the beach. The new course was designed by Les Furber, a Canadian architect and president of Golf Design Services, in a combination of styles dotting the course with palm trees, ponds and bridges. Several hotels are near to the golf club –SuperClubs Breezes, LTI Tuxpan, Bella Costa, Meliá Las Américas Golf & Suites Resort, Meliá Varadero, Sol Club Palmeras and Sol Club Sirenas.

❹ Varadero's Museum

57 St. on Ave. de la Playa, Varadero.

Tel.: (5345) 613189.

Located at a bungalow, the former beach house of wealthy Cuban engineer Leopoldo Abreu, the museum was inaugurated on December 5, 1981. There is an exhibition of historical pieces, as well as a collection of decorative arts and speleology. Among the exhibits you will find archeological evidence 2,000 years old, personal objects of former Varadero resident and US billionaire Irénée Dupont, an embalmed border patrol dog, and pieces from the Literacy Campaign and the most important local traditions, such as the Varadero regattas.

❺ Plaza América Convention Center

Sur Expressway, Km 11½, Las Américas, Varadero. Tel.: (5345) 667895, 668509, 668508.

This Center offers visitors a perfect combination of facilities, services and technology. Modern and functional, the center has highly qualified congress organizers, multilingual simultaneous interpretation, room clerks, technical teams and support staff. There are 10 meeting rooms of different capacity and the plenary room with 500 seats. In the building there is also Varadero's largest mall with dozens of outlets, restaurants, bars and coffee-shops, as well as opticians' facilities and drug stores.

(26) special municipality

Isle of Youth

The Cuban archipelago second largest island, located on Southwest Cuba, is part of Los Canarreos archipelago, together with over 600 keys and islets. Several names have identified it through time. The aborigines called it Camarcó, but on his second voyage Columbus christened it as La Evangelista on June 13, 1494. That was the name used by corsairs, pirates and smugglers that made of the place one of their havens in the Caribbean, so much so, that some believe it to have inspired British novelist Robert L. Stevenson for his *Treasure Island*.

A view of Nueva Gerona with de Las Casas Range in the background.

The Island of the Thousand Names, as many call it, was later officially known as Isle of Pines, until 1975, when it was renamed Isle of Youth because of the many so called "country schools", as well as for the students from Africa and other countries that had been granted scholarships to study there. A little more than 100 kilometers away from Batabanó, once it was also a settlement of Japanese farmers and immigrants from the Cayman Islands, the latter arriving between 1903 and 1910, when they founded the town of Jacksonville –at present Cocodrilo.

Today this special municipality offers its visitors the possibility of exploring coral reefs of extraordinary beauty thanks to services provided by the international diving center at El Colony Hotel, located on the premises of the Punta Francés National Marine Park. Another site of interest is black-sand Bibijagua Beach, close to two museums: Presidio Modelo, a prison to where Fidel Castro was sentenced, and El Abra Farm, linked to José Martí, Cuba's Apostle for Independence. These attractions are accompanied by Punta del Este's No. 1 cave, considered by speleologists the Sistine Chapel of Caribbean cave paintings, with more than 200 works.

A land of citrus fruit and first quality marble, Isle of Youth also excels in artistic and utilitarian ceramics. This is also the land of *sucu-sucu*, the native musical rhythm that has reached Cayo Largo del Sur, a wonderful tourist destination with 24 kilometers of beaches. Other suggestions of this small Cuban island are diving in over 30 sites, bird watching in the midst of large populations of mangrove, and visits to the neighboring Iguana, Rico and Rosario keys.

Western Cuba

The sunset at El Colony Hotel.

A marble quarry.

Capital: Nueva Gerona.

Area: 3,056 Km^2.

Population: 86,000 plus.

Boundaries: To the north with Batabanó Gulf; to the East with the waters of the island's shelf and the province of Matanzas; and to the West with the waters of the island's shelf and the province of Pinar del Río.

Economy: Industrial-agrarian.

Main Products: Citrus fruits, electric power, construction materials, food industry.

Relief: The territory is flat, with the North Plain as a point of interest, where you can find the Casas, Caballos and La Cañada Hill Ranges, and the South Plain with an area of 850 Km^2. The highest point is La Cañada Range, with 303 m.

Access: The Isle of Youth has an international airport and also another servicing national flights. At Cayo Largo there is the Vilo Acuña International Airport, where large-sized planes can land and as many as 300 passengers are serviced every hour. There are daily flights from Havana to Cayo Largo and the latter is also a point of departure for excursions to other tourist destinations. From Batabanó Port, at the province of Mayabeque, there is a ferry service to and fro the Isle of Youth.

The dock at Nueva Gerona.

Isle of Youth

Sites of interest

(27) Nueva Gerona

The capital of the Isle of Youth is a small town surrounded by hills by the Las Casas River. Along 39th St. its busiest artery flanked by portals and thick columns, there is a movie theater, a drugstore, post office, the bank, the hospital, stores, bars and restaurants.

El Pinero Memorial

33 St., between 26 and 28, Nueva Gerona.

Tel.: (5346) 323195.

In downtown Nueva Gerona, the capital of this special municipality, and near the Las Casas River's Malecón you will find El Pinero National Monument. Today you can only see the boat's hull, at present located in *terra firma* at its namesake square. The local population used to wait for arrivals and departures of El Pinero, built in Philadelphia in 1901, as an important event.

(28) Model Prison

Delio Chacón Residential, Nueva Gerona. Tel.:(5346) 325112.

About 5 Km to the South of Nueva Gerona stands the Model Prison, a unique facility in Latin America for its size and panoptic design. It is made up of 34 buildings, besides the security system's sentry boxes and the perimeter fence. The project was based on a prison at Jolliet, Illinois, and its construction took from October 1925 to February, 1932, during the government of President Gerardo Machado. One of the cells was occupied by Pablo de la Torriente Brau, who wrote the book *El Presidio Modelo*, which denounces the horrors of the prison, where other important political figures of the time also were. A group of the participants of the attack on Moncada Barracks in Santiago de Cuba, which took place on July 26, 1953, arrived to this prison on October 13 of that same year, and four days later arrived the group's leader, a young lawyer by the name of Fidel Castro, who remained here for 20 months.

Isle of Youth

Sites of interest

㉙ Museum at El Abra Farm

Siguanea Highway, Km. ½.

Inaugurated on January 28, 1944, the museum exhibits objects, documents and other pieces related to José Martí's stay in the Isle of Pine. Martí arrived at the farm on late October, 1870, after being released from a Havana prison where he had been sentenced to hard labor. At El Abra he stayed for two months, and subsequently left for Havana to be deported immediately to Spain. During his sojourn at the farm, young Martí occupied the first bedroom of the second body of the house. Among other pieces, the museum exhibits part of the belongings he used at the farm, an autographed book by his friend Fermín Valdés Domínguez, and a replica of the shackles he wore at the San Lázaro quarry.

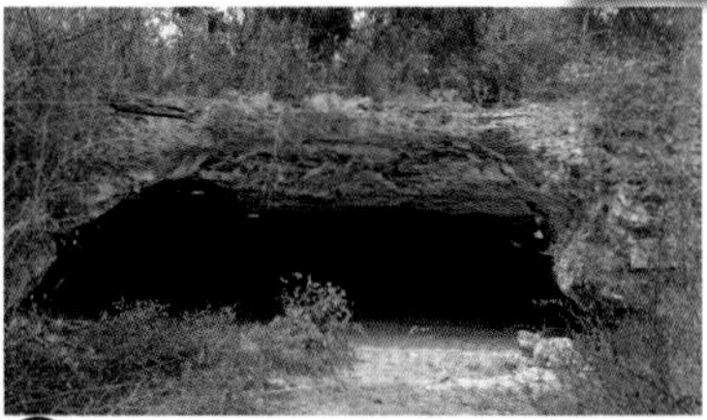

㉚ Punta del Este (Eastern Point)

Southeast tip of the Isle of Youth.

With a rich biodiversity due to its exuberant vegetation and varied terrestrial and sea wildlife, the place is famous for its four-cave system, particularly the number 1, where 213 paintings by aborigines can be found, almost a third of all known in the country. Because of its importance, Cuban academician Fernando Ortiz called it "the Sistine Chapel of Caribbean cave paintings". Ceilings and walls are adorned with concentric circles in harmonious and interrupted colored series, alternating red and black, and sometimes the white of the rock itself, although there other shapes.

㉛ Bibijagua Beach

Northwest Isle of Youth, some 8 Km from Nueva Gerona.

The beach stands out from others in the island and in the rest of Cuba because of the black color of its sand, the result of the erosion of black marble. Very near to the Model Prison, it has a modern hotel and other facilities.

Isle of Youth

Sites of interest

(32) Punta Francés National Marine Park

Isle of Youth's Southwest tip, 22 Km away from the town of Crocodile and 122 Km from Nueva Gerona.

The place that served as refuge for Cuba's first inhabitants witnessed the visits of many corsairs and pirates from the 16th to the 19th centuries. Underwater research at the cove on Francés Cape in 1978 served for selecting the first 40 diving sites. This has evolved into the International Diving Center at El Colony Hotel. Since 1982, it is the venue of international events of underwater photography, national championships (1994), and treasure searching (1996). Cuban world champion diver in apnea Déborah Andollo has set here several records.

(33) El Colony Hotel

Siguanea Highway, Km 42, Isle of Youth.

Tel.: (5346) 398181.

Built in the 1950s, it is located at Siguanea Cove on Isle of Youth's southern coast. Nearby is the marina, with boats for professional diving and fishing, equipped with first aid kits, oxygen, GPS system, and sonar. For underwater activities, there are 56 diving centers, several with important colonies of coral, gorgonia and sponges, besides the existence of underwater caves, passageway and tunnels. The following diving sites are ones of special beauty: Pared de Coral Negro (Black Coral Wall), Túnel del Amor (Tunnel of Love), Cueva Azul (Blue Grotto), El Pasaje Escondido (Hidden Passageway), Cueva de los Sábalos (Tarpon Cave), Piedra de Coral (Coral Stone), El Salto (The Waterfall), Anda del Pirata (Pirate's Anchor), Paraíso de las Levisas (Chupare Stingray Paradise) and Pequeño Reino (Little Kingdom).

Western Cuba

(34) Cayo Largo del Sur

Eastern tip of Los Canarreos archipelago.

The key has 24 Km of excellent beaches, as well as numerous facilities catering to visitors. With a high degree of conservation, the coral reef barriers are complemented by the neighboring islets where there is a great number of species of flora and wildlife, including iguanas, pelicans and turtles. A tourist destination *par excellence*, isolated and quiet, it is located on the eastern tip of Los Canarreos archipelago, 135 Km from Nueva Gerona, 125 Km from Cienfuegos province, and 177 Km from Havana and Varadero. There is a lodging infrastructure worthy of the most demanding of tastes, among them Sol Cayo Largo, Sol Pelícano, Isla del Sur and Playa Blanca hotels, with the addition of marinas and diving centers. Cayo Largo del Sur offers the possibility of flying to Isle of Youth, visiting that island, sailing in yachts and catamaran boats and hopping to Cayo Iguana and other neighboring islets.

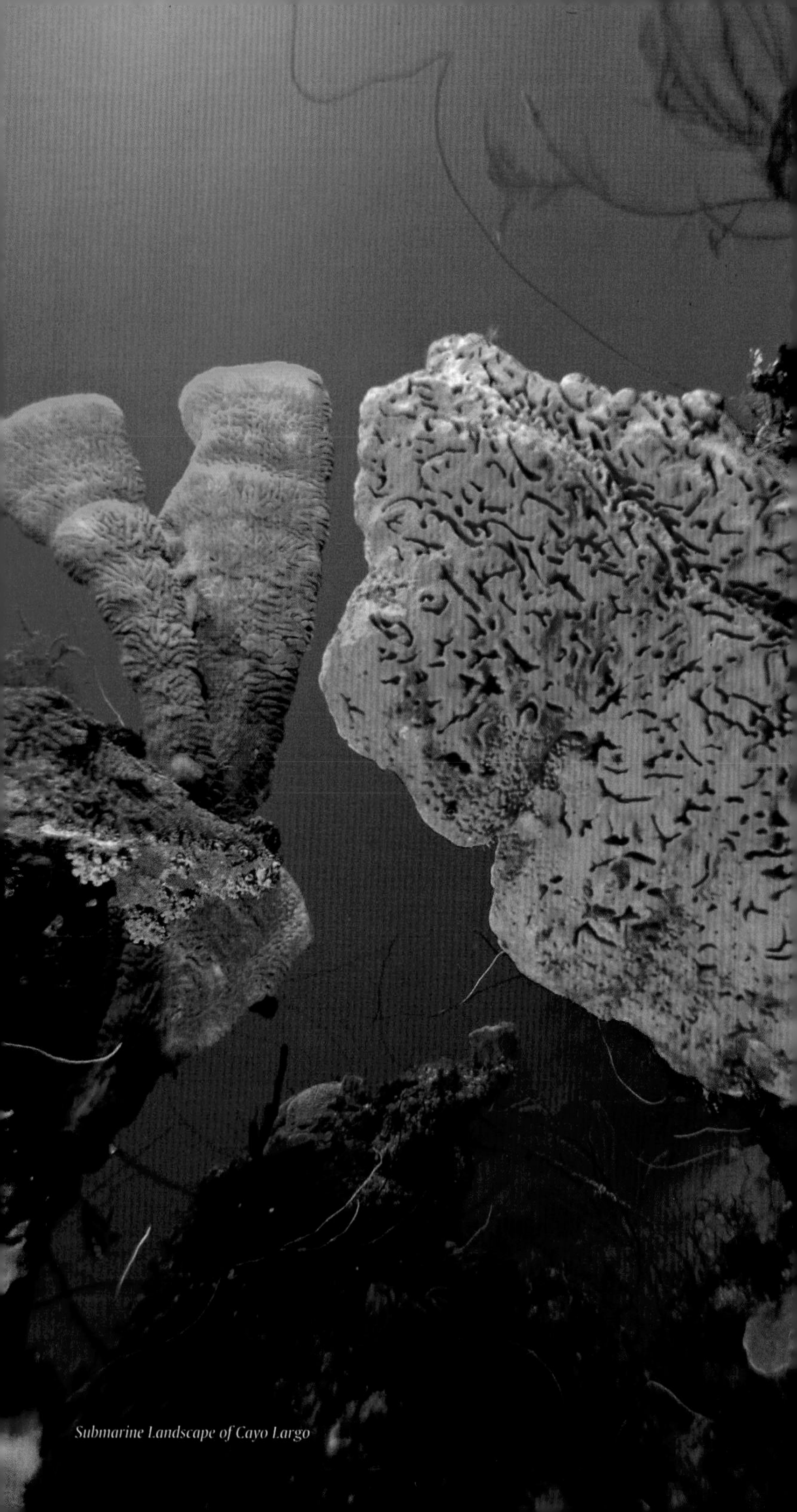

Submarine Landscape of Cayo Largo

A Journey Through Central Cuba

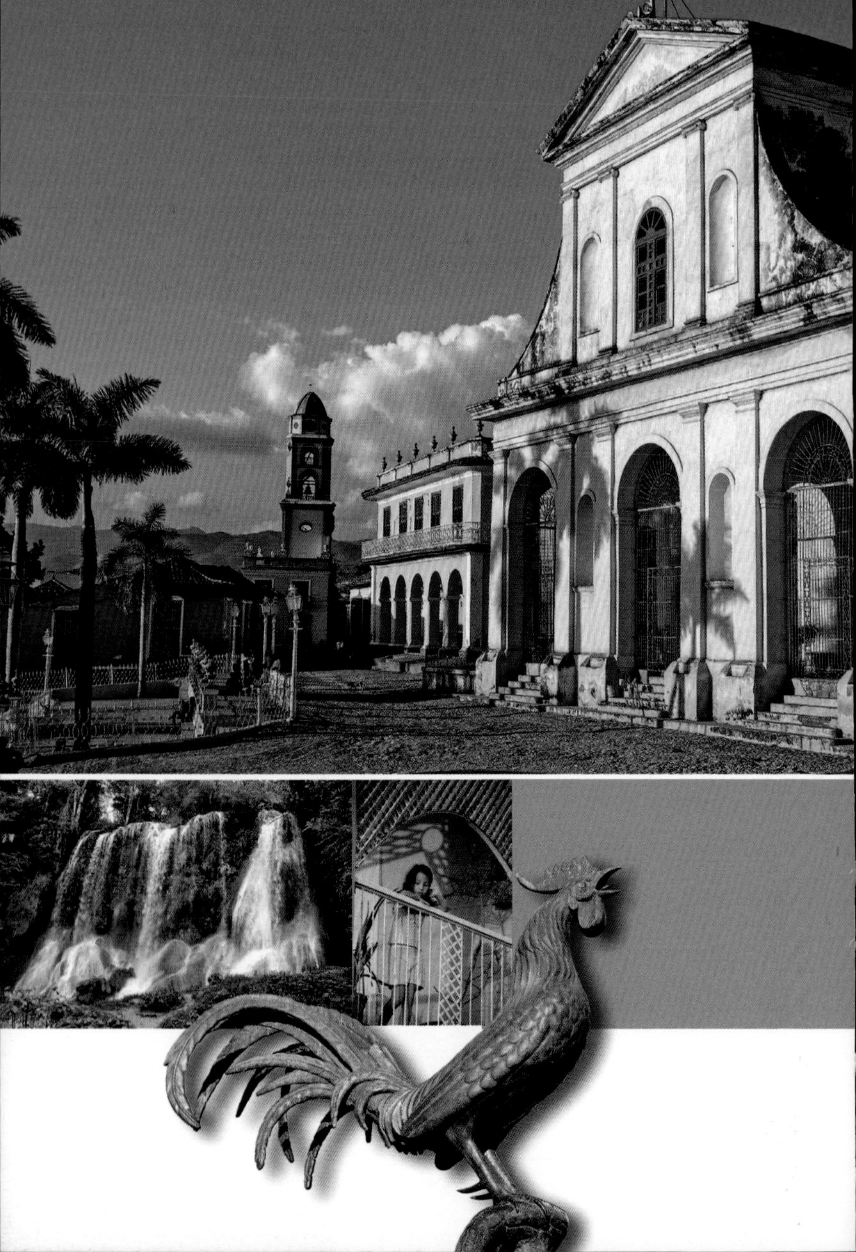

central
Cuba

Five provinces form this region –Cienfuegos, Villa Clara, Sancti Spíritus, Ciego de Ávila and Camagüey– with more than 2 million people. One of its characteristics is its great plains, although it includes the Escambray Range, one of the most important mountain systems in Cuba.

If we draw a path through the region we can find many tourist centers, outstanding because of the diversity of their offers. Cienfuegos, known as the Pearl of the South, combines the charm of a city founded by the French in early1819 with the beauty of its coast and the quiet waters of its beaches. Also outstanding are the values that have made its Historical Center a Unesco World Heritage Site.

However, this is not the only city in the region that has such recognition. Trinidad, in the province of Sancti Spiritus, reveals itself as a city frozen in time. Here you breathe in the atmosphere of a town where details of colonial architecture prevail. Further on, at the center of the region, Camagüey is also a World Heritage Site. The land of "tinajones" (large earthenware jars), as it is also known, exhibits a particular trait: regular and small squares and churches spread all over the city. This is the starting point for a visit to Santa Lucía Beach, near Cayo Sabinal.

Speaking about "cayos" (Spanish for keys or islets), the north coast of Villa Clara excels for its stunning beaches and exuberant vegetation. Nearby, Ciego de Avila offers the visitor the chance to discover the Jardines del Rey archipelago, where Cayo Coco and Cayo Guillermo are located, paradisiacal environments where you will find the coral barrier that runs parallel by Cuba's north coast, and even be surprised by a colony of pink flamingoes.

Central Cuba

index

In this section of the guide, you will find general data, references to historic and tourist sites of the five central provinces, as well as of the town of the Santísima Trinidad.

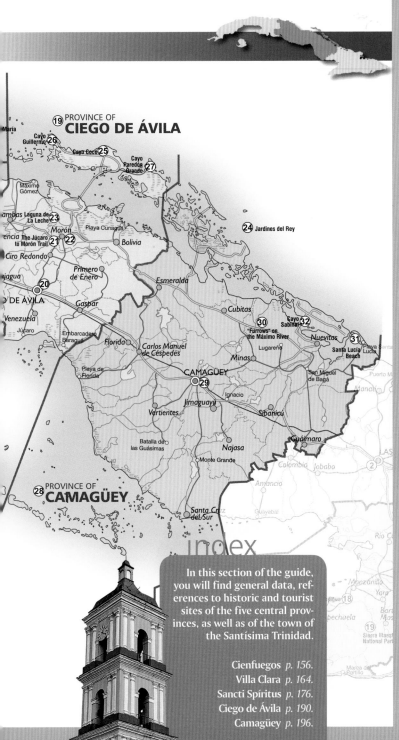

1 province of
Cienfuegos

The Cienfuegos Malecón.

Many consider Cienfuegos, and most of all, its capital, as one of the most beautiful in the country. No wonder they call the city "The Pearl of the South", or also "Beautiful City by the Sea." Because of it, singer/songwriter Beny Moré, one of its most beloved sons, immortalized it in a song. French Louis de Clouet founded the city in 1819, and named it Fernandina de Jagua. A main characteristic of the town are its wide and rectilinear streets, good taste and refinement, as well as its beautiful neoclassic and eclectic buildings.

Its Historical Center, declared by Unesco World Heritage Site in 2005, is considered a singular model of 19th century urban planning in Cuba and the Caribbean. Its orthogonal design is characterized by compact construction, stylistic homogeneity, and the magnificence of its main buildings. The restoration of streets and constructions is a palpable reality for those who decide to walk around the city that boasts a long and beautiful Prado Promenade. The Prado ends at the exact place where the Malecón begins –the junction with Punta Gorda, a neighborhood that still displays its antique splendor in wooden houses, as well as Valle Palace and the Jagua Hotel.

With an undeniable sea tradition, Cienfuegos offers a seascape of incomparable beauty at the entrance to the bay, dominated by Jagua Castle, built for the defense of the city against pirates. The Botanical Garden and the Ciego Montero Spa are a must for visitors to this province, also famous for the Rancho Luna and Inglés beaches.

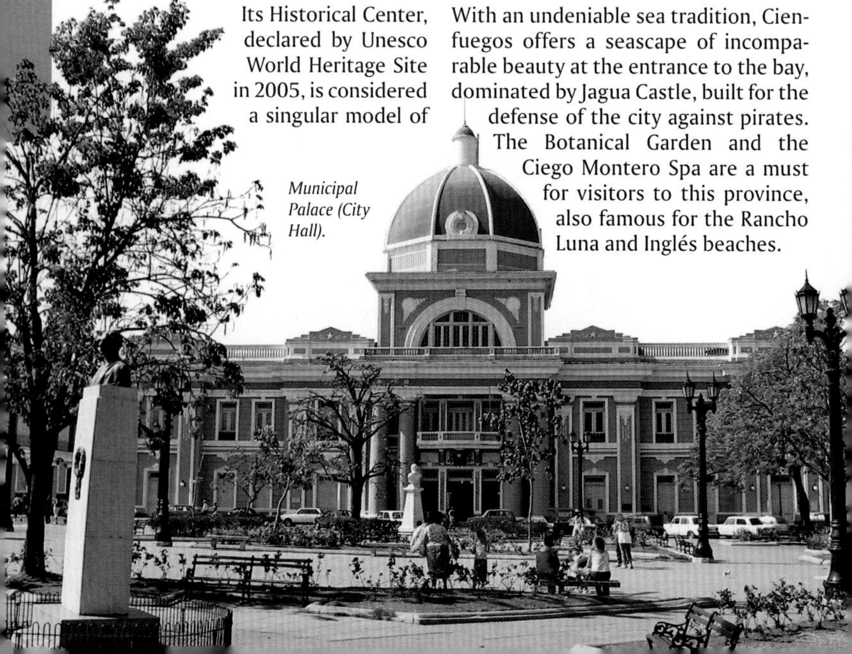

Municipal Palace (City Hall).

A view of Cienfuegos Bay.

Capital: Cienfuegos.

Area: 4,180 Km².

Municipalities: Cienfuegos, Cruces, Palmira, Lajas, Aguada de Pasajeros, Rodas, Abreu and Cumanayagua.

Population: 400,000.

Boundaries: To the North with the province of Villa Clara; to the East with the province of Sancti Spíritus; to the South with the Caribbean Sea; and to the West with the province of Matanzas.

Economy: Industrial-agrarian and livestock, fishing, and a busy port.

Main products: Cane sugar, power generation, and food and chemical industries.

Relief: Mainly plains, although approximately 15% of the surface is over 100 m high The elevations are located in Southeast Cienfuegos, on the portion of the Escambray Mountain Range belonging to this province. Cienfuegos main geographical accident is Jagua Bay, around which is concentrated the province's life.

Access: By air, through the Jaime González International Airport. By land, through the National Highway and the railroad that connects Cienfuegos with the central branch line. The highway network interconnects all urban areas and tourist, economic and cultural points of interest.

Additional information: The Martín Infierno Cave, a National Monument since 1990, has the world´s biggest stalagmites, as well as gypsum flowers, the only existing ones in Cuba; a butterfly bat colony, the smallest in the world, and elephant ear's stalactites.

Punta Gorda neighborhood.

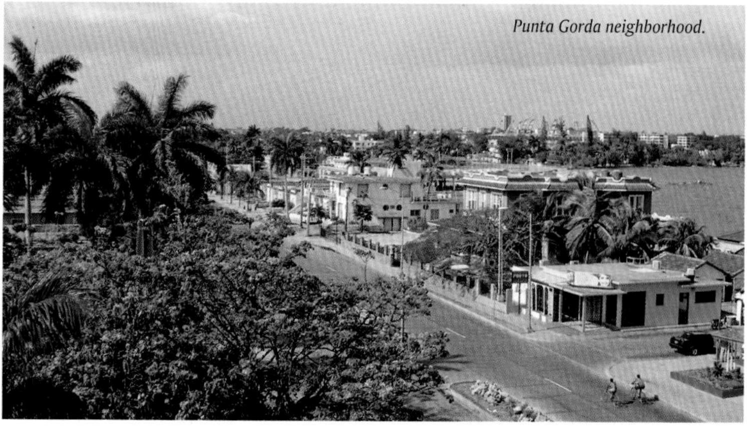

② A map of the city of **Cienfuegos**

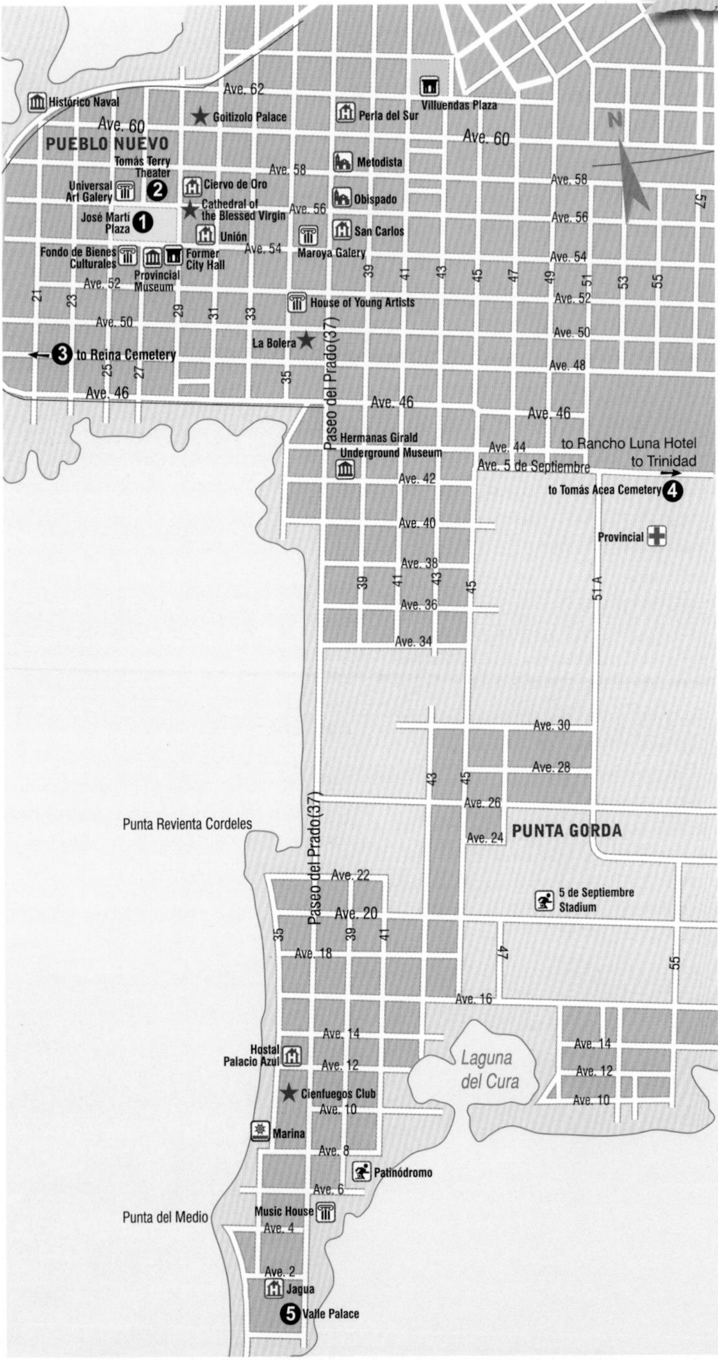

Cienfuegos

Sites of interest

❶ José Martí Plaza

54th and 56th Avenue, between 25 and 29 Ave.

There is a large granite rose that signals the exact spot where the town of Fernandina de Jagua was founded under a mahogany tree on April 22, 1819. It also serves as the zero point from where all the city`s streets were traced. Through the years, before bearing the name of José Martí Plaza, it had several names –Ramírez Square, Main Square, Recreation Square and Independence Square. The main political, administrative, and social buildings surround the plaza, as well the Cathedral of the Blessed Virgin, the Town Hall, the Tomás Terry Theater, the old San Lorenzo College, the former Casino Español (Spanish Club) and at present the Provincial Museum, the Ferrer Palace (House of Culture), El Bodegón (Spanish for Tavern) Palatino and several private homes.

❷ Tomás Terry Theater

2703, 56th Ave., on 27th, Cienfuegos
Tel.:(5343)513361.

Named after Tomás Terry, a plantation owner and local patron of the arts, the theater was built in 1890 with an impressive façade and frescos on the ceiling. Many famous artists have honored this stage, such as Italian tenor Enrico Caruso, French actress Sara Bernhardt and Mexican movie star Jorge Negrete.

Cathedral of the Blessed Virgin facing Martí Plaza.

Cienfuegos

❸ Reina Cemetery

50th Ave. and 7th, St, Cienfuegos.

Located on West Cienfuegos and considered an authentic museum of funeral arts, the Reina Cemetery was declared a National Monument. Although its proximity to the sea has been damaging, it still displays its original layout and has examples of French and Italian statuary art. One of the most famous is Sleeping Beauty, the source of many stories. Previously the cemetery was placed on a block limited by the Santa Elena-Velazco-Santa Cruz-Casales streets, but in 1839 it was relocated to the present site in order to protect the population from the risk of infection from corpses of the victims of cholera or other maladies.

❹ Tomás Acea Cemetery

5 de Septiembre Avenue. Tel: (5343) 525 257.

Also considered an architectural jewel and designed as a garden with paths and fruit trees, the Tomás Acea substituted the old Reina Cemetery. It has an elegant administrative building of classic design with thick columns and drawings of the time, preceded by an impressive entrance. Located on East Cienfuegos, it is the work of two local architects, Pablo Donato Carbonell and Luis Felipe Ros. It constitutes a valuable example of construction in 1926 and of American modern building concepts at the time.

❺ Valle Palace

37 St, between 0 and 2 Ave, Punta Gorda, Cienfuegos. Tel.: (5343) 551 003.

One of the most amazing buildings in the city, located at the Punta Gorda neighborhood by Jagua Bay, it was a wedding gift for Amparo Suero Rodríguez, married to wealthy businessman Acisclo del Valle Blanco. The idea to build a unique mansion came to them while traveling in Spain. The eclectic-designed home was constructed between 1913 and 1917, at a cost of 1.5 million pesos by French, Arab, Italian and Cuban builders with much of the materials (such as marble, alabaster, bronze, glass and ceramics) imported from Spain, Italy and the United States. Currently it hosts a restaurant annexed to the Jagua Hotel and a *bodegón* (Spanish tavern) for fans of art and fine cuisine.

Cienfuegos
Sites of interest

③ Jagua Castle *Jagua Castle Hamlet. Tel.: (5343) 965 402.*

For safeguarding the area, Spain built a stonework fortress at the bay's entrance. Engineer Joseph Tantete began it in 1733, and 12 years later it was officially inaugurated under the name of Our Lady of the Angels of Jagua Castle. Located on a small hill, the fortress has been painstakingly restored to welcome visitors, who will learn of the legend of the Lady in Blue, a mysterious woman who haunted halls and rooms at night, terrorizing the guards. The story goes that one of the guards was found one morning in a state of shock, wringing a blue piece of cloth in his hands. He never recovered and had to be committed to an asylum for the insane. By the fort, a fishing town can be reached by boat from Pasacaballos Hotel, Cienfuegos Port or Punta Gorda.

④ El Nicho

Known for its cascades, caves, natural pools and trails, the natural reserve El Nicho, on the Cienfuegos Escambray Mountain Range, reveals itself as a scientific and ecological area of great importance because of its abundant wildlife and varied flora.

Cienfuegos

Sites of interest

⑤ Botanical Garden

136 Central Street, Pepito Tey, Cienfuegos
Tel: (5343) 545 115.

The Cienfuegos Botanical Garden located near the present Pepito Tey Sugar Mill, on the highway to Trinidad, in Sancti Spiritus province, is considered the most important on the island, not only for its age, but also for its valuable plant collection, some of them the only of its kind in the Americas and other regions of the planet. With an area of 97 hectares, it was founded by US businessman Edwin F. Atkins, who bought the Soledad sugar mill in the late 19th century. His intention was to create a botanical research center that would allow him to improve sugar cane in his lands for a better yield. In 1901, under his sponsorship, the Harvard Botanical Station for Tropical Research and Sugar Cane Investigation is founded on the premises. In 1919, Atkins passed on the management of the institution to Harvard University, which left Cuba in 1960. Currently the garden has more than 417 different species, of which approximately 500 are unique specimens, represented by plants of over 670 types of 125 different families, most of them trees. Seventy percent of the plants at the Garden are from Asia, Africa, Oceania and the Americas.

Benny Moré, The Most of Rhythm

Cienfuegos prides itself for being the birthplace of Maximiliano Bartolomé Moré, aka Benny Moré, a self-made musician who sang with several groups until he created his own "Giant Band". Born on August 24, 1919 in the town of Santa Isabel de las Lajas, he is also known as ¨El Bárbaro del Ritmo¨ (The Most of Rhythm) and has inspired with its unique voice several generations in Cuba and abroad. El Benny, as he was fondly called by his fans, passed away in the early 1960s. Every year on the day of his death, he is remembered at his hometown, particularly at the Benny Moré International Festival. For some years, his bronze statue, lovingly made by Cuban sculptor José Villa Soberón, winner in 2008 of the National Award of the Arts, stands on the Cienfuegos Prado Promenade.

The statue of Benny Moré on the Cienfuegos Prado Promenade.

Central Cuba

⑥ province of
Villa Clara

Vidal Plaza and La Caridad Theater.

A group of families of the neighboring town of San Juan de los Remedios came to these lands to get away from the coast threatened by pirate attacks. Under the shadow of a tamarind tree, they founded the town and celebrated the first mass on July 15, 1689. At the time, they could not imagine that Villa Clara would become the meeting point for travelers who cross the country from one end to the other. Santa Clara, its capital, was also for many years the capital of the former province of Las Villas, which then included the present provinces of Cienfuegos, Sancti Spíritus and Villa Clara.

Today this is an attractive city for many reasons, among them its historical significance due to an important battle led by Ernesto "Che" Guevara. The battle hastened the end of the Fulgencio Batista regime. Because of it, Santa Clara is also known as Che's City. It is also his final resting place, where he lies in a mausoleum together with some of his revolutionary comrades that fought at his side in Bolivia.

Besides its history, the territory is also admired for its architectural heritage and the popular traditions of the town of San Juan de los Remedios, famous for its "parrandas" (carnival parades). It is also a preferential site for those who prefer exploring the virgin keys on the northeast: Las Brujas, Santa María, Francés, Cobo and Ensenachos. The province also has natural resources such as the mineral medicinal waters at Elguea Spa, as well as the Hanabanilla reservoir, of excellent conditions for trout fishing.

Remedios Church.

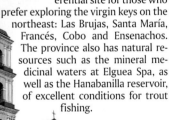

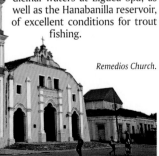

Provincial Palace

Capital: Santa Clara.

Area: 8,662.4 Km².

Municipalities: Santa Clara, Corralillo, Quemado de Güines, Sagua la Grande, Santo Domingo, Ranchuelo, Cifuentes, Camajuaní, Encrucijada, Remedios, Caibarién, Placetas and Manicaragua.

Population: 800,000 plus.

Boundaries: To the North with the Atlantic Ocean; to the East and the South with the province of Sancti Spíritus; and to the west with the provinces of Cienfuegos and Matanzas.

Economy: Industrial-agrarian. Predominance of cane sugar industry.

Main Products: Home electric appliances, heavy industry machinery, textiles, chemical products, paper, food industry, marble, tobacco and citrus fruits.

Relief: Its coast, characterized by swampy and low areas, is 191 Km long on the north, and is its only maritime border. The greater heights are Pico Tuerto (923 m) in the Trinidad Mountain Range, and Guaniquical Mountain Range (869 m).

Access: The Island's two main routes, Central Highway and the National Expressway, converge here and link the territory with West and East Cuba. Flights arrive at the provincial capital's airport and at an airfield in Cayo Las Brujas. Both can handle medium and small aircraft. The territory is linked to the northern keys by a causeway over the sea.

Additional Information: The famous thermal and mineral medicinal waters of Elguea are in the territory.

Fountain of the Boy with the Unfortunate Boot, at Vidal Plaza.

Façade of the Museum of Decorative Arts.

⑦ A map of the city of **Santa Clara**

EL VAQUERITO
to Camajuaní
SANTA CATALINA
to Remedios
CIRCUNVALACIÓN
N
Tomás Ruiz
Ana Pegudo
Ave. de la Liberación
Conrado Benítez
Nelson Villariño
Obdulio Morales
Campo
Campo Interior
Félix Huergo
A. Álvarez
R. Ruiz del Sol
Che Monument
The Armored Train Monument
Aurelio Janet Sports Center
CAPIRO
Capiro Outlook
Ernesto Che Guevara
Miguel Gutiérrez
Chiqui Pedraza
to Ciego de Ávila
SANDINO
Burro Perico
Augusto César Sandino
Ave. 9 de Abril
Ave. Sandino
BRISAS DEL CAPIRO
Carretera Central a Placetas
Carretera Central
Cubanicay
Maceo
E. P. Morales
C. Quintero
Unión
Ave. 26 de Julio
Bonachea
Bella Vista
San Juan
Ceiba
VIGÍA
Misionero
5ta Escambray
ESCAMBRAY NORTE
Colón
J. de la Luz y Caballero
Hospital
Clínico Quirúrgico
Barcelona
Pasaje Risquet
9na.
VILLA JOSEFA
Prolongación de Colón
Ave. Marta Abreu
ESCAMBRAY
CIRCUNVALACIÓN
CARDOSO
Ave. 7 de Diciembre
Pediátrico
Clínico Quirurgico
Materno
to Manicaragua

❶ Leoncio Vidal Plaza

Marta Abreu, Rafael Tristá, Máximo Gómez and Luis Estévez Streets.

At a meeting of the Santa Clara city commission on March 4, 1899, councilman Enrique del Cañal proposed to name the plaza in honor of Cuban patriot Leoncio Vidal Caro, a native of Ceja del Pablo, Corralillo. Previously this space was known as Parade Grounds, Main Square, and Constitution Square. Since its creation, the plaza has undergone many changes that have erased elements of its previous design, such as the Greater Parish, demolished in 1923, and the beautiful and long-missed pergola once located at the entrance. There is still the Obelisk, inaugurated on July 15th, 1886 on the 197th anniversary of the town's foundation, in memory of two illustrious priests. Father Juan Martín Conyedo (1687–1761) and Father Francisco Hurtado de Mendoza (1724-1803). Other elements still remaining at the plaza are the gazebo built in 1911; the fountain of the Boy with the Unfortunate Boot, and several monuments, including one built to honor the notable patriot and patron Marta de los Ángeles Abreu de Estévez.

❷ La Caridad Theater

Vidal Plaza, between Lora and Máximo Gómez, Santa Clara. Tel.:(5342)205548.

La Caridad Theater was inaugurated on September 8, 1885, under the patronage of Marta de los Ángeles Abreu de Estévez, in order to donate its proceedings to charity and perpetuate her father´s memory. Its decor and other details of interior design are outstanding. At present, thanks to a rigorous restoration process, the magnificence the building had at its opening can once again be admired.

3 El Carmen Plaza

Máximo Gómez St., between San Pablo and Conyedo, Santa Clara.

The plaza is located on top of a hill where the mass for the foundation of Santa Clara was heard on July 15, 1689, under a leafy tamarind tree. According to popular legends, the settlers at San Juan de los Remedios, terrorized by the constant attacks of corsairs and pirates, decided to emigrate inland seeking safer terrain. They found a place with beautiful rivers and abundant vegetation and decided to stay. Nothing documents the story, but it remains as a legend for enriching Santa Clara traditions. Yet, there was a tamarind tree planted at the right wing of the Church of Our Lady of Carmen. Here rises a monument dedicated to the 18th century original families, a concrete pillar covered in marble from the Isle of Pines, currently Isle of Youth.

4 Santa Clara Libre Hotel

6 Vidal Plaza, between Tristá and P. Chao, Santa Clara. Tel.: (5342) 207548 al 50.

Formerly the Santa Clara Hilton Grand Hotel, built in 1954, the building ended the neoclassic and eclectic architecture that predominates around Vidal Plaza. Commissioned by local tycoon Orfelio Ramos, it is the city's highest building. On the first floor there is a movie theater named at that time as Cloris Theater. Currently it bears the name of war hero Camilo Cienfuegos. In the Battle for Santa Clara, the Revolutionary Army took the building in combat.

5 Decorative Art Museum

Vidal Plaza, on Luis Estévez, Santa Clara. Tel.: (5342) 205 368.

Located at the center of Santa Clara, it is housed in an 18th century building where fans, furniture, porcelains, lamps, textiles, paintings, dressing accessories and sculptures from the 17th to the 20th centuries are on display. Among other exhibits, you will find the lingerie of the Martí-Bance family and some personal objects of well-known Cuban poet Dulce María Loynaz del Castillo.

Villa Clara

Sites of interest

❻ The Armored Train Monument

Camajuaní Highway on the railroad crossroad. Tel.:(5342) 202 758.

The work of Cuban sculptor José Delarra, the monument is a memento of one of the most relevant events near the end of the Cuban insurrection against the Batista dictatorship –the Battle of Santa Clara, led by Ernesto Che Guevara and his Rebel Army troops. On December 29, 1958, the rebels attacked and took the armored train sent from Havana, thus ending the battle. The monument has five statues representing the rebels' actions, and four of the original wagons and the bulldozer used to rip-off the railroad tracks.

❼ Monument to Commander Ernesto Che Guevara

Los Desfiles Avenue, Santa Clara. Tel.: (5342) 205 985.

Inaugurated on December 28, 1988 to commemorate the 30th anniversary of the Battle of Santa Clara, it was designed by architect Jorge Cao Campos and sculptor José Delarra. The monument includes a museum and mausoleum where, since October 17, 1997, lie Che's remains together with those of the revolutionaries that died fighting in the Bolivia guerrilla campaign led by Guevara. It exhibits some of Che's personal objects and exhibits a chronological reconstruction of his lifetime.

Foto: Alberto Díaz Korda

Foto: Osvaldo Salas

Ernesto Guevara

Ernesto Guevara, known as Che to his comrades first and the whole world later (Rosario, Argentina, June 14, 1928-La Higuera, Bolivia, October 9, 1967), was one of the top Commanders of the Cuban Revolution (1953-1959) that brought to Cuba a new political system. From 1959 to 1965, he was a key government figure in the formation of the new Cuba. He held several important posts in the administration, mainly in the economic area –Minister of Industry, Chairman of the National Bank, and heading diplomatic missions abroad.

Convinced of the need to extend armed struggle to the Third World, Che Guevara proposed the creation of several guerrillas in Latin America. Between 1965 and 1967, he fought in Congo and Bolivia. Captured in Bolivia after being wounded, he was assassinated on October 9, 1967. This famous portrait, taken by Alberto Díaz (Korda), has become one of the most reproduced icons in the world, both in its original form and in multiple versions.

⑧ Hanabanilla Lake

Located on a large valley in the midst of the Escambray Mountain Range, this is the only lake surrounded by mountains in Cuba. It is ideal for trout fishing, hiking, climbing, and admiring the many varieties of orchids that grow in this place, as well as different specimens of Cuban wildlife.

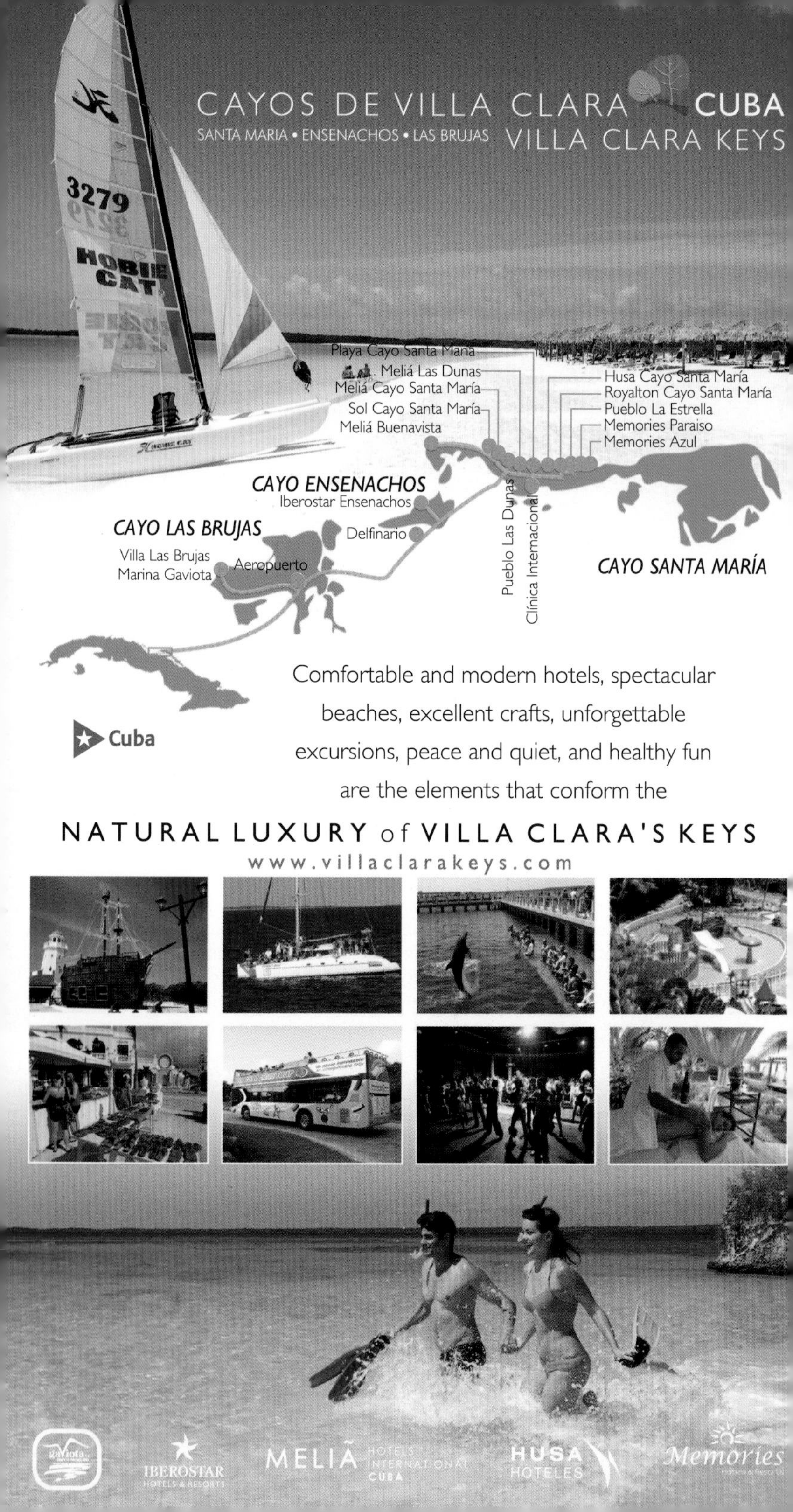
CAYOS DE VILLA CLARA CUBA
SANTA MARIA • ENSENACHOS • LAS BRUJAS
VILLA CLARA KEYS
3279
HOBIE CAT
Playa Cayo Santa María
Meliá Las Dunas
Meliá Cayo Santa María
Sol Cayo Santa María
Meliá Buenavista
Husa Cayo Santa María
Royalton Cayo Santa María
Pueblo La Estrella
Memories Paraiso
Memories Azul
CAYO ENSENACHOS
Iberostar Ensenachos
Delfinario
CAYO LAS BRUJAS
Villa Las Brujas
Marina Gaviota
Aeropuerto
Pueblo Las Dunas
Clínica Internacional
CAYO SANTA MARÍA
Cuba
Comfortable and modern hotels, spectacular beaches, excellent crafts, unforgettable excursions, peace and quiet, and healthy fun are the elements that conform the
NATURAL LUXURY of VILLA CLARA'S KEYS
www.villaclarakeys.com
gaviota
IBEROSTAR
HOTELS & RESORTS
MELIÃ
HOTELS INTERNATIONAL CUBA
HUSA
HOTELES
Memories

Villa Clara

Sites of interest

⑨ Las Brujas, Santa María and Ensenachos Keys

These keys (or "cayos" in Spanish) are linked to the mainland by a 50 Km causeway. White sand beaches, crystal-clear waters, sea bottoms of exceptional beauty, a large coral reef and colonies of flamingos give to these keys the characteristics of Paradise.

⑩ San Juan de los Remedios

To the left side streets in the town of Remedios and to the rights the impressive gold plated altar in St. John the Baptist Greater Parish Church.

San Juan de los Remedios is the eighth town founded by Spanish conquistadors on the island in the first quarter of the 16th century. It has attractions such as St. John the Baptist Greater Parish Church, one of the most important of its kind in the country, with polychrome decoration on its ceilings and unique sculptures. Alejandro García Caturla's house, on Camilo Cienfuegos Street, exhibits musical instruments, portraits, and personal objects that belonged to this 20th century great Cuban musician, born in Remedios in 1906.

However, undoubtedly, the "parrandas" (carnival parades) are the distinctive feature of the region. There is even a museum that shows the history of these parades in photographs, musical instruments, costumes and handcrafted objects. According to tradition, an imaginary line splits the town's Main Square in half. The neighborhoods thus divided "battle" each other on behalf of their "barrios", San Salvador and El Carmen, represented by a rooster and a hawk respectively. On December 24, when the clock at the Greater Parish Church strikes 9:00 pm, the competition begins with each side displaying its creative abilities, imagination and a whole year´s efforts making costumes, ornate poles, floats, fireworks, and traditional music.

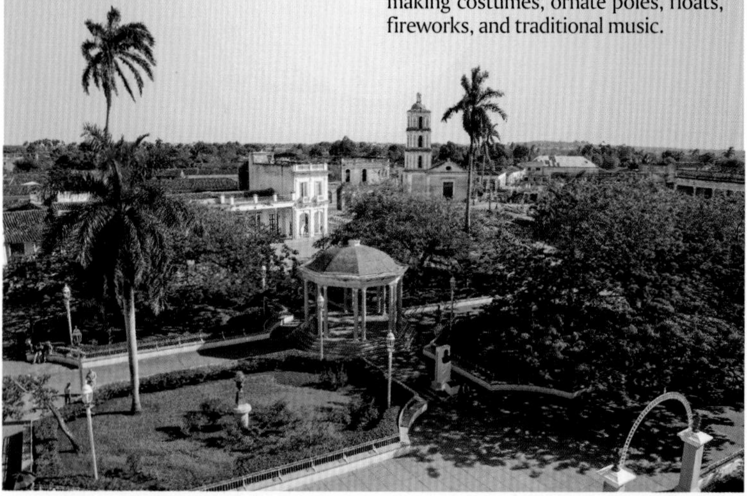

Parrandas of Remedios.

11 province of
Sancti Spíritus

Sancti Spíritus is privileged for having in its territory two of the first seven towns founded by Spanish conquistador Diego Velázquez in 1514: the Santísima Trinidad (Holy Trinity) and the present capital of the province, Sancti Spiritus. The former was founded in the Aborigine chieftainship of Guamuhaya. As it was customary at the time, the land chosen for the town was designed as a rectangle, with the Royal Square in the middle, and around it the church and the public buildings. Nowadays many of these buildings, some of them converted into museums and other family homes, attract the attention of visitors to Trinidad, where there is large valley with several ruins of former sugar mills.

Sancti Spiritus, the Land of the Holy Spirit, was born among palm leaves and wood until it became a town with narrow streets, interior patios, tiled roofs, bridges, large and small. The city can be toured today with the nostalgia for the past. The Greater Church, built in 1680 and considered the city's most ancient building, is one of its most emblematic, together with the legendary bridge over the Yayabo River, the only of its kind in Cuba, with 5 romantic style monumental arches.

From the peace of this colonial environment, you can reach the no less peaceful site of Topes de Collantes, in the part of the Escambray Range pertaining to the province; keep on going until you reach the Ancón Peninsula and is neighboring keys; and finally enjoy the famous Mayajigua lakes.

Serafín Sánchez Plaza.

Greater Parish Church.

Capital: Sancti Spíritus.

Area: 6,779.81 Km².

Municipalities: Sancti Spiritus, Taguasco, Jatibonico, Yaguajay, Cabaiguán, Trinidad, Fomento and La Sierpe.

Population: 460,000 plus.

Boundaries: To the North, with the Old Bahamas Channel; to the East, with Ciego de Ávila province; to the South, with the Ana María Gulf and the Caribbean Sea; and to the West with Cienfuegos and Villa Clara provinces.

Economy: Industrial-agrarian, livestock.

Main products: Cane sugar, tobacco, coffee, rice, tubers, vegetables and a variety of fruits. Forest resources are also exploited as well as cattle, hogs and poultry. There is some fishing activity, especially in Casilda, Trinidad.

Relief: Varied, mainly plains, and in a lesser degree mountains and hills.

Access: Main accesses are through the Central Highway, the National Expressway, North and South circuits and the Central Railroad –the North Line and Sancti Spíritus-Tunas de Zaza Branch. It has two national airports at the cities of Sancti Spiritus and Trinidad.

⑫ A map of the city of **Sancti Spíritus**

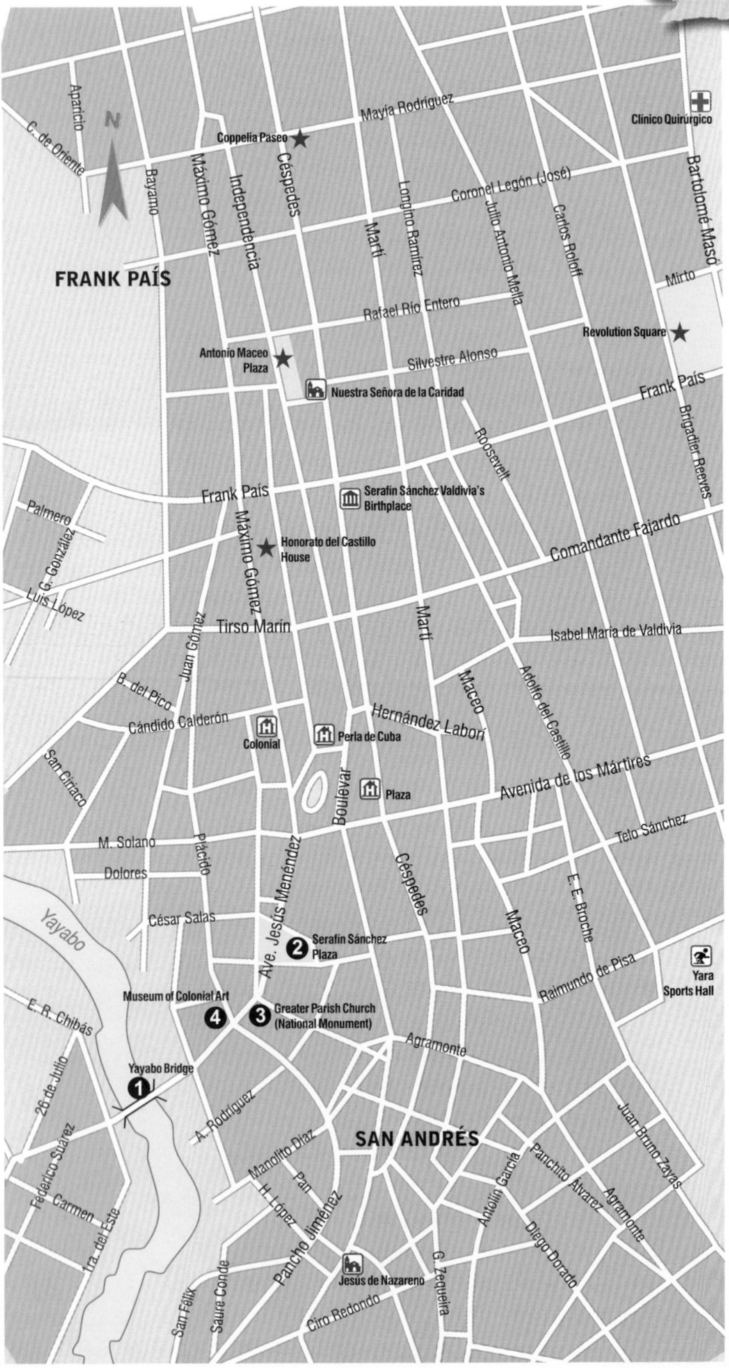
N
FRANK PAÍS
SAN ANDRÉS
Coppelia Paseo
Clínico Quirúrgico
Antonio Maceo Plaza
Nuestra Señora de la Caridad
Revolution Square
Serafín Sánchez Valdivia's Birthplace
Honorato del Castillo House
Colonial
Perla de Cuba
Plaza
Serafín Sánchez Plaza
Museum of Colonial Art
Greater Parish Church (National Monument)
Yayabo Bridge
Yara Sports Hall
Jesús de Nazareno
Yayabo
Aparicio
C. de Oriente
Bayamo
Máximo Gómez
Independencia
Céspedes
Martí
Longino Ramírez
Julio Antonio Mella
Carlos Roloff
Bartolomé Masó
Mayía Rodríguez
Coronel Legón (José)
Mirto
Rafael Río Entero
Silvestre Alonso
Frank País
Brigadier Reeves
Roosevelt
Palmero
G. González
Luis López
Comandante Fajardo
Tirso Marín
Isabel María de Valdivia
Juan Gómez
B. del Pico
Cándido Calderón
Hernández Laborí
Maceo
Adolfo del Castillo
San Ciriaco
Boulevar
Avenida de los Mártires
Telo Sánchez
M. Solano
Dolores
Plácido
Ave. Jesús Menéndez
E. E. Broche
César Salas
Raimundo de Pisa
E. R. Chibás
Agramonte
26 de Julio
A. Rodríguez
Manolito Díaz
Juan Bruno Zayas
Federico Suárez
Pan
H. López
Antolín García
Panchito Álvarez
Carmen
1ra. del Este
Pancho Jiménez
Diego Dorado
G. Zequeira
San Félix
Saure Conde
Ciro Redondo

Sancti Spíritus

Sites of interest

❶ Yayabo Bridge

This bridge on the Yayabo River is one of Sancti Spiritus' greatest architectural icons. Considered the only one of its kind in Cuba, it is approximately 85 m long and over 9 m high. Its finest feature is its five huge arches of a marked Romanesque style. It was built with local materials –bricks, slaked lime and sand– and its construction ended in the first half of the 19th century.

❷ Serafín Sánchez Plaza

Independencia and Máximo Gómez Streets.

The city's main plaza is surrounded by important buildings, including the Principal Theater, the Provincial Museum, the Central Library, and the vintage Perla de Cuba Hotel, one of the most exclusive in the island at the beginning of the 20th century. With large glass works and Sevillian tiled floors, at present it houses the Center for the Patrimony. The plaza, declared a National Monument, honors Serafin Sanchéz, a local patriot of the War of Independence. The house where he was born is located at Céspedes Street and exhibits valuable objects belonging to the Sánchez Valdivia family as well as of other patriots.

❸ Greater Parish Church

58 Agramonte Oeste Street.

Tel.: (5341) 324 855.

The wainscoting of the main nave, and the vaulted ceilings of the Chapel of the Christ of Humanity and Patience, turn the church into one of the most outstanding buildings in Sancti Spiritus' Historical Center. The second oldest church existing in Cuba, it was finished in 1680. Its tower, built in 1819, for a time was the highest in the island. Initially it was 20 m high, but lightning damaged the dome, and in mid 19th century it was rebuilt in its present form.

Sancti Spíritus

Sites of interest

❹ Museum of Colonial Art

74 Plácido Street, on Jesús Menéndez.
Tel.: (5341) 325 455.

Its collection of furniture, china, and fans, among many other objects, make this museum the place to visit for discovering the lifestyle of the colonial period. It is located in a house belonging to the second half of the 18th century, the first two-story building, with hundreds of doors and windows. The house underwent several transformations by its former owners, the Valle Iznaga family and has the architectural characteristics of the 19th century.

⑬ San José del Lago Spa

Mayajigua, Sancti Spíritus.

Hydrocarbonaceous, calcic, magnesian, lukewarm and bacteriologically pure waters that are colorless and tasteless, suitable for medicinal baths distinguish this spa located on Mayajigua, on the northern part of the province.

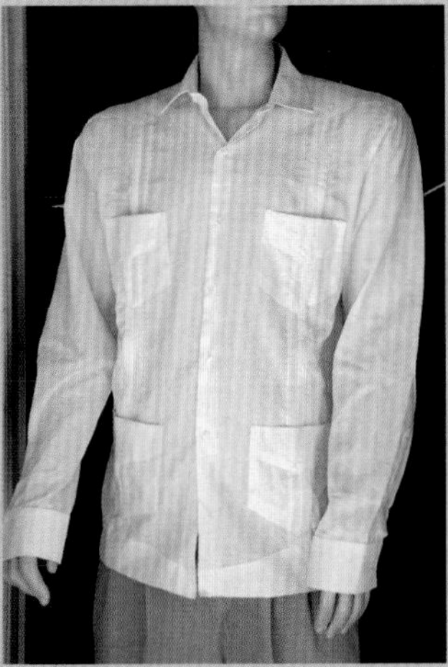

The guayabera

The guayabera is a kind of shirt long linked to Cuban history. The garment allegedly originated in Sancti Spiritus, where since 2007 exists a socio-cultural project dedicated to its revival. The project already has dozens of guayaberas that once belonged to worldwide figures, such as Gabriel García Márquez and Miguel Ángel de Asturias. Recently the Cuban Government declared that the guayabera should be the regular attire for officials participating in diplomatic events.

⑭ Zaza Dam

Approximately 8 Km to the East of Sancti Spiritus on the highway to the province of Ciego de Ávila, the Zaza Dam, the largest in the country, is teeming with trout and perch. It is an ideal place for fishing lovers.

⑮ Topes de Collantes Natural Park

With sites of impressive beauty, such as the waterfall of the Caburní River and Vega Grande, it is located in the Guamuhaya Mountain Range standing out for its endemic wildlife and flora, among the latter giant tree ferns. There is a spa at this peaceful environment of the Escambray.

Sancti Spíritus

Sites of interest

16 Trinidad

The so-called Museum City of Cuba, founded by Diego Velázquez in 1514, flourished between the 17th and 19th centuries thanks to sugar cane and slave trade. There are still buildings that show the splendor of the time, declared a World Heritage Site by Unesco in 1988, along with famous Valle de los Ingenios (Sugar Mill Valley).

Trinidad offers a varied range of architectural details, ranging from artistic balconies to iron grates, stairs and multicolored façades. This colonial jewel has a Main Square surrounded by magnificent 18th century buildings such as the Brunet and Sánchez Iznaga Palaces, and the Church of the Holy Trinity. Here Spanish and African traditions are blended and flourish in a culture passed on from one generation to the other. Besides its urban center, Trinidad has other attractions such as the natural and archaeological Reserve Valle de los Ingenios, the Escambray Mountain Range and its beaches.

A wedding at Trinidad.

An aerial view.

⑯ A map of the city of **Trinidad**

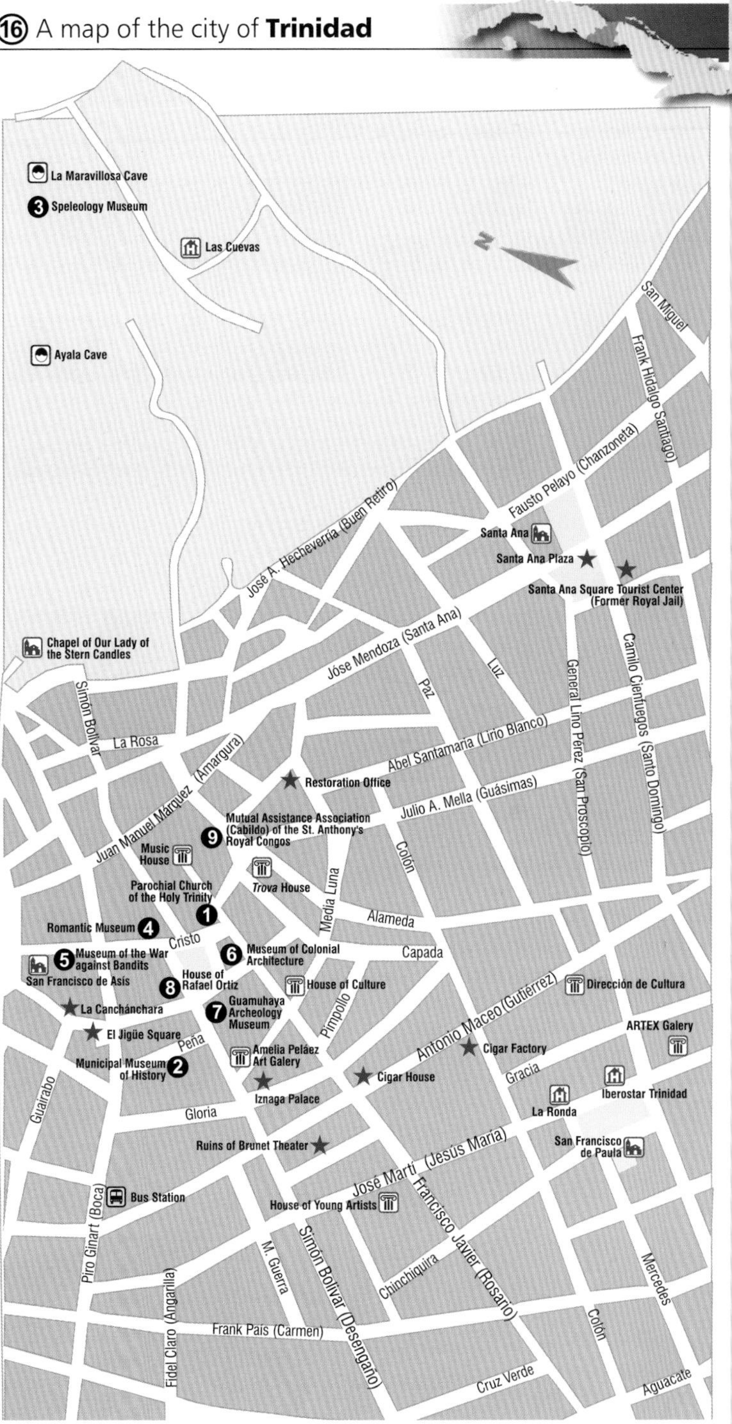

La Maravillosa Cave
3 Speleology Museum
Las Cuevas
Ayala Cave
San Miguel
Frank Hidalgo Santiago
Fausto Pelayo (Chanzoneta)
José A. Hecheverría (Buen Retiro)
Santa Ana
Santa Ana Plaza
Santa Ana Square Tourist Center (Former Royal Jail)
Chapel of Our Lady of the Stern Candles
Jóse Mendoza (Santa Ana)
Luz
Paz
General Lino Pérez (San Proscopio)
Camilo Cienfuegos (Santo Domingo)
Simón Bolívar
La Rosa
Abel Santamaria (Lirio Blanco)
Restoration Office
Juan Manuel Marquez (Amargura)
Julio A. Mella (Guásimas)
9 Mutual Assistance Association (Cabildo) of the St. Anthony's Royal Congos
Music House
Colón
Trova House
Parochial Church of the Holy Trinity
1
Media Luna
Alameda
Romantic Museum 4
Cristo
5 Museum of the War against Bandits
6 Museum of Colonial Architecture
Capada
San Francisco de Asís
House of Rafael Ortiz 8
House of Culture
Dirección de Cultura
La Canchánchara
Guamuhaya Archeology Museum 7
Pimpollo
Antonio Maceo (Gutiérrez)
ARTEX Galery
El Jigüe Square
Peña
Cigar Factory
Amelia Peláez Art Galery
Municipal Museum of History 2
Gracia
Cigar House
Guairabo
Iznaga Palace
Iberostar Trinidad
La Ronda
Gloria
Ruins of Brunet Theater
San Francisco de Paula
José Martí (Jesús María)
Bus Station
House of Young Artists
Francisco Javier (Rosario)
Piro Ginart (Boca)
M. Guerra
Simón Bolívar (Desengaño)
Chinchiquira
Mercedes
Fidel Claro (Angarilla)
Frank País (Carmen)
Colón
Cruz Verde
Aguacate

Trinidad

Main Square.

Jigüe Square.

Squares

Trinidad has many squares, large and small, among which you can find the Santa Ana, close to Main Square, Jigüe Square, and Triple Cross, on the Northwest end of the Historic Center, at the neighborhood known as El Calvario. The latter, with three wooden crosses installed around 1826 in its center, became the final point of Catholic processions on the Holy Week and the Corpus, which gave the city a great importance since the very beginning of the conquest and colonization.

Triple Cross Square.

Santa Ana Square.

Carrillo Square.

1 Parochial Church of the Holy Trinity

Main Square, Trinidad.

This 1892-built church with a neoclassic façade is composed of four naves. A neo-gothic altar to the Virgin of Mercy displays on its rear a painting by Cuban artist Antonio Herr. The church also has an 18th century wooden image of the Lord of the True Cross, made in Spain. Legend goes that the sculpture departed from the Port of Barcelona in 1731 for Vera Cruz as destination. Yet, on three consecutive occasions, the ship that transported it was diverted by winds to Casilda, 6 Km from Trinidad. On its fourth attempt for Mexico, the Captain decided to leave behind part of the cargo, among which was a chest containing the Christ. Locals believed this was a signal from Heaven and since then they worship the image.

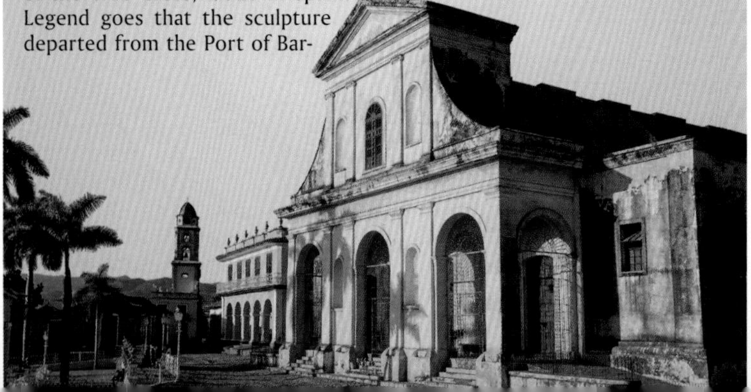

Trinidad

❷ Municipal Museum of History

423 Bolívar St., between Gustavo Izquierdo and Rubén Martínez Villena, Main Square. Tel.: (5341)994460.

The museum is located in a building commissioned by Mariano Borrell Padrón, one of the city's sugar barons. In 1841 it was bought by María de Monserrate, who a year later married Cantero, a landowner. Since then it became the Cantero Palace, and subsequently the family remodeled it as a sumptuous neoclassic mansion. Based on collections of objects, maps and monuments related to the Cantero family, the Museum describes the history of Trinidad. The facility is also dedicated to piracy, the plantations at Sugar Mills Valley, slavery and the Independence Wars. From its tower, you can enjoy a beautiful sight of the city.

❸ Speleology Museum

Las Cuevas Hotel, Santa Ana.

Located in a 3,700-Km^2 cave, 1 Km northeast from the center and very close to Las Cuevas Hotel, a legend says that a young aborigine girl, by the name of Caucubú, hid there when her lover Naridó was murdered. In homage to their love, a fountain was built for bringing happiness to lovers who drink its water. In full-moon nights, Caucubú appears at the entrance of Wonderful Cave, looking for Naridó.

❹ Romantic Museum

52 Hernández Echerri St., on Simón Bolívar, Main Square. Tel.: (5341) 994 363.

The building that houses the museum was built in 1812 for the wealthy Borrell family. In its rooms, it recreates the environment of a classical colonial Trinidad residence between the years 1830–1860, exhibiting furniture and decorative objects from the 18th and 19th centuries.

❺ Museum of the War against Bandits

Hernández Echerri St., on Guinart. Tel.: (5341) 994 121.

The Museum occupies the building where the Church and Convent of St, Francis of Assisi once stood, from the 18th century up to 1892. Since then the building was used for different purposes and in time it deteriorated to the point of demolition. Of the original building, only the tower and its clock are still standing. The facility became a museum on June 1, 1934. Its exhibits are related to the last stage of the Cuban independence process (1952-1959), and to the War against Bandits.

Trinidad

6 Museum of Colonial Architecture

83 Ripalda Street, between Hernández Echerri and Martínez Villena, Main Square. Tel.: (5341) 993 208.

Located in the former mansion of the Sanchez Iznaga family, it is dedicated to Trinidad's different architectural styles and the building techniques used throughout the colonial period.

7 Guamuhaya Archeology Museum

457 Simón Bolívar St., between Fernando Hernández Echerri and Martínez Villena, Main Square. Tel.: (5341) 993 420.

Located in the former Padrón Manor, it exhibits artifacts from aboriginal communities settled here prior to the arrival of the Spaniards, as well as objects of value from the city and the surrounding valleys pertaining to the colonial period. Its walls, doors and ironworks are the best evidence of local artisanship and the flourishing of the city in the 18th and 19th centuries.

8 House of Rafael Ortiz

Rubén Martínez Villena St. on Bolívar, Main Square. Tel.: (5341) 994 432.

The house, built between 1800 and 1809 by city Mayor Rafael Ortiz de Zúñiga, is at present the Benito Ortiz Borrell Universal Art Gallery, where pieces by Antonio Herr, Juan Oliva, Benito Ortiz, Antonio Zerquera and David Gutiérrez are on exhibit.

9 Mutual Assistance Association (Cabildo) of the St. Anthony's Royal Congos

168 Isidro Armenteros St., Trinidad.

This is a sample of syncretism between Spanish and African cultures. Patron saint of the institution, St. Anthony of Padua is identified with the Yoruba deity Oggun. His celebration day in the Catholic liturgy is on June 13. The story tells that a group of former slaves brought to Cuba from the Congo bought the house in 1845, and then in 1856 founded the Cabildo to keep their spiritual patrimony alive. The original drums for the "toque" (ritual celebration) to St. Anthony-Oggun are still here on display.

Trinidad

Horseback-riding residents in Trinidad.

The place to taste a "Canchánchara", a popular traditional drink made with sugar cane spirits, honey and limejuice.

Iberostar Trinidad Hotel.

A Trinidad stone-paved street.

Trinidad

⑰ Valle de los Ingenios (Sugar Mill Valley)

Declared by Unesco a World Heritage Site, it takes its name from the many sugar mills ("ingenios" in Spanish) in the valley in the late 18th and early 19th centuries. Twelve kilometers northeast of Trinidad, this great open-air museum exhibits 70 archaeological sites, including the ruins of sugar mills, parts of industrial machinery, and utilitarian objects. From the "Loma del Puerto" (Port Hill) lookout at 122 m above sea level, there is a spectacular view of the entire valley. Nevertheless, the Manaca-Iznaga community is one of the most interesting spots in the valley from the historical and architectural point of view, for the majority of its mills and facilities are still standing. The famous tower of Manaca-Iznaga, built by Alejo Iznaga, called the slaves to the brutal toiling in the sugarcane plantations and served as a lookout for overseeing the huge sugarcane fields. The legend goes that the two Iznaga brothers, Pedro and Alejo, were in love with the same woman and decided to settle the issue by building a monument each whose magnitude would define the winner. Alejo built the 45 m high tower, while Pedro opened a 28 m-deep well.

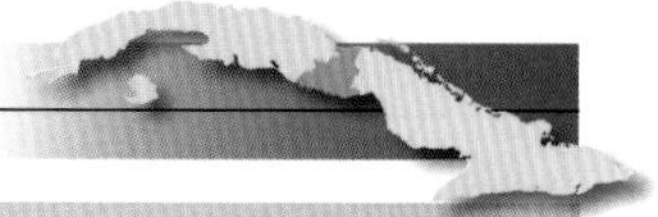

Trinidad

⑱ Ancón Peninsula

Located about 10 Km south of Trinidad, the Ancon Peninsula has a beautiful namesake beach on its South coast. From a pier near the Ancon Hotel, boats take divers to the magnificent coral barrier reef. On the rocky shores near María Aguilar beach, there are lagoons where you can snorkel and watch myriads of tropical fish. On the other side of the bay, in front of the peninsula, there is the old port of Casilda, a stopping point for those heading to the beaches. It was once one of the most thriving ports on the island when sugar trade flourished in Trinidad.

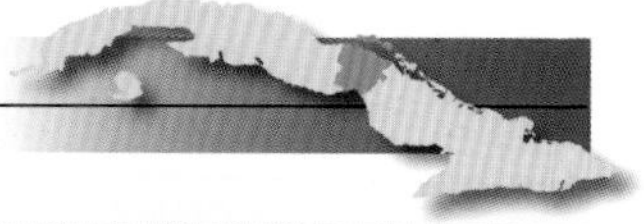

(19) province of
Ciego de Ávila

Cayo Guillermo.

Jardines del Rey Archipelago (Gardens of the King) is the tourist treasure of the province, offering paradise-like environments not only for the quality of its beaches, but also for the different number of wildlife species in the area and the high degree of conservation of the marine and land ecosystems. Joined to the mainland by a causeway, Cayo Coco and Cayo Guillermo keys stand out among the many beautiful islets that form the archipelago. There are several 4- and 5-star all-inclusive beachfront hotels.

Ciego de Ávila has two well-known lakes: La Redonda, ideal for trout fishing, and Laguna de la Leche (Milk Lake) thus named for the color of its water. North of Milk Lake you will find Turiguanó Island, a cattle-raising community built in the early sixties on the side of Turkey Hill (Loma del Pavo) in the style of traditional Dutch homes. There are also about 40 bird-hunting reserves surrounding the great swamps and lakes to the North of Morón, as well as near Cunagua Hill. The best known are Aguachales de Falla, Chicola, Canal La Yana and Puente Largo. Trout fishing is also great at Puente Largo, as well as at Liberación Dam on the town of Florencia, an area of great natural beauty in East Ciego de Ávila.

Beside these natural attractions, the visitor can stop at the province's capital, founded in 1840, and enjoy the classic constructions of this period with its large verandas, neoclassic columns and Creole roof tiles. Traditional celebrations similar to the Remedios "parrandas", in the province of Villa Clara, also characterizes life in Ciego de Ávila, the venue for shows led by those living in neighborhoods of descendants of Jamaican and Haitian immigrants.

The Entrance to the Cayo Coco causeway.

Laguna de la leche (Milk Lake).

Capital: Ciego de Ávila.

Area: 6,946 Km^2.

Municipalities: Ciego de Ávila, Morón, Chambas, Florencia, Ciro Redondo, Baraguá, Majagua, Bolivia, Primero de Enero and Venezuela.

Population: Close to 420,000.

Boundaries: To the North with the Old Bahamas Channel; to the west with the province of Camagüey; to the South with the Gulf of Ana María; and to the West with the province of Sancti Spiritus.

Economy: Industrial-agrarian. Sugar cane industry predominates, but there is also food production, chemistry, steel and mechanical industry, light industry and construction materials. Tourism is an important source of income for the province.

Main Products: There are significant deposits of limestone, gypsum, rock salt and oil.

Relief: Mainly flat with very fertile lands and a large great reserve of underground water.

Access: Land communication is mainly through the Central Highway that crosses the province from West to East, and the North Circuit Highway, as well as other secondary roads. It has also two air terminals, the Máximo Gómez International Airport and another one at Jardines del Rey for domestic flights. A causeway links Jardines del Rey Archipelago to the national highway system.

Additional Information: It has two protected natural areas: the wildlife refuge at Loma de Cunagua and the one at Cayo Ana María. There are also other important natural areas, such as the great swamps north of Ciego de Ávila, recognized as a Ramsar Site. Part of West Ciego de Ávila towards Florencia Municipality is inside the Buenavista Reserve of the Biosphere.

One of Ciego de Ávila's main streets.

(20) A map of the city of **Ciego de Ávila**

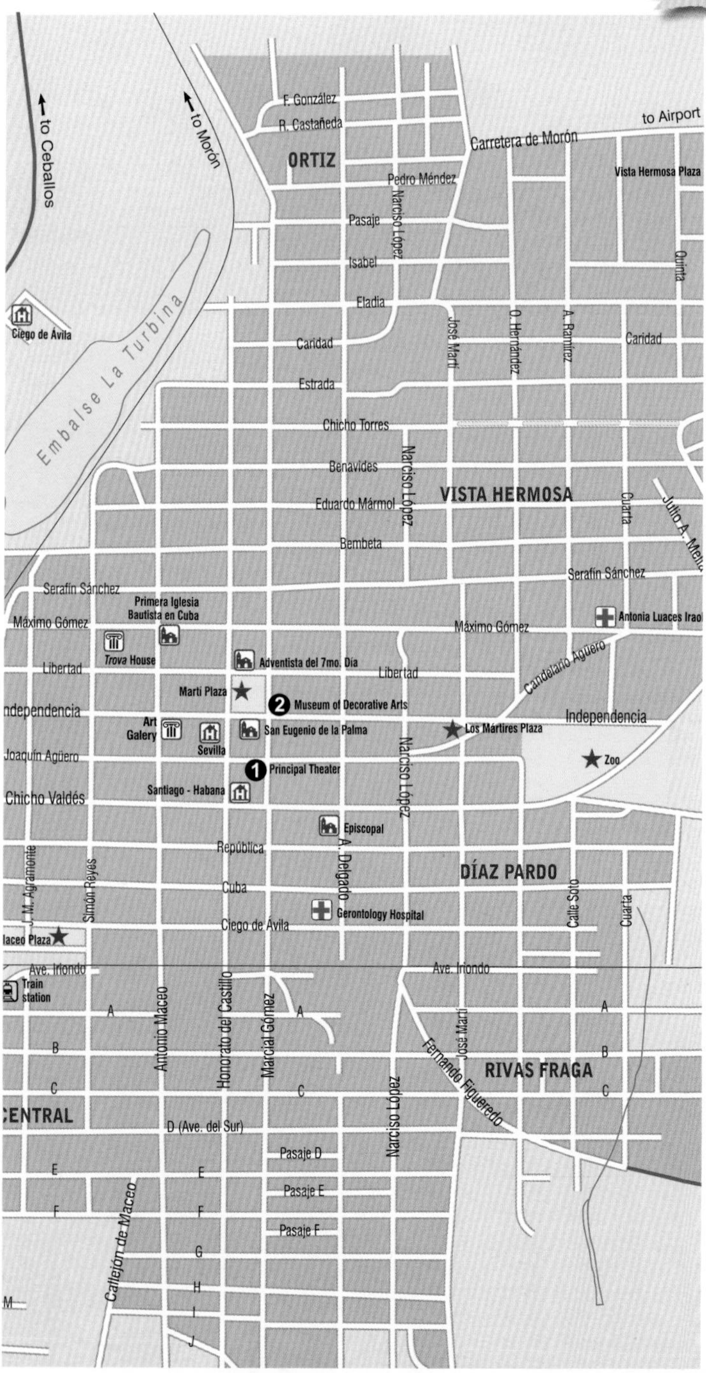

to Ceballos
to Morón
to Airport
F. González
R. Castañeda
ORTIZ
Carretera de Morón
Vista Hermosa Plaza
Pedro Méndez
Narciso López
Pasaje
Isabel
Eladia
Quinta
Ciego de Ávila
Embalse La Turbina
Caridad
Estrada
José Martí
O. Hernández
A. Ramírez
Chicho Torres
Benavides
Eduardo Mármol
VISTA HERMOSA
Cuarta
Julio A. Mella
Bembeta
Serafín Sánchez
Primera Iglesia Bautista en Cuba
Máximo Gómez
Antonia Luaces Iraola
Trova House
Adventista del 7mo. Día
Libertad
Candelario Agüero
Marti Plaza
Museum of Decorative Arts
Independencia
Art Galery
Sevilla
San Eugenio de la Palma
Los Mártires Plaza
Zoo
Joaquín Agüero
Principal Theater
Chicho Valdés
Santiago - Habana
Episcopal
República
A. Delgado
DÍAZ PARDO
J. M. Agramonte
Simón Reyes
Cuba
Gerontology Hospital
Calle Soto
Maceo Plaza
Ciego de Ávila
Ave. Iriondo
Train station
A
Antonio Maceo
Honorato del Castillo
Marcial Gómez
B
Fernando Figueredo
RIVAS FRAGA
C
CENTRAL
D (Ave. del Sur)
Pasaje D
E
Pasaje E
F
Pasaje F
Callejón de Maceo
G
H
I
J
M

Ciego de Ávila

Sites of Interest

❶ Principal Theater

13 Joaquín Agüero St., between Marcial Gómez and Honorato del Castillo, Ciego de Ávila.

Inaugurated on March 2, 1927, it is one of the best examples of the eclectic architecture typical of Ciego de Avila, and having one of the best acoustics in the country. The marble used in this building was imported and crafted by Giovanni di Marco. Several Cuban and foreign artists, such as Jorge Negrete, Ernesto Lecuona and Libertad Lamarque, among others, have performed at the Principal.

❷ Museum of Decorative Arts

2 Marcial Gómez St., on Independencia, Ciego de Ávila.

Built during the period of constructive frenzy in Ciego de Ávila, up to the first half of the 20th century, this monumental building on Zero Corner constitutes a great example of the eclectic architecture of the area. It also exhibits collections of decorative art divided in different sections, such as ceramics, glass, paintings, furniture, metal, stones, music records, and watches and clocks. Rooms are decorated in the styles of the 19th and 20th centuries, offering a historic view of the city's homes as well as a panorama of decorative art.

㉑ The Júcaro to Morón Trail

Surrounding Morón there are ruins of fortifications, part of the 17-league defensive trail built by the Spaniards to prevent the passing through of the Cuban Liberation Army during the East to West invasion. Experts consider the Trail one of the most important engineering works in Spanish America.

Ciego de Ávila

㉒ The Morón Rooster

There are several versions about the origin of the name of Morón, second city in importance in the province of Ciego de Ávila, which link it to a low elevation and from where in Spain came the original settlers, some of them from the Sevillian town of Morón de la Frontera. Morón, located in Central Cuba, is also known for the sculpture of a rooster that greets visitors at the city's entrance, and whose history is related to an incident at the Sevilian town in the colonial period. The story goes that there were public disorders because of the political situation. One of the town's officials, called The Rooster for its arrogance and ostentation, was severely beaten. The event gave origin to the popular folk song that says: "You have been left/like the Morón rooster/featherless and clucking at its best". The neighbors placed on the La Peña Promenade a plucked rooster that in the 1950s inspired the neighbors of Morón in Cuba to raise a similar one, a popular project obstructed by politicians. Years later, the rooster was placed on a pedestal and taken down several times, until unknown hands destroyed it. Neighbors longed for the return of the symbol of their town, and on May 2, 1982, a new rooster was put in place. The statue by Rita Longa and Armando Alonso (the latter the artist who made the previous one) is cast in bronze and accompanied by a watch tower and amplifiers to broadcast its singing all over the entire town.

㉓ Laguna de la Leche (Milk Lake)

Cuba's largest natural body of fresh water –approximately 130 million cubic meters in an area of 67 Km^2– is close to Morón. Its name derives from the calcium sulfate and gypsum sedimentation in its bottom.

Central Cuba

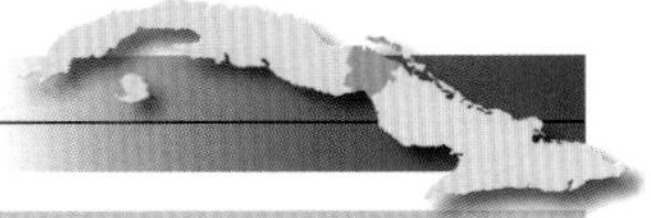

㉔ Jardines del Rey (Gardens of the Kings)

An archipelago of approximately 400 uninhabited keys, also part of the larger Sabana-Camagüey Archipelago, and named as Garden of the Kings by Spanish conquistador Diego Velázquez in 1514 in honor of King Ferdinand of Spain. Locals say that these keys and islets served as haven for corsairs and pirates, and some claim that US writer and winner of the Nobel Prize of Literature in 1954, Ernest Hemingway, loved to sail among these islets. Virgin beaches, one of the world's grandest coral reefs (400 Km long), little explored territories and one of the largest pink flamingo colonies in the region, are some of the attractions in this northern area of the province. There are comfortable hotel facilities at Cayo Coco and Cayo Guillermo.

㉕ Cayo Coco

With an area of 370 Km^2, marshes and 22 Km of white sandy beaches, the key is a natural reserve, almost 90 percent of its territory covered by vegetation that serves as refuge for many wildlife species, none of them dangerous. Outstanding among these is a large colony of pink flamingos. La Güira, which recreates a settlement of wood coal makers of the many in existence at Cayo Coco in the early 20th century, and the Boar's Cave, are two of the places worth visiting. Cayo Coco's beaches are protected by an extensive coral barrier reef and have several lagoons. There are two trekking trails: the Loma del Puerto Dune, and Las Dolinas. The key has an international airport that can service large-sized aircraft.

㉖ Cayo Guillermo

Immortalized by Ernest Hemingway in his posthumous novel *Island in the Stream*, it has an area of 13.2 Km^2 and three 4 Km-long beaches, among which Pilar Beach stands out for its magnificent landscape and calm water. At this small key linked to Cayo Coco by a causeway, you will find the highest dunes in the Caribbean islands, up to 15 m high.

㉗ Cayo Paredón Grande

Another one of the islets in Jardines del Rey, its sea bottom is magnificent. The Diego Velázquez lighthouse stands out built on a rocky headland by Chinese coolies in 1859. The causeway that runs through Cayo Coco and Cayo Romano also links Paredón Grande to the mainland.

(28) province of
Camagüey

Entirely different tourist destinations, but equally attractive, are offered by the province of Camaguey. This vast territory of plains combines the history of its capital city with the beauty of its beaches, such as Santa Lucía, the majesty of the Cubitas Mountain Range and the Jardines del Rey Archipelago to the North, as well as the Jardines de la Reina (Gardens of the Queen) Archipelago to the South.

The once-called Santa María del Puerto Príncipe, founded on February 2, 1514 on a spot at the north coast known as Punta Guincho, and finally moved to its actual site in 1528, boasts one of the country's best preserved historical centers, awarded by Unesco the title of World Heritage Site in 2008. A labyrinthine design of its streets, many large and small squares and numerous ancient churches, form the oldest part of the city.

This is a land of great historic and cultural traditions and of prominent figures. Cuban patriot Ignacio Agramonte, who rose in arms against the Spanish colonial government in 1868, leading the people of Camagüey, lives in the memory of all. Agramonte, whose great military deeds in the battlefield gave him the nickname of El Mayor, is worshipped throughout the country.

This was also the home of Silvestre de Balboa, the author of the first Cuban literary work, an epic poem written in 1608 called *Mirror of Patience*. Two centuries later, on March 23, 1814, the city became the birthplace of Gertrudis Gómez de Avellaneda, the most important woman writer of her time in the Spanish language. This is also the hometown of Nicolás Guillén, considered Cuba's National Poet, as well as of other famous artists, such as painter Fidelio Ponce de León. At present, a vivid cultural life reflects on several events, also in the Camagüey Ballet –a well-known dance company both in Cuba and abroad–, and in the Camagüey Folkloric Dance Ensemble. The San Juan of Camagüey is a traditional festivity born between 1725 and 1728 that has become the most popular in the region. The festivities begin on January 24 and last a whole week, characterized by dances, floats, "comparsas" (parades) and congas.

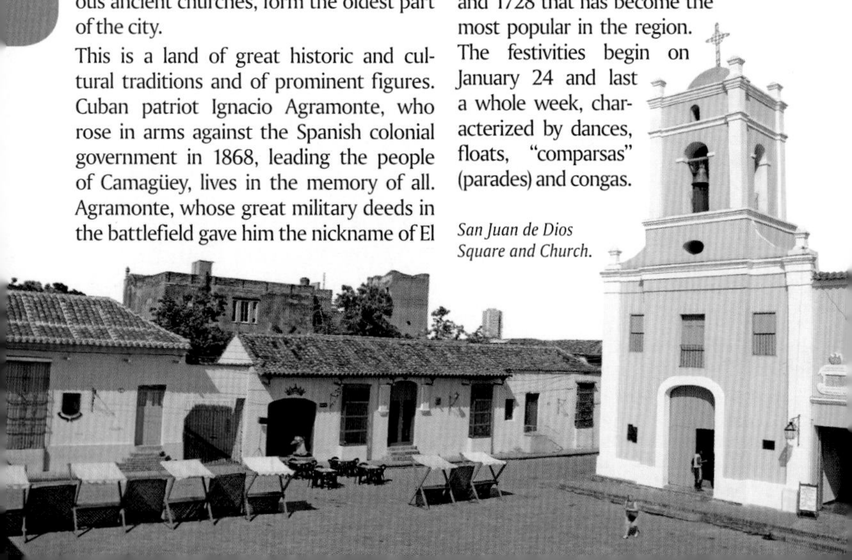

San Juan de Dios Square and Church.

Church and Cemetery of the Christ.

Church of La Merced.

Capital: Camagüey.

Area: 15,615 Km^2.

Municipalities: Camagüey, Esmeralda, Nuevitas, Guáimaro, Santa Cruz del Sur, Florida, Sierra de Cubitas, Minas, Sibanicú, Najasa, Vertientes, Jimaguayú and Carlos Manuel de Céspedes.

Population: 783,000 plus.

Boundaries: To the North, with the Old Bahamas Channel; to the East, with the province of Las Tunas; to the South, with the Caribbean Sea; and to the West, with the province of Ciego de Ávila.

Economy: Industrial-agrarian, predominantly sugar cane industry and cattle raising, as well as food production and mining.

Main Products: Electric power, construction materials, metallurgy.

Relief: This is the most level Cuban province, with not many heights, except for the Cubitas, Najasa and Maraguán mountain ranges. The highest elevation is Cerro Tuabaquey, with 339 m.

Access: By air, through the Ignacio Agramonte International Airport and by land through the national highway system. There is also an airfield at Santa Lucia for medium- and small-sized aircraft.

The tower and altar at the Church of the Sacred Heart.

㉙ A map of the city of **Camagüey**

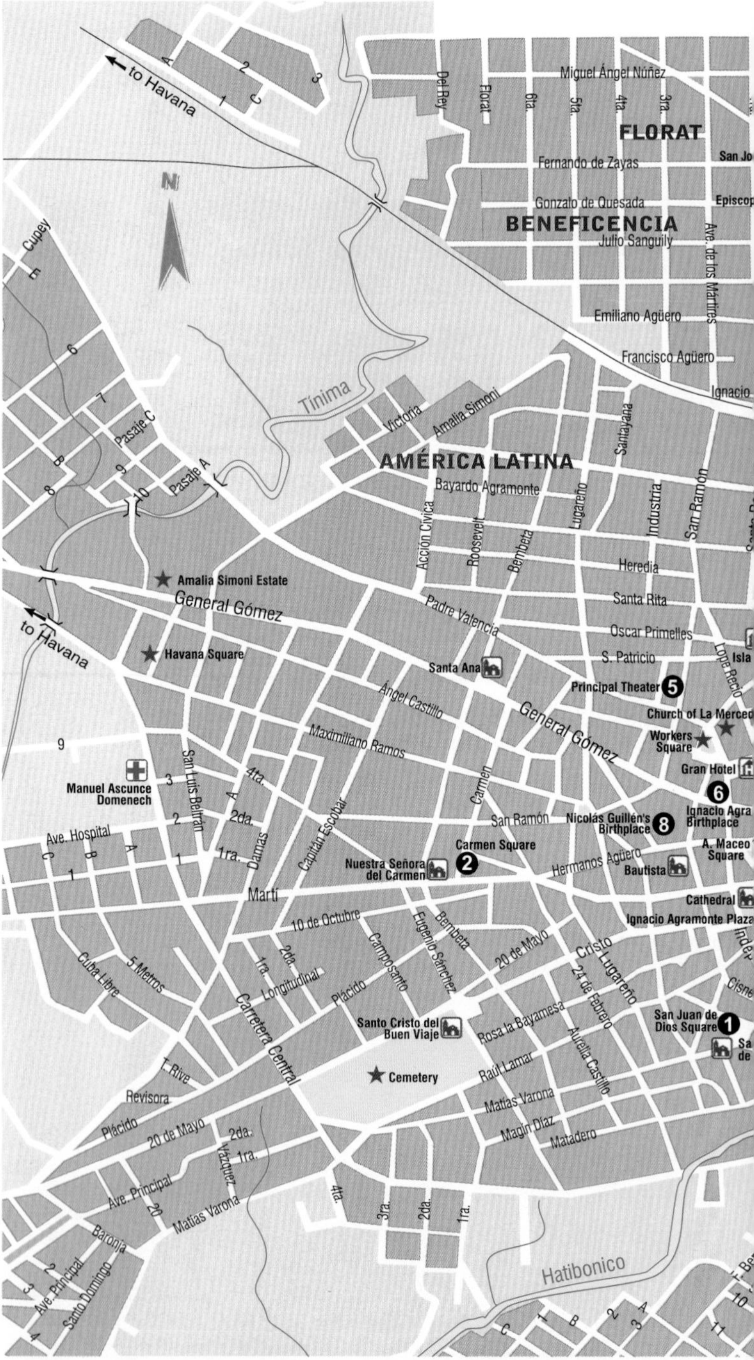

Central Cuba

LA VIGÍA
LAS MERCEDES
LA NORMA
SARATOGA
LA ZAMBRANA
GARRIDO
LA CARIDAD
Manuel R. Artola
Fernando de Zayas
Julio Sanguily
Tomás Betancourt
Andrés Sánchez
Puerto Príncipe
Ignacio Agramonte
Ave. Carlos J. Finlay
to Airport Ignacio I. Agramonte
Nuevitas-Santa Lucía
Joaquín de Agüero
Miguel Benavides
Luis A. Varona
Jaime Noguera
Teniente Cañón
General Pancho Varona
Carlos Mola
Chino Manuel
Barberán
Ramón Ro
Joaquín Collar
5ta. la Mía
Luis C. Romero
Enrique Villuendas
Quiñones
Esteban Varona
José Ramón Silva
Fidel Céspedes
Calixto García
Teniente Miranda
Oscar Primelles
Coronel Labrada
Pablo Lombida
Vergues
Coronel Pichardo
Central
Roloff
La Norma
Plaza
Colón
San José
América
Avellaneda
San Fernando
Padre Olallo
Jaime
Soledad Square
Ignacio Agramonte
Río
Ángel Ciro Betancourt
Vate Morales
Ave. 26 de Julio
Tarafa
Montreal
José Arango
Ignacio Agramonte
Ave. Van Horne
Gonzalo Moreno
Cornelio Porro
Braulio Pena
Ismael Bello
Manuel Suárez
Pasaje B
Avenida 2da.
Pasaje A
1ra.
Domingo Parra
to Las Tunas
to Minas
Youth Square
Sagrado Corazón de Jesús
Ignacio Agramonte Revolution Square
Cándido González Stadium
Plaza of the Legends
Barberán y Collar Monument
Zoo
Country Club Plaza
Palace of Marriage
Ave. de la Libertad
San Joaquín
Fondo Cubano de Bienes Culturales
Freyre
Victoria
Carretera Central al Hotel Camagüey a Las Tunas
Camagüey Ballet
Ojo de Agua
F. Rodríguez
Nolasco Rodríguez
Cuba
General de la Vega
Pancha Agramonte
Domingo Puente
Coronel Bringas
Sociedad Patriótica
María del Rosario
Nuestra Señora de la Caridad
Dolores Betancourt
Pediatric Hospital

Camagüey

Sites of Interest

❶ San Juan de Dios Square

San Juan de Dios and San Rafael St., Camagüey.

The square was built in 1728, when the Church and the Hospital already existed. In its surroundings is the city's first important architectural grouping. The Church of San Juan de Dios has the only representation of the Holy Spirit in human form existing in Cuba. Here is also the former San Juan de Dios Convent-Hospital, which at present houses part of the Office of the City's Historian, the agency charged with restoration work in the city.

❷ Carmen Square

Hermanos Agüero, Honda and Carmen, St., Camagüey.

This is another well-preserved architectural environment in Camagüey. Facing the square is the Church of Our Lady of El Carmen, built in the early 19th century and the only one with two towers in the city.

❸ Ignacio Agramonte Plaza

República e Ignacio Agramonte St., Camagüey.

The foundational site of the city, it has had different names throughout the years: Main Square or of the Greater Church, then Constitution Plaza, Recreational Plaza, and Plaza of the Queen. Finally, in 1899 it received its present name: Ignacio Agramonte Plaza, after the Cuban patriot. Surrounding the plaza are, among others, the Metropolitan Cathedral, the City Hall, the Provincial Library, the Patricio Ballagas House of Trova, the Nicolás Guillén Research Center, and the birthplace of physician and microbiologist Carlos J. Finlay, who discovered that the mosquito was the transmitting agent of yellow fever.

Camagüey

City of "tinajones"

Camagüey is also known as land of "tinajones" (very large earthenware jars), which are seen everywhere around the city, particularly in homes. Based on the typical Andalusian jars once used for storing grain, wine, oil and other liquids, the tinajón became the alternative that immigrant potters from Spain found for storing water. Though the tinajones were widely made on this region since the 17th century, they were not exclusive to the area, for they were also found in the provinces of Trinidad and Sancti Spiritus, the West Indies (Jamaica) and even in South America (Chile and Peru), the latter a heritage of the Inca civilization. Though tinajones made of the red clay found in the Cubitas Mountain Range existed since 1600, none has been found bearing that date. The earliest are from 1760. All houses in Camaguey had at least one tinajón. The water contained inside its cool round walls was used for drinking and cooking, and usually it was offered to visitors, many of whom married and settled in Camaguey. The tradition is to tell the grooms at weddings: "That guy drank water from a tinajón". In 1900, there were some 16,000 tinajones, but today there are only about 2,500.

❹ Soledad Square

República and Agramonte St., Camagüey.

Named after the Church that stands there, neighbors popularly call it Plaza del Gallo (Rooster Square), after a namesake store no longer in existence. The current building is from 1776 and an exponent of Cuban colonial Baroque.

❺ Principal Theater

64 Padre Valencia St., between Tatán Mendéz and Lugareño, Camagüey.

Built in 1850, at present it is the seat of the Camagüey Ballet. It also hosts important cultural events.

❻ Ignacio Agramonte's Birthplace

459 Ignacio Agramonte Ave. between Independencia and Cisneros.

Located in a building that is an example of stately mansions in the 18th century, the memorial museum offers a view of domestic life in those times and comprehensive information on Ignacio Agramonte, born in a room on the second floor on December 23, 1841. Inaugurated as museum in 1973, it has seven rooms exhibiting photocopies, actual documents, photographs, furniture and personal effects that belonged to the Agramonte family and to the patriot himself.

[redacted]

Oriente Sugar Mill, built in 1844 in the present municipality of Sidunch. The

preserved monumentary complex of Cuban sugar industry.

Camagüey

Sites of Interest

❼ Country Club Plaza

Next to La Caridad neighborhood and between the Hatibonico River and the Juan del Toro Stream.

The green heart of Camagüey, the Gonzalo de Quesada Plaza, popularly known as Casino Campestre (Country Club), is the largest within a city in Cuba. It has luxuriant trees and beautiful statues. An example of the latter is the monument dedicated to the 1933 Seville-Camagüey flight (Seville-Havana in official Spanish records) by pilots Mariano Barberán and Joaquin Collar. The modern hotel Cuatro Vientos in Santa Lucía Beach bears the name of the airplane used in the flight.

❽ Nicolás Guillén's Birthplace

253 Hermanos Agüero St., Camagüey

Tel:(5332) 293706.

This house was originally a family home from the second decade of the 19th century. Nicolás Guillén Batista, who in time became Cuba's National Poet, was born in an adjoining room on July 10, 1902. It currently hosts the Nicolás Guillén Research Center and a small museum dedicated to the poet.

(30) "Furrows" on the Máximo River

One of the natural beauties of Camagüey is the Furrows on the Máximo River, which form a pool of snow-white calcareous rock and extends some 500 meters down the river. This place, one of the most particular on the planet, was formed some 28 million years ago. For its beauty and singularity, it has been declared a National Monument.

(31) Santa Lucía Beach

This beach of white sand and turquoise warm waters is ideal for diving due to its proximity to the second largest coral barrier reef in the world. The reef runs from East to West for 400 Km along the Sabinal, Guajabal, Romano and Cruz keys, up to Varadero. The main tourist area has a 20 Km-long beach with several diving sites, which offer divers not only the possibility of observing the remains of sunken ships in the 19th and 20th centuries, but also a unique show in which expert guides feed friendly sharks.

(32) Cayo Sabinal

Part of a protected area together with Cayo Romano and Cayo Guajabal keys, Sabinal has an area of 335 Km^2 and approximately 30 virgin beaches. Access is through a causeway, or by catamaran from Santa Lucía Beach. You can visit the Colón Lighthouse (1894) and the ruins of the San Hilario Fort (1831), used as base of operations by corsairs and pirates. Wild horses and cattle, sheep, deer, hutias (an edible Caribbean rodent), iguanas and turtles live in the keys.

Hotel on Santa Lucía Beach

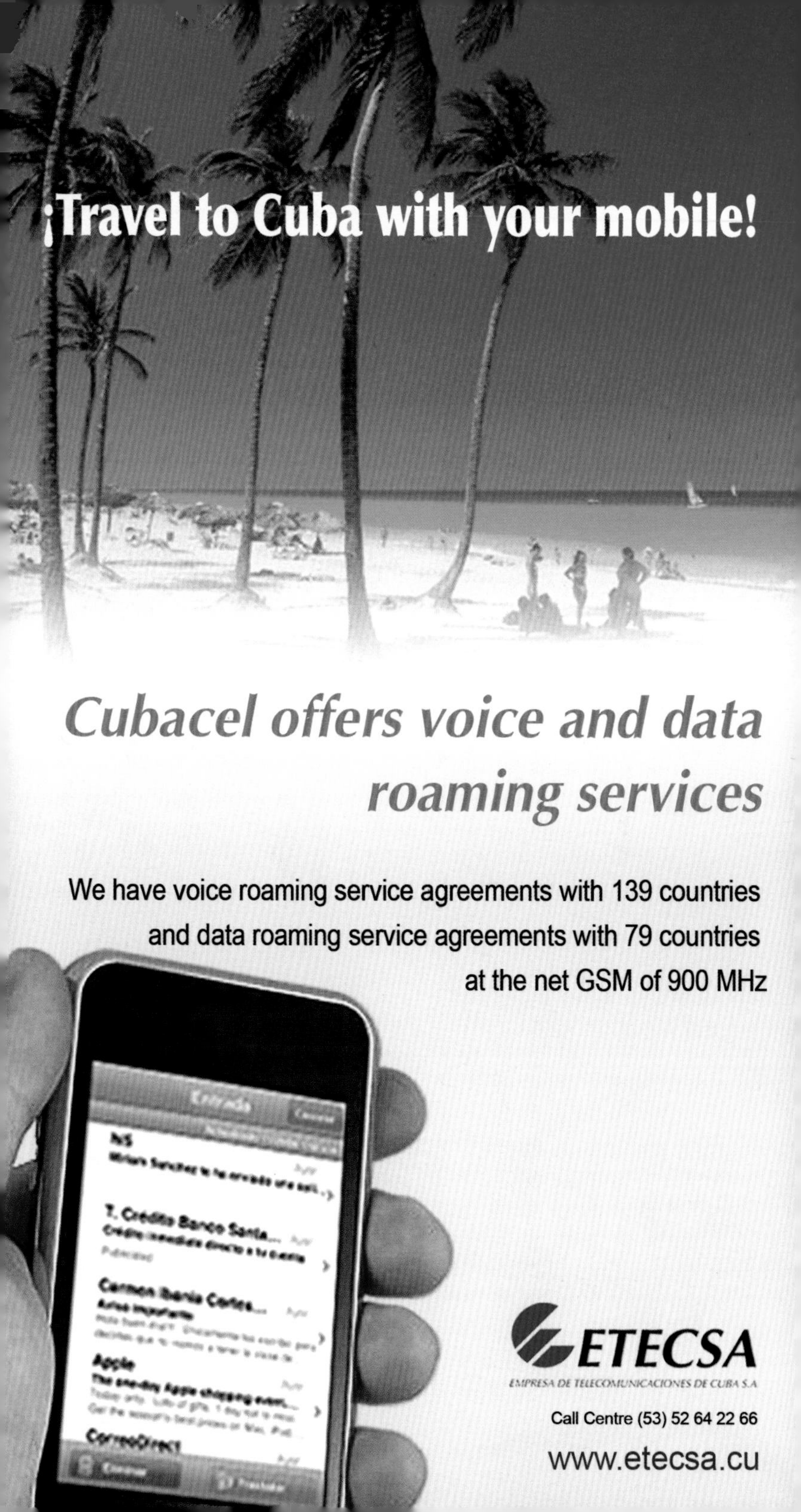
¡Travel to Cuba with your mobile!
Cubacel offers voice and data roaming services
We have voice roaming service agreements with 139 countries and data roaming service agreements with 79 countries at the net GSM of 900 MHz
ETECSA
EMPRESA DE TELECOMUNICACIONES DE CUBA S.A
Call Centre (53) 52 64 22 66
www.etecsa.cu

A Journey Through
East
Cuba

east
Cuba

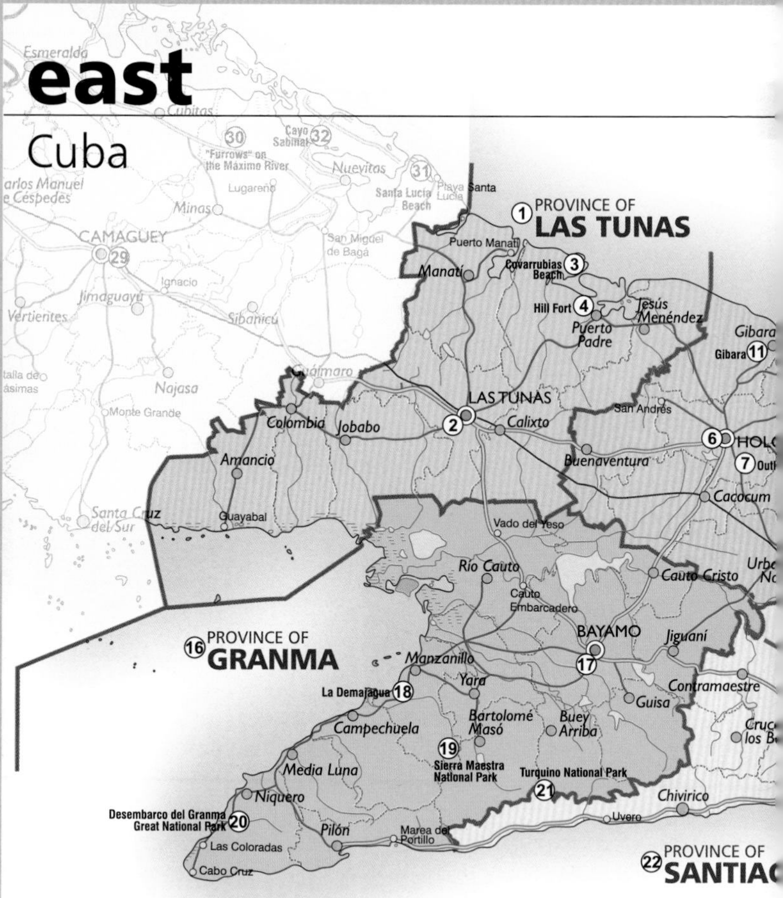

High mountains, long rivers, bays of spectacular beauty and outstanding geographical features, make East Cuba a region of privileged natural beauty. Formed by the provinces of Las Tunas, Holguín, Granma, Santiago de Cuba and Guantánamo, the region is highlighted by the majesty of the Sierra Maestra Mountain Range, and the abundant natural wealth safeguarded in protected areas comprising several national parks.

Although with certain differences in culture and traditions, there are common characteristics to Cuba's eastern provinces. Among them is Santiago de Cuba, whose namesake capital is the country's second largest city. The trip by road to Santiago from the Cruz Cape area is fascinating, for the highway borders the steep foothills of the Sierra Maestra, which at several places seem to plunge into the Caribbean Sea.

Holguín has excellent beaches and an important archaeological site, while Guantanamo, the easternmost province, gives you the opportunity to visit the Stone Zoo Museum or tour Baracoa, the first town founded in Cuba. Guantánamo is famous for being the place where the US Naval Base is located, which can be seen from Los Malones outlook, on the highway to Baracoa.

It was on this region of the country where Cuba's War of Independence began on October 10, 1868, when Carlos Manuel de Céspedes, known as the Father of the Nation, freed his slaves and rose in arms against Spanish colo-

nial domination. Here is also the city of Bayamo, cradle of Cuban nationality, where our national anthem was sung for the first time. It was also in this region where in 1895 the second stage of the independence war was reinitiated under the lead of outstanding patriots such as José Martí, Antonio Maceo and Máximo Gómez. Years later, in 1953, Fidel Castro and his revolutionary comrades attacked the Moncada Barracks in Santiago de Cuba, and in 1956, after being imprisoned and gone into exile, landed at the head of 82 men at Las Coloradas Beach, in the province of Granma. Subsequently, the Sierra Maestra was the place where the Rebel Army reorganized to fight the Batista dictatorship and eventually reach victory in 1959.

index

The following section offers general information and references about historical and tourist sites, as well as curios and characters of the region.

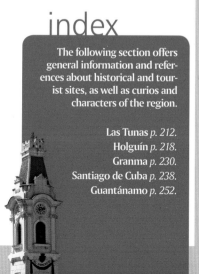

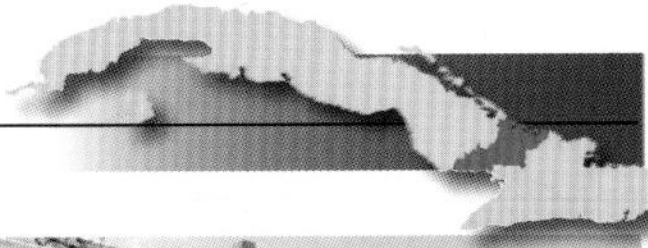

① province of
Las Tunas

Three aboriginal regions formed this part of the country at the arrival of Spanish Conquistadors: Maniabón and Boyucá to the North and Cueybá in Central South. In 1603, in the region of the old chieftainship, existed the "Hato de las Tunas", so called due to the good conditions for raising cattle (hato is Spanish for herd), fertile lands rich in pastures and where there was an abundance of "tunas" (Spanish for prickly pear). The region had several names, until in 1976, with the new political and administrative division of the country, adopted the current name of Las Tunas.

Centuries went by before the region took off and little by little became the bordering city between the Central and Eastern regions. The coexistence of several styles characterizes its oldest part, where there are still some examples of colonial architecture, as well as details of art deco and rationalism. Although Las Tunas has not yet fully developed its tourist potential, it has great attractions, particularly on its north coast, where you will find Covarrubias Beach, at Puerto Padre. The province is famous for the National Cucalambeana Festival, a feast of traditional popular culture in honor Juan Cristóbal Nápoles Fajardo (aka El Cucalambé), a 19th century Cuban poet who wrote on pastoral themes.

Capital: Las Tunas.

Area: 6,588 Km².

Municipalities: Las Tunas, Puerto Padre, Jesús Menéndez, Manatí, Majibacoa, Amancio, Colombia and Jobabo.

Population: 500,000 plus.

Boundaries: To the North, with the province of Camaguey and the Atlantic Ocean; to the East with the province of Holguín and the Guacanayabo Gulf; and to the West with the province of Camaguey.

Economy: Industrial-agrarian, mainly sugar cane industry.

Main Products: Sugar cane, stainless steel products, building materials, among others.

Relief: Mainly flat, with fertile well-irrigated soils. Its main elevations are the Cañada Honda Mountains, 219 m high.

Access: Known as the balcony of East Cuba, it is crisscrossed by the Central Highway and the Central Railway. In the capital city, there is a domestic flight terminal.

② A map of the city of **Las Tunas**

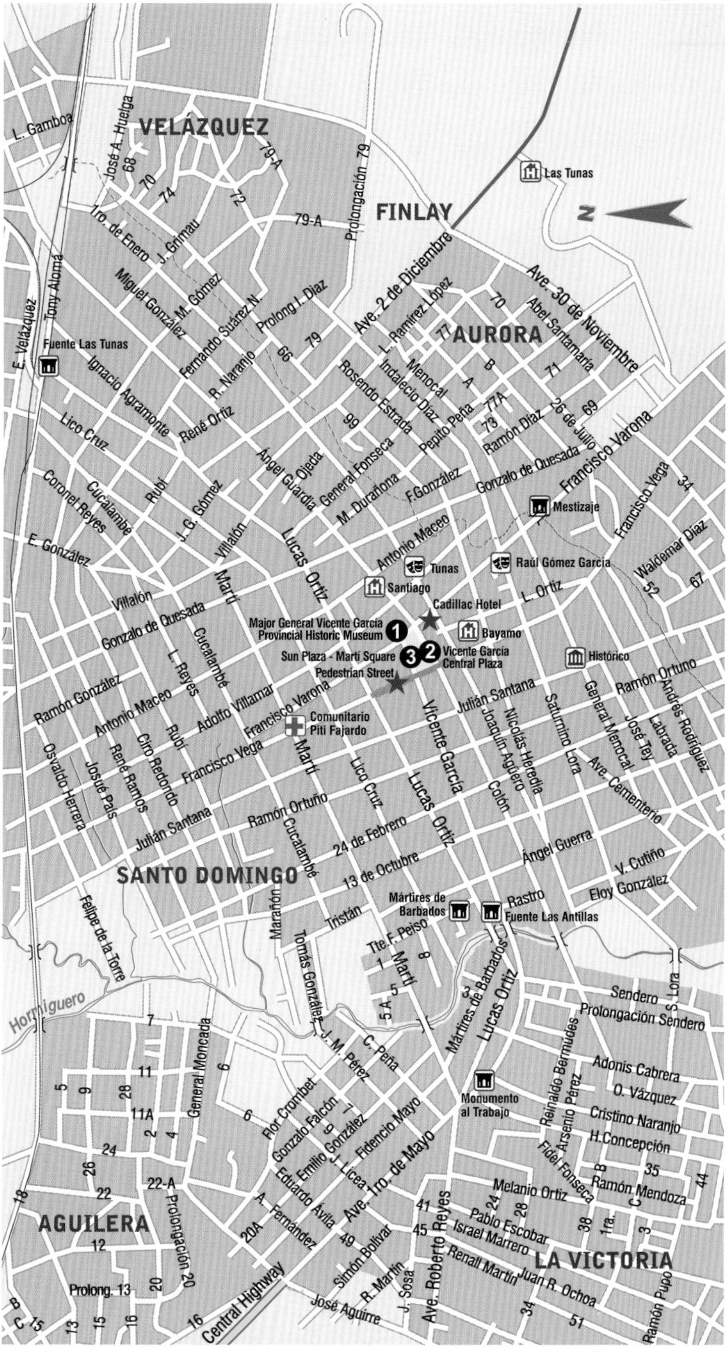

Las Tunas

Sites of Interest

❶ Major General Vicente García Provincial Historic Museum

Francisco Varona St., between Angel Guarda and Adolfo Villamar St., Primero, Las Tunas. Tel:(5331) 348201.

The museum is housed in a building of eclectic architectural style located in the city's historic center. It treasures evidence of the city's history and patrimony.

❷ Vicente García Central Plaza

Vicente García St. on Francisco Varona St.

Originally Main Square, it has several commemorative monuments of high patrimonial value, such as the sculpture of Vicente García and busts of Mario García Menocal and Federico Capdevila.

Las Tunas

❸ Sun Plaza - Martí Square

Ángel Guarda St., between Francisco Varona and Francisco Vega, Las Tunas. Tel.: (5331)47913.

Inaugurated on March 25, 1995, it was designed by architect Domingo Alás Rosel as a tribute to Cuba's National Hero José Martí. It includes a sundial, a calendar, a solar reflector and Marti´s bronze effigy by Rita Longa. There is also a ceramics mural by artist Pedro Escoba, representing the participation of Las Tunas citizens in the Cuban War of Independence in 1895.

A pedestrian Street in Las Tunas.

The Cadillac Hotel made the short list of the 2011 National Conservation Prize.

Las Tunas

Sites of Interest

③ Covarrubias Beach

Puerto Padre Municipality, Las Tunas.

Towards west of Puerto Padre we find Malagueta Bay, an ideal scenery with great conditions for bird watching. On the bay's northern area, facing the open sea, there is Covarrubias Beach; across it and not too far away, there is a 30 feet-deep spot known as Los Patabanes. There is also a beachfront hotel.

The sculpture capital

Since the creation of the province of Las Tunas Province, there was a budding movement of amateur and professional sculptors. For that reason, the idea cropped up of carrying out a national event of that artistic expression. In 1977, on its third edition, it had reached national fame and had the presence of the great Cuban sculptress Rita Longa. Since then, participants committed themselves to donate works to the province for locating them in public spaces and keep the movement alive. Las Tunas became, step by step, the sculpture capital in Cuba with hundreds of original works disseminated throughout its territory.

④ Hill Fort *Puerto Padre Municipality, Las Tunas.*

Rising 34 m above sea level, it welcomes visitors to Puerto Padre, known as the Blue Town of the Windmills. Built in mid-1869 by the Corps of Engineers of the Spanish Army, the fort became the most important expression of the triple defensive system with which the Spaniards planned to defend the town. Typologically Hill Fort, declared a National Monument in 1981, is the only one of its kind in the country, and in its construction rough masonry was used, based on local elements like limestone and sand. Although Spain believed it impregnable, a Cuban unit that was part of Major General Vicente García's forces attacked and occupied the fortress in the early hours of February 14, 1877.

Street in Puerto Padre, Las Tunas

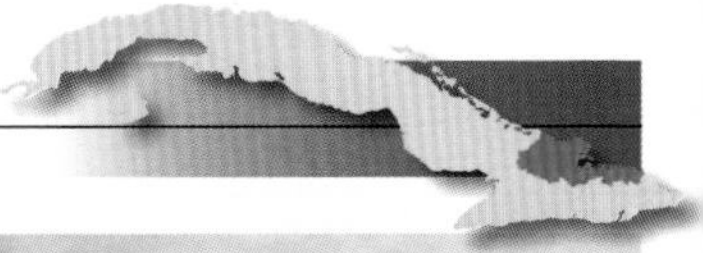

(5) province of
Holguín

Guardalavaca beach.

Hundreds of kilometers of its north coast with excellent beaches and keys, as well as the majesty of valleys and mountain, make this province one of the main tourist destinations areas in the country. The provincial capital, set between Mayabe Hill and Loma de la Cruz (Hill of the Cross) and known as "city of plazas", boasts a perfect design of its streets, adorned by several of said public spaces. Many places and institutions are named after Major General Calixto Garcia, Holguín's main historic figure, who excelled during Cuba's independence wars.

Hill of the Cross.

Among Holguin's attractions you can find the largest Aborigine burial site in the West Indies, as well as the city of Banes, considered Cuba's archeological city. As if that were not enough, there is also Bariay, where Columbus made his first landing in Cuba, and which made him exclaim his famous phrase: "This is the most beautiful land humans eyes have ever seen"

Also of great beauty, the city of Gibara is outstanding for the excellent state of conservation of its Spanish colonial architecture. For lovers of diving, there is the unique option of the Blue Tank of Caletones, a flooded cave, which has the peculiarity of being located below the main rout of migratory birds in the region. Another place worth visiting is Cayo Naranjo, at its namesake bay, a true aquarium in the middle of the sea, and Cayo Saetía, at the mouth of Nipe Bay, and considered the largest game preserve in the country.

Bariay, where Columbus first landed in Cuba.

A view with the Columbus Mosque in the background, an elevation that the Admiral described in his logbook.

Capital: Holguín.

Area: 9,293 Km^2.

Municipality: Holguín, Antillas, Banes, Sagua de Tánamo, Mayarí, Gibara, Moa, Rafael Freyre, Urbano Noris, Báguanos, Cueto, Frank País, Cacocum and Calixto García.

Population: Over 1 million inhabitants.

Boundaries: To the North it borders with the Atlantic Ocean; to the east with the province of Guantanamo; to the South, with the provinces of Santiago de Cuba and Granma, and to the West with the province of Las Tunas.

Economy: Industrial-agrarian.

Main Products: Minerals (iron, nickel, cobalt and chrome), steel and mechanical industry, sulfuric acid, building materials, wood products, textile industry, food industry and others.

Relief: Mountainous terrain rich in minerals. There are many beaches along the province's North coast. The open air cobalt and nickel deposits are the biggest in the world. This territory outstands for the aborigine community archaeological findings. It also has the largest bay in Cuba, the Nipe Bay, and its tallest point is Cristal Peak, at 1,231 m above sea level.

Access: By air, through Frank País International Airport; by land through the Central Highway; and by sea, by Puerto Vita International Marina.

Julio Grave de Peralta Plaza, also called San Isidoro or Plaza of the Flowers.

⑥ A map of the city of **Holguín**

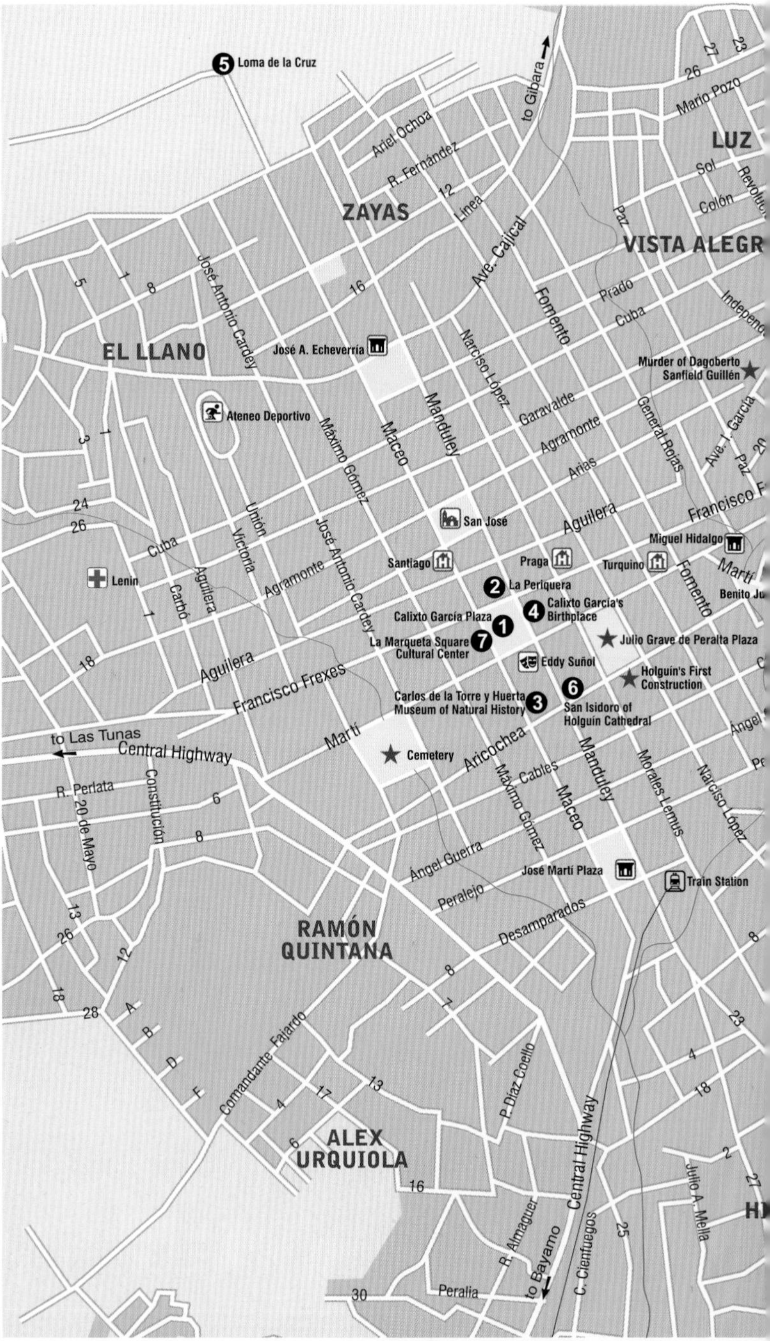

Loma de la Cruz
to Gibara
ZAYAS
LUZ
VISTA ALEGR
EL LLANO
José A. Echeverría
Ateneo Deportivo
San José
Santiago
Praga
Turquino
Miguel Hidalgo
Lenin
La Periquera
Calixto García Plaza
Calixto García's Birthplace
La Marqueta Square Cultural Center
Julio Grave de Peralta Plaza
Eddy Suñol
Holguín's First Construction
Carlos de la Torre y Huerta Museum of Natural History
San Isidoro of Holguín Cathedral
Murder of Dagoberto Sanfield Guillén
Cemetery
José Martí Plaza
Train Station
to Las Tunas
Central Highway
RAMÓN QUINTANA
ALEX URQUIOLA
to Bayamo
Central Highway

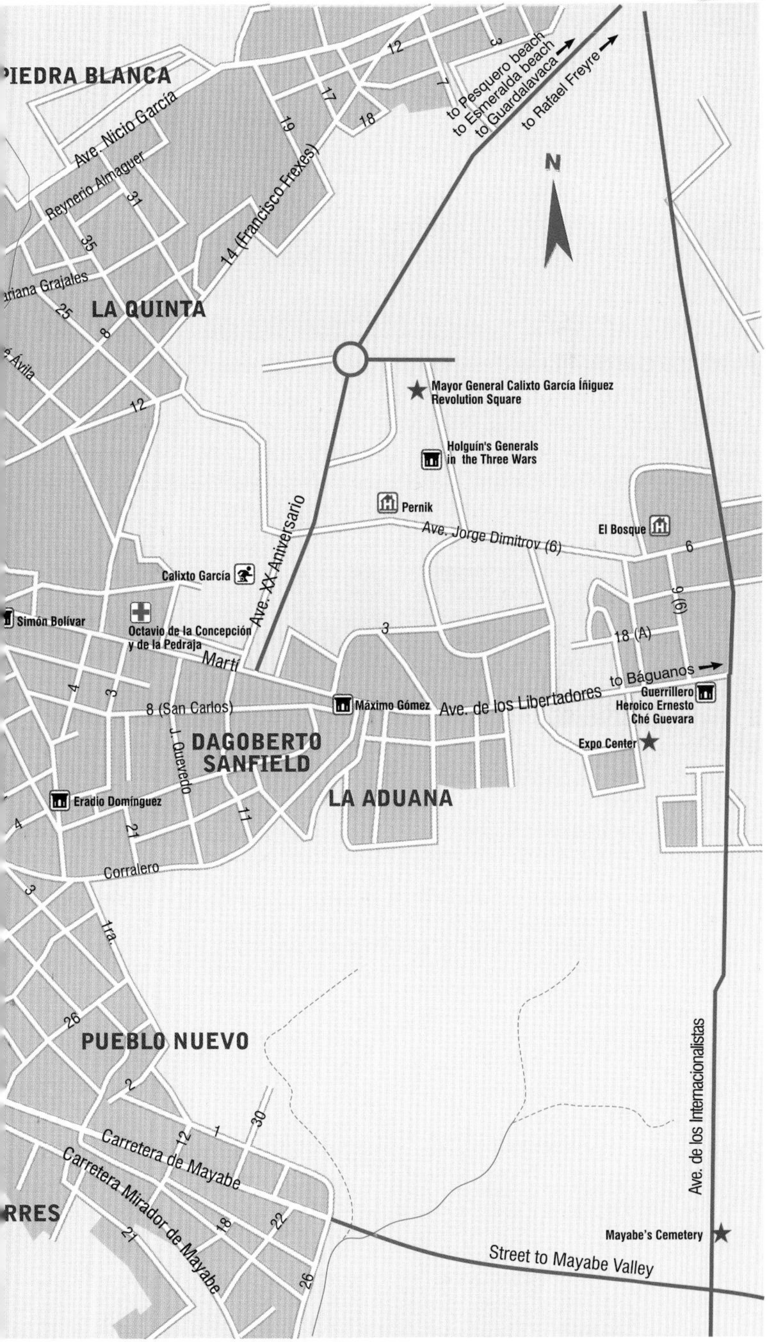
PIEDRA BLANCA
Ave. Nicio García
Reynerio Almaguer
14 (Francisco Frexes)
to Pesquero beach
to Esmeralda beach
to Guardalavaca
to Rafael Freyre
N
LA QUINTA
Mayor General Calixto García Íñiguez Revolution Square
Holguín's Generals in the Three Wars
Pernik
Ave. Jorge Dimitrov (6)
El Bosque
Ave. XX Aniversario
Calixto García
Simón Bolívar
Octavio de la Concepción y de la Pedraja
Martí
8 (San Carlos)
Máximo Gómez
Ave. de los Libertadores
to Báguanos
Guerrillero Heroico Ernesto Ché Guevara
Expo Center
18 (A)
J. Quevedo
DAGOBERTO SANFIELD
LA ADUANA
Eradio Domínguez
Corralero
PUEBLO NUEVO
Carretera de Mayabe
Carretera Mirador de Mayabe
Ave. de los Internacionalistas
Mayabe's Cemetery
Street to Mayabe Valley

Holguín

Sites of Interest

❶ Calixto García Plaza *Frexes, Libertad and Maceo Streets.*

Built in 1719-1720, this plaza is the former Main Square. In 1898, it was given its current name. In 1916 a statue of Calixto García was placed the center of the plaza, where it still stands. Today it is a particularly cultural space surrounded by La Periquera Museum, the Ballado Gallery, the Marti Movie Theater, the Rodrigo Prats Operetta House, and the Suñol Theater, among others.

❷ La Periquera

198 Frexes St., between Libertad and Maceo. Tel.: (5324) 463395.

A famous and historic site in Holguín, located in a neoclassic building with great arcades and ample rooms, and which Spaniard Francisco Rondán commissioned in 1860. The residence, built across Main Square, the present Calixto García Plaza, served as shelter for Spanish troops when Cuban independence fighters attacked the city. According to one of the most credible versions, since then the place was called "La Periquera" (Spanish for parakeet cage), in reference to the color of the Spanish Army's uniforms. At present the building houses a museum that exhibits archeological pieces related to Cuban Aborigines, as well as documents and historic testimonials associated to the Independence War. In its rooms symbols that identify the territory and important works of art are on display. It is also a center of intellectual attraction where national and international meetings are held.

Holguín

Sites of Interest

❸ Carlos de la Torre y Huerta Museum of Natural History

129 Maceo St., between Martí and Luz Caballero. Tel.: (5324)423935.

Founded on May 31, 1969, it offers a view of Cuban nature, particularly from Northeast Cuba. Most of its pieces are donations made by Professor José García Castañeda, and by the Guamá Museum, the first one in Holguin. It has among other collections, samples of malacology, ornithology, lepidoptera, insects, rocks, minerals and paleontology, the latter with the most perfect example of fossil found in Cuba.

❹ Calixto García's Birthplace

147 Miró St., Holguín.

This museum is a memorial of Major General Calixto García Íñiguez. Originally the Garcías residence, it preserves photographs, documents and other objects related to the life and military feats of this great patriot. It also has a Reference Center on Cuba's wars of independence.

❺ Loma de la Cruz (Hill of the Cross)

With a height of 261 m above sea level, it is named after a wooden cross that stands at its top. For many it is a protecting symbol, for others a depository of promises and for others still a unique ornament. The first cross was placed on the hill in 1790, by Friar Francisco Antonio de Alegría, Prior of Holguín's Franciscan community. The present cross is the third and like the original one is made from *caguairan* (a Cuban type of fir), for this precious wood grows in abundance in the forests of Bariay. The hiking to the Hill of the Cross, although it has intermediate resting spots with benches along its 458 steps, is particularly hard. At present there is a road that leads to the back side of the hill to admire one of the greatest views of the city. Every year on May, the Hill of the Cross is visited by hundreds of Cuban and foreign artists that join the locals in the May Processions, a traditional regional feast.

A view of the city from atop the Hill of the Cross.

East Cuba

Holguín

Sites of Interest

❻ San Isidoro of Holguín Cathedral

Manduley St., between Luz Caballero and Aricochea.

The former Parochial Church of Holguín, it constitutes a place of worship for believers. In the Cathedral's archives, the books where baptisms, marriages and deaths were registered since 1731 are still treasured.

❼ La Marqueta Square Cultural Center

Mártires, Martí, Máximo Gómez and Luz Caballero Streets.

Located in the midst of Holguin's urban conglomerate, La Marqueta Square Cultural Center is an important site in the city. Originally created in 1848 as a market, at present is a place where locals meet.

Pool area at Mayabe Tourist Center.

Pancho the donkey is specially addicted to beer.

⑦ Outlook of Mayabe

High on a hill in the outskirts of the city, you will find the Mirador de Mayabe (Mayabe Outlook), which offers a great view of the vast namesake valley that borders Holguín.

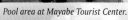

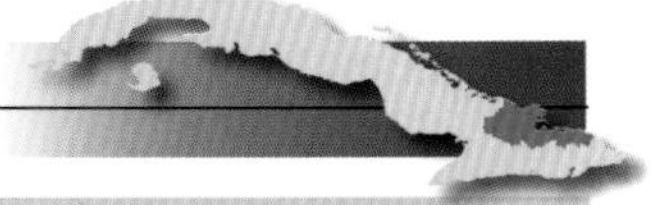

Typical symbols in Holguín

The symbol of the city is the La Periquera's Doorknocker, created in 1990. It is a replica of one of the wrought-iron doorknockers, representing a woman's face of neoclassic design, used on the entrance door to the above-mentioned La Periquera. The symbol was designed by sculptress Caridad Ramos as a symbol of friendship and it is awarded to outstanding national and international figures who through their work have contributed to the well-being of society.

Another symbol is the Holguin Ax, a ceremonial piece of the agrarian and ceramicist Aborigine groups that inhabited Cuba at the time of the Spaniards' arrival in the 15th century. Made of olive green peridotite, the Ax of Holguín bears a distinctive seal that set it apart from others of its type. It represents a masculine anthropomorphic figure with a diadem on the top and arms crossed over the chest. It is awarded to institutions and persons of outstanding performance in different fields.

⑧ Banes

Officially, 96 sites have been registered in the municipality of Banes, declared the archaeological capital of Cuba. In its urban center you can visit the Bani Cuban Aborigine Museum, the only one of its kind in the country, which has on display the most complete collections of objects from Aboriginal cultures in the West Indies. At present, at Chorro de Maíta Site Museum there is a cemetery and a Taíno village that recreate Aboriginal life on the island.

⑨ Chorro de Maíta Archaeological Site

305 General Marrero St., between Céspedes and Martí, Banes.

Hiking up the mountain on a rough road to the town of Yaguajay town, in the municipality of Banes, you can find the first cemetery found in Cuba of agrarian and ceramicist Aborigine groups. There is evidence of all the different burial forms found not only in Cuba, but also in the Caribbean, and even some forms that had never been previously registered. It is believed that Chorro de Maíta might have been a contact point with other cultures.

⑩ Bariay Bay

Bariay Bay is located east of Gibara, with an islet in its center named Bariay Key. On arriving to this point on October 28, 1492 aboard La Niña, la Pinta and La Santa Maria, Christopher Columbus wrote in his journal that this was mainly a flat region with many palm trees, water springs, exuberant vegetation, varied fauna and extremely benevolent. At the area you can see the Maniabón Hills, and Columbus' Mosque, also called by locals Bariay´s Tit for its shape. The encounter of the two cultures is registered there with a monument raised at Sabaneta Point in 1992 to commemorate the 500th anniversary of Columbus' arrival to Cuban territory.

The Seat of the Humberto Solás International Festival of Low-Budget Films.

⑪ Gibara

What at Bariay was seen at a distance with many precautions, in Gibara became the first contact between European and Cuban Aboriginal cultures. It is said that on November 1, 1492, Columbus sent boats ashore in order to establish contact with the local population. Founded on January 16, 1817, the town developed until it was given the category of city. Located in Northwest Holguín and at the namesake municipality, Gibara treasures many historical, cultural and patrimonial values, besides being a rich source of traditions. The city has been the permanent seat of the Humberto Solás International Festival Low-Budget Films.

Boats at Gibara Bay.

⑫ Guardalavaca, Esmeralda and Pesquero Beaches

Crystal clear warm waters and fine white sand are the characteristics of these beaches, as well as thick green coastal vegetation, bordering a unique rolling terrain. Close to Esmeralda Beach is the Bahia de Naranjo Natural Park, and very near to Guardalavaca the above mentioned Chorro de Maíta and Banes.

⑬ Bahía de Naranjo Natural Park

With an area close to 4,047 acres, on the coast there are stretches of mangrove and coastal scrub, as well as trees endemic to the region. The park offers the possibility of walking through Las Guanas and Peñón-Conuco eco-tourist trails, besides yacht cruises, a visit to the aquarium to see dolphins and sea lions perform, as well as a taste of seafood specialties or typical Creole dishes in the countryside. As lodging it has a comfortable cabana built on a small key by the aquarium, and two rustic cabanas mimicking the customs of local farmers, located on solid ground by the sea.

⑭ Saetía Key

Located at the entrance of Nipe Bay, it is the biggest game preserve in the country. In its 42 Km^2, more than half of the islet area is covered by forest that serves as shelter for a varied wildlife, among which you can find white-tailed deer, wild pig, buffalo, ostrich and hutias, among other species.

⑮ La Mensura National Park

Located in the heights of Pinares de Mayari, this is the second national park in the province and one of the three most modern in Cuba. It constitutes an important component of the biodiversity in the Cuban archipelago because of its endemism, those species in danger of extinction, as well as their capacity to adapt to the extreme ecological conditions of the site. Nature at Holguín offers other attractions, such as the Alexander von Humboldt National Park, at the Toa Ridge Reserve of the Biosphere, as well as Sierra de Cristal, the Gibara Chair, Colorado Hill (also known as Columbus Mosque) and Yaguajay Hill.

16 province of
Granma

The main altar at Bayamo's Higher Parochial Church.

The Father of the Nation Carlos Manuel de Céspedes.

Closely related to Cuban history, this province of East Cuba is an attractive tourist destination for those who enjoy both history and nature. A region of marked contrast due to the presence of the Sierra Maestra, the vast plains of the Cauto River and the warm waters of the Caribbean Sea, is known as the Cradle of the Nation, besides housing many of the country's historic sites.

This is the province where the Father of the Nation Carlos Manuel de Céspedes was born; where in 1868 the War of Independence began; where the National Anthem was sung here for the first time, and where Cuba's National Hero José Martí died in combat. Years later, in 1956, revolutionaries led by Fidel Castro came on the Granma yacht and landed in the province to start again the war against Batista's tyranny that ended with the definite triumph of the Cuban Revolution in 1959.

Bayamo and Manzanillo are the largest and most important cities in the province. The former was burned down by local citizens on January 12, 1869 to avoid surrendering it to the Spaniards; while the latter the main port is famous for the gazebo on its plaza, for many one of the most beautiful in the country. Granma is also known for its natural parks, which are abundant in wildlife and flora and in landscapes of great beauty. From Cape Cruz to La Plata, on the road to Santiago, in a land of valleys and mountains, you can find the Sierra Maestra and Desembarco del Granma Parks, the latter declared a World Heritage Site by Unesco. Further on, at Bartolomé Masó Municipality bordering Santiago de Cuba, there is the Turquino National Natural Park. Another attraction is the Marea del Portillo tourist center, a striking combination of valleys, mountains, a river and the sea.

Granma Yacht.

Cauto Valley.

Capital: Bayamo.

Area: 8,375 Km².

Municipalities: Bayamo, Manzanillo, Campechuela, Jiguaní, Niquero, Bartolomé Masó, Buey Arriba, Guisa, Media Luna, Pilón, Río Cauto, Yara and Cauto Cristo.

Population: Over 830,000.

Boundaries: To the North it borders with the provinces of Las Tunas and Holguin; to the East with Holguin and Santiago de Cuba; to the South with the province of Santiago de Cuba and the Caribbean Sea; and to the West with the Guacanayabo Gulf.

Economy: Industrial-agrarian, livestock.

Main products: Sugar cane, rice, cocoa, products from the sea and marble.

Relief: Formed by plains as well as mountain ranges. Part of the Sierra Maestra Mountain Range, the largest and highest in the country, is located in the province. The highest point is La Bayamesa with 1,730 m above sea level. It has many rivers, among them the Cauto, the longest in Cuba with 343 Km.

Access: There are 2 airports, the Sierra Maestra in Manzanillo, and the Carlos Manuel de Céspedes in Bayamo. By land, Central Highway connects Granma with the rest of the provinces. A highway that borders the foothills of the Sierra Maestra reaches Marea del Portillo, the province's main tourist destination.

Marea del Portillo Hotel.

The Gazebo at Manzanillo.

Bayamo's Revolution Square.

⑰ A map of the city of **Bayamo**

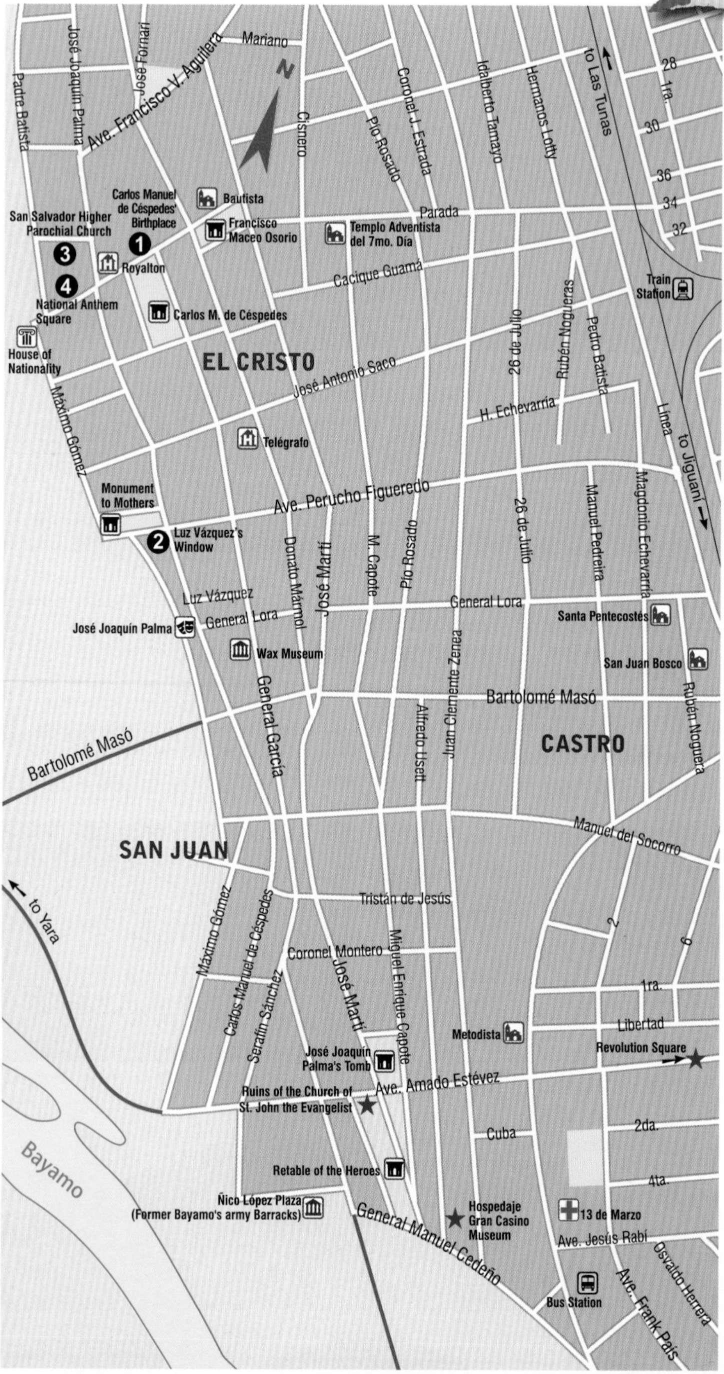

Cespedes Park.

Bayamo

Tower of St. John the Evangelist Church, the entrance to the first cemetery in Cuba.

Founded in 1513, this is the second of the seven towns established in Cuba by Diego Velázquez. Squares, stately mansions and an ancient cathedral shaped the city. Ten days after the beginning of the Ten-Year War in 1868, Bayamo was declared Capital of the Republic in Arms. Two events happened at the time that would mark forever the history of the city and of the country: on October 20, 1868 the people sang here the National Anthem for the first time; and on January 12, 1869 that same people burned down the city to avoid surrendering it to overwhelming Spanish forces. These and other important events of the island's history that took place here turned it into the Cradle of Cuban Nationality and made Bayamo worthy of the title of National Monument City. One of the most deeply rooted traditions is horse-drawn carriages, which you can use for touring the narrow streets and sight-seeing along its main buildings and squares.

❶ Carlos Manuel de Céspedes' Birthplace

57 Antonio Maceo St. between José Joaquín Palma and Donato Mármol, Bayamo. Tel.: (5323)423864.

This house is a museum that reveals different sides of Cuban patriot Carlos Manuel de Céspedes, the Father of the Nation. Objects and original documents are on display while the rooms recreate the way of life of Cuban landowners in the late 19th and early 20th centuries The house stands in the city's Historical Center, across Bayamo's former Main Square.

❷ Luz Vázquez´s Window

160 Carlos Manuel de Céspedes St., between Perucho Figueredo and Lora, Bayamo.

This was the home of Luz Vázquez Moreno, the beautiful woman who inspired the first Cuban romantic ballad, "La Bayamesa" (Woman of Bayamo), sung for the first time on March 27, 1851. Though there are still some details to be researched, there is a certainty that the song was originated when Luz Vázquez had a row with her husband Francisco del Castillo Moreno. In order to make amends, he requested Carlos Manuel de Céspedes and José Fornaris to help him gain her love again. This way, the three friends wrote the lyrics and the music of La Bayamesa, which was sung at Luz's closed window by tenor Carlos Pérez.

La Bayamesa

Do you remember, gentle Bayamesa,
That you were my resplendent sun,
And smiling on your languid forehead
A soft kiss I stamped with ardor?
Do you remember that on a happy time
I was ecstatic with your pure beauty,
And on your bosom I bowed my head,
Moribund of joy and love?
Come and appear smiling at your window.
Come and listen lovingly to my song.
Come, do not sleep, attend to my crying.
Give relief to my somber pain.
Remembering past glories,
Let us dissipate, my love, all sadness,
And let us bow together our heads
Moribund of joy and love.

❸ San Salvador Higher Parochial Church

National Anthem Square, Bayamo.

Due to the burning of the city on January 12, 1869, the city lost many important examples of religious and domestic architecture, among which was its main Church, consecrated to the Holy Savior. Of the sacred patrimony of that temple, only the Chapel of Our Lady of Grief is still standing, which was built in 1740 next to the Higher Parochial Church. Both buildings that form a unique complex of sacred art are located at the National Anthem Square. Promoted to the rank of cathedral when the Bayamo-Manzanillo dioceses was proclaimed, the church witnessed the first patriotic concerns of the Cuban people.

❹ National Anthem Square

Maceo, Padre Bautista, José Joaquín Palma, Máximo Gómez and Céspedes St., Bayamo.

The venue for many festivities in Bayamo, as well as of relevant historic events such as the entrance of the independence fighters to the city on October 29, 1868, when the people asked musician and poet Pedro "Perucho" Figueredo to write the lyrics of the then called Bayamo's Anthem, a patriotic march that later became the Cuban national anthem.

⑱ La Demajagua Plantation

Located 13 Km from Manzanillo, at La Demajagua began the War of Independence when Carlos Manuel de Céspedes freed his slaves. The Cuban flag was also handcrafted here and raised for the first time to summon Cubans to fight for their freedom. The land, along with the sugar mill, the house and the slaves' dwellings were razed by Spanish forces on October 17, 1868. Since then it was completely abandoned and in ruins, and served as pastureland for a long time, until it became La Demajagua National Park on 1968.

⑲ Sierra Maestra National Park

The park extends through three of Cuba's eastern provinces –Granma, Santiago de Cuba and Guantánamo– and was declared a preserved rural area in 1980. This mountainous region is the most important mountain range in the country and has a great variety of climates and soils, a notable diversity of landscapes, the island's deepest caverns, and exuberant flora of a marked endemism, distributed in a territory considered the most valuable geo-botanic complex in the country.

Granma

Sites of Interest

⑳ Desembarco del Granma (Landing of the Granma) Great National Park

Considered by many a true paradise, this National Park was declared a World Heritage Site by Unesco in 1999. Located on the western part of the Sierra Maestra, it has an area of 27,000 hectares characterized by very well-preserved beautiful crags and high vertical scarps. There are many landscapes with waterfalls, pools, exuberant vegetation and a varied wildlife. At the park there are dozens of archaeological sites in areas like El Guafe, formed by ceremonial caves and burial sites.

㉑ Turquino National Park

With a unique natural beauty that has witnessed many historical events, the Park's main mission is to protect one of the best-preserved mountain ecosystems in the country. It is located in the West-Central Sierra Maestra and extends to territories belonging to the municipalities of Guamá (province of Santiago de Cuba) and Bartolomé Masó (Granma).

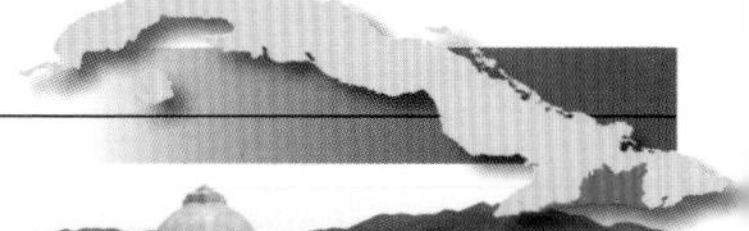

(22) province of

Santiago de Cuba

San Pedro de la Roca Castle.

A distinguishing trait of Santiago de Cuba is its hospitality. "Santiagueros" (Spanish for the inhabitants of Santiago) are open-natured, friendly and communicative. They are the first to open their doors in this Eastern province, the epicenter of many important events, such as the 1868 and 1895 Independence Wars; and later, in 1953, the scene of the attack to Moncada Barracks, led by Fidel Castro, as well as other significant events of the underground struggle of the 26th of July Movement.

Its namesake capital is a land of contrasts where mountains and sea converge. Located on the margins of a large bay with the Sierra Maestra as a backdrop, the "most Caribbean of all Cuban cities" has over 20 museums and is a lively city either by day or by night, adorned by its very warm climate with the hustle and bustle of its people. After the Haitian revolution by Toussaint L'Ouverture in 1791, scores of French immigrants arrived. They not only introduced coffee plantations, but also their culture. With the comings and goings many of the present traditions of this province were created. Its famous carnival was influenced by the festivities of slaves and in time became an all-out popular party, where the conga, parades and floats, as well as the unmistakable sound of the Chinese horn and drum cannot be absent. Add to this the "Tumba francesa", a musical and dance tradition that became a representative element of the culture of Black slaves in East Cuba, particularly in its southern part: Baracoa, Guantánamo and Santiago de Cuba. For that reason the La Caridad Eastern Society of Tumba Francesa was declared in 2003 by Unesco a masterpiece of World Oral and Immaterial Patrimony.

But Santiago is much more than that, for it is the cradle of the son and the bolero, and where traditional trova and choral singing are deeply rooted, and where you can taste the best rum in the country. Its House of the Caribbean is an important institution that promotes the famous Caribbean Festival. As a tourist destination, it also offers the possibility of enjoying its well-preserved nature at Baconao Park, part of the Sierra Maestra Natural Park, at the Gran Piedra Mountain Range, and in other ecological reserves of the area. For divers, the coral reefs are a great attraction with a high degree of conservation and the presence of some 70 species on the insular shelf.

Moncada Barracks.

Fraternidad coffee plantation.

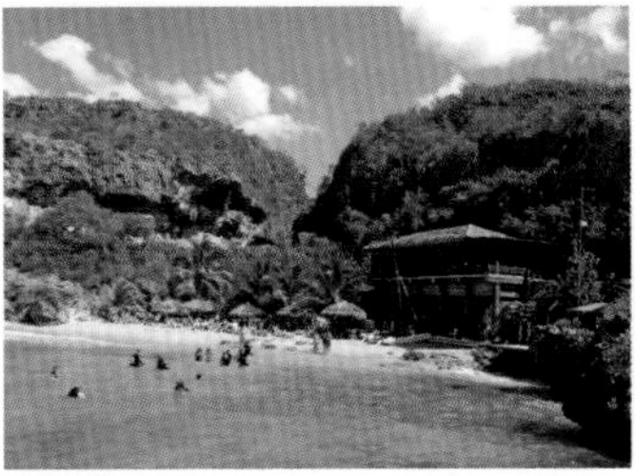

Baconao Park.

Gran Piedra, at 1,225 meters above sea level.

Capital: Santiago de Cuba.

Area: 6,156 Km^2.

Municipalities: Santiago de Cuba, San Luis, Palma Soriano, Guamá, Tercer Frente, Segundo Frente, Contramaestre, Songo-La Maya and Mella.

Population: Over 1 million.

Boundaries: To the North, it borders with the province of Holguin; to the East with the province of Guantanamo; to the South with the Caribbean Sea; and to the West with the province of Granma.

Economy: Industrial-agrarian, mainly coffee and sugar industries.

Main Products: Electric Power supply, sugar, cement and a wide range of steel and mechanical products.

Relief: A mainly mountainous territory, with the greatest extension of the Sierra Maestra Mountain Range, with the Real del Turquino Peak at 1,974 m above sea level, the highest point in the country, as well as other elevations such as the Cuba Peak (1,874 m), the Suecia Peak (1,734 m), and La Gran Piedra (1,225 m).

Access: Linked to other provinces by the highway and railway network. By air, through the Antonio Maceo International Airport. By sea through Guillermón Moncada Port and Punta Gorda International Marina.

The statue of hero Frank País facing the Santiago de Cuba Bay.

The entrance to the Santiago de Cuba Bay.

23 A map of the city of **Santiago de Cuba**

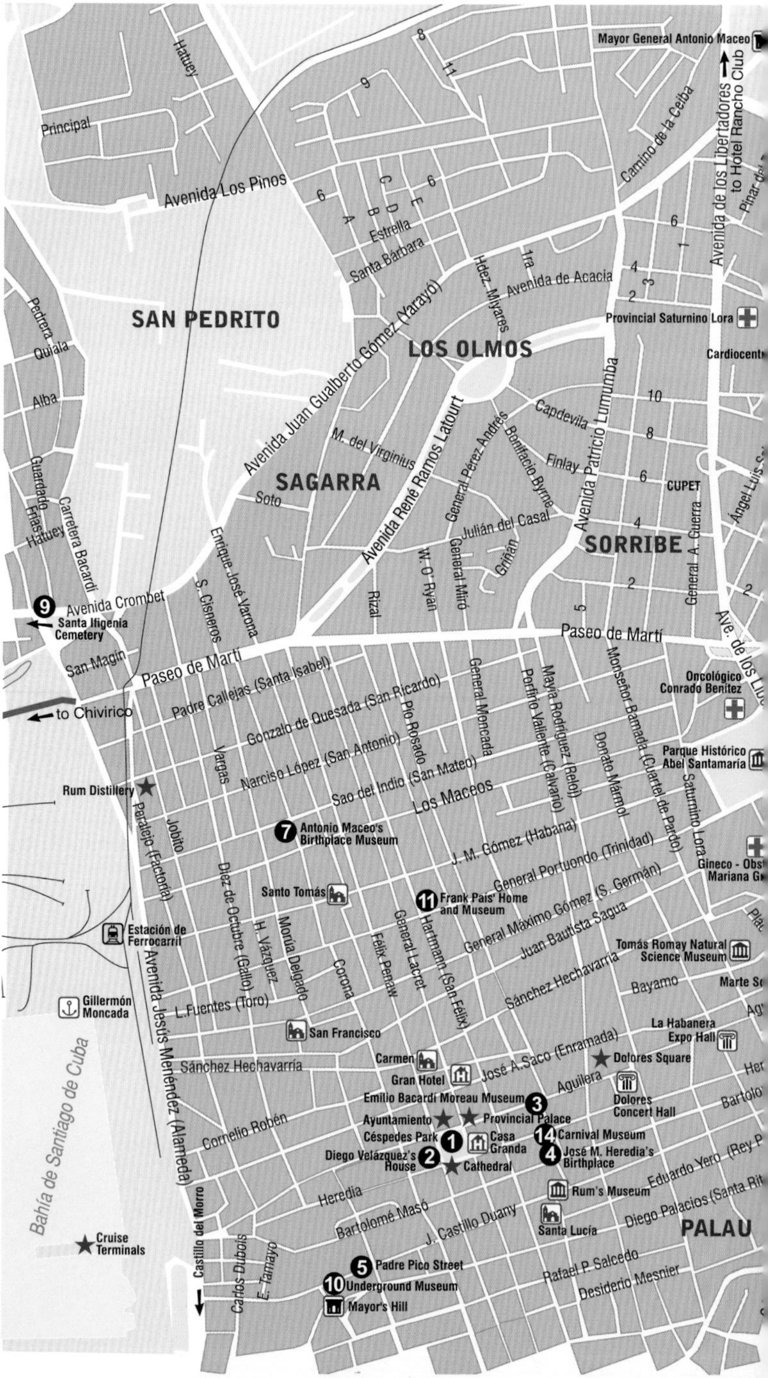

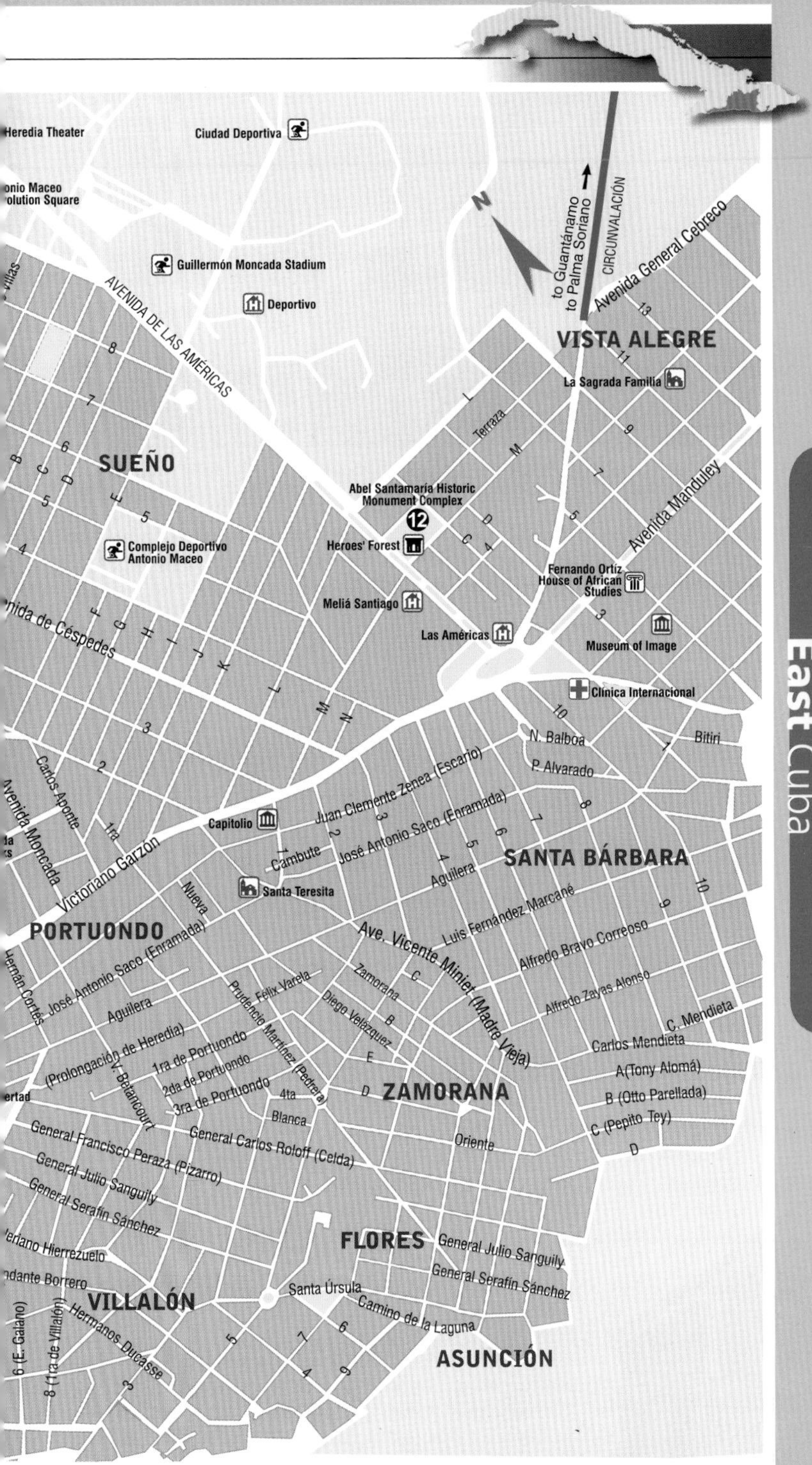
Heredia Theater
Ciudad Deportiva
Revolution Square
Guillermón Moncada Stadium
Deportivo
AVENIDA DE LAS AMÉRICAS
to Guantánamo
to Palma Soriano
CIRCUNVALACIÓN
Avenida General Cebreco
VISTA ALEGRE
La Sagrada Familia
Terraza
SUEÑO
Abel Santamaría Historic Monument Complex
12
Heroes' Forest
Avenida Manduley
Complejo Deportivo Antonio Maceo
Fernando Ortiz House of African Studies
Meliá Santiago
Las Américas
Museum of Image
Clínica Internacional
N. Balboa
Bitiri
P. Alvarado
Carlos Aponte
Avenida Moncada
Juan Clemente Zenea (Escario)
José Antonio Saco (Enramada)
Capitolio
Cambute
SANTA BÁRBARA
Aguilera
Victoriano Garzón
Santa Teresita
Nueva
Luis Fernández Marcané
PORTUONDO
Ave. Vicente Miniet (Madre Vieja)
Alfredo Bravo Correoso
Hernán Cortés
Zamorana
Alfredo Zayas Alonso
Félix Varela
Diego Velázquez
C. Mendieta
Carlos Mendieta
Prudencio Martínez (Pedrera)
(Prolongación de Heredia)
1ra de Portuondo
2da de Portuondo
3ra de Portuondo
V. Betancourt
4ta
Blanca
ZAMORANA
A (Tony Alomá)
B (Otto Parellada)
C (Pepito Tey)
General Francisco Peraza (Pizarro)
General Carlos Roloff (Celda)
Oriente
General Julio Sanguily
General Serafín Sánchez
Hierrezuelo
Borrero
FLORES
VILLALÓN
Santa Úrsula
Camino de la Laguna
6 (E. Galano)
8 (1ra de Villalón)
Hermanos Ducasse
ASUNCIÓN

East Cuba

Santiago de Cuba

Sites of Interest

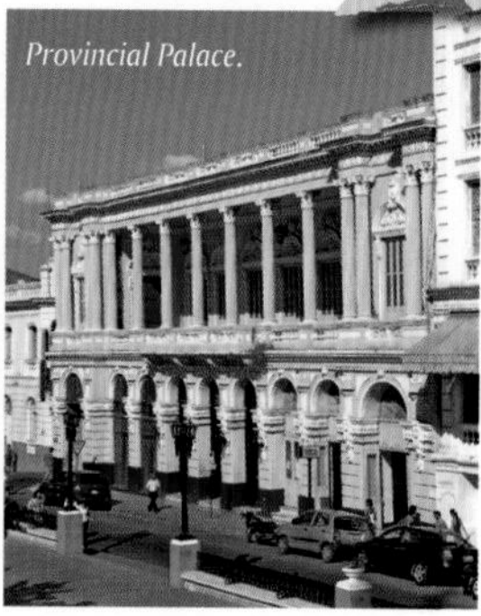

Provincial Palace.

❶ Céspedes Park

Calles Aguilera, San Pedro, Heredia, y Santo Tomás, Santiago de Cuba.

Santiago's most important plaza is also its most animated. Buildings of varied architecture surround it: the former Town Hall, Diego Velázquez's house, the Cathedral, the former San Carlos Club and the Casa Granda Hotel.

Santiago de Cuba´s Cathedral.

❷ Diego Velázquez´s House

Céspedes Park, Santiago de Cuba.

Located on a corner across Céspedes Plaza, this was the home of conquistador Diego Velázquez and a valuable sample of colonial architecture. Built between the years 1516 and 1530, experts consider it the oldest Spanish construction of its type still standing in Latin America. The building, the seat of the first Government of the island, is remarkable for its many Mudejar architectural and decorative elements. At present it is a museum that relives the colonial atmosphere of an early Cuban home. It displays a valuable collection of furniture, as well as other exhibits.

Interior patio of Santiago de Cuba's Town Hall.

3 Emilio Bacardí Moreau Museum

Carnicería St., between Aguilera and Heredia, Santiago de Cuba.

The first institution of its kind in Cuba was inaugurated in 1899. Its patron and promoter was Don Emilio Bacardí, Santiago de Cuba's first mayor. It treasures valuable pieces of pre-Columbian culture, national art and Cuban history, among the latter, a tail coat that belonged to Cuba's National Hero José Martí, as well as personal objects of Carlos Manuel de Céspedes, the Father of the Nation. On exhibit there is an Egyptian mummy brought to Cuba by Bacardi himself as well as Peruvian *paraca* mummies brought to the country by the founders of the museum. The museum has an important collection of colonial paintings, as well as works of the Spanish Renaissance and others by relevant modern Cuban painters such as Wifredo Lam and René Portocarrero.

4 José M. Heredia's Birthplace

206 Heredia St., between San Félix and Pío Rosado, Santiago de Cuba.

For its historical and architectural values, José Maria Heredia's birthplace was converted into a museum to preserve one of the relics of the colonial period in Santiago de Cuba. It exhibits documents, paintings and other objects, and is also the seat of the Center for Heredia Studies, an institution created to research the life of the first romantic poet in America.

5 Padre Pico Street

Laid out in 1899 by order of Mayor Emilio Bacardí to honor Catholic priest Bernardo del Pico Redin, is one of the city's best known streets. It is a natural viewpoint and its steps are one of the entrances to El Tivoli neighborhood, a venue par excellence of Santiago's famous carnival. The street has 52 steps –13 sections of 4 steps each– and 12 landings.

6 Marte Square

Victoriano Garzón Avenue on Aguilera St.

One of the city's most central sites, it was constructed in the late 18th century as part of the development of Santiago to the East. The square honors the independence of Cuba. A decree by city hall on June 12, named it Liberty Square, but locals kept referring to it by its old name: Marte Square. It is one of the favorite sites in Santiago, since fans gather here to discuss about any sport.

Santiago de Cuba

❼ Antonio Maceo's Birthplace Museum

207 Los Maceo St., between Corona and Rastro, Santiago de Cuba.

Located in the historical center of Santiago de Cuba, it was inaugurated on December 5, 1974. It exhibits objects linked to the family and military life of Antonio Maceo Grajales, Mayor General of the Cuban Liberation Army, known as the Bronze Titan, born in this house on June 14, 1845.

❽ Moncada Barracks

General Portuondo St., between Moncada and Los Libertadores Ave., Santiago de Cuba. Tel.: (5322) 661 157.

History was made when the Moncada Barracks were attacked by a group of young revolutionaries, led by Fidel Castro. The plan was to take over the Barracks and then head to the mountains near Santiago the Cuba to fight Fulgencio Batista's dictatorship. After the triumph of the Revolution, the Moncada became a school (Ciudad Escolar 26 de Julio) and there is a museum in one of the facilities that relive the events that took place on July 26, 1953.

❾ Santa Ifigenia Cemetery *Crombet Avenue, Juan G. Gómez.*

Located northwest of the city, close to the once called Camino Real (Main Road) of the island, the cemetery is the final resting place not only of Cuba's famous sons and daughters, but also of important figures from abroad. Buried here are José Martí; Carlos Manuel de Céspedes; generals of the Wars of Independence such as José Maceo, Flor Crombet and Guillermón Moncada, as well as other Cuban heroes of the 19th and 20th centuries. Emilio Bacardi, the city's first mayor; Francesco Antommarchi, Napoleon Bonaparte's personal physician; Pepe Sánchez, the creator of the bolero in Cuba, also rest in peace here.

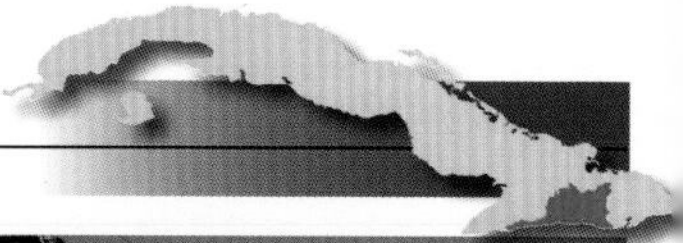

⑩ Underground Museum

1 Rabí St., between San Carlos and Santa Rita, Santiago de Cuba.

Located on Intendente Hill, in the Tivoli neighborhood, the museum treasures part of the history related to the underground movement during the war against the Batista dictatorship, particularly the city's role and actions in cities and town in support of the Rebel Army and the 26th of July Movement.

⑪ Frank País' Home and Museum

226 San Bartolomé St., between Habana and Maceo, Santiago de Cuba. Tel: (5322) 652 710.

This was the home of Frank País's family since 1939. On November 30, 1964 it became a museum. The exhibits show the private life of the leader of the Santiago armed uprising on November 30, 1956.

⑫ Abel Santamaría Historic Monument Complex

Trinidad St., between Calle Nueva and Central Highway, Santiago de Cuba. Tel.: (5322) 624119.

Formed by a museum, a library and a monument, the institution is located on the lot once occupied by the Saturnino Lora Civilian Hospital, scene of the armed action taken by 23 young revolutionaries led by Abel Santamaria Cuadrado on July 26, 1953 as part of the attack on Moncada Barracks. Months later, on October 16, Fidel Castro, leader of the revolutionary movement, stood trial here for these actions in a small study for nurses. At this significant trial, Fidel, who represented himself, gave his closing arguments in a speech known as "History Will Absolve Me."

⑬ Heredia Theater

Avenue of the Américas on Dolphins Avenues.

This is Santiago de Cuba's most important cultural center, named after José María Heredia, the Western Hemisphere's first romantic poet. It is the only theater designed and built in Cuba after the revolutionary triumph of 1959. Specialized in programming, organization and promotion of artistic performances, expositions, festivals, congresses, conventions, conferences, and other national and international events, the facility has an area of 72,000 m^2 and is the permanent venue of Expocaribe International Fair.

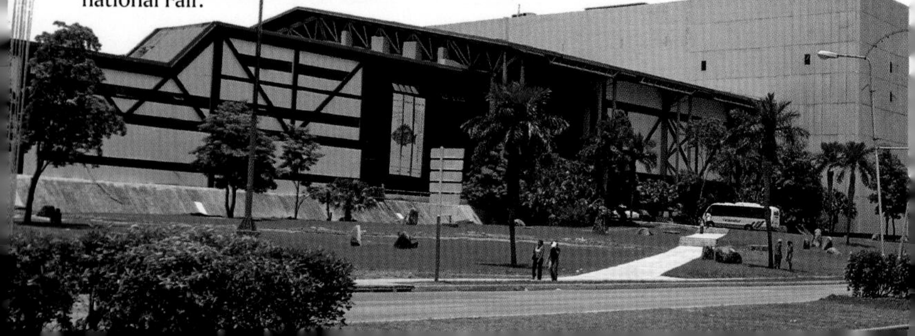

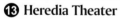

Street in Santiago de Cuba

Santiago de Cuba

Sites of Interest

⓮ Carnival Museum

303 Heredia St. on Carnicería, Santiago de Cuba. Tel.: (5322) 626 955.

Songs, dances and other manifestations that came to the island from the African continent have found a space in festivities such as the carnival, to which Santiago has dedicated a museum to preserve this cultural heritage. Its rooms are totally dedicated to the history of that popular feast, quite different from others celebrated in Cuba because of Spanish, African and French-Haitian elements. Such a fusion of cultures brought a larger diversity of dances and rhythms, costumes and other distinctive traits that make of the Santiago Carnival the most spectacular in Cuba. One of its characteristics are the conga parades, among them the one from the neighborhood of Los Hoyos (Hijos del Cocoyé) and the Paso Franco, accompanied by several types of drums and the Chinese horn.

The museum, inaugurated on June 7, 1983, details the different stages of this popular manifestation that in the month of July fills the city with music and dancing. Considered among the three major popular festivities in the country, the Santiago Carnival was originated in the July 25 procession dedicated to St. James the Greater. At the institution are exhibited models of floats, trophies awarded, banners, costumes, capes and street props, as well as the musical instruments of the associations that participate in the feasts: Carabalí Council, Tumba Francesa and Santiago Conga.

⓯ Antonio Maceo Revolution Square

Los Delfines Ave. on the corner to Las Américas.

Located at the entrance of Santiago de Cuba, it is considered the most significant monument of the 20th century raised in the city. For honoring Antonio Maceo, local sculptor Alberto Lezcay made a 16 m high statue, the tallest in the country.

East Cuba

Santiago de Cuba

Sites of Interest

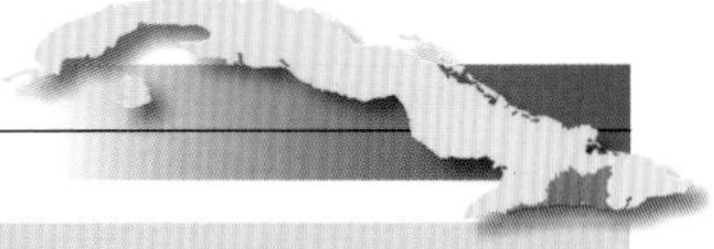

㉔ Shrine of the Virgin of El Cobre

Santiago del Prado Hill, El Cobre, Santiago de Cuba.

The history of the shrine is linked to a legend that has been modified with the passing of time. It tells that three humble men, a white man, a mulatto, and a black man found the image of the Virgin of Charity floating in the water at Nipe Bay. They decided to bring it to El Cobre mines, where they built her a chapel. At present, it is a required destination for the faithful of Cuba's patron saint in order to make offerings or ask for favors from the Virgin. The offerings are kept in the Chapel of Miracles, where you can find an assorted collection of precious stones, gold jewelry and the medal awarded to US writer Ernest Hemingway for the Nobel Prize of Literature in 1954, which he donated to the Virgin. Pilgrims and tourists take home as souvenirs small stones freckled with copper from the old mines, as simple souvenirs or for protection from evil. The image of the Virgin of Charity is kept in a glass display case at the "Dressing Room", where the faithful go to pray and place flowers at her feet.

Views of the Santiago Bay from Morro Castle.

㉕ Morro Castle

Morro Highway, Km. 7½.

Tel.: (5322) 691 569.

Construction of San Pedro de la Roca Castle, known as Morro Castle, began on 1638, –designed by Italian military engineer Juan Bautista Antonelli– and spanned until the early 18th century. Its main objective was to protect the city from the attack of pirates and corsairs that roamed the Caribbean Sea at the time. In 1997 Unesco declared it a World Heritage Site, due to its extraordinary historic and architectonic values and as a unique sample of Renaissance architecture in the Caribbean.

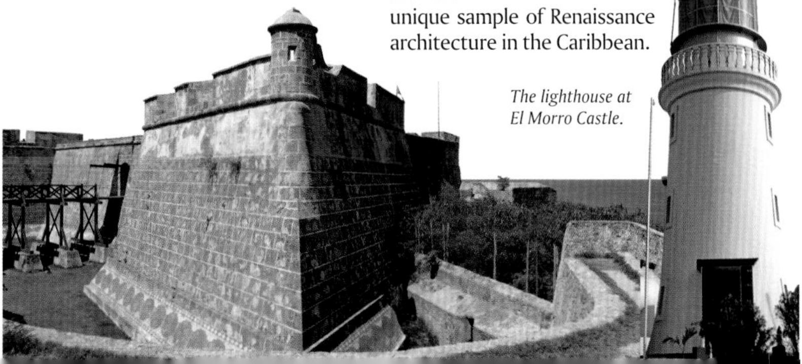

The lighthouse at El Morro Castle.

㉖ Baconao Park

20 Km from Santiago de Cuba.

This is a vast region along Santiago's South coast up to the province of Guantanamo, declared by Unesco in 1987 a Natural Reserve of the Biosphere. The park has many features that characterize it, both for its untamed nature and its archaeological values. It has many attractions, including:

La Gran Piedra (The Great Boulder) (Siboney Highway and Gran Piedra Highway, Km. 14): A huge boulder of volcanic origin, 51 m long and almost 39 m wide, with 459 stone steps to the top that serves as an outlook with an altitude of 1,225 m above sea level. On a clear night it is possible to see Jamaica's lights, and on clear days with good visibility you can see both the North and the South coasts of the Eastern region. Studies have confirmed the Gran Piedra Mountain Range as the main destination of the French immigrant settlers in the 19th century, for there are still ruins of dozens of coffee plantations.

La Isabelica Ethnographic Museum (Gran Piedra Highway, Km. 14, Santiago de Cuba): Declared by Unesco a World Heritage Site on November 29, 2000, it is part of the coffee plantations created by the French immigrants and its Haitian slaves. It is an example of the plantation economy that recreates French-Haitian family life at the time, with exhibits of well-preserved period furniture and examples of decorative art.

Aquarium: It has a 30 m-deep underwater tunnel and a dolphin show

Siboney Farm Museum. (Siboney Highway, Km. 13 ½): Once used as headquarters of the revolutionaries that attacked the Moncada Barracks on July 26, 1953, it allows to know the events and preparations prior to the action and its consequences.

Baconao Lake: A Taíno Aborigine village is reproduced here. There is also a restaurant whose specialty is seafood.

Prehistoric Valley: The work of sculptor Dagoberto Ramos, who filled the site with life-sized reproductions of creatures from the Jurassic period.

Land Transportation Museum: This original exhibition consists of over 2500 scale reproductions, from the origin of the wheel and its evolution up to present-day vehicles.

Museum of Natural Science: Naturalized specimens of sea wildlife and birds, as well as typical minerals of the area.

A landscape in the Sierra Maestra.

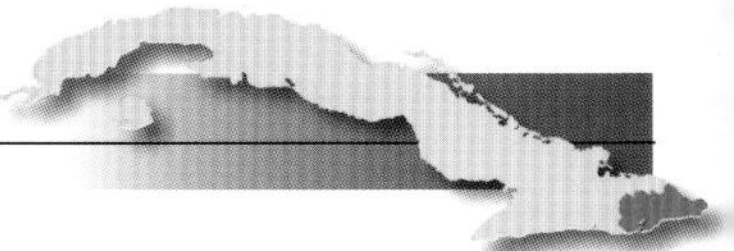

27 province of
Guantánamo

With an Aborigine name that means "land between rivers" the easternmost province of Cuba is filled with history, for Cuba's first town, Baracoa, was founded in this region in 1511. French and Haitians settled in the area and in a short time developed the cocoa, fruit and coffee plantations in the mountains, and left their imprint in agriculture and customs, at present still alive in the population. In the province, there still are traces of Aboriginal settlements in Caridad de los Indios, Manuel Tames Municipality, a fact of cultural and ethnic importance.

The name of the region became world-famous through the song "Guantanamera", composed in 1928 by Joseíto Fernández. This region is also known for its music genres such as *changüí*, *nengón* and *quiribá*, and for the *Tumba Francesa* a folk dance brought by Haitian immigrants.

Capital: Guantánamo.

Area: 6,168 Km^2.

Municipalities: Guantánamo, Baracoa, Yateras, Imías, Niceto Pérez, Caimanera, El Salvador, Maisí, Manuel Tames and San Antonio del Sur.

Population: 510,000 plus

Boundaries: To the North, it borders with the province of Holguin and the Atlantic Ocean; to the East with the Windward Passage; to the South with the Caribbean Sea; and to the West with the province of Santiago de Cuba.

Economy: Industrial–agrarian, mainly sugar and food industries.

Main products: Coffee, sugar cane, cocoa and coconuts, as well as a wide variety of food crops.

Relief: Two main different geographical features: Guantanamo Valley, with plains and an ample closed bay; and the mountain area, which covers 75% of the territory with the Sagua-Baracoa Mountain Range as its main feature.

Access: There are 2 important airports: Mariana Grajales Airport in Guantánamo, and Gustavo Rizo Airport in Baracoa. The province is linked to the rest of the country by the national highway system and the railway network.

A woman in the country crushing coffee beans.

"Guateque", a traditional festivity in the country.

The Lighthouse at Maisí Point, Cuba's easternmost tip.

㉘ A map of the city of **Guantánamo**

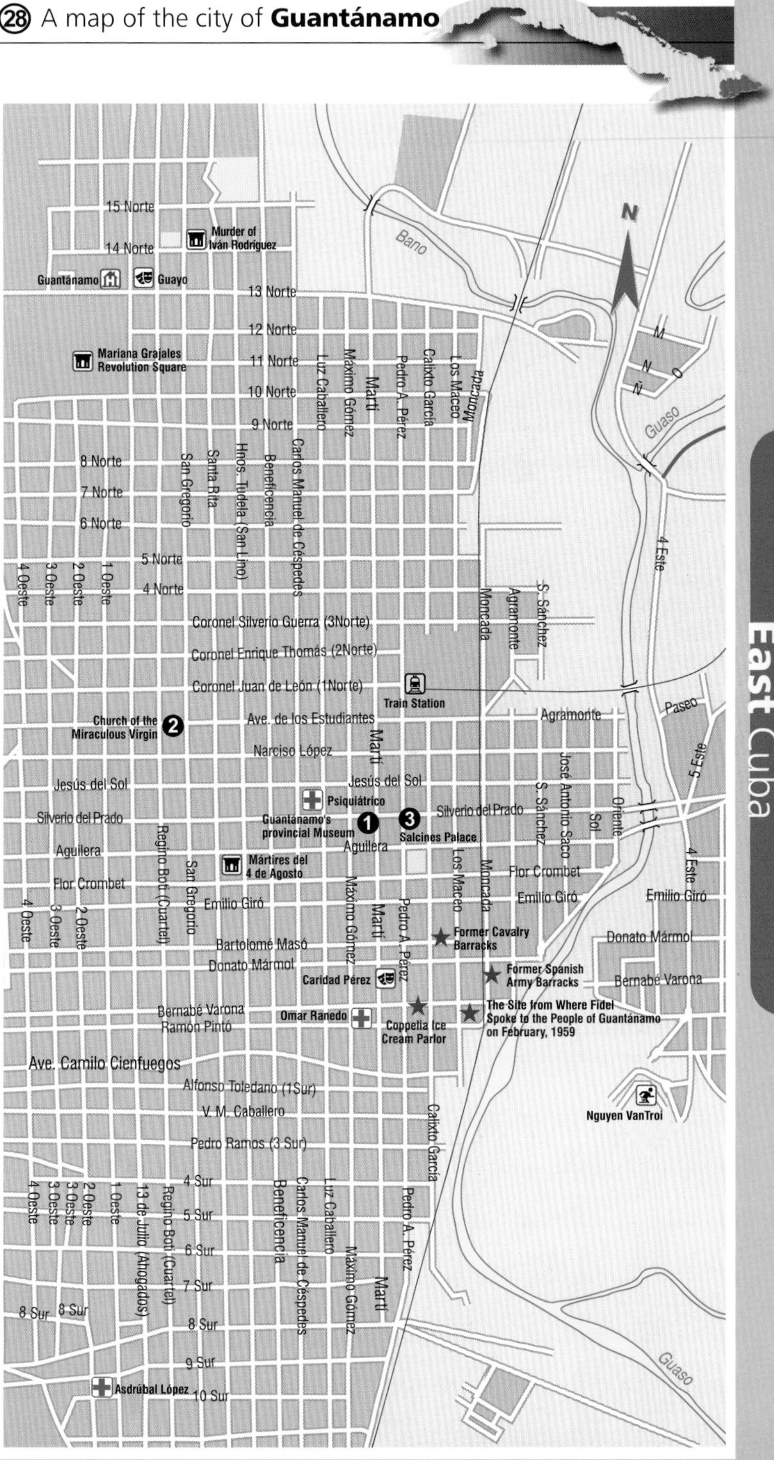
N
15 Norte
14 Norte
Murder of Iván Rodríguez
Guantánamo
Guayo
13 Norte
12 Norte
11 Norte
10 Norte
9 Norte
Mariana Grajales Revolution Square
Bano
Guaso
M
N
Ñ
O
Luz Caballero
Máximo Gómez
Martí
Pedro A. Pérez
Calixto García
Los Maceo
Moncada
8 Norte
7 Norte
6 Norte
5 Norte
4 Norte
San Gregorio
Santa Rita
Hnos. Tudela (San Lino)
Beneficencia
Carlos Manuel de Céspedes
4 Oeste
3 Oeste
2 Oeste
1 Oeste
4 Este
Moncada
Agramonte
S. Sánchez
Coronel Silverio Guerra (3Norte)
Coronel Enrique Thomás (2Norte)
Coronel Juan de León (1Norte)
Train Station
Church of the Miraculous Virgin
Ave. de los Estudiantes
Narciso López
Agramonte
Paseo
5 Este
Jesús del Sol
Silverio del Prado
Aguilera
Flor Crombet
Psiquiátrico
Guantánamo's provincial Museum
Salcines Palace
Silverio del Prado
José Antonio Saco
S. Sánchez
Sol
Oriente
Regino Botí (Cuartel)
San Gregorio
Mártires del 4 de Agosto
Emilio Giró
Flor Crombet
Emilio Giró
4 Este
Emilio Giró
Donato Mármol
Bernabé Varona
Former Cavalry Barracks
Former Spanish Army Barracks
Bartolomé Masó
Donato Mármol
Caridad Pérez
The Site from Where Fidel Spoke to the People of Guantánamo on February, 1959
Bernabé Varona
Ramón Pintó
Omar Ranedo
Coppelia Ice Cream Parlor
Ave. Camilo Cienfuegos
Alfonso Toledano (1Sur)
V. M. Caballero
Pedro Ramos (3 Sur)
Nguyen VanTroi
Calixto García
4 Sur
5 Sur
6 Sur
7 Sur
8 Sur
9 Sur
10 Sur
13 de Julio (Ahogados)
Regino Botí (Cuartel)
Beneficencia
Carlos Manuel de Céspedes
Luz Caballero
Máximo Gómez
Martí
Pedro A. Pérez
8 Sur
Asdrúbal López
Guaso

East Cuba

Guantánamo

Sites of Interest

❶ Guantánamo's provincial Museum

804 Martí St. on Prado, Guantánamo. Tel.: (5321) 32 5872.

It shows the development of the province through time with valuable objects of Aborigine culture and collections that are examples of its history and traditions.

❷ Church of the Miraculous Virgin *821 Paseo St., between San Gregorio and Cuartel, Guantánamo.*

The church is an example of the rationalist style with a marked brutalist influence. It is a construction of reinforced concrete with a triangular roof imitating the traditional "vara en tierra", a kind of leant-to in the Cuban countryside where farmers keep their tools. Its privileged location on one of Guantánamo highest elevations turns it into one of the city's most outstanding feature. Its concrete tower topped by a Latin cross can be seen from any slightly rising point of the city. Since 2008, it is the seat of the Guantánamo-Baracoa Bishopric.

❸ Salcines Palace

802-804 Pedro Agustín St. Silverio del Prado.

One of the most significant buildings in the city's historical center, named after engineer and architect José Lacita de Jesús Salcines, who was in charge of its construction between 1916 and 1918. Its most relevant feature is the sculpture of Fame, placed at the top of the palace´s dome, specially made for the building by Italian Amerigo J. Chini. Due to its cultural and artistic importance and taking into consideration the results of a survey, the sculpture became the symbol of the city on December 1, 1993.

Guantánamo

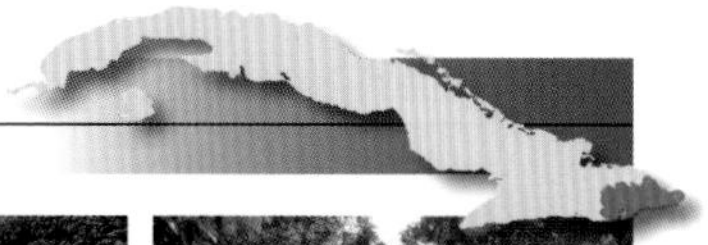

㉙ Stone Zoo

San Lorenzo Farm, Yateras Municipality, Guantánamo.

The Stone Zoo was created by self-taught sculptor Angel Iñigo Blanco, a member of a farming family. The park is located in the municipality of Yateras, 24 Km from the city of Guantánamo, in San Lorenzo Farm. Inaugurated on December 21, 1977, the zoo consists of life-sized stone animal placed in areas resembling their own environments. There are more than 400 specimens, such as lions, elephants, snakes and even tiny animals.

㉚ Alexander von Humboldt National Park

Extending through the provinces of Holguín and Guantánamo, this is one of the most important parks in the Caribbean. It is named after German scientist Alexander von Humboldt, an outstanding figure of his time, who visited Cuba on two occasions: from December 19, 1800 to March 15th, 1801, and on the second time sometime between April and May, 1804. With a high degree of preservation, the park has one of the greatest vegetation density and of endemic species in the world. Two percent of all flora species of the world are found here. The park is the basic nucleus of the Toa Ridge Reserve of the Biosphere, a Unesco World Heritage Site.

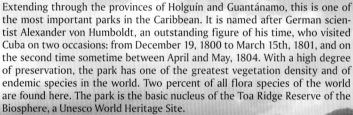

(31) Baracoa

The city of Baracoa.

La Farola.

Estuary of the Miel river.

Our Lady of the Assumption of Baracoa, Cuba's oldest town, was founded by Diego Velázquez on August 15, 1511 at the beginning of the island's colonization. Bathed by the Miel River and surrounded by mountain ranges, at present it is called "landscape city," "city of rains," "city of mountains", and "city of waters," the latter as reference to the Arawak term Baracoa, meaning "existence of the sea."

Christopher Columbus.

Baracoa was Cuba's first capital until 1515, when the seat of the government was moved to Santiago de Cuba. Like other settlements, the town was a constant target of pirate and corsair attacks. For that reason, the conquistadors built several forts, such as Matachín, La Punta and Seboruco Castle, preserved up to date and the town's major attractions. Add to this its horseshoe bay, the Baracoa Anvil and the parish church where the Holy Cross of the Vine is venerated, the oldest historical relic of the encounter of the two cultures in the New World. The story goes that Columbus himself planted the cross on Baracoa soil on December 1, 1492.

In the late 18th century and up to 1804, over 100 French families came to the region fleeing the Haitian revolution. They encouraged honey production and introduced the latest techniques in coffee growing and coconut oil extraction, as well as in banana plantations.

Physical features of the aborigines can still be seen in many Baracoans, and the town is also famous for its particular treats, such as "bacán", a kind of green plantain tamale, "ajiaco" stew, fish cooked in milk, and the celebrated "cucurucho", a ground coconut and pineapple desert wrapped in a piece of palm leaf.

Access to the town is an adventure in itself, through a winding road along the mountains, known as La Farola, with 11 suspension bridges. Its highest point is Altos de Cotilla, 600 m above sea level.

An overview of Baracoa with the Anvil in the background.

Mule driver in the mountains.

㉛ A map of the city of **Baracoa**

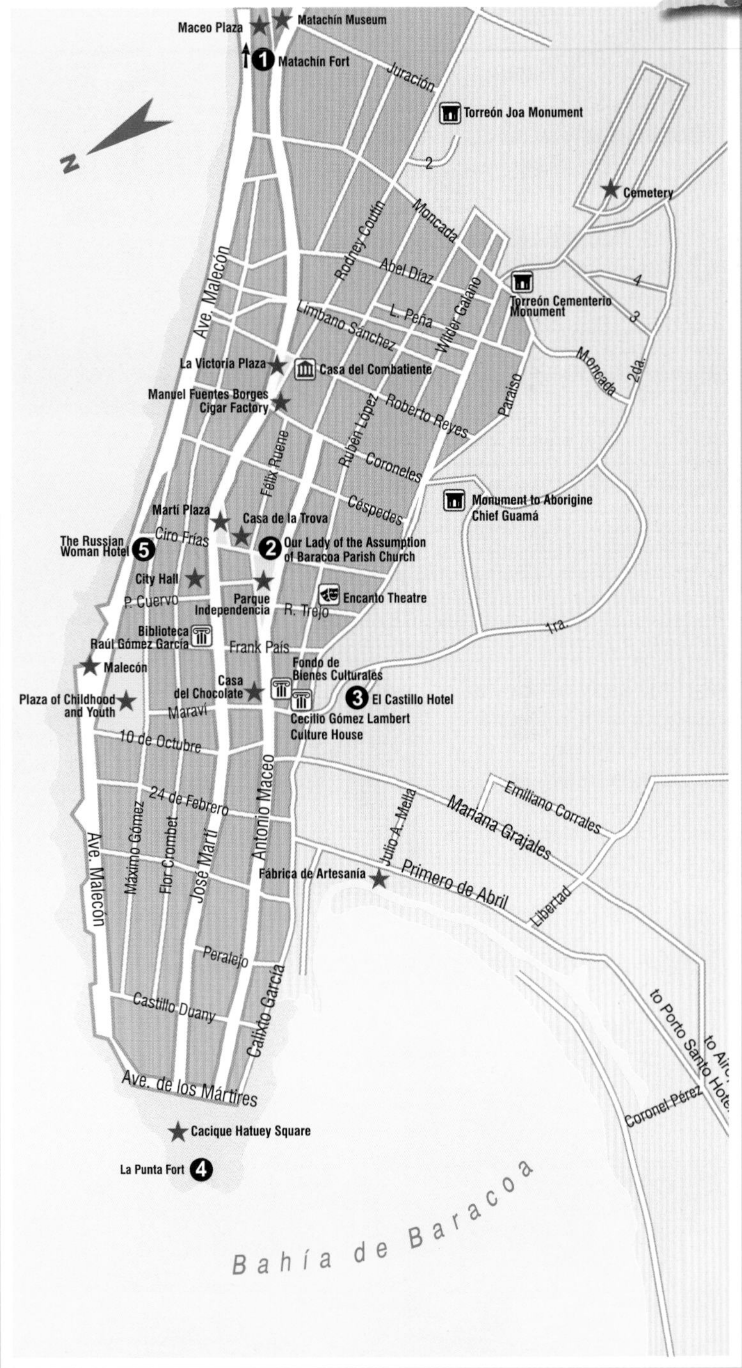
Maceo Plaza
Matachín Museum
1 Matachín Fort
Juración
Torreón Joa Monument
2
Cemetery
Moncada
Rodney Coutín
Abel Díaz
Torreón Cementerio Monument
4
3
Ave. Malecón
L. Peña
Wilder Galano
Limbano Sánchez
Moncada
2da.
La Victoria Plaza
Casa del Combatiente
Manuel Fuentes Borges Cigar Factory
Roberto Reyes
Paraíso
Rubén López
Félix Ruene
Coroneles
Céspedes
Monument to Aborigine Chief Guamá
Martí Plaza
Casa de la Trova
Ciro Frías
The Russian Woman Hotel 5
2 Our Lady of the Assumption of Baracoa Parish Church
City Hall
P. Cuervo
Parque Independencia
R. Trejo
Encanto Theatre
1ra.
Biblioteca Raúl Gómez García
Frank País
Malecón
Fondo de Bienes Culturales
Casa del Chocolate
3 El Castillo Hotel
Plaza of Childhood and Youth
Maraví
Cecilio Gómez Lambert Culture House
10 de Octubre
24 de Febrero
Antonio Maceo
Emiliano Corrales
Mariana Grajales
Julio A. Mella
Ave. Malecón
Máximo Gómez
Flor Crombet
José Martí
Fábrica de Artesanía
Primero de Abril
Libertad
Peralejo
Castillo Duany
Calixto García
Ave. de los Mártires
Coronel Pérez
Cacique Hatuey Square
La Punta Fort 4
Bahía de Baracoa

Baracoa

Palace of the Government.

Toa River.

The Malecón at Baracoa.

1 Matachín Fort

Martí St. on Malecón, Baracoa.

Northwest of the city, at Esteban Point, across the Miel River inlet, and opposite to the old Majana Fort, stands Matachín, the second construction by Royal Decree. It is known as Matachín since the early 19th century, for according to local sources every day two steers were slaughtered to feed Spanish troops. On October 18, 1981 it was inaugurated as Municipal Museum, and since then it displays an overview of Cuba's history. There are also samples of Cuban Aboriginal culture, the story of the celebrated Russian Woman and the collections of autochthonous flora and wildlife. Of the latter, there are specimens of the multicolored polymita snails and the Cuban solenodon.

2 Our Lady of the Assumption of Baracoa Parish Church

Across the city's Main Square.

The current Church, located across the city's Main Square and very close to the former Town Hall, was built in 1807. On August 14, 1833 an igneous meteorite crashed into the building and partially destroyed it. It was largely repaired in 1886, and in the early 20th century two side towers were added in the shape of narrow pyramids, which do not exist at present. The Cross of the Vine, the oldest historical relic of the encounter of the two cultures in the New World is within the church's walls. It is the only one of its kind in the Caribbean and allegedly made of wood from a local forest by Columbus' men.

Baracoa

❸ Seboruco de Santa Bárbara Castle

Calixto García St., Paraíso, Baracoa.

Located on the Northwest part of the city, on the side of a hill more than 100 m above sea level, it was the third and most important construction of the town's defense system in the 18th century. During the 1970s it was turned into a hotel and renovated in 1992. The castle is part of the tourist path of the area and from the site there is a full and magnificent view of the city and its surroundings.

Monument on Duaba Beach as a memorial to the landing of Antonio Maceo and a group of patriots, on April 1, 1895.

❹ La Punta Fort

Burén Point, Baracoa.

Part of the city's defense system in the 18´s century, it is located Northwest of Baracoa, on Burén Point, at the port's entrance. At present it is a restaurant

The Baracoa Anvil.

❺ The Russian Woman

Once upon the 1920s Magdalena Menasses, later known as The Russian Woman, arrived in Baracoa. Many still speculate about the reasons that the daughter of a former advisor to the Czar took refuge in Cuba's first town. Some say that she came fleeing the Russian Revolution; others claim that she was attracted by the economic advantages and the weather of the region. But whatever the reason, she became a celebrity, the object also of many a discussion whether she was the model for the character of Vera in Cuban novelist Alejo Carpentier's *The Rites of Spring*. At present, by the Baracoa Malecón this mystery woman's former home, has been transformed into a small hotel where photos and some of her belongings are on display.

Baracoa

The symbol of Baracoa's wildlife is the endemic *Polymita picta* snail. This is a land mollusk, remarkable for the extraordinary variations and combinations of colors in their shells. Naturalists have acknowledged six different species: *picta*, *muscarum*, *sulphurosa*, *versicolor*, *venusta* and *brocheri*. All of them are tree-dwellers and live on different plants, particularly bushes, and especially on coffee trees. They feed on fungus and lichen attached to the bark and leaves of their hosts, thus contributing to the plants' health. They are easily recognizable, for their color striped shells seem hand painted and stand out against the intense green of vegetation. According to a local legend, an Aboriginal chieftain wanted to offer a gift to a beautiful woman and he went out to catch the colors of the sun, the greens of the mountains, the pink of the flowers and the white of the sea foam. But when he wanted to catch the blue in the sky, he was surprised by darkness and had to settle for the black of night. At present, because the snail is an endangered species collecting them is forbidden to avoid the disappearance of these jewels from the face of the Earth.

Mata Bay.

The home of Faustino Lobaina, a Baracoan.

Yumurí River in Guantánamo.

Useful information

In this chapter you will find Cuba's current migratory, customs and health regulations, as well as other useful tips and references on where to go for tourist information on Cuba.

HOW TO GET TO CUBA

The island's main point of entry is the José Martí International Airport in Havana, although there are other airports throughout the country that connect Cuba with over 40 cities in the world. You can also come by boat to marinas and ports that welcome visitors, including those in their own crafts.

MIGRATORY REGULATIONS

Visitors must have an updated passport or a travel document issued on their behalf and the appropriate visa or tourist card. Citizens of countries with which Cuba has free visa agreements just need their passports. Tourist cards can be obtained at Cuban consulates abroad. There are two types of cards: for individual tourists and for those traveling in groups. Businessmen, journalists performing their duties and Cuban-born persons nonresident in the country or having another nationality should present a visa issued by a Cuban Consulate. Passports of residents in the United States are not stamped on entering the country.

Travelers who wish to extend their stay in Cuba or change the designation with which they entered the country should address their hotel's Tourism Bureau or the nearest one at their destination.

REGULATIONS

CUSTOMS REGULATIONS

On passenger traffic:

Passengers should declare to Customs all items that are not part of their personal belongings.

Passengers arriving in Cuba as tourists:

Regulations included in the June 4, 1954 Convention on Customs Facilities for Tourists, which Cuba has signed, will be applied to tourists arriving to Cuba.

Personal items imported by tourists, on condition that they are for their own use, that they carry them or are included in their baggage, and that they are exported on leaving the country will be temporarily admitted free of duties and taxes.

Tourists may bring with them under the terms of temporary import, along with clothes, toiletries and other objects explicitly personal, the following items:

- Personal jewelry
- One photographic or film camera, together with a reasonable amount of film, cassettes and accessories.
- Binoculars
- One portable musical instrument.
- One portable slide or film projector and accessories, plus a reasonable amount of slides or films.
- One portable sound reproduction set, including recorders, portable compact disc readers, and Dictaphones with tapes and discs.
- One portable radio receiver.
- One mobile or cellular phone
- One portable TV set
- One portable typewriter
- One personal computer and accessories
- One portable calculator
- One baby carriage
- Toys (only minors)
- One wheelchair
- Sports equipment

EXEMPT ARTICLES

Passengers may bring the following articles and products exempt from payment of customs duties:

- Their personal effects such as clothing and any new or used articles that they may reasonably need for their personal use, depending on the circumstances of their trip, days and intermediate stays.

- Articles or products subject to payment when its value is less than $50.99 pesos.

- Ten kilograms of medical products, as long as they are transported in a separate piece of luggage and independent of other articles, and in their original package, such as: finished pharmaceutical products, as long as they are not included among medical products whose import is not authorized or subject to special requirements.

- Scientific, technical, art and literature books, musical scores, discs, audio tapes, slides and films for educational purposes, wheelchairs, prosthesis when they replace or substitute an organ or part of it, and equipment, books or materials for the blind, medals, decorations and prizes awarded abroad, and the products that as temporary imports may bring citizens from other countries in their conditions as artists, sportsmen, experts, scientists, journalists and filmmakers, passengers in transit and persons who arrive to the country under special circumstances, and all those who are granted this benefit by international agreements of which Cuba is part.

ON IMPORT

As passengers, individuals can only import articles or products with no commercial value. The total value of said articles or products included in the luggage of passengers, subject to payment of Customs rights and which are not part of their personal belongings, cannot exceed a value of $1,000 pesos.

BOTH AT ENTRANCE TO AND EXIT FROM THE COUNTRY, PASSENGERS MAY NOT CARRY:

Narcotic drugs and psychotropic or hallucinogenic substances, except those for medical use accompanied by the appropriate medical certificates; explosives, firearms and ammunition, except with the express authorization of the competent body; blood- related products; literature, articles and objects considered pornographic, obscene or contrary to the general interests of the Cuban nation; protected species by the Convention on International Trade of Threatened Species of Wild Fauna and Flora, unless a permit has been issued by the appropriate authority. (CITES permit.)

ON LEAVING THE COUNTRY PASSENGERS MAY NOT TAKE WITH THEM:

More than three units of a Cuban produced medical product, except those for continuing treatment, according to the duration of said treatment and supplied with a certificate of the health center, and in the case of non-permanent residents in Cuba, with an appropriate official invoice.

National heritage works or with museum value; books, brochures and serial publications dated more than 50 years ago, as well as Editorial "R" books if they do not have the Export Certificate from the Cultural Works Registry.

Cuban handmade cigars in an amount exceeding 50 units, if the traveler does not have the official invoice from the store where they were purchased.

Lobster in any quantity and form of packaging.

Cash in an amount exceeding $5,000 USD or its equivalent in other currencies that have not been declared on entering the country or without the Bank's appropriate authorization.

More than $100.00 Cuban National Currency (CUP) or more than $200.00 Cuban Convertible Pesos (CUC).

Manuscript books; incunabular (books published from 1440 to 1500); books, brochures and foreign serial publications printed from the 16th to the 18th centuries (1501 -1800); books, brochures and serial publications published in Cuba in the 18th century; books and brochures that bear the seal of libraries belonging to the National System of Public Libraries or other information systems, as well as of Cuban organizations and institutions.

Pieces and collections with numismatic value without the authorization of the Numismatic Museum or of Cuba's Central Bank are not exportable. If you purchase new paintings and sculptures at authorized points of sale, make sure that they have the seal which authorizes their export or request the appropriate permit, an indispensable requirement to take them with you.

ON THE EXPORT OF ROLLED CIGARS

On leaving the country, passengers must verbally declare to Customs all the rolled cigars they are carrying or have packed in their luggage.

A passenger may take with him, provided he/she complies with the established requisites for the export of rolled cigars:

1. Up to twenty (20) units of separate rolled cigars without submitting any document.
2. Up to fifty (50) units of rolled cigars on condition that they are in their original package, closed, sealed and with the official established hologram; otherwise export is not authorized.
3. If the number exceeds the fifty (50) units of rolled cigars, the passenger must submit the official invoice from the store chain authorized to market Cuban rolled cigars. Said invoice must cover all the rolled cigars to be exported, which must be in their original package, closed, sealed and with the official established hologram.

The export without commercial character of leaf tobacco, seals and/or supplies related to the tobacco industry is not allowed.

The export without commercial character by passengers, postal or messenger service of machine made cigarillos under three (3) grams per unit, in any registered brand and in the original package, are not subject to restriction or to special requisites, unless the export is for profit.

ON THE EXPORT OF FLORA AND WILDLIFE SPECIES

Individuals that import, re-export and introduce sea-related threatened species of flora and wildlife protected by the Convention on International Trade of Threatened Species of Wild Fauna and Flora (CITES), must obtain a permit from the Center of Environmental Management and Inspection, an agency of the Ministry of Science, Technology and the Environment.

Passengers that classify as tourists may take with them on leaving the country up to three 3 specimens of conch shells (*Strombus gigas*) as personal objects. The export of conch meat (*Strombus gigas*), shells containing meat or live animals that do not have the appropriate CITES permit is not allowed.

Passengers that classify as tourists may import up to three (3) specimens of conch shells (*Strombus gigas*) as personal objects.

REGULATIONS

ON THE EXPORT OF NATIONAL HERITAGE GOODS

The export of part or the whole of a work considered a Cultural National Heritage or with museum value is not allowed, unless accompanied by a previous and express authorization from the Ministry of Culture's National Council of Cultural Heritage.

A cultural work or one of museum value may not be re-exported without submitting the certificate of temporary or definitive import from Customs at the time of its import to the country.

Works of art made in Cuba from the 16th to the 19th centuries, whether by Cuban or foreign artists, as well as works of art created by Cuban artists born between 1900 and 1960 have been declared a Cultural Heritage of the Nation. The works of these artists can only be taken from the national territory with the express authorization of the Ministry of Culture's National Council of Cultural Heritage and through the National Cultural Works Registry.

In order to export a cultural product that has not been declared part of the Nation's Cultural Heritage, any Cuban or foreign individual must request the appropriate exit permit or export certificate from the Ministry of Culture's National Cultural Works Registry.

No export certificate is required for artistic or utilitarian handicrafts in its different manifestations, or for contemporary ornaments sold in stores and utensils of domestic use (glasses, jugs, dishes, and cutlery).

EXIT TAX

Exit tax at Cuban international airports is 25.00 CUC.

SANITARY REGULATIONS

Sanitary regulations are restrictive only for visitors from countries where yellow fever and cholera are endemic, or from those that have been declared zones of infection by the World Health Organization. In such cases, an International Certificate of Vaccination is mandatory. The import of animal and vegetable natural products is restricted. Animals may be imported accompanied by the appropriate certificate.

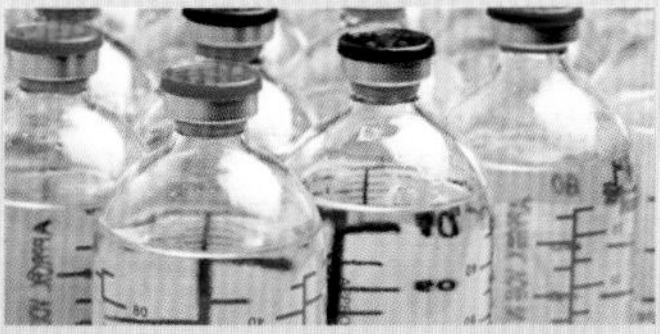

For further information on Customs regulations, please visit the General Customs of the Republic of Cuba's web site: http://www.aduana.co.cu, or call 8838282, 8837575 and 8819732 (all of them in Havana).

Cuba's time zone

Cuba's time zone is the GMT - 05:00 and is coincidental with the Eastern Standard Time in the US. Cuba has the same time as New York, Miami, Washington and the East coast of the US and Canada. From March to October, daylight saving time is adopted and clocks are set one hour ahead of normal time.

What to Wear

Most of the year weather is warm, so the use of light, fresh clothes is recommended. Nevertheless, visitors must bear in mind that from late October to March cold fronts are frequent. In December and January lower temperatures of 10 degrees Celsius (50 F) are sometimes reported. For this time of year a light wool or gabardine sweater is recommended. In the rainy season (May to October), it is advisable to have a light raincoat.

Informal wear (jeans, shorts, T shirts, etc.) are acceptable almost anywhere; but for the theater, de luxe restaurants, concert halls, business meetings and other places more formal wear is required.

Electric current and TV signal

In Cuba, electric current is 110 V and 60 Hz; although in newer buildings you may also find 220 V and 50 Hz. Electric equipment with French type round prongs should have an adaptor for American type flat prong outlets.

TV signals in Cuba use the American NTSC standard. There are five public TV channels and in most hotels there is satellite TV.

Transportation and car rental

Cuba has a road infrastructure and a transportation system that links the whole country, as well as tourist destinations and places of interest. The most used means is bus transportation with two main companies –Astro and Vía Azul. It also has an infrastructure for air transportation connecting the main cities and tourist destinations, as well as the railway that links the most important cities, but is far from the comfort and standards of developed countries.

At most cities and tourist destinations you can find taxis, as well as several car and microbus rental companies in most hotels and at agencies in every city and tourist destination. To rent a car you need a valid driver's license and your passport. There are also private taxis available in every city with a slightly lower price than those of government tourist companies. Traffic signals use the international system and driving is on the right side of the road.

Unit of measure

The official measuring standard is the International Unit System.

Telephone communication

Cuba's infrastructure guarantees direct telephone communications with any place on the country or with any part of the world.

To make an international call from Cuba you must dial:

1

119 + country code + city code + telephone number.

For example: If you wish to call someone in Toronto, Canada, dial:
119 (international prefix from Cuba) + 1(Canada's code)
+Toronto code + ___________________required telephone number

In order to guarantee success, check international codes before dialing.

To call Cuba from abroad, dial:

2

International selection prefix + 53 + area code + telephone number.
For example: In order to call from Italy to Varadero, Matanzas, dial:
00 international selection prefix
+ 53 (Cuba's code)
+ 45 (area code)
+ ________________required telephone number.

In order to call a cell phone in Cuba, dial:

3

International selection code + 53 + required mobile phone number.
Cell phones in Cuba begin with 5.

All calls to cell phones in Cuba from abroad are free of charge for the call's recipient.

In order to call long distance in Cuba, dial:

4

International selection code + Area code + Required telephone number.

0 (from Havana)

01 (from any other province)

In order to guarantee success, make sure to dial the appropriate number and codes.

For example: For calling Santa Clara, Las Villas from Havana, follow these instructions:

0 selection code

(( )) wait for higher tone (except for subscribers of digital centrals)

+ 42 Santa Clara code

+ ______________required telephone number.

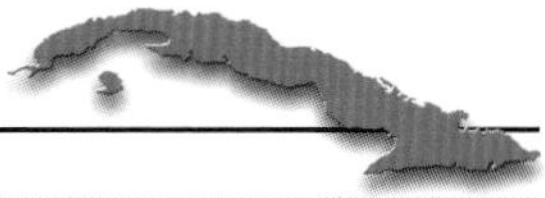

National Telephone Codes

Pinar del Río 48.

Artemisa 47 (Bahía Honda, San Cristóbal and Candelaria 48).

Havana 7.

Mayabeque 47.

Matanzas 45.

Island of Youth 46.

(Cayo Largo del Sur 45).

Cienfuegos 43.

Villa Clara 42.

Sancti Spíritus 41 (Condado, El Pedrero and Topes de Collantes 42).

Ciego de Ávila 33 (Mamanantuabo 32).

Camagüey 32.

Las Tunas 31.

Holguín 24.

Granma 23.

Santiago de Cuba 22.

Guantánamo 21.

On arriving to Cuba you can get cell phone service from Cubacel. You can either hire a phone or bring your own and activate it. Contact Cubacel through its telephone number 5 2642266 or by email at cubacel@cubacel.cu, cubacel@cubacel.com. Visit its webpage at www.cubacel.cu.

For further information, please visit www.etecsa.cu.

Internet access

There is Internet access at most hotels and at important tourist facilities. At many cities and tourist destinations there are cybercafés. Connection is generally by modem (*dial up*) and is not very fast.

Photographs

You can take photos and tape video freely in any part of the country, except at restricted areas as indicated by signs, such as military zones and others. Museums and some sites of interests have specific regulations. For color photographs, the best time of day is between 09:30 and 11:30, and after 16:30.

Medical attention and Health insurance

With general primary healthcare services and a network of high quality hospital facilities, Cuba also has institutions dedicated to the treatment of dermatological conditions, pigmentary retinosis and ophthalmological diseases, among many others.

There are also international pharmacies and clinics, as well as opticians. More than 95 percent of hotels have a house physician for guaranteeing primary attention to guests.

Since May 2010, visitors must have travel insurance with medical coverage that includes medical expenses or a medical expenses insurance policy. Either one should cover Cuba. The policy should be taken out at the point of departure for Cuba. A traveler that exceptionally has no insurance policy at the moment of arrival can take out a policy that covers insurance and assistance with a Cuban insurer at the airport, port or marina of arrival. Travel insurance taken out with Cuban insurance companies has round the clock and all year round assistance service to the traveler in Cuba through Asistur. (www.asistur.cu).

Currency

The national currency is the Cuban peso, equal to 100 cents. There are 1, 3, 5, 10, 20, 50 and 100 pesos bills; and 1, 2, 5, and 20 cents coins, as well as 1 and 3 pesos coins. At foreign exchange outlets (CADECA), you can buy/sell Cuban convertible pesos (CUC). The present exchange rate is 20-25 Cuban pesos for 1 Cuban convertible peso. The official exchange rate of the convertible peso to the US dollar is 1:1 in the whole country, both for exchange operations in the entrepreneurial sector and for visitors and locals at CADECA. A 10 percent tax is still in force for buying convertible pesos with US dollars.

Cuban convertible pesos (CUC)

Cuban pesos

Forms of payment

The official currency is the Cuban peso and its import and export is not allowed. The convertible peso (CUC) is equivalent to the US dollar and has the same use in the national territory. US dollars are no longer in circulation. Tourists are advised not to bring US dollars, for there is a 10 percent tax when exchanging it for Cuban currency. At international marinas, cruiser terminals and duty free shops in airports, you may pay with US dollars, for the 10 percent tax is included in the price of products.

You may pay directly in Euros in Varadero, Cayo Largo, Jardines del Rey, Santa Lucía Beach in Camagüey, Covarrubias Beach in Las Tunas and on all beaches in Holguín (Guardalavaca, Don Lino, Esmeralda, Pesquero). Any foreign currency, including US dollars, may be changed into convertible pesos (CUC) at airports, banks and hotels, as well as change them back on leaving the country. There are CADECAs all over the country for changing foreign currency into Cuban pesos and convertible pesos. There are several banking entities in the country with modern technology and interconnectivity. Prices at tourist facilities are set in CUC. Bacal, Transcard, Visa and MasterCard credit cards are accepted as long as they are not issued by US banks or their branches. There are also national payment systems issued by the Banco Financiero Internacional (BFI card) and the Red card issued by Banco de Crédito y Comercio, Metropolitano, Popular de Ahorro and BICSA.

For information about rates of exchange of the CUC with other currencies, visit the Cuba's Central Bank website at http://www.bc.gov.cu

Safety in Cuba

Cuba is one of the safest countries in Latin America with a relatively low rate of violent crimes. Assaults are very uncommon, although it is recommended to take precautions at night and away from the city's center or in isolated places.

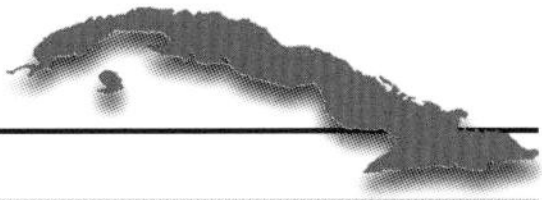

CUBA'S TOURIST INFORMATION

Main Cuban tourist destinations

Havana.
Varadero.
Holguín.
Jardines del Rey
(Cayo Coco and Cayo Guillermo).
Cayo Largo del Sur.
Santiago de Cuba.
Santa Lucía de Cuba.
Trinidad.
Cienfuegos.
Pinar del Río.
Península de Zapata.
Villa Clara.
Granma.
Las Tunas.
Baracoa.

Lodgings

Cuba has an ample offer in lodgings all over the country, ranging from de luxe resorts to 2, 3, 4 and star hotels, bungalows, apartho-tels, hostels, villas, tourist communities, spas and even private homes

Several Cuban hotel chains operate in the island, as well as companies from other countries, such as Sol Meliá, Accor, Barceló, Occidental Hoteles, IberoStar, LTI, Red Deer, Sandals, Blau Hoteles and Superclub, among others.

Cubanacán: With over 70 hotels and 15,000 rooms, the leader of the Cuban tourist industry is also associated with solid international hotel chains. Besides its city hotels, it has positioned its sun and sand brands Brisas and Club Amigo. It also is beginning to position Horizontes, with hotels in natural environments.

Gran Caribe: Its hotels are well known for their excellence and quality and are found in Havana, Varadero, Cayo Largo, Cayo Guillermo, Cayo Coco, Santiago de Cuba and Cienfuegos. It also has other facilities, such as restaurants and night clubs.

Gaviota: Among its objectives are the promotion and sale of hotel and tourist services, as well as health care, water sports, fishing, diving and other offers. It also guarantees a trustworthy and safe Nature tourism.

Islazul: Targeting mainly domestic tourism, the chain has hotel facilities as well as others in beaches, cities and Nature all over the country.

Habaguanex: Sole manager in Old Havana of every type of industry, hotel facilities, restaurants and other activities for tourism in the Historical Center.

Popular Camping Consortium: Focused on camping and ecotourism.

Web pages on tourist development in Cuba

Portal of tourism in Cuba (www.cubatravel.cu).
Cubanacán (www.cubanacan.cu)
Gran Caribe (www.gran-caribe.com).
Gaviota (www.gaviota-grupo.com).
Habaguanex (www.habaguanex.cu).
Islazul (www.islazul.cu).
Cubamar (www.cubamarviajes.cu).
Cubatur (www.cubatur.cu).
Transtur (www.transturcuba.com).
Publicitur (www.publicitur.com).
Infotur (www.infotur.cu).
Cuba's Convention Bureau (www.cubameeting.co.cu).

CUBA'S TOURIST INFORMATION

Tourism Offices abroad

For the promotion of Cuba's tourism abroad and to strengthen the product's positioning, the country has offices in its main markets.

Argentina /928 Marcelo T. de Alvear St. (4th floor) C.F., Argentina/Tel.: (54-11)-4326-7810 / 4326-7995/ info@turismodecuba.com.ar.

Benelux/ Bierstraat, 12B 3011 XA, Low Countries/Tel.: (0031)10 2136403/ direccion@nunaarcuba.nl; info@nunaarcuba.nl.

Canada (Montreal) / 2075 Rue University Bureau 460, Montreal Quebec H3A 2L1, Canada/Tel.: 514- 875 8004/ http://www.gocuba.ca.

Canada (Toronto)/ Cuba Tourist Board, 1200 Bay St., Suite 305 Toronto, Ontario M5R 2A5, Canada/Tel.: 1-416-362-0700 through 02/ info@gocuba.ca/ http://www.gocuba.ca.

China /Room 303, Building 6, 93 Wanda Plaza, Jianguo Road, Chaoyang District, 100022, China/Tel.: 86-10- 5820 6825 / director@cubatravel.cn; inf@cubatravel.cn.

France/ 280 Boulevard Raspail Paris 75014, France/Tel.: 33 (0) (1-45) 38-9010/ ot.cuba@wanadoo.fr.

Germany /Kaiserstrasse 8 Frankfurt D-60313, Germany/Tel.: 0049 (069) 288322 and 23/ info@cubainfo.de / http://www.cubainfo.de.

Italy /30 Via Fara, Milan 20124, Italy/Tel.: (0039-02) 6698-1463/ info@cuba-si.it/ http://www.cuba-si.it.

Mexico/ 71 Shakespeare St., Apt. 302 Col. Anzures C.P 11590 Del. Miguel Hidalgo, Mexico/Tel.: (00 52 55) 5250-7974 / 5255-0663/ direccion@conocecuba.com.mx.

Russia /Kutuzovski Prospekt 9/2, kv. 66 Moscow 112248, Russia/Tel.: (7-095) 933 5986/ cubaturismo@mtu-net.ru.

Spain/ 50 Paseo de La Habana, Ground Floor D, CP: 28036, Madrid 28036, Spain/Tel.: 34-91-411-3097/ info@descubracuba.es / http://www.descubracuba.com.

Sweden/ 26 B Karlbergsvägen, 113 27, Postal Address: Box 45140, 104 30, Sweden /Tel.: 46 8 315360/ info@vivacuba.se/ www.vivacuba.se.

United Kingdom/ 54 Shaftesbury Avenue (first floor) London WC 2H8JT, UK/Tel.: (0-207) 240-6655/ tourism@travel2cuba.co.uk /www.travel2cuba.co.uk.

Venezuela/ Francisco de Miranda Ave., Torre Provincial Building. B Tower, 10th floor, Ofic. 104 Chacao, Caracas, Venezuela/Tel.: 58212 2672268 / ofiturven@cantv.net.

Travel agencies

Amistur / 406 Paseo St., between 17 and 19, Havana/Tel.: (537) 8332374.

Cubadeportes/ 706 20 St., between 7th and 9th, Miramar, Havana/ Tel.: (537) 2040945.

Cubamar / 3rd St., between 12 and Malecón, Havana/Tel.: (537) 8301220.

Cubanacán Travel Agency, Head Office/71 17A St., between 174 and 190, Havana/Tel.: (537) 2089920.

Cubatur, Head Office /410 15 St., between F and G, Vedado, Havana/Tel.: (537) 835 2902, 835 3790.

Ecotur/ 34 St., between 49 and 49 A, Kohly, Havana/Tel.: (537) 2045188.

Gaviota Tours, Head Office /2833 47th Ave., between 28 and 34, Kohly, Havana / Tel. (537) 2047526, 2079481.

Havanatur, Head Office/ 3rd St. on 74, Miramar, Havana/Tel.: (537) 2019752.

Paradiso, Head Office / 23 St. on P St., Vedado, Havana/ Tel. (537) 8365380.

San Cristóbal /110 Oficios St., between Lamparilla and Amargura St., Old Havana/ Tel.: (537) 8619171.

Sol y Son Los Viajes/ 64 23rd St., on P St., Vedado, Havana/Tel.:(537) 8330294.

Universitur /768-1 30St., between Kohly Ave. and 41, Nuevo Vedado, Havana/Tel.: (537) 555557.

CUBA'S TOURIST INFORMATION

Ministry of Tourism Territorial Delegations

Pinar del Río

Maceo núm. 117 e/ Antonio Tarafa y Rafael Morales, Pinar del Río/ Tel.: (5348) 754803/e-mail: infotur@minturpr.co.cu .

Havana

Calle 110 núm. 318 e/ 3ra y 5ta, Miramar, Playa/Tel.: (537) 204 5555, 2069778/ e-mail: delegado@mintur.cha.cyt.cu.

Matanzas-Varadero

1ra. Avenida e/ 13 y 14, Varadero, Matanzas/ Tel.: (5345) 667163, 612953, 667379/ Fax: (5345) 667379/ e-mail: delegado@mintur.var.cyt.cu.

Isle of Youth

Empresa Turística Gran Caribe Cayo Largo/ Archipiélago Canarreos, Isla de la Juventud/ Tel.: (5345) 24 8155/Fax: (5345) 24 8212/e- mail: director@dtcls.tur.cu.

Cienfuegos

Calle 37 núm. 1406 e/ 14 y 16. Punta Gorda, Cienfuegos/Tel.: (5343) 551631, 551107/ Fax: (5343) 551632 /e-mail: delegado@mintur.cfg.cyt.cu.

Villa Clara

Calle. Maceo núm. 453 e/ Caridad y Carretera Central /Tel.: (5342) 218611, 208600/ Fax: (53 42) 208600 / e--mail: minturvc@mintur.vcl.cyt.cu.

Sancti Spíritus-Trinidad

Vicente Sullam núm. 13 e/ Pablo Pi y Cándido Benítez, Trinidad, Sancti Spíritus/ Tel.: (5341) 96 443, 96 377/ Fax: (5341) 96378/ e-mail: delegado@mintur.tdad.tur.cu, minturss.secre@enet.cu.

Ciego de Ávila

Máximo Gómez núm. 82 e/ Honorato del Castillo y Ciego de Ávila / Tel.: (5333) 26 6641, 26 6402/ Fax: (5333) 26 6300/ E-mail: zamora@mintur.cya.cyt.cu.

Camagüey-Santa Lucía Beach

Céspedes y Carretera Central, Rpto. Jayamá/Tel.: (5332) 271851, 272162/ Fax: (5332) 287149/ e-mail: bertica@mintur.cmg.cyt.cu.

Las Tunas

Calle Francisco Varona 298, Las Tunas / Tel.: (5331) 37 2717/ 37 1512.

Granma

Calle Martí núm. 178 e/ Saco y Figueredo, Bayamo, Granma/ Tel.: (5323) 42 6969/ Fax: (5323) 42 7399 / e-mail: delegado@minturgr.co.cu.

Holguín

Calle Habana núm. 13 e/ Libertad y Maceo/ Tel.: (5324) 461417, 424133; 468500/ e-mail: deleg@mintur.hlg.tur.cu.

Santiago de Cuba

Carretera Central esquina Yarayó s/n, Santiago de Cuba/Tel.: (5322) 62 9047, 62 3894/ Fax: (5322) 68 6118/e-mail: delegado@mintur.cu.co.

Guantánamo

Calle Calixto García num. 1057 e/ Mármol y Varona, Guantánamo/ Tel.:(5321) 35 5991/ Fax: (5321) 35 5818/ e-mail: minturgt@enet.cu.

CUBA'S TOURIST INFORMATION

Tourist Information Centers in Cuba (INFOTUR)

All over the country there is a network of tourist information centers (INFOTUR) where you can get additional information to complement this directory, as well as for knowing other details (www.infotur.cu).

5ta. on 112, Miramar / 5th on 112, Miramar, Havana/ Tel.: (537) 2047036.

13 St., Downtown Varadero/ 1st. Ave. on 13 St., Acuazul Hotel, Varadero/ Tel. (5345) 66 2966/ 66 2961.

Baracoa/ 129 A Maceo St., between Frank País and Maravi, Guantánamo/ Tel.: (5321) 641781.

Camagüey/ Ignacio Agramonte International Airport, Finlay Ave., Km 7½, Office 4, Zone 4, Camagüey/ Tel.: (5332) 26 5805 / 26 5807.

Céspedes Plaza/ 701 Lacret 701 St. on Heredia, Santiago de Cuba/ Tel.: (5322) 669401.

Ciego de Ávila / Honorato del Castillo St., 12-Story Building, Ciego de Avila/ Tel.: (5333) 209109.

Cienfuegos / 37 St. on 18, Cienfuegos/ Tel.: (5343) 514653.

Frank País International Airport/ Bayamo Highway, Km 15/ Holguín/ Tel.: (5324) 474774.

Granma /178 Martí St., between Saco and Figueredo, Granma/ Tel.: (5323) 422599.

Guanabo/ 5th Ave., between 468 and 470, Guanabo, Havana /Tel.: (537) 7964139.

Guantánamo Hotel / 13 Norte St. on Ahogados, Guantánamo/ Tel.(5321) 385838.

Hicacos Mall/ 1st. Ave., between 44 and 46, Varadero/ Tel.: (5345) 667044.

Holguín /Pico Cristal, Libertad St. on Martí, Holguín/ Tel.: (5324) 425013, 425003.

Jardines del Rey Airport/ Cayo Coco/ Ciego de Ávila/ Tel. (5333) 309109.

José Martí International Airport, Terminal 3/ Wajay Highway, Km 3 ½ , Havana/ Tel. (537) 2664094.

Las Tunas /298 Francisco Varona St., Las Tunas/ Tel.: (5331) 37 2717/ 37 1512.

Obispo/ 524 Obispo St., between Bernaza and Villegas, Old Havana/ Tel.: (537) 8663333 / 8664153.

Pinar del Río's MINTUR Delegation/ 117 Maceo St., between Antonio Tarafa and Rafael Morales, Pinar del Río, Tel.: (5348) 754803.

Quitrin / Obispo on San Ignacio, Old Havana/ Tel.: (537) 8636884.

Santa María del Mar/Las Terrazas Ave., between 10 and 11, Sta. María, Playas del Este, Havana/ Tel.: (537) 7971261.

Santiago Airport/ Antonio Maceo International Airport, Santiago de Cuba/ Tel.: (5322) 692099/ 692113/ 698864 .

Trinidad /Camilo Cienfuegos on Santa Ana, Sancti Spíritus/Tel.: (5341) 99 8257-58.

Villa Clara/ Abel Santamaría Cuadrado International Airport, Maleza Highway, Km 11, Villa Clara/Tel.: (5342)214402/ 227546.

Viñales /63B Salvador Cisneros St., , Viñales, Pinar del Río/Tel.: (5348) 796263 .

Vueltabajo Hotel/103 Martí St. on Rafael Morales, Pinar del Río/Tel.: (5348) 728616.

CUBA'S TOURIST INFORMATION

Nature

Cuba has magnificent natural sceneries, and besides its proven beauty several areas have been acknowledged by UNESCO as Reserves of the Biosphere. The country also has an important number of protected areas.

National Parks

Guanahacabibes National Park, Pinar de Río.

La Güira National Park, Pinar del Río.

Viñales, Pinar del Río.

Caguanes, Sancti Spíritus.

Topes de Collantes National Park, Sancti Spíritus.

La Mensura National Park, Holguín.

Bahía de Naranjo Natural Park, Holguín.

Cristal Peak, Holguín.

Sierra Maestra National Park, Granma.

Turquino National Park, Granma and Santiago de Cuba.

Granma's Landing Great National Park, Granma.

Alexander von Humboldt National Park, Holguín and Guantánamo.

Punta Francés Marine National Park, Isle of Youth.

Reserves of the Biosphere .

Guanahacabibes, Pinar del Río.

Rosario Mountain Range, Pinar del Río.

Zapata Swamp, Matanzas.

Buenavista Park, Sancti Spíritus-Villa Clara-Ciego de Ávila, part of which is Caguanes Park.

Alexander von Humboldt National Park, Holguín and Guantánamo.

Baconao.

Ramsar Sites (wetlands ecosystem of international importance)

Zapata Swamp.

Buenavista Park, Sancti Spíritus-Villa Clara-Ciego de Ávila, part of which is Caguanes Park.

Delta of the Cauto River.

Other natural parks

Metropolitan Park, Havana.

Lenin Park, Havana.

Country Club, Camagüey.

CUBA'S TOURIST INFORMATION

Events

Congresses, conventions and meetings, among other events, have a special importance in Cuba, one of the first destinations in Latin American for this type of tourism. There are convention centers in the country equipped with modern computing and communications system, as well as exhibition sites, which have the added value of the ability and professionalism of the staff in charge of organizing events.

Havana

Chamber of Commerce /661 21 St., El Vedado/Tel.: (537)8381452, 8333042.

Cuba's Convention Bureau / Neptuno Hotel, 3rd. St., between 70 and 74, Miramar, Playa/Tel.:(537) 2048273, 2048274.

EXPOCUBA/ Rocío Highway, Km 3½, Calabazar/Tel.: (537) 6974252, 6974253.

Havana Convention Palace / 146 on 11 Ave., Playa/Tel.: (537) 2096435, 2080523.

Pabellón Cuba/ 266 N St., La Rampa, El Vedado/Tel.: (537) 8323511.

PABEXPO/ 174 17 St., Playa/Tel.: (537) 2710758.

Matanzas

Plaza América/ Sur Expressway, Km 11½, Varadero/Tel.: (5345)668163.

Villa Clara

EXPOCENTRO/Arcoiris, Santa Clara/ Tel.: (5342)293374.

Camagüey

Conventions Bureau/Céspedes Jayamá, Camagüey/Tel.: (5332) 271851, 272162.

Holguín

EXPOHOLGUÍN/244 Libertadores St./ Tel.: (5324)480315, 482280.

Guantánamo

Pabellón Guantánamo/P.A. Pérez/Tel.: (5321)322208.

CUBA'S TOURIST INFORMATION

International and National Airports

Abel Santamaría/ Maleza Highway, Km 11, Santa Clara/ Tel.:(5342) 209138 / 227525 / 227551 (International).

Antonio Maceo/ Ciudamar Highway, Km 2 ½ , Santiago de Cuba/ Tel.: (5322) 69 8614/69 8612 (International).

Cayo Las Brujas/ Cayo Las Brujas, Northeast Keys, Villa Clara/ Tel.:(5342) 350009 – 350064 (International).

Frank País/ Central Highway to Bayamo, Km 11 ½, Holguín/Tel.(5324) 474630 (International).

Ignacio Agramonte/ Finlay Ave., Km. 7½, Camagüey/Tel.:(5332) 26 1010 / 26 7292 (International).

Jaime González / Caonao Highway, Km 3, Cienfuegos/ Tel.:(5342) 551328 (International).

Jardines del Rey/ Cayo Coco, Ciego de Ávila/ Tel.: (5333) 309106 and 309161 to 65 (International).

José Martí /Van Troi Ave. on Final, Havana/ Tel.: (537) 2664644 (International).

Switchboard: 2751200 and 6420100.

Flight Information: 2664133 and 649 5666.

Lost and Found Baggage: 2751424 – 6426172 - 2751374 / Waiting List: 2751456 / Complaints: 6426742.

Juan Gualberto Gómez/ Mártires de Barbados Ave., Km 5, Matanzas/Tel.:(5345) 613016/ 247015(International).

Sierra Maestra / Cayo Espino Highway, Km 7, Manzanillo, Granma/ Tel.:(5323) 57 7520 /57 7401 (International).

Vitalio Acuña / Cayo Largo, Isle of Youth / Tel.: (5345) 248181 - 248364 (International).

Alberto Delgado /Alberto Delgado, Sanctí Spíritus/ Tel.: (5341) 99 6393 (National).

Carlos Manuel de Céspedes/ Bayamo to Holguín Highway, Bayamo, Granma/ Tel.: (5323) 42 7514/ 42 7916 (National).

Gustavo Rizo/ Jaitecico Highway, Guantánamo/ Tel.: (5321) 645376 (National).

Hermanos Ameijeiras/ Rafael Martínez, Las Tunas/ Tel.:(5331) 346873 (National).

Joaquín de Agüero/ Palmas de Lucía, Santa Lucía Beach, Camagüey/ Tel.:(5332) 33 6362 (National).

La Coloma/ Pinar del Río (National) /Tel.: (5348) 750106.

Mariana Grajales/ Paraguay Highway, Guantánamo/ Tel.:(5321) 355912 (National).

Máximo Gómez / Caunao Highway, Km. 3, Ciego de Ávila (National)/ Tel.: (5333) 266003.

Orestes Acosta / R. Monterrey, Holguín/ Tel.: (5324) 607012, 607916 (National).

Rafael Cabrera/ Highway to the Airport, Km 5, Isle of Youth / Tel.: (5346) 322300 and 322531.

CUBA'S TOURIST INFORMATION

Airlines

Aerocaribbean/Calle 23 núm. 64, Vedado, Plaza de la Revolución, Havana/ Tel.:(53 7) 8327584.

Aeroflot/ 5ta.Ave e/76 y 78, Edificio Barcelona, Ofic. 208, Centro de Negocios Miramar, Playa, Havana/Tel:(537) 2043200, 2043758/Fax:(53 7) 2045593.

Aerogaviota/ Ave. 47 núm. 2814, Reparto Kohly. Playa, Havana/Tel:(53 7) 2030668, 2030686/ Fax:(53 7) 2042621.

Aeropostal/ Hotel Habana Libre Tryp, Plaza de la Revolución, Havana/ Tel:(537) 8384000, 8384203 .

Aerotaxi/ Calle 24 y Ave. de la Playa, Varadero, Matanzas/Tel:(5345) 667540, 612929.

Aerotaxi /Calle 27 núm. 102 e/ M y N, Vedado, Plaza de la Revolución, Havana/ Tel:(537) 8334064/ Fax:(537) 8334063.

Aerovaradero S.A. (TAME)/ Calle 23 núm. 64, Vedado, Plaza de la Revolución, Havana/Tel:(537) 8330012, 8334126/ Fax:(537) 8334126.

Aerovías Caribe/Calle 23 núm. 64, Vedado, Plaza de la Revolución, Havana/Tel:(53 7) 8333621, 8334423/ Fax:(537) 8333871.

Air Canada/Calle 23 y P, El Vedado, Havana/ Tel:(537) 8363226, 8363227.

Air Europa/ 5ta.Ave, e/ 76 y 78, Edificio Santiago, Centro de Negocios de Miramar, Playa/Tel:(537) 204 6904, 666919/Fax:(537) 204 6905 .

Air Europe/ Edificio Lonja del Comercio, piso 2, Oficina M, La Habana Vieja, Havana/Tel:(537) 8666745 .

Air France/ Calle 23 núm. 64 esq. a Infanta, Vedado. Plaza de la Revolución, Havana/Tel.:(537) 8332642/ Fax:(537) 8332634.

ALM, Compañía Antillana de Aviación/ Calle 23 esq. a E, Vedado, Plaza de la Revolución, Havana/ Tel:(537) 8333729, 8333730/ Fax:(537) 8333732.

AOM-French Airlines/ Calle 23 núm. 64, interior, Vedado, Plaza de la Revolución, Havana/ Tel:(537) 8334098, 8333997, 8333783/ Fax:(537) 8333783.

Avianca Sam/ Hotel Nacional de Cuba, Mezanine, Plaza de la Revolución, Havana/ Tel:(537) 8334700, 8334701/Fax:(537) 8334702.

Blue Panorama/23 y L, El Vedado/Tel.: (537) 8360213.

Copa Airlines/ Calle 23 núm. 64, interior, Vedado. Plaza de la Revolución, Havana / Tel:(537) 8331758, 8333657/Fax:(537) 8333951.

Cubana de Aviación.

Calle Chico Valdés núm. 83, Ciego de Ávila/ Tel:(53 33) 22-5316.

Calle Libertad y Martí, Edificio Pico de Cristal, 2do piso Policentro, Holguín/ Tel:(53 24) 42-5707/ Fax:(53 24) 46-8111.

Ave. del Puerto núm. 6, Reparto Rolo Monterrey, Moa, Holguín/ Tel:(53 24) 67916.

Calle Maceo núm. 70 e/ Marcham y Villuenda, Manzanillo, Granma/Tel:(53 23) 2800.

Calle Martí núm. 52 e/ Parada y Rojas, Bayamo, Granma/ Tel:(53 23) 423916.

Calle Santo Tomás e/ Heredia y San Basilio, Santiago de Cuba/ Tel:(53226) 624156, 622290.

Calle Calixto García núm. 817 e/ Prado y Aguilera, Guantánamo/ Tel:(5321) 34533.

Calle Martí núm. 181, Baracoa, Guantánamo/ Tel:(5321) 42171.

Calle 39 núm. 1415 e/ 16 y 18, Nueva Gerona. Isla de la Juventud/ Tel:(5346) 322531, 324259.

Calle 11, Barlovento. Varadero, Matanzas/ Tel:(5345) 613016.

Calle República núm. 400 esq. a Correa, Camagüey/Tel:(5332) 91328, 92156.

Calle Lucas Ortiz esq. a 24 de Febrero, Las Tunas/ Tel:(5331) 42702.

(Domestic Flights)/ Calle Infanta y Humboldt, Vedado. Plaza de la Revolución, La Habana/ Tel:(537) 8334446, 8334950.

(International Flights)/ Calle 23 e Infanta, Vedado. Plaza de la Revolución, La Habana/Tel:(537) 8334949, 8334950, 8334446 al 49/Fax:(537) 8335177 al 79.

Grupo TACA/Hotel Habana Libre Tryp. Plaza de la Revolución, Havana / Tel:(53 7) 8333114, 8333187/ Fax:(537) 8333728.

Iberia/ Centro de Negocios Miramar, en edificio Santiago de Cuba, planta baja, 5ta. Ave, esquina a 76, Miramar, Playa / Tel.:(537) 2043454.

LTU-Balair Condor/ Calle 23 núm. 64, Vedado. Plaza de la Revolución, Havana/ Tel:(537) 8333524, 8333525/ Fax:(537) 8333590.

Martinair Holland/ Calle 23 esq. a E, Vedado. Plaza de la Revolución, Havana/ Tel:(537) 8333729, 8333730/Fax:(537) 8333732.

Martinair Holland/ Aeropuerto Internacional Juan G. Gómez, Varadero, Matanzas/Tel:(5345) 253624/ Fax:(5345) 253624.

Mexicana de Aviación/ Calle 23 núm. 64, Vedado, Plaza de la Revolución, Havana/Tel:(537) 8333533, 8333532.

TAAG/ Calle 23 núm. 64, interior, Vedado. Plaza de la Revolución, Havana/ Tel:(53 7) 8333527, 8333528/Fax:(53 7) 8333049.

Embassies in Havana, Cuba

Algeria / 5ta. Ave. núm.2802 esq. a 28, Miramar / Tel.: (537) 2042835, 2042538.

Angola/5ta. Ave. núm.1012 e/ 10 y 12, Miramar / Tel.: (537) 2044391-92, 2042474.

Antigua and Barbuda /5ta. Ave. núm. 6407, esq. a 66 Miramar/ Tel.: (537) 2079756.

Argentina/ Calle 36 núm.511 e/ 5ta. y 7ma., Miramar /Tel.:(537) 2042565, 2042549, 2042972, Consular Section, Tel (537) 2042573.

Austria/ Ave. 5ta.A núm.6617 esq. a 70, Miramar / Tel.: (537) 2042394, 2042825.

Azerbaijan/ 5ta. Ave. núm.9608 e/ 96 y 96 A, Miramar /Tel.: (537) 2079280.

Bahamas/ 5ta. Ave. núm.3006 e/30 y 32, Miramar / Tel.: (537) 2069918, 2069919.

Barbados/ Calle 18 No. 715 e/ 7ma y 31, Miramar /Tel.: (537) 212-5894, 212-5895.

Belarus/ Calle 5ta.A núm.6405 e/ 64 y 66, Miramar / Tel.:(537) 2047330-31.

Belgium/ Calle 8 núm.309 e/ 3ra. y 5ta., Miramar / Tel.: (537) 2044806.

Belize/ Calle 5ta A núm. 3608 e/ 36 y 36 A, Miramar /Tel.: (537) 2043504.

Benin /Calle 20 núm.119 e/ 1ra. y 3ra., Miramar / Tel.: (537) 2042179.

Bolivia/ Calle 3ª núm. 3601 e/ 36ª y 38, Miramar / Tel.: (537) 2042426/2079501.

Brazil/Lonja del Comercio, Lamparilla núm. 2, 4to. Piso, Old Havana/Tel.: (537) 8669051-52, 8669080, 8662910, Consular Section, Tel.: (537) 8616791.

Bulgaria /Calle B núm.252 e/ 11 y 13, Vedado / Tel.: (537) 8333125, 8333126.

Burkina Faso/ Calle 40 núm. 516 e/ 5ta.A y 7ma., Miramar /Tel.: (537) 2042217, 2042895.

Cabo Verde/ Calle 20 núm. 2001 esq. a 7ma., Miramar /Tel.: (537) 2042979 y 2125296.

Cambodia/ 5ta. Ave. núm.7001 e/ 70 y 72, Miramar /Tel.: (537) 2041496.

Canada/ Calle 30 núm.518 esq. a 7ma. Ave., Miramar /Tel.: (537) 2042516-17, 2042527, 2042382.

Chile / Calle 33 núm.1423 e/ 14 y 18, Miramar / Tel.: (537) 2041222, 2041223.

Colombia/ Calle 14 núm.515 e/ 5ta. y 7ma., Miramar /Tel.: (537) 2049644, 2049645, 2041248. General Consulate, Tel.: 2041246/47.

Congo /5ta. Ave. núm.1003 e/ 10 y 12, Miramar, La Habana/Tel.: (537) 2049055.

Costa Rica, 5ta. Ave núm. 6604, e/ 66 y 68, Miramar/ Tel (537) 2046938.

Cyprus /Calle 5ª Ave núm. 8409, e/ 84 y 86, Miramar /Tel.: (537) 2125228/5229.

Czech Republic/ Ave. Kohly núm.259 e/ 41 y 43, Nuevo Vedado /Tel.: (537) 8833201, 8833467.

Djibouti / Calle 22 núm. 518 esq. a 7ma, Miramar /Tel.: (537) 2079622 y 2141113.

Dominica/Calle 36 núm. 507 e/ 5ta. y 7ma., Miramar /Tel.: (537) 2141096.

Dominican Republic/ Ave. 5ta. núm.9202 e/ 92 y 94, Miramar /Tel.: (537) 2048429, 2048430.

Ecuador/ Ave. 5ta.A núm. 4407 e/ 44 y 46, Miramar /Tel.: (537) 2042034 - 2042868 y 2141425.

Egypt/ 5ta. Ave. núm.1801 esq. a 18, Miramar / Tel.: (537) 2042441, 2042542.

El Salvador/Calle 24 núm. 307, e/ 3ra y 5ta, Miramar/Tel.: (537) 212-5612 y 212-5902.

Equatorial Guinea / 3rd. Ave. núm. 1001, e/ 10 y12, Miramar /Tel.: (537) 2041720, 2069675.

Ethiopia/ 5ta. Ave. núm.6604 Apto. 3 e/ 66 y 68, Miramar /Tel.: (537) 2069905.

European Union / 5ta. Ave. núm. 2007 esq. a 22, Miramar /Tel.: (537) 2040327, 2040357, 2040201, 2040299, Apartado Postal 11300.

FAO / Calle 154 núm.301, Rpto. Náutico /Tel.: (537) 2086411-13.

France / Calle 14 núm. 312 e/ 3ra. y 5ta., Miramar /Tel.: (537) 2013131, 2013121 y 2013118 (Emergencies)

Gambia/ Calle 24 núm.307 e/ 5ta. y 3ra., Miramar /Tel.: (537) 2049242.

Germany/Calle 13 núm.652 esq. a B, El Vedado / Tel.: (537) 8332569, 8332539, 8332460, Consular Section, Tel.: (537) 8333188.

Ghana/ 5ta. Ave. núm.1808 esq. a 20, Miramar / Tel.: (537) 2042153, 2042613.

Greece/ 5ta. Ave. núm.7802 esq. a 78, Miramar / Tel.: (537) 2042854, 2042995.

Grenada/ 5ta. Ave. núm.2006 e/ 20 y 22, Miramar /Tel.: (537) 2046764, 2048890.

Guatemala / Calle 20 núm. 301 e/ 3ra. y 5ta., Miramar /Tel.: (537) 2043417-19, 2048173.

Guinea Bissau/ 5ta. Ave. núm.8203 e/ 82 y 84, Miramar, La Habana/Tel.: (537) 2045742.

Guinea/ Calle 20 núm.504 e/ 5ta. y 7ma., Miramar /Tel.: (537) 2041894.

Guyana/ Calle 18 núm.506 e/ 5ta. y 7ma., Miramar /Tel.: (537) 2042249, 2069740.

Haiti/ Calle 7ma. núm. 4402 esq. a 44, Miramar / Tel.: (537) 2045421-22.

Holy See/ Calle 12 núm.514 e/ 5ta. y 7ma., Miramar /Tel.: (537) 2042700, 2042296.

Honduras/ Calle 3ra. núm.123 e/ 78 y 80, Edificio Habana, 1er. Piso, Oficina 102, Centro de Negocios de Miramar, Miramar /Tel.: (537) 2045496.

Hungary/ Calle G núm. 458 e/ 19 y 21, Vedado, La Habana/Tel.: (537) 8333365, 8333346.

India/ Calle 21 núm.202 esq. a K, Vedado / Tel.:(537) 8333169, 8333777, 8381700.

Indonesia /Ave. 5ta. núm.1607 esq. a 18, Miramar /Tel.: (537) 2049618, 2049963,2040046.

Islamic Republic of Iran /5ta. Ave. núm.3002 esq. a 30, Miramar /Tel.: (537) 2042597, 2042675, 2042950.

Embassies in Havana, Cuba

Italy / 5ta. Ave. núm. 402 esq. a 4, Miramar /Tel.: (537) 2045615.

Jamaica/ Calle 22 núm.503 e/ 5ta. y 7ma., Miramar /Tel.: (537) 2042908, 2046959 y 2069024.

Japan /Centro de Negocios Miramar. Edif. Jerusalén, 5to.piso Ave. 3ra. esq. a 80, Miramar /Tel.: (537) 2043508, 2043355, 2043598, 2043507, 2048904.

Kazakhstan /5ta. Ave. núm.2203 e/ 22 y 24, Miramar /Tel.: (537) 2069963.

Kuwait/ Hotel Nacional de Cuba (Provisional) /Tel.: (537) 8365769, Ext. 673 y 605, Fax (537) 8365055.

Laos /5ta. Ave. núm.2808 esq. a 30, Miramar /Tel.: (537) 2041057, 2041059.

Lebanon/ Calle 17-A núm.16403 e/ 164 y 174, Siboney /Tel.: (537) 2086220, 2086221.

Libya/ Calle 14 núm.1402 esq. a 7ma., Miramar / Tel.: (537) 2042192, 2042892.

Malaysia/ 5ta. Ave. núm.6612 e/ 66 y 68, Miramar /Tel.: (537) 2048883-84.

Mali/ Calle 36-A núm.704 e/ 7ma. y 42, Miramar / Tel.: (537) 2045321.

Mexico/ Calle 12 núm. 518 esq. a 7ma. Ave., Miramar /Tel.: (537) 2047722-25, 2042553, 2042583, 2042909, 2042498. Consular Section, Ave 7ma. núm.1206, Tel.: 2141433/38.

Mongolia/ Calle 66 núm. 505 esq. a 5ta.-A, Miramar, La Habana/Tel.: (537) 2042763.

Mozambique/ 7ma. Ave. núm. 2203 e/ 22 y 24, Miramar /Tel.: (537) 2042443, 2042445, 2079918.

Namibia/ Calle 36 núm.504 e/ 5ta. y 5ta.-A, Miramar / Tel.: (537) 2041428, 2041430.

Netherlands/ Calle 8 núm.307 e/ 3ra. y 5ta., Miramar /Tel.: (537) 2042511-12, 2042534, 2042708.

Nicaragua/ Calle 20 núm.709 e/ 7ma. y 9na., Miramar /Tel.: (537) 2041025, 2046323, 2045387, 2079641.

Nigeria / 5ta. Ave. núm.1401 e/ 14 y 16, Miramar/ Tel.: (537) 2042898, 2042091, 2049567.

Norway/ Calle 30 núm.315 e/ 3ra. y 5ta. Ave., Miramar / Tel.: (537) 2040696, 2044410-11.

Order of Malta/ Calle 182 núm. 115, e/ 1ª y 3ª, Reparto Flores / Tel.: (537) 2723350 y 052957663.

Pakistan / 5ta. Ave. núm.2606 e/ 26 y 28, Miramar /Tel.: (537) 2141151/52.

Panama / Calle 26 núm.109 e/ 1ra. y 3ra., Miramar/Tel.: (537) 2040858, 2041673.

Paraguay/ Calle 34 núm.503 e/ 5ta. y 7ma., Miramar /Tel.: (537) 2040884.

Peru /Calle 30 núm.107 e/ 1ra. y 3ra., Miramar / Tel.: (537) 2042632, 2043570. Consular Section, Tel.: 2042477.

Philippines/ 5ta. Ave. núm. 2207 esq. a 24, Miramar /Tel.: (537) 2041372, 2041551, 2041553.

PHO-WHO/ Calle 4 núm.407 e/ 17 y 19, Vedado / Tel.: (537) 8382526, 8382527.

Poland/ Calle G núm. 452 esq. a 19, Vedado /Tel.: (537) 8332439-40.

Popular Democratic Republic of Korea/ Calle 17 núm. 752 esq. a Paseo núm.752 /Tel.: (537) 2049055, 8332313.

Popular Republic of China / Calle C e/ 13 y 15, Vedado /Tel.: (537) 8333005, 8333614.

Portugal / Ave. 7ma. núm. 2207 esq. a 24, Miramar /Tel.: (537) 2042871, 2040149.

Qatar /Ave. 3ra. núm.3407 e/ 34 y 36, Miramar / Tel.: (537) 2040587, 2040590.

Rumania/ Calle 21 núm. 307 e/ H e I, Vedado /Tel.: (537) 8333322, 8333325.

Russia/ 5ta. Ave. núm. 6402 e/ 62 y 66, Miramar / Tel.: (537) 2042628, 2041080, 2041085, 2042686.

Sahrawi Arab Democratic Republic / 5ta. Ave. núm.8206 e/ 82 y 84, Miramar /Tel.: (537) 2041499, 2041045.

Saint Lucia/ Calle 12 núm. 511 E/ 5ta. y 7ma., Miramar /Tel.: (537) 2069609/10.

Saint Vincent and the Grenadines/ Centro de Negocios Miramar, Edif. Jerusalén, Oficina 403, 3a. Ave. e/ 76 y 78, Miramar /Tel.: (537) 2069783.

Serbia/ 5ta. Ave. núm. 4406 e/ 44 y 46, Miramar / Tel.: (537) 2042488, 2042607.

Slovakia / Calle 66 núm. 521 e/ 5ta.B y 7ma., Miramar /Tel.: (537) 2041884, 2041885.

South Africa /5ta. Ave. núm.4203 esq. a 42, Miramar /Tel.: (537) 2049671-76.

Spain/ Calle Cárcel núm. 51, esq. a Zulueta /Tel.: (537) 8668025, 8668026.

Sri Lanka/Calle 32 núm.307 e/ 3ra. y 5ta., Miramar, La Habana/Tel.: (537) 2042649, 2042562, 2079915.

State of Palestine/ Calle 20 núm.714 e/ 7ma. y 9na., Miramar /Tel.: (537) 2042556, 2079626.

Suriname/ Centro de Negocios de Miramar. Edificio Jerusalén. Oficina 106, Calle 3ª e/ 78 y 80, Miramar, La Habana/ Tel.: (537)2079559/2079563.

Sweden /Calle 34 núm. 510 e/ 5ta. y 7ma., Miramar, La Habana/Tel.: (537) 204 2831.

Switzerland/ 5ta. Ave. núm.2005 e/ 20 y 22, Miramar, La Habana /Tel.: (537) 2042611.

Syria/ Calle 20 núm.514 e/ 5ta. y 7ma., Miramar / Tel.: (537) 2042266, 2042434.

Timor L'Este /Calle 40ª núm.301, esq. a 3ra., Miramar /Tel.: (537) 206991/2125225/2079856.

Trinidad and Tobago/ 5ta. Ave. núm.6603 e/ 66 y 68, Miramar /Tel.: (537) 2079603.

Turkey / 5ta. Ave. núm.3805 e/ 36 y 40, Miramar / Tel.: (537) 2041204-05, 2042237, 2042933.

Ukraine /5ta. Ave. núm. 4405 e/ 44 y 46, Miramar /Tel.: (537) 2042586, Consular Section, Tel.: (537) 2042374.

UNESCO /Calzada núm. 551 esq. a D, Vedado, La Habana /Tel.: (537) 8321840, 8327741, 8327638, 8321787, 8333438.

Embassies in Havana, Cuba

UNICEF /Ave.1ra.-B núm.15802 esq. a 158, Rpto. Náutico, La Habana /Tel.: (537) 2086307, 2086094.

United Kingdom/ Calle 34 núm. 702 e/ 7ma. y 17, Miramar /Tel.: (537) 2142200, 2041771-72.

United Nations Development Program (UNDP) / Calle 18 No 110 e/ 1ra. y 3ra., Miramar/Tel.: (537) 2041512 -2041513- 2041515.

United States Interest Section/ Calzada e/ L y M, Vedado /Tel.: (537) 8333543-47, 8333551-59.

Uruguay/ Calle 36 núm.716 e/ 7ma. y 9na., Miramar /Tel.: (537) 2042311.

Venezuela / Calle 20 núm. 20512, e/ 5ta. y 7ma., Miramar /Tel.: (537) 2042662, 2042612, 2042497, 2042631.

Viet Nam/ 5ta. Ave. núm.1802 esq. a 18, Miramar, / Tel.: (537) 2041501.

World Food Program (WFP) / Calle 36 núm.724 e/ 7ma. y 17, Miramar /Tel.: (537) 2042039.

Yemen/ 5ta. Ave. núm.8201 e/ 82 y 84 Miramar / Tel.: (537) 2041506, 2043222, 2041509.

Zimbabwe/ 5ta. Ave núm. 1405, e/ 14 y16, Miramar /Tel.: (537) 2042837, 2042857.

General Consulates

Colombia/Calle 14 núm. 515, e/ 5ta y 7ma, Miramar, Havana/ Tel.: (537) 204-1246 y 204-1247/ Telefax: 204 1249/clahabana@cancilleria.gov.co.

Costa Rica/ 5ta Ave núm. 6604, e/ 66 y 68, Miramar, Havana/Tel.: 204 6938/Telefax: 204-6937/ cricacon@ceniai.inf.cu.

Dominican Republic/ Ave. 3ra, núm. 4609, e/ 46 y 60, Miramar, Havana/Tel.: (537) 204 3152 y 204 3154.

Russia/ Calle 66 núm. 318, esq. 5ta Miramar, Playa, Havana/ Tel.: (537) 2041074/Telefax: 2041987/ ruscons@enet.cu.

Spain/ Calle Zulueta núm. 2, esq. a Cárcel, HAvana/Teléfonos: 8686868/Telefax: 866 8015/ cog. lahabana@maec.es/ Work and Immigration Section at Lonja del Comercio, Oficina 4E. Lamparilla núm. 2, Old Havana, Tel.: (537) 8669014 y 8636029.

Venezuela/ 5ta Ave. núm. 1601, esq. a 16, Miramar, Havana/ Tel.:(537) 2079797/ Fax: (537) 2079790.

Consulates

San Marino / 5ta Ave. núm. 7806, esq. a 80, Apto. núm. 306, Miramar, Havana.

Honorary Consulates

Bangladesh / 3ra. Ave. núm. 2403, e/ 24 y 26, Miramar, Havana/Tel.: (537) 2040093 y 2040094/ banglacons@mincobre.co.cu.

Canada/ Holguín/Hotel Atlántico, Suite 1, Guardalavaca, Holguín/Tel.: (024) 430320.

Canada/ Varadero/Calle 13 núm. 422 e/ 1ra. y Camino del Mar, Varadero, Matanzas/Tel.: (045) 612078/Fax: (045) 667395.

Cyprus / Línea núm. 756, e/ Paseo y 2, Plaza de la Revolución, Havana/Tel.: (537)8302243/ 8801313/ 8806262.

Denmark/Paseo de Martí, Prado núm. 20, Apto. 4-B, Centro Habana/Tel.:(537) 8668128, 8668144 y 8669110.

Finland/ Calle 140, núm. 2101, e/ 21ª y 23, Cubanacán, Havana/Tel.:(537) 2040793

Mali/ Calle 13 núm. 507 Apto. 1, e/ D y E, Vedado, Havana/ Tel.: (537) 8329148.

Monaco/ Calle 36 núm. 108, e/ 3ra y 1ra, Miramar, Havana/Tel.: (537) 2045458/ Fax: 2049875/ monaco@enet.cu.

Spain/ Camagüey/ Calle Artola núm. 360 e/ Capdevila y Joaquín Agüero, Camagüey/ Tel.: (032) 283330.

Spain/ Santa Clara/ Carretera Central núm. 23, e/ 2da y 3ra, Santa Clara, Villa Clara/Tel.: (042) 203458.

Spain/ Santiago de Cuba/ Calle 11 núm. 203, e/ Fernández Mercané y Bravo Correoso, Santiago de Cuba/ Tel.: (022) 643030.

Thailand/ Calle 5ta Ave. esq a 80, Edif. Raffaello, 2do piso, Ofic. 210, Miramar, Havana/ Tel.: (537) 2044849.

Fire Festivities, Santiago de Cuba.

tourist directory

The present chapter of the guide is divided in three sections: **Western, Central,** and **Eastern regions**, which include the following headings: **Lodgings, Restaurants and Coffee-shops, Night Centers, Stores, Attractions, Water Sports,** and **Health Services.**

Lodgings

Pinar del Río

★★★ **Cabo de San Antonio Villa** (International Diving Center) / Guanahacabibes, San Antonio Cape, Sandino / Tel.: (5348) 757656 and 57 / comercial@mlagorda.co.cu / Fax: (5348) 757655.

★★★ **Horizontes La Ermita Hotel** (Nature) / La Ermita Highway, Km 1½, Viñales / Tel.: (5348) 796071 / reserva@ermita.co.cu / Fax (5348) 796069.

★★★ **Horizontes Los Jazmines Hotel** (Nature) / Viñales Highway, Km 25, Viñales / Tel.: (5348) 796205 / reserva@vinales.hor.tur.cu / Fax (5348) 796215.

★★★ **Horizontes Rancho San Vicente** (Nature) / Puerto Esperanza Highway, Km 33, Viñales / Tel.: (5348) 796201 and 796221 / reserva@vinales.rancho.co.cu / Fax: (5348) 796265.

★★★ **Islazul Mirador Hotel** (Nature) / 23 St. at the End, San Diego de los Baños, Los Palacios / Tel.: (5348) 778338 / carpeta@mirador.sandiego.co.cu/ Fax: (5348) 548866.

★★★ **María La Gorda Villa** (International Diving Center), Guanahacabibes Peninsula, Sandino / Tel.: (5348) 77 8131 / comercial@mlagorda.co.cu / Fax: (5348) 778077.

★★★ **Vueltabajo Hotel** (City) / 103 Martí St., on Rafael Morales / Tel: (5348) 759381 to 83/ reserva@vueltapr.co.cu

★★ **Aguas Claras Camping** (Nature) / Viñales Highway, Km 7 ½, Pinar del Río / Tel.: (5348) 778426-778427 / aguasclaras@enet.cu / Fax: (5348) 778426 / (Reservations at Cubamar).

★★ **Dos Hermanas Camping** (Nature) / Moncada Highway, Km 3, Viñales / Tel.: (5348) 793223 and 796167 (Reservations at Cubamar).

★★ **Horizontes Cayo Levisa** (Beach) / Palma Rubia Highway, La Palma / Tel.: (5348) 756501 to 05 / reservas@cayolevisa.co.cu / Fax: (5348) 756506.

★★ **Laguna Grande Hotel** (Nature) / Simón Bolívar Farm, Sandino / Tel.: (5348) 423823 and 423453 / Fax: (5348) 423453.

★★ **Pinar del Río Hotel** (City) / Martí St. on Final, Autopista / Tel.: (5348) 755070 to 74 reserva@hpr.co.cu / Fax: (5348) 771699.

Artemisa

★★★★ **Moka Hotel** (Nature) / Havana-Pinar del Río Expressway, Km 51, Las Terrazas Community, Candelaria / Tel: (5348) 578600 to 02 / hotel.carpeta@terraz.co.cu / Fax: (5348) 578605.

★★★ **Horizontes Soroa Villa** (Nature) / Soroa Highway, Km 8, Candelaria / Tel: (5348) 523534 and 523556 / reserva@hvs.co.cu / Fax: (5348) 523861.

★★★ **Las Yagrumas Hotel** (Nature) / 40 St., between Final and Río, San Antonio de Los Baños Expressway / Tel.: (5347) 382351-384460-63 / reservas@yagrumas.co.cu

Havana

★★★★★ **Iberostar Parque Central Hotel** (City) / Neptuno St., between Prado Promenade and Zulueta, Old Havana / Tel.: (537) 8606627-29 / reservations2@hotelparquecentral.cu / Fax: (537) 8606630.

★★★★★ **Marqués de San Felipe y Santiago Hotel** (City) / Oficios St., on Amargura, San Francisco Square, Old Havana Tel.: (537) 8649191 / reservas@sanfelipehabaguanex.cu

★★★★★ **Meliá Cohíba Hotel** (City) / Paseo, between 1st. and 3rd. St., El Vedado, Plaza / Tel.: (537) 8333636 / reservas1.mco@solmeliacuba.com / Fax: (537) 8344555.

★★★★★ **Meliá Habana Hotel** (City) 3rd. Ave., between 76 and 80, Miramar, Playa / Tel.: (537) 2048500 / jefe.reservas.mha@solmeliacuba.com / Fax: (537) 2048505.

★★★★★ **Nacional de Cuba Hotel** (City)/ O St. on 21, El Vedado, Plaza/ Tel.: (537) 8363564-67/ reserva@gcnacio.gca.tur.cu / Fax: (537) 8336517.

★★★★★ **Santa Isabel Hotel** (City) / 9 Baratillo St., between Obispo and Narciso López, Old Havana / Tel.: (537) 8608201 / comercial@habaguanexhsisabel.co.cu / Fax: (537) 8608391.

★★★★★ **Saratoga Hotel** (City / 603 Prado Promenade, on Dragones, Old Havana / Tel.: (537) 8681000 / info@saratoga.co.cu / Fax: (537) 8681001.

★★★★★ **Tryp Habana Libre Hotel** (City)/ L St., between 23 and 25 St., El Vedado, Plaza/ Tel.: (537) 8346100/ reservas1.thl@solmeliacuba.com

★★★★ **Ambos Mundos Hotel** (City) / 153 Obispo St., on Mercaderes, Old Havana / Tel.: (537) 8609530 / comercial@habaguanexhamundos.co.cu / Fax 8609532.

★★★★ **Armadores de Santander Hotel** (City) / 4 Luz St., on San Pedro, Old Havana / Tel.: (537) 8628000 / comercial@santander.co.cu

★★★★ **Beltrán de Santa Cruz, Hotel** (City) / 411 San Ignacio St., between Muralla and Sol, Old Havana / Tel.: (537) 8608330 / gerencia@bsantacruz.co.cu

★★★★ **Blau Arenal** (Beach)/ Itabo Lagoon, between Sta. María del Mar and Boca Ciega, East Havana / Tel.: (537) 7971272-7971275/ reservas@arenal.get.tur.cu

★★★★ **Comodoro Hotel** (City) / 3rd Ave. on 84 St., Miramar, Playa / Tel.: (537) 2045551 / reservas@comodor.cha.cyt.cu

★★★★ **Conde de Villanueva Hotel** (City) / 202 Mercaderes St., on Lamparilla, Old Havana / Tel.: (537) 8629293 / reservas@cvillanueva.co.cu / Fax (537) 8629682.

★★★★ **Copacabana Hotel** (City) / 4404 1st. Ave., between 44 and 46, Miramar, Playa / Tel.: (537) 2041037 / reserva@copa.gca.tur.cu / Fax (537) 2042846.

★★★★ **Chateau Miramar Hotel** (City)/ 1st. Ave., between 60 and 70 St., Miramar, Playa / Tel.: (537) 2041952-57 / reservas@chateau.cha.cyt.cu

★★★★ **El Comendador Hotel** (City)/ 55 Obrapía St., on Baratillo St., Old Havana / Tel.: (537) 8605628 / reserva@habaguanexhvalencia.co.cu

★★★★ **El Mesón de La Flota** (City) / 257 Mercaderes St., between Amargura and Teniente Rey, Old Havana/ Tel.: (537) 8633838 /reservas@mflota.co.cu

★★★★ **El Viejo y el Mar Hotel** (City) Marina Hemingway / 5th. Ave. on 248 St., Marina Hemingway Residential, Playa/ Tel.: (537) 2046769-7623/ reserva@hmar.mh.cyt.cu

★★★★ **Florida Hotel** (City) / Obispo St. on Cuba, Old Havana / Tel.: (537) 8624127 / comercial@habaguanexhflorida.co.cu / Fax: (537) 8624117.

★★★★ **H10 Panorama Hotel** (City) / 3rd. on 70 St., Miramar, Playa / Tel.: (537) 2040100 / comercial@panorama.co.cu / reservas@panorama.co.cu/ Fax: (537) 2044969.

★★★★ **Habana Riviera Hotel** (City) / Paseo on Malecón, Plaza / Tel.: (537) 8364051 / reserva@gcrivie.gca.tur.cu

★★★★ **Inglaterra Hotel** (City) / 416 Prado Promenade on San Rafael St., Old Havana / Tel.: (537) 8608593-97 / reserva@gcingla.gcaturcu

★★★★ **La Pradera Hotel & Spa** (City) / 230 St., between 15 A and 17 St., Siboney, Playa / Tel.: (537) 2737467 / comercial@pradera.cha.cyt.cu

★★★★ **Los Frailes Hotel** (City) / 8 Teniente Rey St., between Oficios and Mercaderes St., Old Havana / Tel.: (537) 8629383 / comercial@habaguanexhfrailes.co.cu / Fax: (537) 8629718.

★★★★ **Marqués de Prado Ameno Hotel** (City) / 253 O'Reilly St., between Cuba and Aguiar, Old Havana / Tel.: (537) 8624127 / comercial@habaguanexhflorida.co.cu / Fax: (537) 8624117.

★★★★ **Mercure Sevilla Hotel** (City) / 53 Trocadero St., between Prado Promenade and Zulueta, Old Havana / Tel.: (537) 8608560/ reserva@sevilla.gca.tur.cu / Fax: (537) 8608875.

★★★★ **Occidental Miramar** (City) / 5th Ave., between 72 and 76, Miramar, Playa / Tel.: (537) 2043584 / reserva@miramar.co.cu / Fax : (537) 2048159.

★★★★ **Palacio O'Farrill Hotel** (City) / 102-108 Cuba St., on Chacón, Old Havana / Tel.: (537) 8605080 / comercial@ofarrill.co.cu / Fax: (537) 8605083.

★★★★ **Palco Hotel** (City)/ 146 St., between 11 and 13 St., Siboney, Playa/ Tel.: (537) 2047235/ reserva@hpalco.palco.cu

★★★★ **Plaza Hotel** (City) / 267 Ignacio Agramonte St., Old Havana / Tel.: (537) 8608583 / reserva@plaza.gca.tur.cu / Fax: (537) 8608869.

★★★★ **Presidente Hotel** (City) / 110 Calzada St., El Vedado, Plaza / Tel.: (537) 8381801 / reservas@hpdte.gca.tur.cu / Fax: (537) 8382956.

★★★★ **Raquel Hotel** (City) / 103 Amargura St., on San Ignacio, Old Havana / Tel.: (537) 8608280 / reservas@hotelraquel.co.cu / Fax: (537) 8608275.

★★★★ **San Miguel Hotel** (City) / 52 Cuba St., on Peña Pobre, Old Havana / Tel.: (537) 8627656/ reservas@sanmiguel.co.cu /Fax: (537) 8627856.

★★★★ **Tejadillo Hotel** (City) / 12 Tejadillo St., on San Ignacio, Old Havana / Tel.: (537) 8637283 / comercial@habaguanexhtejadillo.co.cu / Fax: (537) 8638830.

★★★★ **Telégrafo Hotel** (City) / 408 Prado Promenade, on Neptuno, Old Havana / Tel.: (537) 8611010 / reserva@telegrafo.co.cu / Fax: (537) 8614844.

★★★★ **Victoria Hotel** (City) / 19 on M, El Vedado, Plaza / Tel.: (537) 8333510 / reserva@victoria.gca.tur.cu

★★★ **Atlántico Los Pinos Villa** (Beach)/ Las Terrazas Ave., Santa María del Mar, East Havana/ Tel.: (537) 7971085/ reservas@clubtropico.co.cu

★★★ **Bello Caribe Hotel** (City) / 158 St. on 31st. Ave., Playa / Tel.: (537) 7639241 / reservas@bcaribe.cha.cyt.cu

★★★ **Hotetur Deauville Hotel** (City) Galiano on San Lázaro, Centro Habana / Tel.: (537) 8668813 / reservas@hdeauville.gca.tur.cu

★★★ **Islazul Bacuranao Villa** (Beach) / Vía Blanca, Km 15 ½, East Havana Beaches / Tel.: (537) 939241 / reservas@bacuranao.co.cu

★★★ **Islazul Lincoln Hotel** (City) / 157 Virtudes St., on Galiano St., Centro Habana / Tel.: (537) 8628061 - 65 / alojamiento@lincoln.co.cu

★★★ **Kohly Bosque Hotel** (City) / 28-A Ave., between 49-A and 49-C St., Kohly, Playa / Tel.: (537) 2049232 / reservas@kohly-gav.tur.cu

★★★ **Los Pinos Villa** (Beach) / 21 Las Terrazas Ave., Santa María del Mar, East Havana / Tel.: (537) 977361 / reservas@complejo.gca.tur.cu / Fax: (537) 7971269.

★★★ **Montehabana Aparthotel** (City) / 70 St. between 5th A and 7th Ave., Miramar, Playa / Tel.: (537) 2069595 / reservas@montehabana.co.cu

★★★ **Neptuno-Tritón Hotel** (City) / 3rd. on 74, Miramar, Playa/ Tel.: (537) 2041606 / reservas@nep-tri.gca.tur.cu

★★★ **Panamericano Hotel** (City) / A St. on Central Ave., Cojímar, East Havana Tel.: (537) 7661240 / alina.morales@epr.islazul.tur.cu

★★★ **Park View Hotel** (City)/ Colón St. on Morro, Old Havana/ Tel.: (537) 8613293/ comercial@parkview.co.cu / Fax: (537) 8636036.

★★★ **Saint John's Hotel** (City) / O St., between 23 and 25, El Vedado, Plaza / Tel.: (537) 8333740 / reserva@stjohns.gca.tur.cu

★★★ **Tarará Villa Hotel** (Beach) / 9 St. between12 and 14 St., Ciudad Tarará, East Havana / Tel.: (537) 7983166 / 7983163 / tarara@cimex.com.

★★★ **Valencia Hostel** (City)/ 53 Oficios St., on Obrapía, Old Havana / Tel.: (537) 8671037 / reserva@habaguanexhvalencia.co.cu

★★★ **Vedado Hotel** (City)/ 244 O St. on 25 St. / El Vedado, Plaza. / Tel.: (537) 8364072/ reserva@vedado.gca.tur.cu

★★ **Colina Hotel** (City) / 23 L St., between 27 and Jovellar, Plaza / Tel.: (537) 8364071 / reservas@colina.gca.tur.cu

★★ **Islazul Atlántico Aparthotel** (Beach) / Las Terrazas Ave., between 11 and 12, Sta. María del Mar, East Havana Beaches / Tel.: (537) 971494 / jefrecep@terrazas.hor.tur.cu

★★ **Islazul Caribbean Hotel** (City) / 164 Prado Promenade, between Colón and Refugio, Old Havana/ Tel.: (537) 8608241/ reservation@lidocaribbean.hor.tur.cu

★★ **Islazul Lido Hotel** (City) / 210 Consulado St., between Ánimas and Trocadero St., Old Havana / Tel.: (537) 8671102 / lcarp@lidocaribbean.hor.tur.cu

★★ **Las Terrazas Aparthotel** (Beach) / Las Terrazas Ave., between 10 and Rotonda, Santa María del Mar, East Havana / Tel.: (537) 7971344 / jefrecep@terrazas.hor.tur.cu

★★ **Mariposa Hotel** (City) / Novia del Mediodía Expressway, Km 6½, Arroyo Arenas, La Lisa / Tel.: (537) 2049137 / comercio@maripos.cha.cyt.cu

★★ **Mirador del Mar Villas** (Beach) / 11th St., between 1st. and 3rd. Ave., Santa María del Mar, East Havana / Tel.: (537) 7971262 / infomirador@pleste.islazul.tur.cu / (Reservations only through agencies).

★★ **Tropicoco Hotel** (Beach)/ Banderas Ave. on Las Terrazas, East Havana / Tel.: (537) 7971371/ reservas@htropicoco.hor.tur.cu

Mayabeque

★★★★ **Breezes Jibacoa** (Beach) / Arroyo Bermejo Beach, Santa Cruz del Norte Tel.: (5347) 295122 / reservationsmanager@breezesjibacoa.tur.cu / Fax (5347) 295150.

★★★ **Trópico Gran Caribe Club** (Beach) /Vía Blanca Km 60, Jibacoa, Santa Cruz del Norte Tel.: (5347) 295205-07-16 / reserva@clubtropico.gca.tur.cu

★ **Los Cocos Camping** (Nature) / Jibacoa, Santa Cruz del Norte / Tel.: (5347) 295231-32 / (Reservations through Cubamar).

Matanzas-Varadero

★★★★★ **Barceló Marina Palace Hotel** (Beach) / Sur Expressway, Varadero / Tel.: (5345) 669966 / marinapalace.res@Barcelo.co / Fax: (5345) 667022.

★★★★★ **Barceló Solymar Hotel** (Beach) / Las Morlas Highway, Km 4½, Varadero / Tel.: (5345) 614499 reserva@solymar.gca.tur.cu / reserva@resortsolymar.gca.tur.cu / Fax: (5345) 611086.

★★★★★ **Iberostar Laguna Azul Hotel** (Beach) / Km 23, Francés Point, Varadero / Tel.: (5345) 667900 / comercial@laguna.co.cu.

★★★★★ **Iberostar Playa Alameda Varadero** (Beach) / Punta Hicacos Natural Park, Varadero reservas@beachalamedavaradero.co.cu / Tel.: (5345) 668833.

★★★★★ **Iberostar Varadero** (Beach) / Las Morlas Highway, Km 16, Hicacos Point, Varadero / Tel.: (5345) 669999 / comercial@iberostar.co.cu and reservas@iberostar.co.cu / Fax: (5345) 668899.

★★★★★ **Meliá Las Américas** (Beach) / Sur Expressway, Varadero / Tel.: (5345) 667600 / reservas1.mla@solmeliacuba.com

★★★★★ **Meliá Varadero** (Beach) / Sur Expressway, Varadero / reservas1.mva@solmeliacuba.com / Tel.: (5345) 667013.

★★★★★ **Paradisus Princesa del Mar Hotel** (Beach) / Las Morlas Highway, Km 19½, Varadero / Tel.: (5345) 667200 / sales@princesadelmar.co.cu and jefe.reservasppm@solmeliacuba.com / Fax: (5345) 667201.

★★★★★ **Paradisus Varadero Hotel** (Beach) / Francés Point, Varadero / Tel.: (5345) 668700 / paradisus.varadero@solmeliacuba.com / Fax: (5345) 668705.

★★★★★ **Sandals Royal Hicacos** (Beach) / Expressway, Km 15, Varadero / Tel.: (5345) 668844 / reservas@sandals.cyt.cu

★★★★★ **Sol Palmeras** (Beach) / Sur Expressway, Las Morlas Highway, Varadero / Tel.: (5345) 667209 / sol.palmeras@solmelia.com

★★★★★ **Tryp Península Varadero Hotel** (Beach)/ Hicacos Point Natural Park, Varadero/ Tel.: (5345) 668800/ jefe.reservas.tpv@solmeliacuba.com/ Fax: (5345) 667246.

★★★★ **Arenas Blancas Club** (Beach) 64 St., between 1st. and Autopista, Varadero / Tel.: (5345) 614450 / rsv@arblcas.gca.tur.cu / Fax: (5345) 614491.

★★★★ **Arenas Doradas Hotel** (Beach) / Varadero Expressway, Km12, Varadero / Tel.: (5345) 668150 / reserva@arenas.gca.tur.cu

★★★★ **Barlovento Club** (Beach) / 1st. St., between 9 and 12, Varadero/ Tel.: (5345) 667140 reserva@ibero.gca.tur.cu / Fax: (5345) 667218.

★★★★ **Be Live Las Morlas Hotel** (Beach) / Las Américas Ave. on A St., La Torre, Varadero / Tel.: (5345) 667230-32 / comercial@morlas.gca.tur.cu Fax: (5345) 667215.

★★★★ **Be Live Turquesa Hotel** (Beach) / Los Taínos Highway, Km 12½, Varadero / Tel.: (5345) 668471 / reservas@turquesa.gca.tur.cu / Fax: (5345) 668495.

★★★★ **Blau Varadero** (Beach) / Las Morlas Highway, Km 15, Punta Hicacos, Varadero / Tel.: (5345) 668168-667545 / reserva@blauvaradero.cyt.cu / Fax: (5345) 667494.

★★★★ **Breezes Bella Costa** (Beach) / Las Americas Ave., Km 3½, Varadero / Tel.: (5345) 667210 reservationsmaneger@breezesbellacosta.tur.cu Fax: (5345) 667713.

★★★★ **Breezes Varadero** (Beach) / Las Américas Ave., Km 3, Varadero/ Tel.: (5345) 667030 / reservationsmanager@breezesvaradero.cyt.cu / Fax: (5345) 667030.

★★★★ **Brisas del Caribe Hotel** (Beach)/ Las Morlas Highway, Km 12½, Varadero/ Tel.: (5345) 668030/ reservas@bricar.mtz.tur.cu / Fax: (5345) 668005.

★★★★ **Coral-Sirenas Hotel** (Beach) / Las Américas Ave. on K St., La Torre, Varadero / Tel.: (5345) 668070-667240 / jefe.reservas.ssc@solmeliacuba.com

★★★★ **Hotetur Palma Real Hotel** (Beach) / 2nd. Ave on 64, Varadero / Tel.: (5345) 614555/ comercial.palmareal@hotetur.com / Fax: (5345) 614450.

★★★★ **Iberostar Taínos Hotel** (Beach) / Las Morlas Highway, Km 12, Varadero / Tel.: (5345) 668656 / reservas@ibstain.gca.tur.cu / Fax: (5345) 668657.

★★★★ **Kawama Resort Club** (Beach) / 1st. Ave. on 0 St, Kawama, Varadero / Tel.: (5345) 614416-21 / reserva@kawama.gca.tur.cu / Fax: (5345) 667334.

★★★★ **Meliá Las Antillas** (Beach) / Las Morlas Highway Km 14, Varadero / Tel.: (5345) 668470 / jefe.reservas.mat@solmeliacuba.com

★★★★ **Memoires La Salina Hotel** (Beach) / Sur Expressway Km 19 ½, Varadero Natural Park / Tel (5345) 667599 / reservas@sirenishotels.co.cu

★★★★ **Mercure Cuatro Palmas Hotel** (Beach) / 62 St. and 1st. Ave., Varadero / Tel.: (5345) 667040 / reservas@gcpalho.gca.tur.cu

★★★★ **Occidental Allegro Varadero Hotel** (Beach) / Sur Expressway Km 11, Varadero / Tel.: (5345) 668288 / reservas@allegrovaradero.co.cu / Fax: (5345) 668414.

★★★★ **Playa Caleta Hotel** (Beach) / Kawama Ave. on Ending, Varadero / Tel.: (5345) 667120 / reservas@beachcaleta.gca.tur.cu / Fax: (5345) 667779.

★★★★ **Playa de Oro Coralia Club** (Beach) / Las Morlas Highway Km 12½, Varadero / Tel.: (5345) 668566 / reservas@poro.gca.tur.cu y comercial@poro.gca.tur.cu / Fax: (5345) 668555.

★★★★ **Puntarena Club** (Beach) / Kawama Ave. on Ending, Varadero / Tel.: (5345) 667125 al 29 reservas@puntarena.gca.tur.cu / Fax: (5345) 667074.

★★★★ **Tuxpan** (Beach) / Las Américas Ave., Varadero / Tel.: (5345) 667560 / reservas@tuxpan.mtz.tur.cu

★★★★ **Varadero Internacional Hotel** (Beach) / Las Américas Ave., La Torre, Varadero / Tel.: (5345) 667038 to 39 / reserva@gcinter.gca.tur.cu

★★★★ **Villa Cuba Resort Club** (Beach) / Las Américas Highway Km 3, La Torre, Varadero / Tel.: (5345) 668280 / vcuba@vcuba.gca.tur.cu / Fax: (5345) 668282.

★★★ **Acuazul-Varazul Islazul Hotel** (Beach) /1st. Ave. on 3rd. St., Varadero / Tel.: (5345) 667132 / facturas@acua.islazul.tur.cu / Fax: (5345) 667229.

★★★ **Aguas Azules Hotel** (Beach)/ Las Morlas Highway, Km 12, Varadero/ Tel.: (5345) 668243 / reservas@aguasazules.tur.cu.

★★★ **Club Amigo Tropical** (Beach)/1st. St., between 21 and 23, Varadero / Tel.: (5345) 613915/ reserva@tropical.hor.tur.cu / Fax: (5345) 617646.

★★★ **Club Amigo Varadero** (Beach) / Las Morlas Highway, Km 12, Varadero / Tel.: (5345) 668243 reservas@.aguasazules.tur.cu

★★★ **Horizontes Batey Don Pedro** (Nature) / Zapata Peninsula, Zapata Swamp, Tel.: (5345) 912825-913324 / carpeta@donpedro.co.cu

★★★ **Hotetur Sunbeach Hotel** (Beach)/ 17 St. between 1st. Ave. and 3rd. Ave., Varadero/ Tel.: (5345) 667490/ reservas@sunbeach.gca.tur.cu

★★★ **Islazul Los Delfines Hotel** (Beach) / 1st. Ave. between 38 and 39, Varadero / Tel.: (5345) 667720-21 / jrecepcion@delfines.hor.tur.cu / Fax: (5345) 667728.

★★★ **Islazul Oasis Hotel** (Beach) / Vía Blanca, Km 130, Varadero / Tel.: (5345) 667380 to 82 / comercial@oasis.islazul.tur.cu / Fax: (5345) 667489.

★★★ **Islazul Sotavento Villa** (Beach) / 13 St. between Avenida and Camino del Mar, Varadero / Tel.: (5345) 667132-34 / facturas@acua.islazul.tur.cu

★★★ **Tortuga Club** (Beach) / 7 St. between Kawama Ave. and Playa, Varadero / Tel.: (5345) 614747 reservas@villatortuga.gca.tur.cu

★★ **Horizontes Guamá** (Nature) / Laguna del Tesoro, Zapata Peninsula / Tel.: (5345) 915551 / comercial@peninsula.cyt.cu

★★ **Horizontes Playa Larga** (Nature)/ Zapata Swamp/ Tel.: (5345) 987294-987206/ recepcion@hplargac.co.cu

★★ **Islazul Canimao Hotel** (Nature) / Varadero Highway Km 4 ½, Canímar, Matanzas / Tel.: (5345) 261014 - 262237 / director@canimao.co.cu / comercial@canimao.co.cu

★★ **Islazul Dos Mares Pullman** (Beach) / 1st. Ave., between 49 and 50, Varadero / Tel.: (5345) 612702 / recepcion@dmares.hor.tur.cu / Fax: (5345) 667499.

★★ **Islazul Herradura Hotel** (Beach) / Playa Ave., between 35 and 36, Varadero / Tel.: (5345) 613703 / carpeta@herradura.co.cu / Fax: (5345) 667496.

★★ **Islazul La Mar Villa** (Beach) / 3rd. Ave., between 28 and 30, Varadero / Tel.: (5345) 614517-614520 / reservas@villalamar.co..cu

★★ **Islazul Mar del Sur** (Beach) / 3rd. Ave. on 30 St., Varadero / Tel.: (5345) 612246 / reservas@mardelsur.hor.tur.cu / Fax: (5345) 666481.

★★ **Playa Girón Hotel** (Beach) / Girón Beach, Zapata Swamp / Tel.: (5345) 984110 / recepcion@hpgiron.co.cu

Isle of Youth -Cayo Largo

★★★★ **Coral Club** (Beach)/ Canarreos Archipelago, Isle of Youth / Tel.: (5345) 248111-118/ reserva@isla.cls.tur.cu

★★★★ **Lindamar Club** (Beach) / Canarreos Archipelago, Isle of Youth / Tel.: (5345) 248111-118 / reserva@isla.cls.tur.cu

★★★★ **Pelícano Sol Hotel** (Beach)/ Canarreos Archipelago, Isle of Youth / Tel.: (5345) 248333-36/ jefe.reservas.spl@solmeliacuba.com

★★★★ **Playa Blanca Hotel** (Beach)/ Canarreos Archipelago, Isle of Youth / Tel.: (5345) 248071 / reservas.pb@beachblanca.gca.tur.cu

★★★★ **Sol Cayo Largo Hotel** (Beach) / Canarreos Archipelago, Isle of Youth / Tel.: (5345) 248260 / j.reservas.sol@solmeliacuba.com

★★★ **International Diving Center El Colony** (Beach)/ Canarreos Archipelago, Isle of Youth / Tel.: (5346) 398181/ reserva@colony.co.cu

★★★ **Isla del Sur Club** (Beach) / Canarreos Archipelago, Isle of Youth / Tel.: (5345) 248111-118/ reserva@isla.cls.tur.cu

★★★ **Marlin Marina Cayo Largo** (Beach) / Canarreos Archipelago, Isle of Youth / Tel.: (5345) 248384 / comercial@marlin.cls.tur.cu

★★★ **Soledad Club** (Beach)/ Canarreos Archipelago, Isle of Youth / Tel.: (5345) 248111-118/ reserva@isla.cls.tur.cu

★★ **Isla de la Juventud Villa** (City) / Isle of Youth / Tel.: (5346) 323035 / servitec@turiisla.co.cu (Reservations through Cubamar).

★★ **Rancho El Tesoro Hotel** (City) / Isle of Youth / Tel.: (5346) 321739 / servitec@turiisla.co.cu (Reservations through Cubamar).

Restaurants and Coffee-Shops

Pinar del Río

Casa de Don Tomás (Cuban cuisine)/ 140 Salvador Cisneros, Viñales/Tel: (5348) 796300.

Cayo Jutías (Cuban cuisine)/Cayo Jutías/ Tel.: (5348) 648317.

Cueva del Indio (Cuban cuisine)/ Puerto Esperanza Highway, Km. 38, Viñales/Tel.: (5348) 796280.

La Casona (Cuban cuisine)/ Martí St. on Colón/ Tel.: (5348) 778263.

La Terraza (Buffet restaurant)/ La Ermita Hotel, Viñales/Tel.: (5348) 796071.

Las Barrigonas (Coffee-shop) / Autopista, Km 120, Consolación del Sur.

Las Magnolias (Seafood specialties)/ Puerto Esperanza Highway, Km. 38, Viñales (5348) 796280.

Lookout at Viñales (Coffee-shop)/ Viñales Highway, Km. 25/ Tel.: (5348) 796205.

Mural of Prehistory (Cuban cuisine)/ Valle de Viñales/ Tel.: (5348)796260.

Palenque de los Cimarrones (Cuban cuisine)/ Los Cimarrones Cave, Km 36, Puerto Esperanza Highway/Tel.: (5348)796290.

San Vicente Farm (Cuban cuisine)/ Puerto Esperanza Highway, Km. 38, Viñales/ Tel.: (5348)796511.

Artemisa

Buenavista (Cuban cuisine)/ Las Terrazas Complex, Candelaria.

Casa del Campesino (Cuban cuisine)/ Las Terrazas Complex, Candelaria.

Centro (International cuisine)/ Soroa Villa, Candelaria/ Tel: (5348) 523534, ext. 1334.

Fonda de Mercedes (Cuban cuisine)/ Las Terrazas Complex, Candelaria.

La Arboleda (Cuban cuisine)/ Candelaria/Tel.: (5348) 598301.

Salto (Cuban cuisine)/ Villa Soroa, Candelaria/ Tel: (5348) 598301.

Havana

1830 (Cuban and international cuisine)/ Calzada on 20 St., El Vedado/ Tel: (537) 8383091 to 92.

A Prado y Neptuno (Italian cuisine)/ Prado Promenade on Neptuno, Old Havana/ Tel: (537) 8609636.

Ailette (Italian cuisine)/ M St., on 17, Vedado, Plaza/Tel.: (537) 8325677.

Al Medina (Arabian cuisine)/ 12 Oficios St., between Obispo and Obrapía, Old Havana / Tel: (537) 8671041.

Amelia (International cuisine)/ 3rd. between 78 and 80, Miramar, Playa / Tel.: (537) 2047311.

Anacaona (International cuisine)/ Saratoga Hotel, Old Havana / Tel: (537) 868 1000.

Artechef (Cuban cuisine)/ 301 3rd. St., Vedado, Plaza/ Tel (537) 8211089.

Bazar 43 (Coffee-shop)/ 43 St. on 22 St., Playa. / Tel.: (537) 2021872.

Bodegón Criollo (Cuban cuisine)/ Monumental Ave., La Cabaña Fortress, East Havana / Tel: (537) 8620617 to 19 ext. 146.

Bodegón Onda (Spanish cuisine)/ El Comendador Hotel, old Havana / Tel: (537) 8671037.

Cabaña (Cuban and international cuisine, chicken specialties)/ 12 Cuba St., Old Havana / Tel: (537) 8605670.

Café 42 (Coffee-shop)/ 5th-A St between 40 and 42, Miramar, Playa.

Café del Oriente (Cuisine d'auteur) /112 Oficios St., on Amargura, Old Havana / Tel: (537) 8606686.

Café El Escorial (Coffee specialties)/Mercaderes on Muralla, Old Square, Old Havana.

Café Taberna Benny Moré (Cuban and international cuisine)/ Mercaderes St. on Teniente Rey, Old Havana / Tel: (537) 8611637.

Café Lamparilla (Cuban home cooking)/ Lamparilla St., between Mercaderes and San Ignacio.

Café Neruda (Coffee-shop and Bar)/355 Malecón Ave., between Manrique and San Nicolás/ Tel.: (537) 8604159.

Cantabria (Cantabrian, Cuban and international cuisine)/ Armadores de Santander Hotel, Old Havana / Tel.: (537) 8628000.

Casa de la Parra (Cuban and Vietnamese cuisine)/ Bernaza on Teniente Rey/ Tel.: (537) 867 1029.

Casona de la Lisa (Cuban cuisine)/ 39th Ave. on 208, La Lisa/ Tel: (537) 2677469.

Castillo de Farnés (Spanish cuisine) / 361 Monserrate St. on Obrapía, Old Havana / Tel: (537) 8671030.

Cojímar (Seafood specialties)/ Tarará Marina, East Havana / Tel: (537) 7665151.

Chef D'Oeuvre (French cuisine)/ Le Select Club, 5th. Ave. and 30 St, Miramar, Playa/ Tel: (537) 2079681.

Don Cangrejo (Seafood specialties)/ 1606 1st. St., Miramar, Playa/ Tel: (537) 2043837.

Don Giovanni (Italian cuisine)/107-109 Empedrado St., between Tacón and Mercaderes/ Tel.: (537) 8671036.

Don Ricardo (Cuban, international and Irish cuisine)/ Palacio O´Farrill Hotel, Old Havana / Tel: (537) 8605080.

Dos Hermanos (Cuban cuisine)/ Port Ave. on Sol/ Tel.: (537) 861 3514.

El Aljibe (Cuban cuisine) /7th. St., between 24 y 26 St., Miramar, Playa/ Tel: (537) 2041583.

El Bambú (Vegetarian cuisine)/ National Botanic Garden, Arroyo Naranjo/ (537)6979170.

El Baturro (Spanish cuisine) / 661 Egido St., between Jesús María and Merced, Old Havana / Tel: (537) 8609078.

El Condado (Cuban cuisine)/ Santa Isabel Hotel, Old Havana / Tel: (537) 8608201.

El Emperador (International cuisine)/ 17 between M and N, Focsa Building, Vedado, Plaza de la Revolución/ Tel: (537) 8324998.

El Floridita (Seafood specialties) /557 Obispo St., on Monserrate, Old Havana /Tel: (537) 8668856.

El Conejito (White meat specialties)/ M on 17, El Vedado, Plaza de la Revolución/ Tel: (537) 8324671.

El Louvre (Coffee-shop)/ Inglaterra Hotel, Old Havana/ Tel: (537) 8608594.

El Palenque (Cuban and international cuisine)/ Ave. 17 between 174 y 190, Siboney, Playa/Tel.: (537)2718167.

El Mandarín (Oriental cuisine)/ 23 St. on M, El Vedado, Plaza de la Revolución/ Tel: (537) 8320677.

El Mediterráneo (International cuisine)/ Parque Central Hotel, Old Havana /Tel.: (537) 8606628 y 29.

El Mercurio (Sandwiches and international cuisine)/ Lonja del Comercio, Plaza de San Francisco, Old Havana/ Tel: (537) 8606168.

El Mesón de la Flota (Spanish cuisine)/ 257 Mercaderes St., between Teniente Rey and Amargura, Old Havana/ Tel: (537) 8633838.

El Paseo (International cuisine)/ Parque Central Hotel, Old Havana/Tel.: (537) 8606628.

El Patio (International cuisine)/54 San Ignacio St., Cathedral Square, Old Havana / Tel: (537) 8671035.

El Pedregal (International cuisine)/ 23rd. Ave. on 198, La Lisa/ Tel: (537) 2737830.

El Polinesio (Oriental cuisine)/ Habana Libre Tryp Hotel, Plaza de la Revolución/ Tel: (537) 3346100.

El Rancho Palco (Cuban cuisine)/ 140 on 19 St., Cubanacán, Playa/ Tel: (537) 2089346.

El Templete (Seafood specialties)/ San Pedro (Port Ave.) on Narciso López/ Tel.: (537) 866 8807 and 864 7777.

Europa (Stylized Cuban cuisine)/ Obispo St. on Aguiar/ Tel.: (537) 864 4484.

Factoría Plaza Vieja (Coffee-shop, grill and home-brewed beers and malt drinks)/ San Ignacio St. on Muralla, Vieja Square, Old Havana/Tel.: (537) 8664453.

Fiesta (Spanish cuisine)/ Marina Hemingway, Playa/ Tel.: (537) 2041150 ext. 333.

Flores (Coffee-shop) / 176 St., between 1st. and 5th. Ave., Flores, Playa/ Tel: (537) 336512.

Havana Club Rum Museum (Coffee-shop) /162 Port Ave., Old Havana / Tel: (537) 8611900, 8623832, 8624108.

Gato Tuerto (International cuisine)/ O St. between 17 and 19, El Vedado, Plaza de la Revolución/ Tel: (537) 8382696.

Guanabo Club (Cuban cuisine)/ 468 between 13 and 15, Guanabo Beach, East Havana / Tel: (537) 7962884.

Jardín del Edén (Kosher food)/ Amargura on San Ignacio, Raquel Hotel / Tel.: (537) 8608280.

Kasalta (Cuban and international cuisine) /5th. Ave. on 2 St., Miramar/ Tel: (537) 2040434.

La Abadía Tapas Bar / 407 Malecón Ave., between Campanario and Manrique Tel.: (537) 864 4432.

La Barca (International cuisine)/ Port Ave. on Obispo/Tel.: (537) 866 88 07, 864 7777 y 861 64 97.

La Bodeguita del Medio (Cuban cuisine)/ 206 Empedrado St. between San Ignacio and Cuba St., Old Havana / Tel: (537) 8671374.

La Carreta (Cuban cuisine)/ 21 on K St., El Vedado, Plaza de la Revolución/Tel.: (537) 8324485.

La Casa del Pescador (Seafood specialties)/ 5th. Ave. between 440 and 442, Boca Ciega Beach, East Havana / Tel: (537) 7963653.

La Casona de 17 (Cuban cuisine)/ 60 17 St., El Vedado, Plaza de la Revolución/ Tel: (537) 8383136.

La Cecilia (Cuban cuisine)/ 5th. Ave. between 110 and 112, Miramar, Playa/ Tel: (537) 2041562.

La Columnata Egipciana (Tea- and Coffee-Shop)/ Mercaderes between Obispo and Obrapía, Old Havana.

La Dichosa (Coffee-shop)/ Obispo St. on Compostela, Old Havana.

La Divina Pastora (Seafood specialties)/ Monumental Ave., La Cabaña Fortress, East Havana / Tel: (537) 8608341.

La Dominica (Italian cuisine)/ 108 O´Reilly St. on Mercaderes, Old Havana / Tel: (537) 8602918.

La Ferminia (International cuisine)/ 18207 5th. Ave., Flores, Playa/ Tel: (537) 2736786.

La Floridiana (Cuban and international cuisine)/ Florida Hotel, Old Havana / Tel: (537) 8624127.

La Fuente (International cuisine)/ 5th.-A St. between 40 and 42, Miramar, Playa/ Tel: (537) 2125821.

La Fuente, Tropicana (Cuban cuisine)/ 72 St on Línea del Ferrocarril, Marianao/ Tel: (537) 2770174.

La Giraldilla (International cuisine)/ 222 St. between 37 and Autopista, La Coronela. La Lisa/ Tel: (537) 2730568.

La Imprenta (Sandwiches and grilled meats)/ 208 Mercaderes St. between Lamparilla and Amargura/Tel.: (537) 8649581.

La Maison (International cuisine)/ 16th St. between 7th. and 9th., Miramar, Playa/ Tel: (537) 2041543 to 48.

La Mina (Traditional Cuban cuisine)/ 109 Obispo St., on Oficios, Old Havana / Tel: (537) 8620216.

La Paella (Paella specialties)/ Valencia Hostelry, Old Havana/ Tel: (537) 8671037.

La Roca (International cuisine)/ 21 St., on M St., El Vedado. Plaza de la Revolución/ Tel: (537) 8363219.

La Terraza de Cojímar (Seafood specialties)/ 161 Calle Real, Cojímar, East Havana / Tel: (537) 7665151.

Las Terrazas de Prado (Coffee Shop)/ Prado Promenade on Genios, Old Havana / Tel: (537) 8632814.

La Torre (International cuisine)/ 55 17 St., Focsa Building, 36th Floor, El Vedado, Plaza de la Revolución/ Tel: (537) 8383088 y 89.

La Torre de Marfil (Cantonese cuisine)/ Mercaderes between Obispo and Obrapía, Old Havana / Tel: (537) 8671038.

Las Ruinas (International cuisine)/ 100 St. and Cortina de la Presa, Lenin Park, Arroyo Naranjo/ Tel: (537) 6438523 y 6431274.

La Vicaria (International cuisine)/ 5th Ave. on 180 St., Flores, Playa/ Tel: (537) 273 9100.

La Zaragozana (Spanish cuisine)/ Monserrate, between Obispo and Obrapía, Old Havana / Tel: (537) 8671040.

Las Palmeras (Cuban cuisine)/ Tallapiedra St. between Alambique and Diaria, Old Havana / Tel: (537) 8628349.

Los Doce Apóstoles (Cuban cuisine)/ Monumental Ave. , La Cabaña Fortress, East Havana / Tel: (537) 8608341.

Monseigneur (International cuisine)/ 21 St. on 0, Vedado/ Tel: (537) 8329884.

Papa´s (International cuisine)/ Marina Hemingway Residential, Playa/ Tel: (537) 2097920.

Pastelería Francesa (Bakery) / Prado Promenade between San Rafael and Neptuno.

Pico Blanco (Grilled specialties)/ Saint John's Hotel, Plaza de la Revolución/ Tel: (537) 8330130 y 8333740.

Pizza Nova La Cova (Italian cuisine)/ Marina Hemingway Residential, Playa/ Tel: (537) 2046969, 2097289.

Plaza (International cuisine)/ Plaza Hotel, Old Havana / Tel: (537) 8608583.

Plaza de Armas (Cuban and international cuisine) / Ambos Mundos Hotel, Old Havana / Tel: (537) 8609530.

Prado (International cuisine)/ Park View Hotel, Old Havana / Tel: (537) 8613293.

Pizza Nova (Italian cuisine)/ 17 on 10, El Vedado, Plaza de la Revolución.

Puerto de Sagua (Seafood paellas and hamburgers)/ 603 Egido on Acosta, Old Havana / Tel: (537) 8671026.

Rossini (Italian cuisine)/ 5th.-A between 40 and 42, Miramar, Playa/Tel: (537) 2125851.

Santo Ángel (International cuisine) Teniente Rey St. on San Ignacio, Old Havana / Tel: (537) 8611626.

Shanghai (Oriental cuisine) / 7th. on 26, Miramar, Playa/Tel. (537) 2042353, 2040382.

Taramar (Seafood specialties) Vía Blanca Km 18, East Havana, Ciudad de La Habana/ Tel: (537) 7961866.

Telégrafo (International cuisine)/ Telégrafo Hotel, Old Havana / Tel: (537) 8611010.

Tocororo (International cuisine) 18 St. on 3rd., Miramar, Playa/ Tel: (537) 2042209.

Vuelta Abajo (Cuban and international cuisine) / 102 Mercaderes St. on Lamparilla, Conde de Villanueva Hotel, Old Havana / Tel: (537) 8629293.

Torrelavega (Coffee-shop)/ Obrapía between Oficios and Mercaderes, Old Havana.

Wakamba (International cuisine)/ O St. between 23 and 25, El Vedado, Plaza de la Revolución/ Tel: (537) 8784526.

Private Restaurants (Paladares)

Popular imagination named as "paladares" these small private restaurants that offer great dishes in atmospheres that generally reflect their owners' good taste. The name originally came from a Brazilian TV soap opera in which its protagonist opens a restaurant under the name of Paladar (Portuguese and Spanish for palate). These establishments can be found at private homes, in a manor's garden, in an apartment's dining room or in a house's main floor. Here are some of the most famous:

Atelier (Cuban and international cuisine)/ 511 5th St., second floor, between Paseo and 2 St., El Vedado, Plaza/ Tel.: (537) 8362025.

Bom Apetite (International cuisine)/ 7210 11 St., between 72 and 74 St., Playa/ Tel.: (537) 2033634.

Café Laurent (International cuisine)/ 257 M St., between 19 and 21 (the pent house), Vedado, Plaza/ Tel.: (537) 831 2090.

D'DOCE (Cuban and international cuisine)/ 508 12 St., between 21 and 23, El Vedado, Plaza/ Tel.: (537) 8369301.

Decameron (Italian and international cuisine)/ 753 Línea St., between Paseo and 2 St., Vedado, Plaza/ Tel.: (537) 8322444.

Din Don (Italian and Cuban cuisine)/ 11th Ave., between 78 and 80, Playa, Tel.: (537) 2030445.

Doña Blanquita (Cuban cuisine), 158 Prado Promenade, between Colon and Refugio, Old Havana/ Tel.: (537) 8674958.

Doña Eutimia (Cuban and international cuisine)/ Callejón del Chorro, Cathedral Square, Old Havana.

Dr. Café (Cuban and international cuisine)/11 25 St. between 1st and 3rd, Miramar, Playa/Tel.: (537) 2034718 y (53) 52680607.

El Carruaje (Cuban and international cuisine)/ 2104 200 St. between 210 and 23, Siboney, Playa/ Tel.: (537) 2714347 and (53) 52635144.

El Diluvio (Cuban and Italian cuisine) / 1705 72 St., between 17 and 19, Playa/Tel.: (537) 2021531.

El Doble 7 (Cuban and international cuisine)/ 11th Ave. between 84 and 86, Playa/ Tel.: (537) 2068966.

El Farallón (Cuban cuisine and pizzeria)/ 361 22 St., on 23, Vedado, Plaza/ Tel.: (537) 8305187.

El Gringo Viejo (International cuisine)/ 454 21 St., between E and F, Vedado, Plaza/ Tel.: (537) 8311946.

El Portal de Calzada (Cuban and international cuisine) / 710 Calzada St. between Paseo and A St., Vedado, Plaza/ Tel.: (537) 8335008.

Habáname (Creative international cuisine) / 23 St., between G and F, El Vedado, Plaza.

La Casa (Cuban and international cuisine, tapas and cocktail Bar) / 865 30 St. between 26 y 41 Nuevo Vedado, Plaza/ Tel.: (537) 8817000.

La Cocina de Lilliam (International cuisine)/ 1311 48 St. between 13 and 15, Playa/ Tel: (537) 2096514.

La Esperanza (Creative and international cuisine) 105 16 St., between 1st. and 3rd. Miramar, Playa/ Tel.: (537) 2024361.

La Fontana (Italian and international cuisine)/ 3ra.-A on 46, Playa/ Tel.: (537) 202 8337 - (53) 52932497 - (53) 52864747.

La Guarida (International cuisine)/ 418 Concordia, between Gervasio and EscoBar, Centro Habana/ Tel.: (537) 8669047.

La Julia (Cuban cuisine)/ 506^{a} O´Reilly St. between Bernaza and Villegas, Old Havana /Tel.: (537)8627438.

La Moneda Cubana (Cuban and international cuisine)/ 152 Empedrado St. between Mercaderes and San Ignacio, Old Havana / Tel.: (537) 8615304 y (53) 52644713.

La Moraleja (International cuisine) / 454 25th St. between J and I St., Vedado. Plaza/ Tel.: (537) 8320963, (53) 52707298 y (53) 52437469.

La Paila (Cuban and international cuisine)/ 88B St. on 51A, Marianao/ Tel.: (537) 2670282.

Le Chanssoniere (International and Cuban cuisine) / 257 J St. between Línea and 15 St., Vedado, Plaza/ Tel.: (537) 8321576.

Los Amigos (Cuban cuisine)/ M St. between 17 and 19, Vedado, Plaza/ Tel.: (537) 8300880.

Lucas Bar & Grill (Cuban and international cuisine) / 13 15th St. between 2nd. and 4th St., Guiteras, East Havana / Tel.: (537) 7662579.

Mamy's (Cuban cuisine)/ 708 16th St. between 7th and 31st St., Miramar, Playa/ Tel.: (537) 2036700.

Mi Jardín (Cuban and international cuisine)/ 68 St. between 5th B y 7th St., Miramar, Playa.

Moneda Cubana (Cuban cuisine)/ 77 san Ignacio St., Old Havana / Tel.: (537) 8673852.

Monguito (Cuban cuisine)/408 L St. between 23 and 25 St. (across the street from the Habana Libre Hotel), Vedado, Plaza.

Monte Barreto (Cuban and international cuisine, cocktail Bar, open round the clock), 783 9th Ave, between 78 and 80, Playa/ Tel.: (537) 2063527.

Nerei (Cuban and international)/ 19 St. on L, Vedado, Plaza/ Tel.: (537) 8327860.

Parrillada de 84 y Quince (Cuban and international cuisine)/ 84 St. on 15 St., Playa/ Tel.: (537) 2063430.

Piccolo (Italian and Cuban cuisine) (forno di legno) / 5th between 502 and 504, Guanabo, East Havana / Tel.: (537) 7964300.

Punto G (Cuban and international cuisine and coffee-shop)/ 17 St. on G, El Vedado, Plaza.

Rancho Verde (Cuban cuisine)/ 10633 Santa Catalina St. between Ave de los Ocujes and Palatino, Cerro/ Tel.: (537) 6416433.

Torrezno (Cuban and vegetarian cuisine)/ 27 Malecón Ave. between Prado Promenade and Cárcel, Old Havana / Tel.: (537)8617476.

Vista al Mar (Cuban and international cuisine)/ 2206 1 St between 22 and 24, Miramar, Playa/Tel.: (537) 2038328.

Restaurants of Spanish Regional Associations

Castropol (Restaurant, Grill, and Video Bar)/ 107 Malecón Ave., between Genios and Crespo, Centro Habana/ Tel.: (537) 8614864.

Centro Asturiano de La Habana/ 309 Prado Promenade, on Virtudes / Old Havana/ Tel.: (537) 8625482.

El Asturianito (Cuban cuisine and pizzeria)/ 563 Prado Promenade between Dragones and Teniente Rey, Old Havana / Tel: (537) 8632985.

El Gijonés (Cuban and international cuisine)/ 309 Prado Promenade on Virtudes St., Old Havana.

El Guajirito (Cuban, international and Spanish cuisine) / 658 Zulueta St., second floor between Gloria and Apodaca, Old Havana/ Tel.: (537) 6822760.

El Tablao de Pancho (Cuban and international cuisine and pizzeria) 660 Zulueta St., second floor, between Gloria and Apodaca, Old Havana/ Tel.: (537) 8617761.

El Trofeo (Cuban cuisine)/ 563 Prado Promenade between Dragones and Teniente Rey, Old Havana / Tel.: (537) 8632985.

La Gaita (Spanish and Cuban cuisine) / 504 Egido St. between Monte and Dragones, Old Havana / Tel.: (537) 8623193.

Los Curros (Cuban, international and Italian cuisin) Santos Suárez St. on Rabí, Diez de Octubre Tel.: (537) 6405822 y 6491465.

Los Nardos (Spanish, Cuban and international cuisine)/ 563 Prado Promenade between Dragones and Teniente Rey, Old Havana/ Tel.: (537) 8632985.

Sociedad Cultural "Rosalía de Castro" (Cuban and international cuisine)/504 Egido St., second floor, between Monte and Dragones St., Old Havana/ Tel.: (537) 8611766.

Restaurants of Chinese Associations (Chinatown)

Chan Li Po (Chinese and Cuban cuisine) / 453 Campanario St., Centro Habana/ Tel.: (537) 8704747).

El Cantonés (Chinese and Cuban cuisine) / 564 Manrique St., Centro Habana/ Tel.: (537) 8632981.

El Gran Dragón (Chinese and Cuban cuisine) 1 Zanja St., Centro Habana/ Tel.: (537) 8615396.

Guang-Zhou (Chinese and Cuban cuisine)/ 1 Zanja St., Centro Habana/ Tel.: (537) 8615229.

La Dinastía Chao (Chinese and Cuban cuisine) / 356 Dragones St., Centro Habana/ Tel.: (537) 8618095.

La Flor de Loto (Chinese, international and Cuban cuisine)/ 313 Salud St., between Gervasio and Escobar, Centro Habana/ Tel.: (537) 8608501.

La Muralla China (Chinese and Cuban cuisine)/ 12 Zanja St., Centro Habana/ Tel.: (537) 8632081.

Li Lom Sai (cocina china y cubana) / 313 Dragones St., Centro Habana/Tel.: (537) 8622757.

Los Dos Dragones (Chinese and (Cuban cuisine)) / 311 Dragones St., Centro Habana/Tel.: (537) 8620909.

Los Tres Chinitos (Chinese, Cuban cuisine and pizzeria)/ 355 Dragones 355 between Manrique and San Nicolás, Centro Habana/ Tel.: (537) 863 3388.

Lung Kong (Chinese and Cuban cuisine) /364 Dragones St., Centro Habana/Tel.: (537) 8625388 y 8632061.

Min Chin Tang (Chinese and Cuban cuisine) / 513 Manrique, Centro Habana/ Tel.: (537) 8632966.

On Ten Tong (Chinese and Cuban cuisine) / 564 Manrique, Centro Habana/ Tel.: (537) 8632981.

Tien Tan (Chinese and Cuban cuisine) / 1 Zanja St., Centro Habana/ Tel.: (537) 8615478.

Wong Kong Ja Tong (Chinese and international cuisine, and pizzeria) / 414 Dragones, Centro Habana/ Tel.: (537) 8632068.

Mayabeque

El Congo (Coffee-shop)/National Expressway, Km 44, Güines/Tel.: (5347) 599283.

Los Morales (Coffee-shop)/National Expressway, Km 74, Nueva Paz.

Havana Club (Coffee-shop)/Vía Blanca Km 44, Santa Cruz del Norte.

Rancho Alto (Coffee-shop)/ National Expressway, Km 26½, San José de las Lajas.

Matanzas-Varadero

Albacora (seafood specialties) / 59 St. on Mar, Varadero/ Tel: (5345) 613650, 667320.

Antigüedades (seafood specialties)/ 1st. between 56 and 58, Josone Park, Varadero/ Tel: (5345) 667329.

Arrecife (Cuban cuisine)/Camino del Mar on 13 St., Varadero/Tel.: (5345) 668563.

Barracuda (Cuban and international cuisine)/ 1st. Ave. between 58 and 59, Varadero/ Tel: (5345) 668991.

Barbecue (Grill)/ Playa Alameda Hotel Varadero/ Tel: (5345) 668822.

Bodegón Criollo (Cuban cuisine) / Playa Ave. on 40 St., Varadero/ Tel: (5345) 667784.

Burgui Varadero (Coffee-shop)/ 1st. Ave. on 43 St., Varadero/ Tel: (5345) 667578.

Café Atenas (Coffee-shop)/ Vigía Square, Matanzas.

Capri (Italian cuisine) / 42 St. between Ave. and Playa, Varadero/ Tel: (5345) 612117.

Castell Nuovo (Italian cuisine) / Calle 1ra. y 11, Varadero/ Tel: (5345) 667786.

Cayo Libertad (International cuisine)/ Marina Varadero Docks/ Tel: (5345) 613730.

Chef Plaza (International cuisine)/ Sur Expressway, Km. 11, Plaza América Mall, Varadero/ Tel: (5345) 668181.

Coral Negro (Seafood specialties)/ 1st. on Punta Blanca, Varadero.

Cuevas de Bellamar (Cuban cuisine)/ Alcancía Farm, Matanzas/ Tel: (5345) 261683.

Dante (Italian cuisine)/ 1st. between 56 and 58, Josone Park, Varadero/Tel: (5345) 667738.

El Criollo International Pharmacy / 1st. and 18 St., Varadero/ Tel: (5345) 614794.

El Galeón (Seafood specialties)/ Gaviota Marina, Varadero / Tel: (5345) 616296.

El Paso (Coffee shop)/ 1st. on 7, Kawama, Varadero.

El Retiro (International cuisine)/ 1st between 56 and 58, Josone Park, Varadero/ Tel: (5345) 667316.

En Familia Plaza América (Coffee-shop)/ Plaza América Mall, Varadero Tel: (5345) 668181.

Esquina Cuba (Cuban cuisine)/ 1st. Ave, on 36 St., Varadero/ Tel.: (5345) 614019.

Guaimaré (Cuban cuisine)/ 1st. between 26 and 27, Varadero/ Tel: (5345) 611893.

Guantanamera (Cuban cuisine) Plaza América Mall, Varadero/ Tel.: (5345) 668181 ext.346.

Halong (Oriental cuisine)/ Camino del Mar on 12, Varadero/ Tel: (5345) 613787.

Kiki´s Club (Italian cuisine)/1st. on 6, Varadero/ Tel: (5345) 612266.

La Barbacoa (Cuban and international cuisine)/ 1st. Ave. on 64, Varadero/Tel: (5345) 667795.

La Cabañita (International cuisine)/ Camino del Mar on 11 St., Varadero/ Tel: (5345) 613787.

La Campana (Cuban cuisine)/ 1st. between 58 and 59, Josone Park, Varadero/ Tel: (5345) 667224.

La Esquina (Cuban cuisine)/ 36 St. on 1st., Ave. Varadero/ Tel: (5345) 614021.

La Fondue / Casa del Queso Cubano (International cuisine)/Ave. 1ra.between 62 and 63, Varadero/ Tel: (5345) 667747.

La Sangría (Cuban and international cuisine)/Calle 1ra., between 8 y 9, Varadero/Tel.(543)612025.

La Taberna (Cuban cuisine)/Camino del Mar between 13 and 14 St., Varadero/ Tel: (5345) 662018

La Terraza (Coffee-shop)/ Sur Expressway, Km. 11, Plaza América, Varadero/Tel: (5345) 668181.

La Vicaria (Cuban and international cuisine)/ 1st. Ave. on 38, Varadero/ Tel: (5345) 614721.

Lai Lai (Chinese cuisine)/ 1st. Ave. on 18, Varadero/ Tel: (5345) 667793.

Las Américas (International cuisine)/ Las Américas Highway, Km. 8 ½, Mansión Xanadú, Varadero/ Tel: (5345) 667388 y 667750.

Las Brasas (Cuban cuisine)/Camino del Mar and 12 St, Varadero/Tel: (5345) 612407.

Mallorca (Cuban and international cuisine)/ 1st. between 61 and 62, Varadero/ Tel: (5345) 667746.

Chapulín Marina (seafood specialties)/Las Morlas Highway, Km. 12 ½, Varadero/ Tel: (5345) 668727.

Mediterráneo (International cuisine)/ 54 on 1st., Varadero/Tel: (5345) 612460.

Mesón del Quijote (Cuban and international cuisine)/ Las Américas Highway, Km. 1, La Torre, Varadero/ Tel: (5345) 667796.

Mi Casita (Cuban and international cuisine) Camino del Mar between 11 and 12 St, Varadero/ Tel: (5345) 613787.

Pizza Caribe (Italian cuisine)/ Varadero Docks/ Tel.: (5345) 667666.

Pizza Nova (Italian cuisine)/ Sur Expressway. Km. 11, Plaza América, Varadero/Tel:(5345) 668181.

Ranchón El Criollito (Cuban cuisine)/ 1st. on 40 St., Varadero/ Tel: (5345) 612180.

Restaurante Chino (Oriental cuisine)/ 54 on 1st., Varadero/ Tel: (5345) 612460.

Rancho El Caney (International cuisine) 1st. Ave. on 40 St., Varadero.

Ranchón El Compay (Cuban cuisine) /54 St. between 1st. Ave, and Playa, Varadero/ Tel.: (5345) 612460, 613525.

Ranchón Josone (Cuban and international cuisine)/ 1st. Ave. between 58 and 59 St., Varadero/ Tel.: (5345) 667738.

Salón de la Reina (International cuisine)/ 1st. between 25 and 26 St., Varadero/ Tel: (5345) 667736, 614702.

Salón Violeta (Italian cuisine)/ 44 on 1st., Varadero/Tel: (5345) 612866.

Isle of Youth

Arco Iris (Seafood specialties)/ El Colony International Diving Center /Tel.: (5346) 398181.

El Cazador (International cuisine)/ El Colony Hotel /Tel.: (5346) 398181.

El Cochinito (Cuban cuisine)/ 39 on 24 St., Nueva Gerona/Tel.: (5346) 322809.

El Galeón (International cuisine) / El Colony Hotel /Tel.: (5346) 398181.

Night Centers

Pinar del Río

Café Pinar (Nightclub)/ 23 Velez Caviedez St., Pinar del Río/ Tel.: (5348) 778199.

María (Bar)/ María La Gorda Diving Center, Pinar del Río/ Tel.: (5348) 778131.

Palenque de los Cimarrones (Nightclub)/ Puerto Esperanza Highway, Km 34, Viñales / Tel.: (5348) 796290.

Ranchón San Vicente (Bar)/ Puerto Esperanza Highway, Km 38, Viñales.

Rumayor Nightclub (Nightclub)/, Viñales Highway, Km 1½ Pinar del Río/ Tel.: (5348) 763051.

Havana

Alí Bar (Nightclub)/ Dolores Ave. on Lucero, Arroyo Naranjo/Tel.: (537) 6938011.

Amanecer (Nightclub)/ 152 15 St., El Vedado, Plaza/Tel.: (537) 8329075.

Café Cantante Mi Habana (Nightclub)/Paseo on 39, Teatro Nacional, Plaza/Tel.: (537)8784275, 8789546.

Casa de la Música Habana (Nightclub)/Galiano, between Neptuno and Concordia, Centro Habana/Tel.: (537)8624165.

Casa de la Música Miramar (Nightclub)/3398 20th St., on 35 St., Miramar, Playa/Tel.: (537)2046147, 2026147.

Chan Chan (Nightclub) / 5th on 248, Marina Hemingway, Playa/Tel.: (537)2044698.

Chévere (Nightclub)/ 49C St. on 28A, Playa/Tel.: (537)2044990.

Club El Trébol (Nightclub)/Vía Blanca, Km 18, Santa María, East Havana/ Tel.: (537) 7971014.

Club Imágenes (Nightclub)/Calzada on C, El Vedado, Plaza /Tel.: (537) 8833606.

Club Le Select (Snack Bar)/2807 28th St. between 5th and 7th, Miramar/Tel.: (537)2079681.

Cocodrilo Humor Club (Nightclub)/ 3rd, between 10 and 12, Plaza/Tel.: (537)8335305.

Copa Room (Nightclub)/ Riviera Hotel, Paseo on Malecón, El Vedado/Tel.: (537) 8344214-18.

Delirio Habanero (Piano Bar)/Paseo on 39, Teatro Nacional, Plaza/Tel.: (537)8784275.

Dos Gardenias (Nightclub) /7th on 26 St., Miramar, Playa/Tel.: (537) 2042353.

El Floridita (Bar)/557 Obispo St., Old Havana /Tel.: (537) 8671300-01.

El Mirador (Bar)/ Morro-Cabaña Great Historic Park, East Havana/Tel.: (537) 8609990.

El Polvorín (Snack Bar)/ Monumental Ave., La Cabaña Fortress /Tel.: (537) 8609990.

Fresa y Chocolate (Cultural Center)/ 23 St. between 10 and 12, El Vedado, Plaza/Tel.: (537) 8339278.

Gato Tuerto (Nightclub)/ O St. on 19, El Vedado, Plaza/Tel.: (537) 8382696.

Guanabo Club (Nightclub)/ 466 St., between 13 and 15, Guanabo, East Havana/Tel.: (537) 7962884.

Guanimar (Nightclub)/ 5th between 466 and 468, Guanabo, East Havana /Tel.: (537) 7962947.

Habana Café (Nightclub)/ Meliá Cohíba Hotel, El Vedado, Plaza/Tel.: (537) 8333636.

Jardines de La Tropical (Nightclub)/ 41 Ave. on 46, Playa/Tel.: (537) 2035322.

Jardines del 1830 (Nightclub)/ 1252 Malecón Ave. on 20, El Vedado, Plaza/Tel.: (537) 8383090-92.

Jazz Café (Nightclub)/ Paseo on 3rd., El Vedado, Plaza/Tel.: (537) 8383556.

La Zorra y el Cuervo (Nightclub) 23 St. between M and N, El Vedado, Plaza/ Tel. (537)8332402.

Longina (Bar)/ 3308 20 St. on 35, Miramar, Playa.

Los Orishas (Nightclub)/ 175 Martí St., between Cruz Verde and Lama, Guanabacoa/Tel.: (537) 6947878.

Macumba Habana (Nightclub)/ 222 St. between 37 St. and Autopista, La Coronela, La Lisa/ Tel.: (537) 2730568.

Nacional Nightclub (Nightclub)/208 San Rafael St., Centro Habana/Tel.: (537) 8632361.

Opus Bar (Bar)/Calzada on D St., El Vedado, Plaza/ Tel.: (537) 8365429.

Parisién (Nightclub)/ Nacional de Cuba Hotel, O St. on 21 St., El Vedado, Plaza/Tel.: (537) 8363564-67 y 8380294.

Piano Bar El Diablo Tun Tun (Nightclub)/ 20 St on 35 St., Miramar, Playa/Tel.: (537) 2044476.

Piano Bar Maragato (Nightclub)/ Florida Hotel, Old Havana/Tel.: (537) 8624127.

Pico Blanco (Nightclub)/ Saint John's Hotel, El Vedado, Plaza/Tel.: (537) 8333740 y 8344187.

Sala Atril (Nightclub)/ Karl Marx Complex, 1st Ave., between 8 and 10 St., Miramar, Playa/Tel.: (537) 2067596.

Salón Rojo (Nightclub)/ Capri Hotel, 21 St. between N and O St., El Vedado, Plaza/Tel.: (537) 8333747.

Salón Rosado Benny Moré (Nightclub)/ La Tropical Gardens, Marianao/Tel.: (537) 2061281.

Son de la Madrugada (Cultural Center)/ 509 18 St., between 5th and 7th Ave., Miramar, Playa/Tel.: (537) 2041212.

Tropicana (Nightclub)/ 72 St., between 41 and 45 St., Marianao/Tel.: (537) 2670174- 2671717 y 2671718.

Turquino (Nightclub)/ Habana Libre Hotel, El Vedado, Plaza/Tel.: (537) 8346100 y 8384011.

Matanzas

Club FM 17 (Nightclub)/ 1st. Ave. on 17, Varadero/ Tel.: (5345) 614831.

Club La Barra 1470 (Nightclub)/ Calzada on Calvo, Cárdenas/Tel.: (5345) 522368.

Club Matanzas (Nightclub)/Vía Blanca, Km 1, Peñas Altas, Matanzas /Tel.: (5345) 253567.

Continental (Nightclub)/ Internacional Hotel, Las Américas Highway, Km 1, Varadero/Tel.: (5345) 667038.

Cueva del Pirata (Nightclub)/ Sur Expressway, Km 10½, Varadero/Tel.: (5345) 667751.

El Jagüey (Nightclub)/Viaducto between Cuní and San Diego, Matanzas/Tel.: (5345) 253387.

Habana Café (Nightclub)/ La Torre, Varadero/Tel.: (5345) 668070.

Havana Club (Disco)/ 62 St. on 3rd St., Varadero/ Tel.: (5345) 665178.

Kastillito (Nightclub)/ Playa Ave. on 49 St., Varadero/Tel.: (5345) 613888.

La Bolera (Nightclub)/ Céspedes between 28 and 29 St, Cárdenas/Tel.: (5345) 525336.

La Cumbre (Nightclub)/Vía Blanca, Km 4½, Matanzas/Tel.: (5345) 265380.

La Rumba (Disco)/ Las Américas Highway, Km 3½, Varadero/Tel.: (5345) 668210.

Mambo Club (Nightclub)/ Las Morlas Highway, Km 14, Varadero/Tel.: (5345) 668243, 668565.

Tropicana (Nightclub)/Vía Blanca, Km 102, Matanzas/Tel.: (5345) 265381.

Isle of Youth

El Patio (Nightclub)/24 St. on 37 St., Nueva Gerona/ Tel.: (5346) 322346.

Mojito (Bar)/ El Colony Hotel, Isla de la Juventud.

Stores

Pinar del Río

Bodegón La Conchita/ San Juan St. on Isidro de Armas St./ Tel. : (5348) 750171/ Supermarkets.

Casa del Ron/ 151 Antonio Maceo St. on Antonio Tarafa St. / Tel.(5348) 778020/ Cuban rum, nonalcoholic beverage, souvenir.

Casa del Tabaco / 162 Antonio Maceo St., between Rafael Morales and Luz Zaldivar St. / Tel. : (5348) 772244/ Specialized Store.

El Comercio/ Martí St., between Rafael Morales and Ormany Arenado St. / Tel.: (5348) 773022/ Supermarket.

El Jamaiquino/ Sandino Mall/ Tel.: (5348) 423624/ Specialized Store.

El Veguero/ Viñales Highway Km 25/ Tel.: (5348) 796080/ Specialized Store.

Estanco del Tabaco/ 157 Antonio Maceo St. between Abraham Lincoln and Antonio Tarafa St./ Tel.: (5348) 778122 / Specialized Store.

Estanco II/ Km 26, Puerto Esperanza Highway / Tel. (5348) 796090/ tobacco.

Hotel La Ermita/ La Ermita Highway Km 1½, /Tel.: (5348) 796394/ General and Specialized Store.

Hotel Los Jazmines Cava/ Viñales Highway Km 23/ Tel.: (5348) 796394/ Specialized Store.

Hotel Los Jazmines/ Viñales Highway Km 23 / Tel.: (5348) 796394 /General and Specialized Store.

Hotel Mirador de San Diego/ 23 St. at the end, San Diego de los Baños/ General and Specialized Store Tel (5348) 548832.

Hotel Pinar del Río/ Martí St. at the end/ Tel.: (5348) 755070/ General Store.

La Aurora/ 57 Martí St., Between Rafael Morales and Ormany Arenado/ Tel.: (5348) 757649/ General Store.

La Guayabita del Pinar/ 189 Recreo St., between Virtudes and Sol/ Tel.:(5348) 752966/ Drinks and handicraft.

María La Gorda/ María la Gorda International Diving Center, La Bajada, Guanahacabibes Peninsula, San Antonio Cape, General Store Tel.: (5348) 778131.

Mural of Prehistory/ Pons Highway, Km 4, Dos Hermanas Valley/ Tel.: (5348) 796402/ General Store.

Patio del Decimista/ 174 Salvador Cisneros St. / Tel. (5348) 796014/ Specialized Store.

Photoclub/ 63B Salvador Cisneros St., Tel. : (5348) 796264/ Photographs and videos.

Pinareño/ 28 Martí St. between Gerardo Medina and Isabel Rubio St. /Specialized Store.

Viñales Complex/ 42 Salvador Cisneros St. on Ceferino Fernández St. / Tel.: (5348) 796358 / General Store.

Artemisa

El Caribe / 48 on 29, Artemisa/ Tel.: (5348) 362436.

El Salado/ Panamericana Highway, El Salado, Baracoa Beach/ Tel. (5347) 378460 / General Store.

Hotel Moka/ Las Terrazas Community/ Tel. (5348) 578656/ General and Specialized Store.

Soroa/ Soroa Highway, Km 8 ½, / Tel.: (5348) 522052/ General and Specialized Store.

Havana

Arte en Boyeros/ 13 Ave., between 8 and 10 St., Santiago de las Vegas/ Specialized Store /Tel.: (537) 6834113.

Arte en Obispo/ Obispo between Compostela and Aguacate/ Specialized Store Tel.: (537) 8644441.

Arte Malecón/ D St. between 1st St. and 3rd, El Vedado/ Specialized Store.

Artehabana Plaza Cultural/ San Rafael on Industria, Centro Habana/ Specialized Store /Tel.: (537) 8608403.

Artesanía Sevilla/ Sevilla Hotel, Trocadero between Prado Promenade and Zulueta, Old Havana/ General Store / Atlántico/Tel.: (537) 8609046.

Bazar Angerona/ 4205 3rd St., between 42 and 44 St., Miramar/ Specialized Store.

Bazar Wifredo Lam/ 22 San Ignacio St., on Empedrado St., Old Havana/ Specialized Store.

Casa del Café/ Baratillo between Obispo and Jústiz St., Old Havana/ Specialized Store Tel.: (537) 8668061.

Casa del Habano Partagás/ 320 Industria St., between Dragones and Barcelona St., Centro Habana / Specialized Store / Tel.: (537) 8668060.

Casa del Habano Vega Robaina/ Meliá Habana Hotel, 3rd.Ave. on 84 St., Miramar/ Specialized Store /Tel.: (537) 2045289.

Casa del Habano/ Nacional de Cuba Hotel, 21 St. on O St., Vedado/Specialized Store /Tel.: (537) 8363564.

Casa Flores/ 5th Ave. on 160 St., Miramar/General Store / Tel (537) 2722310.

Casa LG / Jerusalén Building, Miramar Trade Center / Specialized Store / Tel.: (537) 2046932.

Casa Panasonic/ Jardines Building, 5th Ave., between 112 and 114 St. / Miramar/ Specialized Store.

Casa Pioneer / 5thA between 40 and 42 St., Miramar/ Specialized Store.

Centro Comercial Altahabana/ Boyeros Ave. on 6th St., Altahabana, Boyeros/ General Store /Tel.: (537) 6444280 y 6444278.

Centro Comercial Náutico / 5th Ave., between 152 and 154 St., Playa/ General Store Tel.: (537) 2086212.

Centro Comercial Palco / 188 St. between 5th and 1st Ave. / Flores, Playa/ General Store Tel.: (537) 2732168.

Centro Comercial Tarará/ 19 St. on 6th St., East Havana/ General Store.

Chateau's Store / Chateau Hotel, 1st Ave. on 60 St., Miramar/ General Store / Tel.: (537) 2041952.

Chinese Store/ Miramar Trade Center, 76 St. on 5th, Miramar/ General Store / Tel.: (537) 2040074.

Colección Habana/O'Reilly St. on Mercaderes St., Old Havana/Patrimonial /Tel.: (537) 8513388.

Complejo Morro-Cabaña/ La Cabaña Highway / Specialized Store.

Confecciones Inglaterra/ San Rafael on Prado/ General Store.

D'Talle Boutique/ Oasis Panorama Hotel, 70 St. between 3rd Ave. and 1st Ave./ General Store / Tel.: (537) 2044969.

Deauville/ Deauville Hotel, Galiano on San Lázaro/ General Store / Tel.: (537) 8668148 y 8668812.

Diplomáticos/ Jerusalén Building, Miramar Trade Center / Specialized Store / Tel.: (537) 2046932.

Dita 7ma y 84/ 708 84 St. between 7th y 9th, Ave Miramar/ Specialized Store / Tel.: (537) 2048093.

El Aljibe / 7th Ave. on 26 St., Miramar/ Specialized Store / Tel.: (537) 2041583.

El Cedro/ Occidental Miramar Hotel, 5th Ave. between 72 and 76 St., Miramar/ General Store /Tel.: (537)2043584.

El Pilar/ Port Ave., Los Marinos Club, Old Havana/ General Store.

FotoClub Comodoro/ Comodoro Hotel, 3rd. on 84 St., Miramar/ Specialized Store / Tel.: (537) 2042830.

FotoClub Dos Gardenias/ Dos Gardenias, 7th. Ave. on 26 St., Miramar/ Specialized Store /Tel.: (537) 2049517 y 2069530.

Fotoclub Plaza de la Revolución/ Cobre Ave. between 8 and 10 St., Armonía Villa, Tarará/ Specialized Store.

Galería Comercial Guanabo/ 5th Ave. on 476 St., Guanabo/ General Store.

Galería Comercial Manzana de Gómez/ San Rafael between Monserrate and Zulueta St., Old Havana/ General Store.

Galería Comercial/ Habana Libre Hotel, 23 St on L St., El Vedado/ Boutique / Tel.: (537) 8346100.

Galería de tiendas Palco Hotel / Palco Hotel, 146 between 11 and 13 St., Playa/ General Store /Tel.: (537) 2084080.

Galerías Cohíba/ Meliá Cohiba Hotel, 3rd. on Paseo Ave., El Vedado/ Boutique / Tel.: (537) 8333636).

Galerías Comodoro/ Comodoro Hotel, 3rd. on 84 St., Miramar/ Boutique /Tel.: (537) 2046177.

Galerías Marina Hemingway/ Marina Hemingway, 5th Ave on 248 St. / Boutique/ Tel.: (537) 2049636.

Galerías Neptuno - Tritón/ Neptuno-Tritón Hotel, 3rd. on 70 St., Miramar/General Store /Tel.: (537) 2040506.

General Store/ Riviera Hotel, Paseo on Malecón, Vedado/ General Store / Tel.: (537) 8364051.

Gusto Cubano/ NH Parque Central Hotel, Neptuno between Prado Promenade and Zulueta St./ General Store /Tel.: (537) 8606628.

Imagen Cuba Siglo XXI/ Panorama Hotel, 70 St. between 3rd Ave. on 1st, Miramar/ General Store /Tel.: (537) 2044969.

Jardín Wagner/ Mercaderes between Obispo and Obrapía St., Old Havana/ Flower Shop/ Tel.: (537) 669017.

José Martí International Airport (Terminals 1, 2, and 3)/ Van Troi Ave. on General Peraza St. / General Store / Tel.: (537) 2664324.

La Elegante/ Occidental Miramar Hotel, 5th Ave. between 72 and 76 St., Miramar/ Tel.: (537) 204 3917, 204 3584 ext. 837/ Boutique.

La Habana Sí (All the Recordings)/ 23 on L St., El Vedado/ Specialized Store / Tel.: (537) 8383162.

Legendario/ 1417 Calzada del Cerro St. between Patria and Auditor St., Cerro/ General and Specialized Store.

Longina (All the Recordings)/ 360 Obispo St. between Habana and Compostela St./ Specialized Store /Tel.: (537) 8628371.

Marco Polo/ Mercaderes between Obispo and Obrapía St./Specialized in Spices.

Mercado del Oriente /Mercaderes, between Obispo and Obrapía St. /Patrimonial-Specialized Store /Tel.: (537) 8669569.

Moda y Punto/ 17th Ave. between 174 and 190 St., Siboney, Playa/ General Store.

National Library/ Independencia Ave. on 20 de Mayo St., Plaza/ Specialized Store /Tel.: (537) 8815083.

Palco Bazar / Palace of Conventions, 146 St. between 11 and 13 St., Playa/ Specialized Store /Tel.: (537) 2026011y 2084080).

Perfumería Habana 1791/Mercaderes on Obrapía St., Old Havana/Specialized Store / Tel.: (537) 8613525.

Perfumería/ Copacabana Hotel, 1st Ave. on 44 St., Miramar/ General Store /Tel.: (537) 2040340.

Plaza Nueva Caracol/ 5th Ave. between 464 and 466 St., Guanabo /General Store / Tel.: (537) 7962449.

Residencial Club Habana's Store/ 5th Ave., between 188 and 192 St., Flores, Playa/ General Store / Tel.: (537) 2043300.

Santa María/ Las Terrazas Ave., Santa María/ General Store / Tel.: (537) 7971268.

Siglo XXI Beauty Parlor/ Oasis Panorama Hotel, 70 St. between/ 3rd and 1ra Ave., Miramar/General Store /Tel.: (537) 2040100.

Taberna El Galeón/ Baratillo between Obispo and Jústiz St. / Specialized Store /Tel.: (537) 8668476.

Tres Toneles/5th Ave. on 456 St., Boca Ciega, East Havana/ General Store / Tel.: (537) 7967134.

T-Shirt/ Palacio de Artesanía, Cuba St., between Cuartel and Peña Pobre St. / General Store / Tel.: (537) 8668072.

Variedades/ Meliá Habana Hotel, 3rd. on 82 St., Miramar/ General Store /Tel.: (537) 2048500.

Mayabeque

Casa Verde 1204 21 St., Nueva Paz/Tel.: (5347) 544129.

El Desarrollo/ 11 on 24 St., Santa Cruz del Norte / Tel.: (5347) 294222.

El Mercado/ 47 Ave. on 64 St., San José de las Lajas/ Tel.: (5347) 861253.

El Paraíso/69 St. on 54 St., Güines/ Tel.: (5347) 523428

El Trópico/ Jibacoa Beach, Santa Cruz del Norte / Tel.: (5347) 295203.

Matanzas-Varadero

Aroma de Playa/ 1st. on 42 St. / Specialized Store.

Arte Cubano/1st. Ave. between 12 and 13 St., Varadero/ Specialized Store / Tel.: (5345) 668281.

Bazar Cuba / 64 St. and Autopista/ Specialized Store / Tel.: (5345) 667691.

Benetton/ Sur Expressway, Km 11 ½, Varadero/ Specialized Boutique /Tel.: (5345) 668281.

Boca de Guamá/ Girón Beach Highway, Zapata Swamp/ Specialized Store /Tel.: (5345) 915643.

Boutique Europa/ Sur Expressway, Km 11 ½/ Specialized Store / Tel.: (5345) 668281.

Brisas del Caribe / Las Américas Highway, Varadero/ Specialized Store / Tel.: (5345) 667622.

Casa del Habano Licorera/ 63 St. on 1st. Ave./ Specialized Store / Tel.: (5345) 614719 y 667843.

Casa del Habano/ 63 St. on 1st. Ave., Varadero/ Specialized Store / Tel.: (5345) 614719 y 667843.

Casa del Ron/ 63 St. on 1st. Ave./ Specialized Store /Tel.: (5345) 668393.

Casa del Tabaco/ Sur Expressway, Km 11 ½/ Specialized Store / Tel.: (5345) 668281.

Centro Comercial Hicacos/ 1ra Ave., between 44 y 46 St., Varadero/ Specialized Store.

Coral Negro/ Sur Expressway, Km 11 ½, Varadero/ Specialized Boutique / Tel.: (5345) 668281.

Deportes/Sur Expressway, Km 11 ½, Varadero/ Specialized Store / Tel.: (5345) 668281.

Dos Delfines/ Varadero Dolphinarium, Las Morlas Highway /Specialized Store / Tel.: (5345) 668353.

Elegante/ Sur Expressway, Km 11 ½, Varadero/ Boutique Tel.: (5345) 668281.

Fariani/Sur Expressway, Km 11 ½, Varadero/ Specialized Store / Tel.: (5345) 668281.

Fotoclub Delfinario/Sur Expressway, Km 16, Varadero/ Photographs and Videos.

Fotoclub Plaza/ Sur Expressway, Km 11 ½, Varadero/Photographs and Videos/Tel.: (5345) 668281.

Fotoclub Tropicana/ Varadero Highway, Km 7/ Photographs and Videos.

Giorgio/ Hicacos Mall, 1st. Ave. between 44 and 46 St., Varadero/ Specialized Boutique.

Giorgio/Sur Expressway, Km 11 ½, Varadero/ Specialized Boutique / Tel.: (5345) 668281.

Hicacos/ 1st. Ave., between 33 and 34 St., Varadero/ Specialized Store.

Juan Gualberto Gómez Airport's Stores / Specialized Stores/ Tel.: (5345) 253640.

Karamba/Sur Expressway, Km 11 ½, Varadero/ Specialized Store / Tel.: (5345) 668281.

Laguna del Tesoro/Boca de Guamá, Zapata Swamp/ Specialized Store.

Los Almendros / 1st. Ave., between 33 and 34 St., Varadero/ Supermarket and General Store.

Mediterráneo/ 1st. Ave. on 54 St., Varadero/ Specialized Store / Tel.: (5345) 668985.

Mundo Infantil/ 13 St. between 1st. and Caminos del Mar, Varadero/ Specialized Store.

Peletería/Sur Expressway, Km 11 ½, Varadero/ Boutique Specialized Store /Tel.: (5345) 668281.

Perfumería/Sur Expressway, Km 11 ½, Varadero/ Specialized Boutique / Tel.: (5345) 668281.

Plaza América/ Las Américas Highway, Varadero/ Specialized Store Tel.: (5345) 668181.

Plaza Caracol/ 54 St. on 1st. Ave., Varadero/ Specialized Store Tel.: (5345) 614715.

Plaza Mar del Sur/ 32 St. on 3rd. Ave., Varadero/ Specialized Store.

Puma/Sur Expressway, Km 11 ½, Varadero/ Specialized Boutique / Tel.: (5345) 668281.

Rifle/ Hicacos Mall, 1st. Ave. between 44 y 46 St., Varadero/ Specialized Boutique.

Show Room/ 208 60 St. between 2nd and 3rd Ave., Varadero/ Specialized Store /Tel.: (5345) 611837.

Solymar / 64 St. and Autopista, Varadero/ Specialized Store/ Tel.: (5345) 678990.

Souvenir Cuba /Sur Expressway, Km 11 ½, Varadero/ Specialized Store / Tel.: (5345) 668281.

Souvenir Isla/ 1st. Ave. on 15 St., Varadero/ Specialized Store.

Souvenir Varadero/1st. Ave. on 15 St., Varadero/ Specialized Store.

Ted Lapidus/Sur Expressway, Km 11 ½, Varadero/ Boutique Tel (5345) 668281.

Tienda Caracol (JB)/Sur Expressway, Km 11 ½, Varadero/ Specialized Boutique /Tel.: (5345) 668281.

Varadero Fashion/ Sur Expressway, Km 11 ½/ Specialized Boutique / Tel.: (5345) 668281.

Varadero Sport/ 63 St. between 1st and 2nd Ave./ Specialized Store.

Isle of Youth

Airport/ Cayo Largo/ Boutique /Tel.: (5345) 248123 ext 125.

Barceló Cayo Largo/ Cayo Largo del Sur/ Boutique /Tel.: (5345) 248123 ext 121.

Bucanero/ Cayo Largo/Boutique /Tel.: (5345) 248123 ext 131.

Casa del Tabaco/ Cayo Largo/ Boutique /Tel.: (5345) 248123 ext 211.

El Boulevard / Martí Ave., between 22 and 24 St., Nueva Gerona/ Supermarket and General Store.

El Sucu Sucu/ 2408 Martí Ave., between 24 and 26 St., Nueva Gerona /Specialized Store.

Imagen Cayo Largo del Sur/Tel.: (5345) 248123

Isla del Sur /Cayo Largo del Sur / Boutique /Tel.: (5345) 248123 ext 045.

Joyería Coral Negro/Cayo Largo/ Boutique /Tel. (5345) 248123 ext 211.

La Cubana/ Martí Ave., on 18 St., Nueva Gerona / Supermarket and General Store.

Playa Sirena/Cayo Largo/Boutique.

Sol Cayo Largo/ Sol Cayo Largo Hotel / Boutique /Tel.: (5345) 248123 ext 122.

Sol Pelícano/Cayo Largo del Sur/ Tel.: (5345) 248123 ext. 045.

Attractions and Sites of Interest

Pinar del Río

Casa Garay Distillery/ 189 Isabel Rubio Sur St., between Ceferino Fernández and Frank País St., Pinar del Río/ Tel.: (5348) 752966.

Francisco Donatién Cigar Factory/ Máximo Gómez St., Pinar del Río, Tel.: (5348) 773069.

Gallery of the Visual Arts Provincial Center/ 7 Antonio Guiteras St., between Maceo and Martí St./ Tel.: (5348) 752758.

Guasch Palace/ 202 Martí Este St., on Comandante Pinares St., Pinar del Río.

José Jacinto Milanés Theater/ 60 José Martí St., between Recreo and Colón St., Pinar del Río/ Tel.: (5348) 753871.

Pedro Pablo Oliva's House and Workshop /160 José Martí St., between Volcán and Cuarteles St./ Tel.: (5348) 753117.

Pinar del Rio's Art Museum (MAPRI)/ 9 Martí St., between Velez Caviedes and Rosario St. /Tel.: (5348) 774671.

Provincial Museum of History / 58 Martí Este St. between Colón and Isabel Rubio St., Pinar del Río, Tel (5348) 754300.

Tranquilino Sandalio de Noda Museum of Natural History / 202 Martí St. on Comandante Pinares St./ Tel.: (5348) 753087/ 778493.

Viñales Museum of Paleontology / Dos Hermanas Camping, Moncada Highway, by the Mural of Prehistory / Tel.: (5348) 793223.

Artemisa

Angerona Coffee Hacienda/ Artemisa-Cayajabos Road, Km 5.5, Sousse Farm.

Antonio Maceo Memorial/ San Pedro, Punta Brava, Bauta.

Artemisa Municipal Museum/ 2307 Martí St., between Mártires and Agramonte St., Artemisa/ Tel.: (5347)362191.

Eduardo Abela Gallery/ 3708 58 St., between 37 and 39 St., San Antonio de los Baños/ Tel.: (5347) 384224.

International Museum of Humor / 60 St., between 41 and 45 St., San Antonio de los Baños/ Tel.: (5347)382817.

Havana

Acapulco Movie Theater / 26 St., between 35 and 39 St., Vedado/ Tel.: (537) 8339573.

Actualidades Movie Theater / 262 Bélgica Ave., between Neptuno and Virtudes St. /Tel.: (537) 8615193.

Adolfo Llauradó Theater/ 11 St., between D and E St., El Vedado/ Tel.: (537) 8325373.

Alexander von Humboldt's House / 254 Oficios St. on Muralla St., Old Havana/ Tel. (537) 8639850.

Amadeo Roldán Auditorium/ 512 Calzada St. on D St., Vedado/ Tel.: (537) 8321168.

Aquarium/ 9 Teniente Rey St., between Oficios and Mercaderes St., Old Havana/Tel: (537) 8639493.

Archeology Museum and Laboratory / 12 Tacón St., between O'Reilly and Empedrado St., Old Havana/Tel.: (537) 8604298, 8614469.

Bertolt Brecht Theater/ 13 St. on I St. Vedado/ Tel.: (537) 8329359.

Buendía Theater/ Loma St. on 39 St., Nuevo Vedado/ Tel.: (537) 8816689.

Camera Obscura (Lookout) / Teniente Rey on Mercaderes St., Main Square, Old Havana / Tel.: (537) 8621801 / 8664461.

Carmen Montilla Gallery/ 162 Oficios St., between Amargura and Churruca St., Old Havana/ Tel.: (537) 8668768.

Casa de las Américas/ 3rd. and G St., El Vedado, Plaza /Tel.: (537) 8382706.

Center of Spanish American Culture / 17 Malecón, Old Havana/ Tel.: (537) 8606282.

Chaplin Movie Theater / 23 St. between 10 and 12 St, Vedado/ Tel.: (537) 831101.

Church of St. Francis of Paula (concert hall)/ Leonor Pérez St. on Port Avenue, Old Havana/ Tel.: (537) 8604210.

Convent of St. Francis of Assisi (Concert hall and Museum of Sacred Art) /Oficios St., between Amargura and Churruca St., Old Havana/ Tel.: (537) 8623467.

El Arca Puppet Theater / Port Ave. on Obrapía St., Historic Center/ Tel.: (537)8648953.

El Templete / Baratillo St. on O'Reilly St., Main Square, Old Havana.

El Sótano Theater/ K St., between 25 and 27, Vedado/Tel.: (537) 8320630.

Ernest Hemingway Museum / Vigía St. on Steinhart St., Vigía Estate, San Francisco de Paula/ Tel.;(537) 6910809.

Forma Gallery/ 255 Obispo St., between Cuba and Aguiar St. / Tel: (537) 8620123.

Former San José Warehouses Cultural Center (handicrafts fair)/ Port Avenue, at the end of Paula Poplar Grove Avenue, Old Havana.

Gran Teatro de La Habana/ Prado Promenade on San José St./ Tel.: (537) 8617391.

Guanabacoa Municipal Museum/ 108 Martí St. on Versalles St. / Tel. (537) 7979117, 7972078.

Habana Factory (Contemporary Art and Experimentation Center) / 308 O'Reilly St. between Habana and Aguiar St., Old Havana/ Tel. (537) 864 9518.

Habana Gallery/ 460 Línea St., between E and F St., Vedado/Tel.: (537) 8327101.

Hand-Made Paper Workshop/ 120 Mercaderes St. (Ground floor), between Obispo and Obrapía St., Old Havana/ Tel.: (537)8613356.

Historical Center's Amphitheater / Port Avenue, between Cuba and Peña Pobre St., Old Havana/ Tel.: (537) 8639464.

House of Africa/ 157 Obrapía, between Mercaderes and San Ignacio St., Old Havana/ Tel. (537) 8615798.

House of Chinese Arts and Traditions / 313 Salud, between Gervasio and Escobar St., Centro Habana/ Tel.: (537) 8635450, 8609976, 8639632.

House of Asia/ 111 Mercaderes St., between Obispo and Obrapía St., Old Havana/ Tel.: (537) 8639740.

House of the Obra Pía/ 158 Obrapía St., between Mercaderes and San Ignacio St., Old Havana/ Tel. (537) 8613097.

House of Poetry / 63 Muralla St. (Ground floor), between Oficios and Inquisidor St., Old Havana/ Tel.: (537) 8621801.

House of Arabs/ 16 Oficios St., between Obispo and Obrapía St., Old Havana/Tel.: (537) 862 0082.

House of México/ Obrapía on Mercaderes St., Old Havana/ Tel.: (537) 8618166.

House of Simón Bolívar / 156 Mercaderes St., between Obrapía and Lamparilla St., Old Havana/ Tel.: (537) 8613988.

House of El Vedado/ 664 23 St., Vedado, Plaza de la Revolución/ Tel.: (537) 835 3398.

House of the Green Tiles / 2 St., between 3rd and 5th Ave., Miramar / Tel.: (537)2125282.

House of Víctor Hugo/ 311 O'Reilly St., between Habana and Aguiar St., Old Havana/ Tel.: (537) 8667590-91.

Hubert de Blanck Theater/ Calzada St., between A and B St., Vedado/ Tel.: (537) 8301011.

Hurón Azul Museum/ Paz St., between Constancia and Lindero, Párraga/ Tel. (537) 6438246.

José Martí's Birthplace and Museum / 314 Leonor Pérez St., between Picota and Egido St., Old Havana/Tel.: (537) 8613778.

José Martí Memorial / Paseo on Carlos Manuel de Céspedes, Plaza de la Revolución/ Tel. (537) 8382347.

José Martí National Library / Independencia Ave. on 20 de Mayo St., Plaza de la Revolución/ Tel.: (537) 855442/ 45.

Karl Marx Theater/ 1st. St., between 8 and 10 St., Miramar/ Tel.: (537) 2030801/05.

La Acacia Gallery/ 114 San José St., between Industria and Consulado St., Centro Habana/Tel.: (537) 8613533- 8639364.

La Casona Gallery/ 107 Muralla St. on San Ignacio St., Old Square / Tel.: (537) 8622633.

La Moderna Poesía Bookstore /525 Obispo St. on Bernaza St., Old Havana/ Tel.: (537) 8616640.

La Rampa Movie Theater /23 St. between N and O St, Vedado/ Tel.: (537) 8366146.

Lenin Park / 100 St. and Cortina de la Presa, Havana/ Tel.: (537) 6442721.

Lumière Cinema / 14 Mercaderes St., between Obispo and Obrapía St., Old Havana/ Tel.: (537) 8664425

Mella Theater/ 657 Línea St., between A and B St., Vedado/Tel.: (537) 8335651/8696.

Model of the Historical Center / 114 Mercaderes St., between Obispo and Obrapía St., Old Havana/ Tel.: (537) 8664425.

Morro-Cabaña Complex/ La Cabaña Fortress Road, East Havana/Tel.: (537) 862 4095, 862 4097.

Museum of Chocolate / Mercaderes St. on Amargura St., Old Havana/ Tel.: (537) 8664431.

Museum of Colonial Art / 61 San Ignacio St., Cathedral Square, Old Havana/ Tel.: (537) 8664458.

Museum of Dancing / 251 Línea St. on G St. Vedado/ Tel.: (537) 8312198.

Museum of Decorative Arts / 502 17 St. on D St., Vedado/ Tel.: (537) 8309848.

Museum of Gold- and Silversmithing/ 113 Obispo St., between Oficios and Mercaderes St., Old Havana/ Tel.: (537) 8639861.

Museum of Havana's Pharmacy / Teniente Rey on Compostela St., Old Havana/ Tel.: (537) 8667554.

Museum of Numismatics / 305 Obispo St., between Aguiar and Habana St., Old Havana/ Tel.: (537) 8615811.

Museum of Playing Cards / Muralla St. on Inquisidor St., Old Square/ Tel.: (537) 8601534.

Museum of Rum/ 262 San Pedro (Port Avenue), between Sol and Santa Clara St., Old Havana/ Tel.: (537) 8618051.

Museum of the Castle of the Royal Force / Main Square, Old Havana/ Tel.: (537) 8644488.

Museum of the City / 1 Tacón St., between Obispo and O'Reilly St., Old Havana/Tel.: (537) 8615779.

Museum of the Orishas/ 615 Prado Promenade, between Monte and Dragones St. / Tel.: (537) 8635953.

Museum of the Revolution/ 1 Refugio St., between Zulueta and Monserrate Tel.: (537) 8624093, 8624094.

Museum of San Salvador de La Punta/ Port Avenue on Prado Promenade/Tel.: (537) 8603196.

Museum of Tobacco / 120 Mercaderes St., between Obispo and Obrapía St., Old Havana/ Tel.: (537) 8615795.

Napoleonic Museum / 1159 San Miguel St. on Ronda St. / Tel.: (537) 8791412.

National Museum of Contemporary Cuban Ceramics / Mercaderes St., on Amargura St., Old Havana/Tel.: (537) 8616130.

National Museum of Fine Arts / Trocadero St., between Zulueta and Monserrate St. /Tel.: (537) 8620140, 8615777.

National Museum of Music / 1 Capdevila St., between Habana and Aguiar, Old Havana/ Tel. (537) 8619846.

National Museum of Natural History / 61 Obispo St., Main Square, Old Havana/ Tel.: (537) 8639361, 8620353.

National Puppet Theater/ M St., between 17 and 19 St., Vedado/ Tel.: (537) 8326262.

National Theater / Paseo on 39 St., Plaza/Tel.: (537) 8796011-15.

New Latin American Foundation's Movie Theater / Santa Bárbara Estate, 212 St. on 31 St., La Coronela / Tel.: (537) 2718967 (537) 8629035.

Oswaldo Guayasamín Gallery/ Obrapía St., between Oficios and Mercaderes St., Old Havana/ Tel.: (537) 8613843.

Payret Movie Theater / Prado Promenade on San José St. / Tel.: (537) 8633163.

Riviera Movie Theater / 23 St. between G and H St., Vedado/ Tel.: (537) 8309564.

Planetarium/ Old Square, Old Havana/ Tel.: (537) 864 9544, 864 9545 y 864 9165.

Rene Portocarrero Serigraphy Workshop/ 513 Cuba St. between Teniente Rey and Muralla St., Old Havana/ Tel.: (537) 8623276.

San Felipe Neri Oratorio (Concert hall)/ Aguiar St. on Obrapía St., Old Havana/ Tel.: (537) 8623243.

Taquechel Pharmacy/ 155 Obispo St., between San Ignacio and Mercaderes St., Old Havana/ Tel.: (537) 8629286.

The Automobile Warehouse / 13 Oficios St., between Obrapía and Callejón de Jústiz St., Old Havana/ Tel.: (537) 863 9942.

Theater of the Third Order / Convent of St. Francis of Assisi, Old Havana /Tel.: (5357) 8623467.

Trianón Theater/ Línea St., between Paseo and A St., Vedado/ Tel.: (537) 8309648.

23 y 12 Gallery/ 12 St. on 23, Vedado/Tel.: (537) 8311810.

23 y 12 Movie Theater / 23 St., between 12 and 14 St., Vedado/ Tel.: (537) 8336906.

Víctor Manuel Gallery / 56 San Ignacio St., Cathedral Square /Tel.: (537) 8612955.

Villa Manuela Gallery (UNEAC)/ 406 H St. between 17 and 19 St., El Vedado/ Tel.: (537)832 2391, 832 4571 to 73.

Walloon Showcase Cultural Center / San Ignacio St., between Teniente Rey and Muralla St., Old Havana/ Tel.: (537) 8683561.

Wifredo Lam Contemporary Art Center / 22 San Ignacio St. on Empedrado St. /Tel.: (537) 8612096.

Yara Movie Theater / 23 St. on L St., Vedado /Tel.: (537) 8329430.

Matanzas

Varadero's Amphitheater/ Vía Blanca on Cárdenas Highway.

Castle of San Severino, Museum of the Slaves' Route / Industrial Park, Dubrocq, Matanzas/Tel.: (5345)283259.

El Morrillo Museum/ Entrance to Matanzas Bay and a short distance from the Canímar River's mouth / Tel.: (5345) 286675.

Gener y del Monte Library/ 72 Contreras St., Matanzas.

José Antonio Echeverría's Birthplace/ 560 Jenes St., between Coronel Verdugo and Calzada, Cárdenas/Tel.: (5345)524145.

Museum of Varadero/ 57 St. on Playa Ave. / Tel.: (5345) 613189.

Pharmaceutical Museum of Matanzas/ 49-51 Milanés St., between Ayuntamiento and Santa Teresa/Tel.: (5345) 243179.

Playa Girón Museum / Girón Beach, Zapata Swamp/Tel.: (5345) 984122.

Plaza América Convention Center / Sur Expressway, Km 11½, Las Américas, Varadero/ Tel.: (5345) 667895, 668509, 668508.

Provincial Museum Junco Palace / Milanés St., between Magdalena and Ayllon, Matanzas/Tel.: (5345)243195.

Sauto Theater/ Magdalena St., between Milanés and Medio, La Vigía Square, Matanzas/ Tel.: (5345) 242721.

Mayabeque

Municipal Museum of Güines/ 10005 77 Ave., between 100 and 112/ Tel.: (5347) 522437.

Municipal Museum of Jaruco/ 2102 32 St., between 21 and 23/ Tel.: (5347) 873224.

Municipal Museum of San José de Las Lajas/ 47 Ave. on 74 St. / Tel.: (5347) 863218.

Municipal Museum of Santa Cruz del Norte /207 11-A Ave., between 2 and 4/Tel.: (5347) 294345.

Isle of Youth

Artistic Ceramics Workshop/ 39 St. on 24 St., Nueva Gerona/ Tel.: (5346) 324574 y 322610.

El Pinero Memorial Square / 33 St., between 26 and 28, Nueva Gerona/ Tel.: (5346) 323195.

Martha Machado Gallery/ 39 St. on 26, Nueva Gerona.

Model Prison/ Delio Chacón, Nueva Gerona/ Tel.: (5346) 325112.

Municipal Museum of Nueva Gerona/ 30 St., between 37 and Martí St. /Tel.: (5346) 323791.

Museum House El Abra Farm/ Highway Siguanea Km. ½ /Tel.: (5346) 396206.

Museum of Natural History/ 4625 41 St., Siguanea Highway / Tel.: (5346) 323143.

Water Sports

Because of its location in the Caribbean Sea, at the entrance to the Gulf of Mexico, and its elongated shape, Cuba reveals itself as a paradise for those who love diving. For them, the island and its adjoining islets offer a network of diving centers close to hotel facilities, furnished with equipment that meet international standards. There also several marinas.

Pinar del Río

Boca del Toro (diving)/ Luis Lazo Highway, Km 2½/Tel.: (5348)753844.

Cayo Jutía Palmares (diving)/Los Colorados Archipelago, Minas de Matahambre, Santa Lucía.

Cayo Levisa Cubanacán (diving)/ North Coast of La Palma, Palma Rubia/ Tel.: (5348) 756501.

María la Gorda (diving)/La Bajada, Guanahacabibes Peninsula/ Tel. (5348) 778131/773067.

Havana

Copacabana-Marlin/ 4404 1st St., Miramar/ Tel. (537) 2041037 ext. 6191.

Habana Residential Club, International Diving Center/ 5th Ave., between 188 and 192, Flores/ Tel. (537) 2045700/2043300-09.

Marlin Marina Hemingway /5th Ave. on 248 St., Santa Fe, Tel. (537) 2045088 (International).

Marlin Marina Tarará / House no. 25 at 7th St., 2 and 11, Tarará, East Havana /Tel.(537) 796 0240 / 796 0242.

Matanzas-Varadero

Barracuda - Marlin/ 59 St. on 1st Ave., Varadero/ Tel.: (5345) 667072/613481.

Chapelín-Marlin/ 59 St. on 1st Ave., Varadero/ Tel.: (5345) 667072/613481/611852.

Marlin Marina Varadero Docks/ Varadero Expressway, Km 38 / Tel. (5345) 668060/667456 (International).

Sandals Royal-Marlin/ Sandals Royal Hicacos Hotel, Las Morlas Highway, Km 14, Varadero/ Tel.: (5345) 668844.

Varadero-Gaviota/ Gaviota Marina Varadero, at the end of Sur Expressway /Tel.: (5345) 66 7755 / 66 7756.

Isle of Youth

El Colony International Diving Center /Tel. (53 46) 398181 / 398282.

Marlin Marina Cayo Largo/ Cayo Largo del Sur, Los Canarreos Archipelago / Tel.: (5345) 24 8214 (International).

Health Care

With general primary healthcare services and a network of high quality hospital facilities, Cuba also has institutions dedicated to the treatment of dermatological conditions, pigmentary retinosis and ophthalmological diseases, among many others. International pharmacies and clinics, as well as opticians', are also listed here.

Pinar del Río

Óptica Miramar, Pinar del Río / 56 Martí St., / Tel.: (5348) 778413.

Havana

Camilo Cienfuegos International Center for Pigmentary Retinosis/ 151 L St., between Línea and 13 St., Vedado/Tel.: (537) 8325554 (Ophthalmology) .

Center for Medical and Surgical Research (CIMEQ)/ 216 St. on 11 B St. Siboney / Tel.: (537) 2717668 y 8581000 (Clinical and surgical facility).

Cira García Central Clinic / 4101 20 St. on 41 St. / Tel.: (537) 2044300 (Clinical and surgical facility facility).

Frank País International Scientific Complex/ 19603 51 Ave., between 196 and 200 St. / Tel.: (537) 2627022 ext. 478 (Orthopedics).

Hermanos Amejeiras Hospital/ 701 San Lázaro St., on Belascoaín/ Tel.: (537) 8761000, 8761613, 8761196, 8761607 (Clinical and surgical facility).

HIV Attention Center / El Rincón Highway / Tel.: (537) 6831052/56 (AIDS and Thalasotherapy).

Iberian American Center for Seniors (CITED), Universidad Ave. on 27 de Noviembre St., Vedado/ Tel.: (537) 8382197 y 8382139.

International Center for Neurological Restoration (CIREN)/ 15805 25th Ave., between 158 and 160, Playa/ Tel.: (537) 2715044, 2736777 (Neurology).

International Pharmacy / 41 St., on 20, Miramar/ Tel.: (537) 204 4350.

International Pharmacy and SPA, Comodoro Hotel, / 3rd Ave on 84, Miramar/ Tel.: (537) 204 9385.

International Pharmacy Casa Bella/2603 7th Ave. on 22 St., Miramar/ Tel. (537) 204 7980.

International Pharmacy Guanabo/ 5th Ave., between 472 and 474, Guanabo/Tel.: (537) 7967146.

International Pharmacy Panamericana Villa Resort / Panamericana Villa, Cojímar/ Tel.: (537) 7661157.

International Pharmacy, Habana Libre Hotel / 23 St. on L, Vedado/Tel.: (5348) 831 9538.

International Pharmacy, Marina Hemingway /Marina Hemingway, Barlovento/ Tel.: (53 7) 204 5132.

International Pharmacy, Miramar Trade Center / 3rd Ave. on 82 St., Miramar/ Tel.: (53 7) 204 4515.

International Pharmacy, Sevilla Hotel / Prado Promenade on Trocadero St. / Tel.: (5348) 861 5703.

International Pharmacy, Terminal No. 3/ José Martí International Airport, Terminal No. 3/ Tel.: (537) 266 4105.

Julio Díaz Rehabilitation Center/ 19815 243 Ave., Fontanar Tel.: (537) 6468646 (Rehabilitation).

La Pradera International Health Center/ 230 St. on 15 St., Siboney/ Tel.: (537) 2737467 ext. 403 (Rehabilitation).

Óptica Almendares/ 364 Obispo St., between Compostela and Habana, Old Havana/Tel.: (537) 8608262.

Óptica Miramar/ 7th Ave. on 24 St., Miramar/Tel.: (537)2042269.

Pedro Kourí Institute of Tropical Medicine (IPK) / Mediodía Expressway, Km 6½ / Tel.: (537) 2020427, 2020430, 2020633, 2020451 (Tropical Medicine).

Ramón Pando Ferrer Hospital/ 3104 76 St. / Tel.: (537) 2654893 (Ophthalmology).

William Soler Hospital/ 100 St. on Perla, Altahabana/ Tel.: (537) 6443521(Pediatrics).

Matanzas-Varadero

Barracuda Sub Aquatic Medical Center / 59 St., on 1st. Ave. (Clinical and surgical facility).

International Clinic, Varadero / 60 St. on 1st Ave. / Tel.: (5345) 667710 to 12.

International Pharmacy Plaza América/Convention Center, Las Américas Highway, Varadero/ Tel.: (5345) 668042.

International Pharmacy, Juan Gualberto Gómez International Airport/ Areglatito-Carbonera Highway/ Tel. (5345) 253489.

Miramar Opticians', Cárdenas /Ruiz St., between Calzada and Coronel Verdugo/ Tel.: (5345) 522036.

Miramar Opticians', Varadero / 1rd Ave., between 41 and 43/Tel.: (5345) 667439.

Pharmacy, International Clinic/ 60 St. on 1rd. Ave., /Tel. (5 45) 667710 - 11.

Plaza América SPA and Club/Convention Center, Las Américas Highway, Varadero/ Tel.: 5345) 668181 ext. 233.

Lodgings

Cienfuegos

★★★★ **Casa Verde Hotel** / 37 St., between 0 and 2 St., Punta Gorda, Cienfuegos / Tel.: (5343) 551003 reservas@jagua.gca.tur.cu

★★★★ **Jagua Hotel** (City) / 1 37 St., between 0 and 2 St., Punta Gorda, Cienfuegos / Tel.: (5343) 551003 / reservas@jagua.gca.tur.cu

★★★★ **La Unión, Hotel** (City) / 31 St. on 54, Cienfuegos Tel.: (5343) 451020 / comercial@union.cfg.tur.cu

★★★ **Club Amigo Rancho Luna-Faro Luna** (Beach) / Rancho Luna Highway, Km 17½, Cienfuegos Tel.: (5343) 548012-548020 / comercial@ranluna.cfg.tur.cu

★★★ **Guajimico Villa** (Nature) / Trinidad Highway. Km 42, Cumanayagua, Cienfuegos, / Tel.: (5342) 540947, 451205 / guajimico@enet.cu.

★★★ **Palacio Azul Hostel** (City) / 1 37 St., between 12 and 14 St., Cienfuegos / Tel.: (5343) 555828, 555829 / directorl@hpazul.cfg.tur.cu

★★ **Pasacaballo Hotel** / Pasacaballo Highway, Km 22 ½ / Tel.: (5343) 592100/ jefecarpeta@pasacaballos.cfg.tur.cu

★★ **Punta la Cueva Hotel** / Punta la Cueva Highway / Tel.: (5343) 513956 / jefecarpeta@pcueva.cfg.tur.cu

★ **Yaguanabo Islazul Villa** (Beach) / Trinidad Highway, Km 55, Cienfuegos / Tel.: (5342) 540807/ villa@yaguanabo.cfg.tur.cu

Villa Clara-North Keys

★★★★★ **Ensenachos Iberostar Hotel** (Beach)/ Cayo Ensenachos, Caibarién/ Tel.: (5342) 350300 j.reservas@ensenachos.co.cu

★★★★★ **HUSA Cayo Santa María Beach Resort Hotel** (Beach) / Cayo Santa María, Caibarién, Tel (5342) 350400 / jefe.reservas.Barcelo@cayosantamaria.co.cu

★★★★★ **Iberostar Ensenachos Hotel** (Beach) Cayo Ensenachos, Caibarién / Tel.: (5342) 350300 j.reservas@ensenachos.co.cu

★★★★★ **Meliá Buenavista Planta Real Hotel** (Beach) / Cayo Santa María, Caibarién / Tel.: (5342) 350700 / reservas1.csm@solmeliacuba.com.

★★★★★ **Meliá Cayo Santa María Hotel** (Beach) / Cayo Santa María, North of Caibarién / Tel.: (5342) 350500 / reservas1.csm@solmeliacuba.com

★★★★★ **Meliá Las Dunas Hotel** (Beach) / Cayo Santa María / Tel.: (5342) 350100 / reservas2.mld@solmeliacuba.com

★★★★ **Sol Cayo Santa María Hotel** (Beach) / Cayo Santa María, North of Caibarién / Tel.: (5342) 350200 / reservs2.csm@solmeliacuba.com

★★★ **Cayo Las Brujas Villa** (Beach) / Cayo Las Brujas, Caibarién/ Tel.: (5342) 350199/ reseervas@villa.lasbrujas.co.cu

★★★ **Islazul Elguea Hotel** (Nature) / Corralillo Tel.: (5342) 686298-686292 / carpeta@velguea.vcl.tur.cu

★★★ **Islazul Santa Clara Libre Hotel** (City) / 6 Vidal Plaza, between Tristá and P. Chao St., Santa Clara / Tel.: (5342) 207548 to 50 / armando.perez@mscl.co.cu

★★★ **La Granjita Villa** (City) / Malezas Highway, Km 21½, Santa Clara/ Tel.: (5342) +218190/ reserva@granjita.vcl.tur.cu

★★★ **Los Caneyes Hotel** (City) / Eucaliptos Ave. on the Beltway, Santa Clara / Tel.: (5342) 218140 / comercial@caneyesvc.co.cu

★★ **Brisas del Mar Hotel** (Beach) / At the end of Playa Highway, Caibarién / Tel.: (5342) 351699 / recepcion@brisas.co.cu

★★ **Islazul Hanabanilla Hotel** (Nature) / Hanabanilla Waterfall, Manicaragua/ Tel.: (5342) 208461/ director@hanabanilla.vcl.tur.cu / recepcion@hanabanilla.vcl.tur.cu

★★ **Mascotte Hotel** (City) / 114 Máximo Gómez St., Remedios / Tel.: (5342) 395144-395467/ reservas@mascottevcl.tur.cu

★★ **Río Seibabo Camping** (Nature) / Condado de Güinía de Miranda Highway, Manicaragua / Tel.: (5342) 349832.

Sancti Spíritus-Trinidad

★★★★★ **Cubanacán Plaza Hostel** (City) / 1 Independencia St., between Mártires Ave. and A. Guitera St., Sancti Spíritus / Tel.: (5341) 327102-27124 / aloja@hostalesss.co.cu

★★★★★ **Iberostar Trinidad Grand Hotel** (City) 262 José Martí St., between Lino Pérez and Colón St., Trinidad / Tel.: (5341) 996070-75 / comercial@iberostar.trinidad.co.cu and reservas@iberostar.trinidad.co.cu

★★★★ **Brisas Trinidad del Mar Hotel** (Beach) / Ancón Peninsula, Trinidad / Tel.: (5341) 996500-07 / reserva@brisastdad.co.cu

★★★★ **Kurhotel Hotel** (Nature) / Topes de Collantes / Tel.: (5342)540117/ reserva@topescom.co.cu

★★★ **Ancón Hotel** (Beach) / María Aguilar Highway, Ancón Beach, Trinidad / Tel.: (5341) 996123-29/ reservas@ancon.co.cu

★★★ **Caburní Villa** (Nature) / Topes de Collantes, Trinidad / Tel.: (5342) 540117 / reserva@topescom.co.cu

★★★ **Costa Sur Hotel** (Beach) / María Aguilar Beach, Ancón Peninsula, Trinidad / Tel.: (5341) 996174-78 / reservas@costasur.co.cu

★★★ **Cubanacán Hostal del Rijo** (City) / 12 H. del Castillo St. on Máximo Gómez St., Trinidad / Tel.: (5341) 328588 / aloja@hostalsss.co.cu

★★★ **Horizontes MaDolores** (Nature) / Cienfuegos Highway, Km 1½, Trinidad / Tel.: (5341) 996394 / comercial@dolores.co.cu / alojamiento@dolores.co.cu

★★★ **Islazul Rancho Hatuey Villa** (Nature) / Central Highway, Km 383, Sancti Spíritus/ Tel.: (5341) 361315 / reserva.vrhatuey@islazul.ssp.tur.co.cu

★★★ **Islazul San José del Lago Villa** (Nature) / Mayajigua Highway, Yaguajay / Tel.: (5341) 546108-09 / reserva.loslagos@islazulssp.tur.co.cu

★★★ **Islazul Zaza Hotel** (Nature) / San José Farm, Km 5½, Zaza Lake / Tel.: (5341) 327015 / reserva@hzaza.co.cu

★★★ **Las Cuevas Hotel** (City) / Finca Santa Ana, Trinidad / Tel.: (5341) 996135 / reservas@cuevas.co.cu

★★★ **Los Helechos Hotel** (Nature) / Topes de Collantes / Tel.: (5342) 540117 / reserva@topescom.co.cu

★★ **Islazul Los Laureles Villa** (City) / Central Highway, Km 383, Sancti Spíritus / Tel.: (5341) 361016 / reserva.loslaurele@islazulssp.tur.co.cu

Ciego de Ávila-Cayo Coco and Cayo Guillermo

★★★★★ **Blau Colonial Cayo Coco** (Beach) / Cayo Coco, Morón / Tel.: (5333) 301311 / reservas@blaucolonial.co.cu / Fax (5333) 301384.

★★★★★ **Meliá Cayo Coco Hotel** (Beach) / Cayo Coco, Morón / Tel.: (5333) 301180 / reservas1.mcc@solmeliacuba.com

★★★★★ **Meliá Cayo Guillermo Hotel** (Beach) / Cayo Guillermo, Morón / Tel.: (5333) 301680 / jefe.reservas.mcg@solmeliacuba.com

★★★★ **Be Live Coco Beach Hotel** (Beach) / Cayo Coco, Morón / Tel.: (5333) 302250 / reservas@Beachcoco.co.cu / Fax (5333) 302190.

★★★★ **NH Cristal Laguna Hotel** (Beach) / Hoteles Ave., Cayo Coco, Morón / Tel.: (5333) 301470 / jreserva@hotel-el.co.cu

★★★★ **Sol Cayo Coco Hotel** (Beach) / Cayo Coco, Morón/ Tel.: (5333) 301280 / jefe.reserva..scc@solmeliacuba.com

★★★★ **Sol Cayo Guillermo** (Beach) / Cayo Guillermo, Morón / Tel.: (5333) 301760 / jefe.reservas.scg@solmeliacuba.com

★★★★ **Tryp Cayo Coco** (Beach)/ Cayo Coco, Jardines del Rey, Morón/ Tel.: (5333) 301300/ jefe,reservas.tcc@solmeliacuba.com

★★★ **Be Live Villa Cayo Coco** (Beach) / Cayo Coco, Morón / Tel.: (5333) 302180 / reservas@Beachcoco.co.cu

★★★ **Cojímar Club** (Beach) / Cayo Guillermo, Morón / Tel.: (5333) 301712 / esp.reservas@cojimar.gca.tur.cu / Fax (5333) 301725.

★★★ **Iberostar Daiquirí Hotel** (Beach) / Cayo Guillermo, Morón / Tel.: (5333) 301650 / reserva@ibsdaiq.gca.tur.cu

★★★ **Islazul Ciego Hotel** (City) / Ceballos Highway, Km ½, Ciego de Ávila / Tel.: (5333) 228013 / reserca@enet.cu

★★★ **Islazul Morón Hotel** (City) / Tarafa Ave., Morón / Tel.: (5333) 502230 / reserca@enet.cu / Fax (5333) 502133.

★★ **Santiago Habana** (City) / Honorato Castillo, on Central Highway, Ciego de Ávila / Tel.: (5333) 225725 / reserca@enet.cu

Camagüey-Santa Lucía

★★★★ **Be Live Brisas Santa Lucía Hotel** (Beach) / Turística Ave. at Santa Lucía / Tel.: (5332) 336317-336140 / aloja@brisas.stl.tur.cu / comerc@brisas.stl.tur.cu / Tel.: (5332) 365142.

★★★ **Caracol Club Amigo Hotel** (Beach) / Turística Ave., Santa Lucía / Tel.: (5332) 365158-60 / reservas@caracol.stl.tur.cu / (5332) 365157.

★★★ **Islazul Gran Hotel** (City) / 57 Maceo St., between General Gómez and I. Agramonte St., Camagüey / Tel.: (5332) 292093-94 / reserva@hgh.camaguey.cu / Fax (5332) 293933

★★★ **Mayanabo Club Amigo Hotel** (Beach) / Santa Lucía Beach / Tel.: (5332) 365168-70 / aloja@mayanabo.co.cu

★★★ **Santa Lucía Club** (Beach)/ Santa Lucía Beach / Tel.: (5332) 336109/ xiomara@clubst.stl.tur.cu jjose@club.stl.tu.cu / Fax (5332) 365153.

★★ **Florida Hotel** (City) / Central Highway, Km 531, Florida / Tel.: (5332) 514670 / reservas@hflorida.co.cu

★★ **Islazul Colón Hotel** (City) / 472 República St., Camagüey/ Tel.: (5332) 251520/ reservas@hcolon.camaguey.cu / Fax (5332) 283346.

★★ **Islazul Plaza Hotel** (City) / 1 Van Horne St., between República and Avellaneda, Camagüey / Tel.: (5332) 282457-282435 / reservacion@hplaza.camaguey.cu

★ **Islazul Caonaba Hotel** (City) / Albaina St., on Martí, Camagüey / Tel.: (5332) 414803 / recepcion@caonaba.co.cu

★ **Islazul Isla de Cuba Hotel** (City) / 453 San Esteban St., Camagüey / Tel.: (5332) 292248/ reservacion@hplaza.camaguey.cu / Fax (5332) 257023.

★ **Puerto Príncipe** (City) / 260 Mártires Ave., La Vigía, Camagüey / Tel.: (5332) 282469 / carpeta@hpp.camaguey.cu / Fax (5332) 296117.

Restaurants and Coffee-Shops

Cienfuegos

Club Cienfuegos (Cuban and int. cuisine) / 37 St., between 8 and 12 St., Punta Gorda/Tel.: (5343) /512891.

El Nicho (Cuban and international cuisine)/ Nicho, Escambray/ Tel.: (5343)/433351.

Las Vegas (Cuban and international cuisine)/ La Vega, Trinidad Highway, Km 59, Cienfuegos.

Palacio de Valle (Cuban and international cuisine)/ 37 Ave. between 0 and 2, Punta Gorda, Cienfuegos/ Tel.: (5343)/554441.

Ranchón Aguada (Stopping point)/ National Highway, Km.272, Aguada de Pasajeros.

Ranchón Lajas (Stopping point)/ National Highway, Km.232, Lajas.

Villa Clara

El Curujey (Cuban and international cuisine)/ Camajuaní Highway, Km 5, Caibarién/ Tel.: (5342)/395764.

La Concha (Cuban and international cuisine)/ Central Highway, on Danielito St., Santa Clara/ Tel.: (5342)/218124.

La Ruina (Cuban and international cuisine)/ 6 St. on 15 St., Caibarién.

La Vicaria (Cuban and international cuisine)/ 9 Ave. on 10 St., Caibarién/ Tel.: (5342)/351085.

Sancti Spíritus-Trinidad

Colonial (Cuban and international cuisine)/ Maceo St. on Colón St., Trinidad / Tel.: (5341)/ 996473.

Don Antonio (Cuban and international cuisine)/ Gustavo Izquierdo St., Trinidad / Tel.: (5341)/ 996548.

El Jigüe (Cuban and international cuisine)/ Pino Guinart St. on Real St., Trinidad / Tel.: (5341)/ 996476.

Grill Caribe (Cuban cuisine)/ Ancón Peninsula, Trinidad / Tel.: (5341)/ 996241.

Guachinango (Cuban and international cuisine)/ Guachinango, Trinidad.

La Canchánchara (Coffee-shop)/ Real St., Trinidad.

Manacas Iznaga (Cuban and international cuisine)/ Manacas-Iznaga, Trinidad / Tel.: (5341)/ 997241.

Mesón de la Plaza (Cuban and international cuisine)/ 34 Máximo Gómez St., Sancti Spíritus / Tel.: (5341)/ 328546.

Mesón del Regidor (Cuban and international cuisine)/ Simón Bolívar St. on Real St., Trinidad / Tel.: (5341) 996572-73.

Plaza Mayor (Cuban and international cuisine)/ Real St. on Rosario St., Trinidad / Tel.: (5341) 996470.

Plaza Santana (Cuban and international cuisine)/ Camilo Cienfuegos St. on J. Mendoza St., Trinidad / Tel.: (5341) 996423.

Quinta Santa Elena (Cuban and international cuisine)/ Yayabo Bridge, Sancti Spíritus, / Tel.: (5341)328167.

Vía Real (Cuban and international cuisine)/ Real St., Trinidad/ Tel.: (5341) 996476.

Ciego de Ávila

Finca Oasis (Cuban cuisine)/ Central Highway, Km 22, Este, Baraguá.

Flamingo (Cuban and international cuisine)/ Cayo Coco.

La Casona (Cuban and international cuisine)/ 43 Cristóbal Colón St., Morón.

La Redonda (International cuisine)/ La Redonda Lake, Morón / Tel.: (5333)302489.

La Vicaria (Cuban and international cuisine)/ Central Highway, Ciego de Ávila / Tel.: (5333)266477.

Maribar (Cuban and international cuisine)/ Cayo Guillermo.

Paraíso Palmeras (Cuban and international cuisine)/ 150 Martí St., Morón / Tel.: (5333) 502194.

Presa de Florencia (Cuban and international cuisine)/ F. Chamba Hydraulic Complex, Florencia.

Rancho Palma (Cuban cuisine)/ Morón-Bolivia Highway, Morón.

Ranchón Las Coloradas (Cuban cuisine and seafood specialties)/ Colorada Beach, Cayo Coco.

Camagüey

Bucanero (Cuban and international cuisine)/ La Boca, Santa Lucía Beach / Tel.: (5332) 365226.

Campana de Toledo (Cuban and international cuisine)/ San Juan de Dios Square, Camagüey / Tel.: (5332) 286812.

Colonial (Cuban and international cuisine)/ Ignacio Agramonte St. on República St., Camagüey / Tel.: (5332) 285239.

La Boca (Coffee-shop)/La Boca, Santa Lucía Beach.

Lunamar (Cuban and international cuisine)/ Santa Lucía Mall / Tel.: (5332) 336146.

Rancho King (Cuban cuisine)/ Santa Lucía Highway, Km 35.

Vicaria Pollito (Chicken specialties)/ Nuevitas Highway, Km 5, Camagüey / Tel.: (5332) 261384.

Night Centers

Cienfuegos

Club Cienfuegos (Nightclub)/ 37 St. on 12 St., Cienfuegos/Tel.: (5343)512891.

Club El Benny (Nightclub)/54 Ave., between 29 and 31, Cienfuegos/Tel.: (5343) 551647 and 551105.

Costasur (Nightclub)/ 40 Ave. between 33 and 35 St., Cienfuegos/Tel.: (5343) 525808.

Guanaroca (Nightclub)/ Jagua Hotel, 1 37 St., Punta Gorda, Cienfuegos/Tel.: (5343) 551003.

La Cueva del Camarón (Disco)/ 4 37 St., between 0 and 2 St., Punta Gorda, Cienfuegos/Tel.: (5343) 551214.

La Terraza (Nightclub)/ 37 St., between 8 and 12 St., Punta Gorda, Cienfuegos/Tel.: (5343) 512891.

Villa Clara

Bar Club Boulevard (Nightclub)/ 225 Independencia St., between Maceo and Unión St., Santa Clara/Tel.: (5342) 216236 and 203778.

El Güije (Nightclub)/Independencia St. on Maceo St., Remedios/Tel.: (5342) 363305.

La Terraza (Nightclub)/ Vidal Plaza, Santa Clara/ Tel.: (5342)207548.

Primavera (Nightclub)/ 151 Máximo Gómez St., between Independencia and Martí St., Santa Clara/Tel.: (5342) 203699.

.

Sancti Spíritus

La Canchánchara (Snack Bar)/ Real St., Trinidad/ Tel.: (5341) 996537.

Los Laureles (Nightclub)/ Central Highway, Km 384/ Tel.: (5341)327016.

Ruinas de Brunet (Nightclub)/ Maceo St., Trinidad/Tel.: (5341) 996547.

Ruinas de Lleonci (Nightclub)/ Gustavo Izquierdo St., Trinidad/Tel.: (5341) 996217.

Ciego de Ávila

El Patio de ARTEX (Nightclub)/Libertad St. on Maceo St. /Tel.: (5333) 266680.

La Cueva (Nightclub)/Milk Lake, Morón/ Tel (5333) 502239.

La Cueva del Jabalí (Nightclub)/Cayo Coco, Morón/Tel.: (5333) 301206.

Paraíso Palmeras (Disco)/382 Martí St., between Sergio Antuña and Dimas St., Morón/Tel.: (5333) 502194.

Camagüey

Campana Toledo (Bar)/ 18 San Juan de Dios St., between Ramón Pintó and Pedro Olallo St., Camagüey/Tel.: (5332) 253045.

Copacabana (Nightclub)/ Central Este Highway, between Padre Felipe and Ma. del Rosario St., Camagüey/Tel.: (5332) 253858.

La Bolera (Nightclub)/ Central Este Highway, Camagüey/Tel.: (5332) 287384.

El Colonial (Nightclub)/ 406 Ignacio Agramonte St., between República and Lope Recio St., Camagüey/Tel.: (5332) 285239.

Stores

Cienfuegos

Club Cienfuegos/ 37 St., between 14 and 12 St., Punta Gorda/ General Store.

Faro Luna/ Pasacaballo Highway, Km. 23/ General Store.

Shopping Arcade/ Boulevard on 54 Ave., Cienfuegos/ General Stores, Specialized Stores.

Jagua Shopping Arcade/ 37 St., between 0 and 2 St., Punta Gorda, Cienfuegos/Boutique/ Tel.: (5343) 551312.

Glamour/ 56 Ave. on 35 St., Cienfuegos/ Boutique.

La Casa Mimbre/ 60 Ave. on 35 St., Cienfuegos/ General Store.

Madame Dudot/ La Unión Hotel / 31 St., on 54 St., Cienfuegos/ Boutique.

Marilope/ 3501 35 St., between 16 and 18 St., Cienfuegos/ Specialized Store.

Maroya/2506 54 Ave., between 25 and 27 St. / Specialized Store.

Mercado Habana / 58 Ave. on 31 St., Cienfuegos/ General Store/ Tel.: (5343) 552919.

Mercado Punta Gorda/ 37 St. on 20 St., Cienfuegos/ Supermarket.

Pasacaballo/ Pasacaballo Highway, Km. 26/ Specialized Store.

Punta la Cueva/ Punta la Cueva Highway, Km 3 ½ /Specialized Store/ Tel.: (5343) 512889.

Rancho Luna / Pasacaballo Highway, Km. 22 / Specialized Store/ Tel.: (5343) 548097.

Ranchón La Aguada/ National Expressway, Km 172, Aguada de Pasajeros/ Specialized Store, Tel.: (5343) 562128.

Tabaco Aguada /National Expressway, Km. 172 / Specialized Store.

Terry Theater's Store/ 56 Ave. on 27 St., Cienfuegos/Specialized Store/ Tel.: (5343) 510770.

Villa Clara

Airport Store / Abel Santamaría Airport, Malezas Highway, Km 11, C. Militar/ Specialized Store/ Tel.: (5342) 209138.

Armored Train Museum's Store/ Camajuaní Highway, between Línea and C St. / Specialized Store/ Tel.: (5342) 207368.

ARTEX Bazar /6 Marta Abreu St. on Los Caneyes Highway /Specialized Store/ Tel.: (5342) 206505.

Cacique/ Meliá Las Dunas Hotel, Cayo Santa María/ General Store / Tel.: (5342) 350100.

Casa Cuba/ Occidental Hotel, Cayo Ensenachos/ General Store/ Tel.: (5342) 350333.

Eclipse/ 60 Máximo Gómez St., between Independencia and Martí St., Santa Clara/Specialized Store.

El Primavera/ Máximo Gómez St., between Independencia and Martí St., Santa Clara/ Boutique/ Tel.: (5342) 210372.

Fotoclub Villa Clara/ San Cristóbal St., between Colón and Cuba St. / Specialized Store.

Hanabanilla/ Hanabanilla Hotel / Boutique/ Tel.: (5342) 208461.

Ilusión/ Occidental Hotel, Cayo Ensenachos/Specialized Store/ Tel.: (5342) 250333.

La Casa Grande/ 82 Independencia St., between Rolando Morales and Fructuoso Rodríguez St. / General Store/ Tel.: (5343) 402387.

La Eminencia/ Occidental Hotel, Cayo Ensenachos/Specialized Store/ Tel.: (5342) 350333.

Los Caneyes/ Los Caneyes Hotel/ Los Eucaliptos Ave. / Boutique/ Tel.: (5342) 203775.

Peluquería Destello/ Sol Club Cayo Santa María Hotel, Cayo Santa María/ Specialized Store.

Siguaraya/ 61 Joaquín Paneca St., between Leoncio Vidal and Camilo Cienfuegos, Santa Clara/ Specialized Store/ Tel.: (5342) 481426.

Vega Alta/ Meliá Las Dunas Hotel, Cayo Santa María/ Specialized Store/ Tel.: (5342) 350100.

Sancti Spíritus-Trinidad

Ancón Hotel's Store/ Ancón Hotel, Ancón Peninsula, Trinidad/ Specialized Store/ Tel.: (5341) 996233.

Canchánchara / Rubén Martínez Villena St., Trinidad/ Specialized Store.

Casa de la Trova/ 26 Máximo Gómez St., Sancti Spíritus/ Specialized Store.

Guitarra Mía /474 Antonio Maceo St., between Simón Bolívar and Francisco Javier Zerquera/ Specialized Store.

Hotel Zaza/ Zaza Hotel / Boutique and Specialized Store.

La Rumba/Piro Guinart on Gustavo Izquierdo, Trinidad/ General Store/ Tel.: (5341) 996331.

Las Cuevas/ Las Cuevas Hotel / Specialized Store/ Tel.: (5341) 996627.

Las Cuevas/ Santa Elena Farm/Specialized Store/ Tel.: (5341) 996133.

Las Delicias Minisuper / Francisco J. Zerquera St., Trinidad/ Supermarkets and Stores.

Las Sirenas/ Trinidad del Mar Hotel, Ancón Peninsula / Specialized Store.

Longina /43 Rubén Martínez Villena St. on Simón Bolívar, Trinidad / Specialized Store/ Tel.: (5341) 996626.

Los Helechos/ Los Helechos Hotel, Topes de Collantes/ Specialized Store.

Los Laureles/ Los Laureles Hotel, Central Highway, Km 383/ Specialized Store.

Los Zafiros/302 Lino Pérez St., between José Martí and Francisco Cadahía, Trinidad/ Specialized Store/Tel.: (5341) 992329.

Manaca-Iznaga/Manaca Iznaga Restaurant, Manaca Iznaga, Trinidad/ Specialized Store.

Manacanabo/Manaca-Iznaga, Trinidad/ Specialized Store/ Tel.: (5341) 996338.

Música/29 Fernando Hernández Echerri St., Trinidad/ Specialized Store.

Romantic Museum /52 Fernando Hernández Echerri St. on Piro Guinart and Simón Bolívar, Trinidad/ Specialized Store/ Tel.: (5341) 996627.

Trinidad del Mar/ Trinidad del Mar Hotel, Ancón Peninsula/Specialized Store.

Trinidad/ Francisco J. Zerquera St., Trinidad/ General Store.

Ciego de Ávila

Caracol /at every hotel in Cayo Coco, Cayo Guillermo, as well as at Ciego de Avila and Morón hotels/ General Stores.

Casa de la Trova de Morón/74 Libertad St., between Martí and Narciso López, Morón/Specialized Store/ Tel.: (5333) 504602.

Casa del Tabaco / Tryp Cayo Coco Hotel, Los Hoteles Ave. /Specialized Store.

Catfish /Los Hoteles Ave. /Beauty Parlor.

Chan Chan / Meliá Guillermo Hotel, Cayo Guillermo / Specialized Store.

Daiquirí Beauty Parlor/ Iberostar Daiquirí Hotel, Cayo Guillermo/ Beauty parlor.

Dos Gardenias, ARTEX / Martí St., between Sergio Antuña and Dimas Daniel / General Store/ Tel.: (5333) 502184.

Dos Gardenias/358 Martí St., Morón / Specialized Store/ Tel.: (5333) 502184.

El Carey/NH Hotels, Cayo Coco/ Specialized Store.

El Coral Hotel, Villa Cojímar (ARTEX)/Cayo Guillermo/ Specialized Store/ Tel.: (5333) 301712.

El Jardín/ Martí St., between Callejas and Libertad, Morón/ Specialized Store.

Encuentro Blau Colonial Hotel /Cayo Coco/ Specialized Store/ Tel.: (5333) 301311.

Fotoclub Tryp/ Tryp Cayo Coco Hotel / Los Hoteles Ave. / Specialized Store.

Idilio Iberostar Daiquirí Hotel (ARTEX)/Cayo Guillermo/ Specialized Store.

Jardines del Rey Airport/ Specialized Store/ Tel.: (5333) 266425.

Karamba/Los Hoteles Ave., Tryp Cayo Coco Hotel / Specialized Store.

La Época/ Independencia St., between Maceo and Honorato del Castillo, Ciego de Ávila/ Specialized Store /Tel.: (5333) 207677.

La Vicaria/ Gaviota Cayo Coco Villa, Cayo Coco/ General Store.

Laguna Azul/Los Hoteles Ave., Cayo Coco/ Specialized Store/ Tel.: (5333) 301240.

Logoshop (ARTEX)/ Iberostar Daiquirí Hotel, Cayo Guillermo/ Specialized Store.

Mar Sol (ARTEX)/ Meliá Cayo Coco Hotel / Specialized Store/ Tel.: (5333) 301157.

Camagüey

Camagüey Hotel / Camagüey Hotel, Central Este Highway, Km 4 ½, Jayamá/ General Store/ Tel.: (5332) 272109.

Casa de la Trova/Cisneros St., between Martí and Cristo, Camagüey/ Specialized Store.

Casa del Ron/ Central Este Highway, Km 4 ½ / Specialized Store/ Tel.: (5332) 276331.

El Cartel / Cisneros St., between Hermanos Agüero and Martí, Camagüey/ Specialized Store/ Tel.: (5332) 257293.

El Colonial Complex/ 407 Ignacio Agramonte St., between República and Lope Recio, Camagüey/ Specialized Store/ Tel.: (5332) 285459.

El Sol /Maceo St., between General Gómez and Ignacio Agramonte, Camagüey/ Specialized Store/ Tel.: (5332) 287294.

Futurama Modas/55 Maceo St., between General Gómez and Ignacio Agramonte, Camagüey/ Boutique/ Tel.: (5332) 253055.

Gran Hotel/ 69 Maceo St., between Ignacio Agramonte and General Gómez, Camagüey/ Specialized Store/ Tel.: (5332) 282574.

La Bolera/ Central Highway, between Humbolt and Alonso Fruto, La Caridad / Specialized Store/ Tel.: (5332) 287362.

La Mina /456 República St., between San José and San Martín, Camagüey/ General Store/ Tel.: (5332) 253052.

La Palma /257-259 República St., between Ignacio Agramonte and Finlay, Camagüey/ General Store/ Tel.: (5332) 254725.

Magazine/575 República St., between Línea and Francisquito/Specialized Store/ Tel.: (5332) 296155.

Photoclub Oxio Club/ 278 República St., between Santa Rita and Finlay, Camagüey/ Photographs and Videos/ Tel.: (5332) 257177.

Attractions and sites of Interests

Cienfuegos

Botanical Garden/ 136 Central St., Pepito Tey, Cienfuegos/ Tel: (5343) 545115.

Cienfuegos Provincial Museum /2702 54 Ave., between 27 and 29, Cienfuegos/Tel.: (5343)519722.

Museum of Naval History / 60 Ave. on 21 St., Cayo Loco, Cienfuegos/Tel.: (5343)539361.

Our Lady of the Angels Fortress /Jagua Castle's community /Tel.: (5343)965402.

Reina Cemetery/ 50 Ave on Reina St..

Tomás Acea Cemetery/ 5 de Septiembre Ave. / Tel: (5343) 525257.

Tomás Terry Theater/2703 56 Ave. on 27 Martí St., Cienfuegos/Tel.: (5343)513361.

Valle Palace, 37 Ave., between 0 and 2 Ave., Punta Gorda/Tel.: (5343) 551003.

Villa Clara

Armored Train Memorial / Camajuaní intersection with the Railway / Tel.: (5342) 202758.

Ernesto Guevara Memorial / Ernesto Guevara Revolution Square, Santa Clara /Tel.: (5342) 205668 - 205878 - 205985.

La Caridad Theater/ Vidal Square, between Lora and Máximo Gómez, Santa Clara/Tel.: (5342)205548.

Museum of Decorative Arts / Marta Abreu St. on Luis Estévez, Vidal Plaza, Santa Clara /Tel.: (5342)205368.

Museum of the Remedios Carnival /71 Máximo Gómez St., between Andrés del Río and Alejandro del Río, Remedios.

Villa Clara Provincial Museum/ Abel Santamaría Complex, Main Building, Osvaldo Herrera/Tel.: (5342)203041.

Sancti Spíritus-Trinidad

Carlos de la Torre Museum of Natural History /2 Sur Máximo Gómez St., / Sancti Spíritus /Tel.: (5341)326365.

Guamuhaya Archeology Museum / 457 Simón Bolívar St., between Rubén Martínez Villena and Fernando Hernández, Main Square, Trinidad /Tel.: (5341)993420.

Higher Parochial Church/ 58 Agramonte Oeste St., Sancti Spíritus/ Tel.: (5341) 324855.

Home of Rafael Ortiz (Gallery)/ 43 Rubén Martínez Villena St., Trinidad /Tel.: (5341)994432.

Municipal Museum at Cantero Palace/423 Simón Bolívar St., between Gustavo Izquierdo and Rubén Martínez Villena, Plaza Mayor, Trinidad /Tel.: (5341)994460.

Museum of Colonial Architecture /83 Ripalda St., Main Square, Trinidad /Tel.: (5341)993208.

Museum of Colonial Art / 74 Plácido St. on Jesús Menéndez St., Sancti Spíritus /Tel.: (5341)325455.

Museum of the War against Bandits / Hernández Echerri St., on Pino Guinart (former Convent of St. Francis), Trinidad /Tel.: (5341)994121.

Mutual Assistance Association of the St. Anthony's Royal Congos / 168 Isidro Armenteros St., Trinidad.

Principal Theater/ Máximo Gómez St., Sancti Spíritus/ Tel.: (5341) 325755.

Provincial Museum /11 Céspedes St., between Ernesto V. Muñoz and Ave. de los Mártires, Sancti Spíritus.

Romántic Museum at Brunet Palace /52 Fernando Hernández Echerri St. on Simón Bolívar, Main Square, Trinidad /Tel.: (5341) 994363.

Speleology Museum / Las Cuevas Hotel, Santa Ana.

Ciego de Ávila

Ciego de Ávila Provincial Museum / Honorato del Castillo on Máximo Gómez, Ciego de Ávila /Tel.: (5333)204488.

Morón Municipal Museum /374 Martí St., between Sergio Antuña and Coronel Cervantes, Morón /Tel.: (5333) 504501.

Museum of Decorative Arts /2 Marcial Gómez St., on Independencia, Ciego de Ávila /Tel.: (5333)201661.

Principal Theater/ Joaquín Agüero St. on Honorato del Castillo, Ciego de Ávila /Tel.: (5333) 222086.

Provincial Art Gallery / Independencia St., between Maceo and Honorato del Castillo, Ciego de Ávila /Tel.: (5333)223900.

Camagüey

Ignacio Agramonte Museum / 2 Los Mártires Ave., between Rotario and Andrés Sánchez, Camagüey /Tel.: (5332)282425.

Nicolás Guillén' Birthplace/ 253 Hermanos Agüero St., Camagüey/ Tel.: (5332) 293706.

Principal Theater/64 Padre Valencia St., Camagüey/ Tel.: (5332) 293048.

San Juan de Dios Hospital Museum / San Juan de Dios Square, Camagüey /Tel.: (5332)291388.

Water Sports

Cienfuegos

Guajimico (Diving)/ Cienfuegos-Trinidad Highway, Km 42/ Tel.: (5343) 540946.

Marlin Marina Cienfuegos / 35 St., between 6 and 8 St., Punta Gorda, Cienfuegos/Tel.: (5343) 551241 – 556120 - 551275 (International).

Rancho Luna - Faro Luna - Marlin/ Pasacaballos Highway, Km 18, Rancho Luna Beach / Tel.: (5343) 551699/556120/551241.

Villa Clara

Cayo Las Brujas - Gaviota (Diving)/ Caibarién's North Coast, Cayo Santa María and Cayo Las Brujas/ Tel.: (5342) 350113/ 350013 ext.16.

Sancti Spíritus

Cayo Blanco-Marlin/ Ancón Hotel, Ancón Peninsula, Ancón Beach / Tel.: (5341) 996205- 996670.

Ciego de Ávila

Avalón-Marlin/ Jardines de la Reina Archipelago / Tel.: (5333) 266879 .

Blue Diving-Marlin/ Jardines del Rey/ Tel.: (5333) 308179.

Coco Diving (Cayo Coco)/Jardines del Rey/ Tel.: (5333) 301020.

Green Moray (Cayo Guillermo)/ Jardines del Rey/ Tel.: (5333) 301627.

Marlin Marina Cayo Guillermo/Cayo Guillermo/ Tel.: (5333) 301737 – 301323 - 301516 (International).

Camagüey

Sharks´ Friends-Marlin /International Diving Center, Santa Lucía Beach / Tel.: (5332) 365182.

Health Services

Cienfuegos

International Clinic, Cienfuegos / 202 37 St., between 2 and 4. Punta Gorda/ Tel.: (53 43) 551622.

International Pharmacy at La Unión Hotel / 31 St., between 54 and 56, Cienfuegos/ Tel.: (5343) 451020.

Óptica Miramar, Cienfuegos / 3504 54 Ave. / Tel.: (5343) 551278.

Villa Clara

International Pharmacy at Sol Meliá Cayo Santa María Hotel /Tel.: (5342) 350500.

Medical Station at Barceló Cayo Santa María Beach Resort/ Cayo Santa María/ Tel.: (5342)350400.

Medical Station at Meliá Las Dunas /Cayo Santa María / Tel.: (5342)350100 .

Medical Station at Royal Hideway Cayo Ensenachos/ Cayo Ensenachos/ Tel.: (5342)350300.

Óptica Miramar, Santa Clara / 101 Colón St., between Candelaria and San Miguel, Santa Clara/ Tel. (5342) 208069.

Sancti Spíritus

International Clinic, Trinidad / 103 Lino Pérez Sr. on Anastasio Cárdenas /Tel.: (5341) 996309 - 996492 - 996240.

New Type International Pharmacy / Trinidad del Mar Hotel, Ancón Peninsula / Tel.: (5341) 996500.

New Type Pharmacy, Los Laureles Hotel/ Central Highway, Km 383 / Tel.: (5341) 327016 - 328316.

Ciego de Ávila

International Clinic, Cayo Coco /Los Hoteles Ave. (at the end)/Tel.: (5333) 302158/ 302160/302161.

International Pharmacies / Tryp Cayo Coco Hotel / NH Krystal Laguna Azul Hotel / Iberostar Daiquirí Hotel / International Clinic.

Óptica Miramar, Morón, /298 Martí St., between Serafín Sánchez and Callejas, / Tel.: (5333) 502240.

Camagüey

International Clinic, Santa Lucía / 14 Residencia St., / Santa Lucía Beach / Tel.: (5332) 365300.

International Pharmacy, Santa Lucía/14 Residencia St., Santa Lucía Beach / Tel.: (5332) 36 5300.

Lodgings

Las Tunas

★★★★ **Brisas Covarrubias Hotel** (Beach) / Covarrubias Beach, Puerto Padre / Tel.: (5331) 55530 / reservas@villacovarrubias.co.cu

★★★ **Cadillac Hotel**, (City) / Colón St. on San Francisco St., Las Tunas / Tel.: (5331) 372791, comercial@hotel.tu.co.cu

★★ **Islazul Tunas Hotel** (City) Dos de Diciembre Ave., Las Tunas / Tel.: (5331) 345014/ comercial@hoteltu.co.cu / Fax (5331) 343336.

★ **Cerro de Caisimú Camping** (Nature) / Manatí Highway, Km 18½, El Cerro / Tel.: (5331) 371737.

Holguín

★★★★★ **Paradisus Río de Oro Hotel** (Beach) / Esmeralda Beach, Rafael Freyre / Tel.: (5324) 430090 / jefe.reservas.pro@solmeliacuba.com / Fax: (5324) 430095.

★★★★★ **Playa Pesquero Hotel** (Beach)/ Pesquero Beach, Rafael Freyre / Tel.: (5324) 433530/ dpto.reservas@ppesquero.co.cu / Fax: (5324) 433877.

★★★★ **Blau Costa Verde Hotel** (Beach) / Pesquero Beach, Rafael Freyre / Tel.: (5324) 433510 / reservasl@blau-cv.co.cu / Fax: (5324) 433515.

★★★★ **Cayo Naranjo** (Beach) / Naranjo Bay, Rafael Freyre / Tel.: (5324) 430132 / ventas@marinavita.co.cu

★★★★ **Cayo Saetía Villa** (Nature) / Mayarí / Tel.: (5324) 516900 / comercial@cayosaetia.co.cu

★★★★ **Grand Beach Turquesa Sirenis** (Beach) / Yuraguanal Beach, Rafael Freyre / Tel.: (5324) 433540 / reservas@sirenisbeachtuquesa.co.cu / Fax: (5324) 433545.

★★★★ **Guardalavaca Brisas Hotel** (Beach) / 2 St. Guardalavaca, Banes / Tel.: (5324) 430218 / reserva@brisas.gvc.tur.cu / Fax (5324) 430418.

★★★★ **Playa Costa Verde Hotel** (Beach)/ Pesquero Beach, Rafael Freyre Tel.: (5324) 433520/ reservationsmanager@beachcostaverde.co.cu / Fax: (5324) 433525.

★★★★ **Sol Río Luna-Mares Hotel** (Beach) / Esmeralda Beach, Rafael Freyre/Tel.: (5324) 430060 / jefe.ventas.srm@solmeliacuba.com

★★★ **Atlántico Guardalavaca Club Amigo** (Beach) / Guardalavaca Beach, Banes / Tel.: (5324) 430281 / booking@.clubamigo.gvc.tur.cu / Fax: (5324) 430444.

★★★ **Islazul Don Lino Villa** (Beach) / Playa Blanca Highway, Km 7, Rafael Freyre / Tel.: (5324) 430308 / reserva@donlino.islazul.hgl.tur.cu / Fax: (5324) 430307.

★★★ **Islazul El Bosque Villa** (City) / Jorge Dimitrov Ave., Holguín / Tel.: (5324) 481012 / anamarlenis.nunez@bosque.islazul.tur.cu / Fax: (5324) 481140.

★★★ **Islazul Mirador de Mayabe Villa** (Nature) / Alturas de Mayabe, Km 8, Holguín/ Tel.: (5324) 422160/ reservas@mayabe.islazul.tur.cu

★★★ **Islazul Pernik Hotel** (City) / Jorge Dimitrov Ave., Holguín / Tel.: (5324) 481011 / jrecepcion@pernik.islazul.tur.cu / Fax: (5324) 481011.

★★ **Islazul Cabañas Villa** (Beach) / Guardalavaca Beach, Banes/ Tel.: (5324) 430314/ reservasvc@islazul.hlg.tur.cu.

★★ **Miraflores Hotel** (City) / Calixto García Ave., Miraflores, Moa / Tel.: (5324) 606103 / jcarpeta@miraflores.co.cu

★★ **Pinares de Mayarí Villa** (Nature)/ Mensura Hill, Pinares de Mayarí/ Tel.: (5324) 503308/ comercial@vpinares.co.cu

★ **Silla de Gibara Camping** (Nature) / La Caridad, Rafael Freyre / Tel.: (5324) 421586.

Granma

★★★ **Balcón de la Sierra** (Nature) / Masó Ave., Providencia, Bartolomé Masó, Bayamo / Tel.: (5323) 565513-565523 / carpeta@villagr.co.cu

★★★ **Islazul Bayamo Villa** (City) / Central Highway to Manzanillo, Km 5½, Bayamo / Tel.: (5323) 423102 - 423124 / 426989.

★★★ **Islazul Sierra Maestra Hotel** (City) / Central Highway, Km 1½, Bayamo / Tel.: (5323) 424790 / 7970 (Reservations through Islazul).

★★★ **Las Coloradas Camping** (Beach) / Las Coloradas Beach, Niquero Highway, Km 17, Niquero / Tel.: (5323) 578256.

★★★ **Marea del Portillo Club Amigo** (Beach) Granma Highway, Km 12 ½, Pilón / Tel.: (5323) 597081 / comercial@hfarcar.co.cu

★★★ **Santo Domingo Villa** (Nature) / La Plata Highway, Km 16, Santo Domingo / Tel.: (5323) 565568-13-35 / comercial@islazulgrm.cu

★★ **Horizontes El Yarey Villa** (City) / Santiago de Cuba Highway, Jiguaní / Tel.: (5323) 427256 / economia@yarey.grm.cu / carpeta@yarey.grm.cu

★★ **Islazul Niquero Hotel** (Nature) / 100 Martí St. on Céspedes, Niquero / Tel.: (5323) 592367-68 hniquero@islazulgrm.co.cu

★★ **Islazul Royalton Hotel** (City) / 53 Antonio Maceo St., between General García and J. Palma, Bayamo / Tel.: (5323) 422290-422224 (Reservations through Islazul.).

Santiago de Cuba

★★★★★ **Meliá Santiago Hotel** (City) / M St. on Las Américas Ave., Santiago de Cuba / Tel.: (5322) 687070 / reserva1.msc@solmeliacuba.com

★★★★ **Casagranda Hotel** (City) / 21 Heredia St., between San Pedro and San Félix Martí St., Santiago de Cuba / Tel.: (5322) 653021 / reserva@casagran.gca.tur.cu

★★★★ **Sierra Mar-Los Galeones Hotel** (Beach)/ Chivirico Highway, Km 60, Guamá/ Tel.: (5322) 329110/ resevat@smar.scu.tur.cu

★★★ **Bucanero Club** (Nature)/ Baconao, Km 4½, Arroyo La Costa, Santiago de Cuba/ Tel.: (5322) 399551/ reseva@bucanero.gca.tur.cu

★★★ **Carisol-Los Corales Club Amigo** (Beach) / Baconao Highway, Km 31, Santiago de Cuba / Tel.: (5322) 356122 / reservas@carisol-loscorales.co.scu.cu

★★★ **Costa Morena Hotel** (Beach) / Baconao Highway, Km 38½, Sigua, Santiago de Cuba / Tel.: (5322) 356127 / Fax: (5322) 356160.

★★★ **E San Basilio Hotel** (City), 403 San Basio St., between Calvario and Carnicería, Santiago de Cuba, Tel (5322) 651702 and 651787/ comercial@hostalsb.scu.tur.cu and hotel_e_sanbasilio.scu@tur.cu.

★★★ **El Saltón Villa** (Nature)/ Filé Highway, Puerto Rico, Tercer Frente/Tel.: (5322) 566326/ salton@enet.cu

★★★ **Gaviota Santiago de Cuba Villa** (City) 502 Manduley Ave., Vista Alegre, Santiago de Cuba/ Tel. (5322) 641368 and 641370/ comercial@gaviota.co.cu.

★★★ **Islazul Balcón del Caribe Hotel** (City) / El Morro, Km 4, Santiago de Cuba / Tel.: (5322) 691011 / jcarpeta@bcaribe.co.cu

★★★ **Islazul Las Américas Hotel** (City) / Las Américas Ave. on General Cebreco Martí St., Santiago de Cuba / Tel.: (5322) 642011 / magda@hamerica.scu.tur.co

★★★ **Islazul San Juan Hotel** (City) / Siboney Highway, Km 1½, Vista Alegre, Santiago de Cuba / Tel.: (5322) 687200/ jcarpeta@sanjuan.co.cu

★★★ **Versalles Hotel** (City) / El Morro Highway, Km 1, Altura de Versalles, Santiago de Cuba / Tel.: (5322) 691016 / comercial@hotelversalles.co.cu

★★ **Caletón Blanco Camping** (Nature) / Caletón Blanco Highway, Km 30, Guamá / Tel.: (5322) 26147.

★★ **Islazul Gran Piedra Motel** (Nature)/ Gran Piedra Highway, Km 14, Santiago de Cuba/ Tel.: (5322) 686147 / magda@hamerica.scu.tur.co

★★ **Islazul Libertad Hotel** (City) / 658 Aguilera St., Marte Square, Santiago de Cuba / Tel.: (5322) 627710 reserva@libertad.tur.cu

★★ **La Mula Camping** (Nature) / Granma. Km 120, Guamá / Tel.: (5322) 26262.

Guantánamo-Baracoa

★★★ **Caimanera Hotel** (Nature) / Loma Norte, Caimanera / Tel.: (5321) 499414-416 / caimanera@enet.cu

★★ **El Castillo Hotel** (Nature)/ Calixto García St., Paraíso, Baracoa/ Tel.: (5321) 645224/ reservasps@gavbcoa.co.cu

★★ **Guantánamo Hotel** (City) / 13 Norte St., between Ahogados and 2 Oeste St., Guantánamo / Tel.: (5321) 381015 / hotelgtm@enet.cu

★★ **Islazul La Lupe Villa** (Nature) / El Salvador Highway, Km 3, Guantánamo / Tel.: (5321) 382602-382612 / lupegtm@enet.cu

★★ **La Habanera Hostel** (City) /126 Maceo St., between Frank País and Marabi St., Baracoa / Tel.: (5321) 642337 / reservasps@gavbcoa.co.cu

★★ **La Rusa Hotel** (Nature)/161 Máximo Gómez St., Baracoa/ Tel.: (5321) 643011-643570/ reservasps@gavbcoa.co.cu

★★ **Maguana Villa** (Nature)/ Moa Highway / Tel.: (5321) 645372/ reservasps@gavbcoa.co.cu

★★ **Porto Santo Hotel** (Nature)/ Airport Highway, Jaitesico, Baracoa / Tel.: (5321) 645106/ reservasps@gavbcoa.co.cu

Restaurants and Coffee-Shops

Las Tunas

La Bodeguita (Cuban cuisine)/ 303 Francisco Varona St., Las Tunas/Tel.: (5331) 371536.

La Marina (Coffee-shop)/ Paco Cabrera St., Puerto Padre.

Malecón (Coffee-shop)/ Paco Cabrera St., Puerto Padre.

Parador Cucalambé (Coffee-shop)/ Central Highway, Km 2, Las Tunas.

Holguín

Aldea Taína (Cuban and international cuisine)/ Guardalavaca Beach, Banes/Tel.: (5324) 430422.

Colombo (Cuban and international cuisine)/ Bariay, Rafael Freyre, Banes/Tel.: (5324) 430438.

El Ancla (Cuban and international cuisine)/ Guardalavaca Beach, Banes/Tel.: (5324) 430381.

El Cayuelo (Cuban and international cuisine)/ Guardalavaca Beach, Banes/Tel.: (5324) 430736.

El Faro (Cuban and international cuisine)/ Plaza del Fuerte s/n, Gibara/Tel.: (5324) 434596.

Loma de la Cruz (Cuban and international cuisine)/ Hill of the Cross, Holguín.

Pizza Nova (Italian cuisine)/ Guardalavaca Beach, Banes/Tel.: (5324) 430137.

Salón 1720 (Cuban and international cuisine)/ Frexes St. on Miró St., Holguín/Tel.: (5324) 468150.

Vicaria Banes (Cuban and international cuisine)/ Banes/Tel.: (5324) 802803.

Vicaria Guardalavaca (Cuban and international cuisine)/ Guardalavaca Beach, Banes /Tel.: (5324) 430239.

Granma

El Rápido Hatuey (Coffee-shop)/8 Libertad St., between Guamá and Plaza del Himno, Bayamo.

El Tocororo (Coffee-shop)/ Central Highway to Santiago de Cuba, Bayamo.

La Bodega (Cuban cuisine)/ General García St., Bayamo.

Santiago de Cuba

Café Palmares (Coffee-shop)/ M St., between 6 and Las Américas Ave., Sueño, Santiago de Cuba.

Don Antonio (Cuban and international cuisine)/ Aguileras St., between Calvario and Reloj St., Santiago de Cuba/Tel.: (5322) 652307.

El Cayo (Cuban and international cuisine)/ Cayo Granma, Santiago de Cuba/Tel.: (5322) 690109.

El Cobre (Coffee-shop)/ General Antolín Cebreco St., on Lamboa St., Santiago de Cuba.

El Morro (Cuban and international cuisine)/ El Morro Highway, Santiago de Cuba/Tel.: (5322) 691576.

La Maison (international cuisine)/ Manduley Ave., between 1st and 3rd, Vista Alegre, Santiago de Cuba.

La Rueda (Cuban cuisine)/ 3 Barco St., Siboney, Santiago de Cuba/Tel.: (5322) 39325.

La Teresina (Cuban and international cuisine)/ Aguilera St., between Calvario and Reloj St., Santiago de Cuba/Tel.: (5322) 686485.

Las Enramadas (Coffee-shop)/ Aguilera, between Calvario and Reloj St., Santiago de Cuba.

Matamoros (Cuban and international cuisine)/ Calvario St. on Aguilera, Santiago de Cuba/Tel.: (5322) 686459.

Perla del Dragón (Cuban and international cuisine)/ Aguilera, between Calvario and Reloj St., Santiago de Cuba/Tel.: (5322) 686485.

Punta Gorda (Cuban and international cuisine)/ 1st St., Punta Gorda, Santiago de Cuba/Tel.: (5322) 686219.

Zunzún (Cuban and international cuisine)/ 159 Manduley Ave., Vista Alegre, Santiago de Cuba/ Tel.: (5322) 641528.

Guantánamo

Finca Maraví (Cuban cuisine)/ Cayo Güín, Baracoa.

Finca Toa (Cuban cuisine)/ Mabujabo Highway, Baracoa.

La Punta (Cuban cuisine)/ Baracoa/Tel.: (5321) 641480.

Night Centers

Las Tunas

1913 (Nightclub)/Jesús Menéndez St., between 24 de Febrero and A. Ameijeiras St., Puerto Padre/ Tel.: (5331) 516897.

Bolera (Nightclub)/Francisco Varona St., between Lora and Menocal, Las Tunas/Tel.: (5331) 48668.

El Taíno (Nightclub)/ Central Oeste, Las Tunas Highway /Tel.: (5331) 343823.

Holguín

1720 (Nightclub)/ 190 Frexes St., on Miró St., Holguín/Tel.: (5324) 468150.

La Roca (Disco)/ Guardalavaca Beach, Banes/Tel.: (5324) 30167.

La Rueda (Bar)/ Guardalavaca Beach, Banes/Tel.: (5324) 30167.

Granma

Costa Azul (Nightclub)/1ro. de Mayo St. on N. López St., Manzanillo/Tel.: (5323) 53158.

La Bodega (Nightclub)/34 Plaza del Himno, between Maceo Osorio and General Rabí St., Bayamo.

Parque Granma (Nightclub)/Parque Granma, Almirante Highway, Bayamo.

Santiago de Cuba

La Maison (Nightclub)/ Manduley Ave. on 3rd. St., Vista Alegre, Santiago de Cuba/Tel.: (5322) 641117.

Niágara (Nightclub) /Los Delfines Ave., Heredia Theater, Santiago de Cuba.

San Pedro del Mar (Nightclub)/ El Morro Highway, 619 Aguilera St., Santiago de Cuba/Tel.: (5322)691287.

Santiago Café (Nightclub)/ Meliá Santiago Hotel, Santiago de Cuba/Tel.: (5322) 687070.

Terraza El Quijote (Nightclub)/ Las Américas Hotel, Santiago de Cuba/Tel.: (5322) 687200.

Trip Continental (Nightclub)/ Las Américas Hotel, Santiago de Cuba/Tel.: (5322) 642011.

Guantánamo

Club Nevada (Nightclub)/1008 Pedro A. Pérez St., on Bartolomé Masó St., Guantánamo/Tel.: (5321) 355447.

El Parque (Nightclub)/ Maceo St., Baracoa/Tel.: (5321) 45224.

Stores

Las Tunas

Brisas Covarrubias Hotel's Store / Brisas Covarrubias Hotel /Specialized Store.

Colón Stores /294 Francisco Varona St. on Ángel Guardia /Specialized Store.

El Cucalambé Stopping Point's Store/ Central Oeste Highway, Km. 2½, San Antonio/ General Store.

La Casa Azul /Vicente García St. on Francisco Vega St. / General Store/ Tel.: (5331) 346376.

La Gaviota /Vicente García / Las Tunas/ Specialized Boutique.

La Habanera/ 332 Francisco Varona St. on Lucas Ortiz St., Las Tunas/ Boutique Tel.: (5331) 372711.

Las Antillas Complex / 334 Lucas Ortiz St., between Teniente Peison and Mártires de Barbados St., /General Store.

Las Tunas Hotel's Store / 30 de Diciembre Ave., Las Tunas Hotel /General Store.

Nuevo Milenio/ 249 Francisco Vega St., Primero/ Boutique.

Ranchón La Rotonda's Store /Circunvalación Sur Beltway, Traffic circle to Holguín/General Store.

Tu Mirada /14 Libertad Ave. Puerto Padre Specialized Store/ Tel.: (5331) 515498.

Holguín

Alturas de Mayabe's Store / Mirador de Mayabe Hotel / General Store.

Bella Cubana /68 Martí Ave., between Cárdenas Ave. and T. Esperance St., / Specialized Store/ Tel.: (5324) 803409.

Casa de la Trova El Guayabero's Store /Maceo St., between Frexes and Martí St., Holguín/Specialized Store.

El Bosque / El Bosque Hotel / Specialized Boutique / Tel.: (5324) 468350 and 468289.

El Cuje Cigars / Turey Villa, Guardalavaca Beach / Specialized Store.

El Mojito/ Playa Pesquero Hotel, Pesquero Beach / General Store.

El Paraíso / Las Brisas Villa, Guardalavaca Beach / General Store.

El Ruiseñor/ 30 Independencia St., between Calixto García and Peralta St., Holguín/Specialized Store/ Tel.: (5324) 844329.

El Zunzún / Occidental Grand Beach Turquesa Hotel, Pesquero Beach / General Store.

Fotoclub/Boulevard Guardalavaca/ Photographs and Videos/ Tel.: (5324) 430405.

Guanín / Roca Azul Park, Pesquero Beach / General Store.

Guardalavaca Boulevard / Guardalavaca Mall, Banes / Specialized Store/Tel.: (5324) 460656.

La Cohoba / La Marqueta Square, Holguín/Specialized Store.

La Mariposa / 236 Frexes St. on Máximo Gómez St., Moa/ Specialized Store/ Tel: (5324) 468021.

Perla Marina/Guardalavaca, Holguín/Specialized Store/Tel.: (5324) 430350.

Pico Cristal/Libertad St. on Mart, Holguín/Boutique.

Plaza Comercial 3D / Guardalavaca Beach, across from Guardalavaca Hotel / General Store.

Tobacco Factory's Store /Coliseo Tobacco Factory on 3rd, Peralta/ Specialized Store.

Granma

Balcón de la Sierra / Balcón de la Sierra Villa, Providencia Highway, Km 1/ General Store.

Centro Comercial Telégrafo / 154 Saco St. on Mármol St./General Store.

Guacanayabo / Guacanayabo Hotel, Camilo Cienfuegos Ave. / General Store/ Tel.: (5323) 572998.

Kiosco ARTEX /112 Antonio Maceo St., between 2nd and Frank País Ave./Specialized Store.

La Alondra / Manzanillo Airport, Cayo Espino Highway, Km 7/ Specialized Store.

La Bayamesa/General García St. on Luz Vázquez St. / Specialized Store/ Tel.: 0(5323) 427582.

La Internacional / Marea del Portillo Hotel, Granma Highway, Km 12½/General Store/Tel: (5323) 597016.

La Única / Sierra Maestra Hotel, Highway to Santiago/Boutique/Tel.: (5323) 427419.

Las Rosas /Hotel Farallón del Caribe, Granma Highway, Km 12½/ General Store/Tel.: (5323) 797018.

Mis Anhelos /55 General Rabí St., between General García and Luz and Caballero St.,/ Specialized Store/ Tel.: (5323) 366065.

National Anthem Square/ 20 Maceo St., Bayamo/ General Store/Tel.: (5323) 422896.

Proposiciones /5 General García St., between Maceo and C. Figueredo St., Bayamo/Specialized Store/Tel.: (5323) 427236.

Santiago de Cuba

Casa de la Música /564 Corona St., between Aguilera and Enramadas St., Santiago de Cuba/Specialized Store.

Casa del Habano/ Jesús Menéndez Ave. on Aduana, Santiago de Cuba/ Specialized Store.

Casa Granda / Casa Granda Hotel, San Pedro, Santiago de Cuba/Boutique/ Tel.: (5322) 624027.

Catedral Turística/ Heredia St., between San Pedro and Santo Tomás/ Supermarket/ Tel.: (5322) 686174.

Centro Comercial CUBACENTRO /Santo Tomás St., between San Francisco and San Jerónimo St., Santiago de Cuba/ General Store.

Costa Morena/ Costa Morena Hotel, Baconao Highway / General Store / Tel.: (5322) 356349.

El Cobre/Antolín Cebreco, El Cobre / Boutique/ Tel.: (5322) 346496.

El Morro/ Morro Castle, Morro Highway / Specialized Store/ Tel.: (5322) 617174.

El Quitrín/ 463 San Jerónimo St., between Carnicería and Calvario St., Santiago de Cuba/ Specialized Store.

El Tivolì / Meliá Santiago Hotel, Sueño/ Specialized Store/ Tel.: (5322) 687070.

Foto Club /José A. Saco St., between Félix and S. Pedro St., Santiago de Cuba/ Specialized Store.

La Barrita / Caney Rum Distillery, 703 Peralejo St. / General Store.

La Maison / Manduley Ave., Vista Alegre/Specialized Store/Tel.: (5322) 643932.

Las Américas / Las Américas Hotel / General Store/ Tel.: (5322) 643143.

Las Enramadas / Meliá Santiago Hotel, Sueño/ General Store / Tel.: (5322) 687070.

Plaza de Marte Mall/ Marte Square, Santiago de Cuba/ General Store.

Primor / 302 José A. Saco St., between S. Pedro and S. Félix St. /Boutique.

Souvenir Santiago / Meliá Santiago Hotel, Sueño/ General Store/ Tel.: (5322) 687070.

Teatro Heredia's Store/ Heredia Theater/ Las Américas Ave., Santiago de Cuba / Specialized Store/ Tel.: (5322) 643156.

Vista Alegre Mall/ Caney Highway, between 13 and 15 St., Vista Alegre, Santiago de Cuba/ General Store.

Guantánamo

ARTEX Store /Crombet St., between Los Maceo and Calixto García/Specialized Store.

Baracoa /197 Martí St., between Céspedes and Coroneles Galano St. / Specialized Store/ Tel.: (5321) 645373.

Caimanera /Correos St., between Carril and Carretera / Specialized Store/ Tel.: (5321) 499114.

Fondo Cubano de Bienes Culturales /Crombet St., between Pedro A. Pérez and Calixto García St. / Specialized Store.

Hotel Guantánamo Store /14 Norte St., between 2 and 3 Norte St. / Boutique.

Mercurio / Los Estudiantes Ave. on Santa Rita / General Store/ Tel.: (5321) 355811.

Attractions and Sites of Interests

Las Tunas

Major General Vicente García Memorial Museum /5 Vicente García St., between Francisco Vega and Julián Santana St., Las Tunas /Tel.: (5331) 345164.

Major General Vicente García Provincial Museum / Francisco Varona St., between Ángel Guarda and Adolfo Villamar St., Primero, Las Tunas /Tel.: (5331) 348201.

Mártires de Barbados Memorial Museum / 344 Lucas Ortiz St., betweenTeniente Peisso and Mártires de Barbados St., Las Tunas /Tel.: (5331) 347213.

Plaza Solar Martiana / Ángel Guarda St., between Francisco Varona and Francisco Vega, Las Tunas / Tel.: (5331)47913.

Raúl Gómez García Theater/ 267 Vicente García St., between Lara and Heredia, Las Tunas/ Tel.: (5331) 345113.

Revolution Square / 2 de Diciembre Ave., between Carlos J. Finlay and 30 de Noviembre, Las Tunas / Tel.: (5331)47751.

Holguín

Baní Cuban Aborigines Museum/305 General Marrero St., between Céspedes and Martí St., Banes/ Tel.: (5324)82487.

Birán Historical Site /Cueto/Tel.: (5324)286114.

Calixto García's Birthplace/ 147 Miró St., Holguín.

Carlos de la Torre Museum of Natural History /129 Maceo St., between Martí and Luz Caballero, Holguín /Tel.: (5324)423935.

Chorro de Maíta Site Museum / Yaguajay Hill, Banes /Tel.: (5324)30421.

Eddy Suñol Theater/ 197 Martí St., between Manduley and Maceo, Holguín/ Tel.: (5324) 463161.

La Periquera Provincial Museum/ 198 Frexes St., between Libertad and Maceo St., Holguín/ Tel.: (5324)463395.

Rodrigo Prats Operetta House /113 Martí St., between Maceo and Libertad, Holguín/ Tel.: (5324) 463473.

Granma

Bayamo Provincial Museum / 55 Maceo St., between Donato Mármol and José Joaquín Palma St., Bayamo/Tel.: (5323)424125.

Carlos Manuel de Céspedes' Birthplace / 57 Maceo St., between Donato Mármol and José Joaquín Palma, St., Bayamo /Tel.: (5323)423864.

Celia Sánchez Manduley's Birthplace /11 Raúl Podio St., Media Luna/ Tel.: (5323) 574392.

Homeland Square/ 302 Figueredo St., between 5th Ave. and Antonio Maceo Ave., Bayamo /Tel.: (5323)425132.

José Joaquín Palma Theater/ 172 Carlos Manuel de Céspedes St., between Perucho Figueredo and Lora St., Bayamo/ Tel.: (5323) 424423.

Luz Vázquez's Window / 160 Carlos Manuel de Céspedes St., between Perucho Figueredo and Lora St., Bayamo.

Manzanillo Theater/ Villuendas St. on Maceo St., Manzanillo /Tel.: (5323) 572539.

Santiago de Cuba

Abel Santamaría Plaza and Museum / Trinidad St., between Calle Nueva and Central Highway, Santiago de Cuba/ Tel.: (5322) 624119.

Antonio Maceo Revolution Square / Los Delfines Ave. on Las Américas, Santiago de Cuba/Tel.: (5322) 643053.

Antonio Maceo's Birthplace Museum / 207 Los Maceos St., between Corona and Rastro St., Santiago de Cuba/Tel.: (5322)623750.

Emilio Bacardí Provincial Museum / Pío Rosado St. on Aguilera St., Santiago de Cuba/Tel.: (5322)628402.

Heredia Theater/ Las Américas Ave., between Los Delfines Ave. and Ángel Salazar, Santiago de Cuba/Tel.: (5322) 643768 - 643156 - 643228.

Home of Diego Velázquez/ Céspedes Plaza, Santiago de Cuba.

Home of Frank País/226 San Bartolomé St., between Habana and Maceo St., Santiago de Cuba/ Tel.: (5322)652710.

José María Heredia's Birthplace/ 206 Heredia St., between San Félix and Pío Rosado St., Santiago de Cuba.

José Martí Mausoleum / Crombet Ave., Santiago de Cuba/Tel.: (5322)632723.

La Isabelica Ethnographic Museum / La Gran Piedra Highway, Km. 14, Santiago de Cuba/ Tel.: (5322) 656152.

Moncada Barracks/ General Portuondo St., between Moncada and Los Libertadores Ave. / Tel.: (5322) 661157.

Museum of the Carnival/ 303 Heredia St. on Carnicería St., Santiago de Cuba/ Tel.: (5322) 626955.

Museum of the Underground / 1 Rabí St., between San Carlo and Santa Rita St., Santiago de Cuba/ Tel.: (5322) 624689.

National Museum of Transportation/ Baconao Highway, Km 8½, Santiago de Cuba/Tel.: (5322) 399197.

Oriente Gallery/ 653 Lacret St., between Heredia and Aguilera St., Santiago de Cuba.

San Pedro de la Roca Castle of El Morro / Morro Highway, Km 7½, Santiago de Cuba/Tel.: (5322)691569.

Siboney Farm Historical Museum / Siboney Highway, Km 13 ½, Santiago de Cuba/Tel.: (5322)399168.

Guantánamo

Matachín Fortress, Municipal Museum of Baracoa / Martí St. on Malecón, Baracoa/ Tel.: (5321) 642122.

Provincial Museum / 804 Martí St. on Prado, Guantánamo/ Tel.: (5321)325872.

Salcines Palace/ 802-804 Pedro Agustín St. on Silverio del Prado, Guantánamo.

Universal Bookstore /907 Pedro A. Pérez St., Guantánamo.

Water Sports

Las Tunas

Covarrubias International Diving Center/ Covarrubias Beach /Tel.: (5331) 515530.

Holguín

Blue World (Diving)/ Blau Costa Verde Hotel, Pesquero Beach / Tel.: (5324) 430132/430434 ext: 108 and 107.

Eagle Ray - Marlin/ Guardalavaca Beach / Tel.: (5324) 430316 - 430474 / Fax 430491.

Puerto de Vita Marina /Port of Vita/ Tel.: (5324) 430445 (International).

Sea Lovers (Diving)/ Paradisus Río de Oro Hotel, Esmeralda Beach / Tel.: 5324) 430132/430434 ext: 108.

Granma

Albacora/ Granma Highway, Km 12 ½, Marea del Portillo/ Tel.: (5323) 597139.

Santiago de Cuba

Bucanero - Marlin/ Bucanero Hotel / Tel.: (5322) 691446.

Carisol Los Corales Marlin/ Baconao Highway, Km 40/ Tel.: (5322) 356165/691446.

Marlin Marina Santiago de Cuba / 1st St., Punta Gorda/ Tel.: (5322) 691446/686326 (International).

Punta Gorda International Marina / Marina Santiago de Cuba/ Tel.: (5322) 691446.

Sierra Mar-Marlin/ Brisas Sierra Mar Hotel, Chivirico Highway, Km 60/ Tel.: (5322) 026337/691446.

Health Care

Las Tunas

International Pharmacy / 2 de Diciembre Ave., Las Tunas Hotel / Tel.: (5331) 371510.

Holguín

Guardalavaca International Clinic/ 15 Segunda St., Guardalavaca/ Tel.: (5324) 430312.

Óptica Miramar Holguín, / 212 Frexes St., between Maceo and Mártires/ Tel.: (5324) 421176.

Rehabilitation Clinic Villa Quinqué - Cocal/ Central Highway to Bayamo, Km 6/ Tel.: (5324) 468791 (Rehabilitation).

Granma

International Pharmacy /General García St., between Figueredo and Lora St., Bayamo/ Tel.: (5323) 429596.

Santiago de Cuba

International Clinic / Raúl Puyol Ave. on 10 St., Ferreiro Plaza/Tel.(5322) 642589 / 687001.

International Pharmacy, Meliá Santiago Hotel/ M St. on Las Américas Ave./ Tel.: (5322) 687070.

Óptica Miramar, Santiago de Cuba/Santo Tomás St., between San Basilio and Heredia St. / Tel. (5322) 625259.

Guantánamo

Baracoa International Clinic / 237 Martí St., between Roberto Reyes and Limbano Sánchez St. / Tel.: (5321) 641037-38.

International Pharmacy / Martí St. on Roberto Reyes St. /Tel.: (5321) 641037-38.

International Pharmacy /Crombet St., between Los Maceo and Calixto García St. / Tel.: (5321) 351129.

NAME INDEX

#

A

B

C

D

E

F

G

M

N

O

P

Q

R

S

NOTES

NOTES

NOTES